Praise for *Executive Roadmap to Fraud Prevention and Internal Control: Creating a Culture of Compliance*

"*Executive Roadmap* touches all the bases on corporate fraud. The authors—both experienced fraud investigators and federal law enforcement agents—lay out the history and major milestones of corporate fraud, and discuss with precision the key issues facing today's executives and compliance leaders. The book provides a valuable overview for business leaders looking to develop and implement effective compliance programs and instill a culture of integrity in order to help their organizations defeat the challenges posed by today's sophisticated fraudsters.

—**Jeffrey Eglash, Senior Counsel,**
Litigation & Legal Policy, GE

"Biegelman and Bartow provide great insight into not just *how* fraud occurs inside of companies, but *why*. Preventing fraud requires a solid understanding of both, making this book a must read for any executive who is serious about creating the compliance mechanisms and the corporate culture needed for effective fraud prevention."

—**Aaron G. Murphy, Partner, Latham & Watkins LLP**

"Business leaders would be wise to follow the recommendations in this book. Fraud prevention is more than just creating a set of policies. As the subtitle indicates, it is essential to create a *culture* of compliance. Empty words accomplish nothing. The authors, both experienced fraud examiners, have spent decades investigating fraud, as well as developing strategies to prevent it. This book is an essential tool in creating an antifraud environment in any company."

—**James D. Ratley, CFE, President & CEO,**
Association of Certified Fraud Examiners

"Biegelman and Bartow's *Executive Roadmap to Fraud Prevention and Internal Control* is an essential guide for all who have an interest in eradicating corporate or institutional fraud. Written by experts in detecting and preventing fraud in its myriad forms, this book is a handy source for those who hope to avoid the

predicaments that the authors have seen or in managing the crises that arise when the problems cannot be avoided. The new second edition is an indispensable addition to the libraries of internal compliance and legal officers, and forensic accountants."
—**Joel M. Cohen, Partner, Gibson Dunn & Crutcher, former New York federal prosecutor and liaison to the French Ministry of Justice and OECD**

"Biegelman and Bartow's book offers expert guidance to anyone tasked with understanding and tackling fraud in the workplace. Their straightforward approach informs the reader and provides a roadmap and guidance for implementation of an effective fraud mechanism within any organization—small or large. I plan to provide a copy of the book to my Board of Directors and executive members of management."
—**Lisanne E. S. Cottington, Compliance Officer, Insight Enterprises, Inc.**

"This next edition is extremely timely. It covers key topics that any management member needs to know in today's regulatory climate. These authors have used their extensive corporate and government experience to create a practical and easy to understand compliance guide. A superb resource for any executive."
—**Karen Popp, Partner at Sidley Austin LLP and former federal prosecutor and Associate Counsel to President Clinton**

"With executives increasingly on the hot seat when corporate compliance issues arise, clear guidance regarding risk areas and best practices is invaluable. *Executive Roadmap to Fraud Prevention and Internal Control* contains a timely combination of illustrative stories and practice tips regarding hazards in this complex area. It is a good resource for both corporate executives and the many professionals assisting corporations to prevent or detect fraud and build a culture of legal compliance."
—**Barb Dawson, partner with focus on internal investigations and business litigation, Snell & Wilmer LLP**

"*Executive Roadmap to Fraud Prevention and Internal Control: Creating a Culture of Compliance* is a truly phenomenal book. Martin Biegelman and Joel Bartow have accomplished an incredible achievement: They have flawlessly bridged the chasm between the theoretical/academic and practical/tangible. This is a volume that should *not* be on the bookshelf of every manager interested in compliance and fraud prevention (which should be every manager); it should be dog-eared and open on the *desktop* of every such manager! Kudos to Messrs. Biegelman and Bartow!"

—William J. Kresse, M.S., J.D., CPA, CFF, CFE; Associate Professor, Graham School of Management; Director, Center for the Study of Fraud and Corruption, Saint Xavier University, Chicago

"Biegelman and Bartow have again provided an invaluable resource for leaders in the corporate world who have responsibility for fraud, integrity, and compliance. They send a clear message that addressing fraud is a two part process: establishing robust controls and detection measures and creating a culture of compliance and integrity. This work provides a detailed tour through the world of fraud controls while keeping the importance of culture at the forefront."

—Ronald C. Petersen, Executive Director, Global Security, Ally Financial

"From the perspective of an ethics and compliance practitioner, Martin Biegelman's and Joel Bartow's new offering is a Thanksgiving feast. Too often, companies and organizations get caught up in the moment, and don't stand back to examine the cultural, organizational and historic reasons that fraud exists. Biegelman and Bartow plow that road, and use their insights to offer invaluable tips in the design of effective antifraud programs."

—James D. Berg, Vice President, Chief Ethics and Compliance Officer, Apollo Group Inc.

"Biegelman and Bartow have indeed produced a functional roadmap for the executive to follow in fraud prevention and internal control. This book is a great asset for those engaged in the seemingly endless struggle to control fraud. A "must read" for the industry.

—Raymond L. Philo, MPA, Executive Director,
Economic Crime Institute, Utica College

"As if *Executive Roadmap to Fraud Prevention and Internal Control* wasn't a powerful enough tool for fraud fighters, now Biegelman and Bartow have added fresh insight and advice to the second edition. With compelling updates on costly internal and external fraud and corruption, together with easy-to-read descriptions of latest fraud-fighting technologies, this is a must-read for fraud examiners, auditors, attorneys, and others—whether they've read the first edition or not.

—Peter Goldmann, President, White-Collar Crime 101
LLC/FraudAware

"Fraud borders on the ubiquitous in contemporary corporate culture. This book provides a rich and comprehensive guide to crafting a state of the art fraud deterrence program. While the book is sure to better equip corporate executives and directors in their fight against fraud, I intend to draw heavily upon its content in educating accounting students who represent the CEOs and CFOs of the future."

—Ingrid E. Fisher, PhD, CPA, Associate Professor and
Chair of the Department of Accounting and Law, The
University at Albany-SUNY

"The book's exploration of fraud theories ranging from "rotten apple" to the "potato chip" (can't eat just one!), provides useful examination of the psychology of corporate fraud that explains its recurring nature and offers clues to creating a fraud resistant culture."

—Zachary W. Carter, Partner and head of the Trial
Group, Dorsey & Whitney LLP and former United States
Attorney for the Eastern District of New York

Executive Roadmap to Fraud Prevention and Internal Control

Founded in 1807, John Wiley & Sons is the oldest independent publishing company in the United States. With offices in North America, Europe, Australia and Asia, Wiley is globally committed to developing and marketing print and electronic products and services for our customers' professional and personal knowledge and understanding.

The Wiley Finance series contains books written specifically for finance and investment professionals as well as sophisticated individual investors and their financial advisors. Book topics range from portfolio management to e-commerce, risk management, financial engineering, valuation and financial instrument analysis, as well as much more.

For a list of available titles, visit our Web site at www.WileyFinance.com.

Executive Roadmap to Fraud Prevention and Internal Control

Creating a Culture of Compliance

Second Edition

MARTIN T. BIEGELMAN
JOEL T. BARTOW

WILEY

John Wiley & Sons, Inc.

For general information on our other products and services or for technical support, please contact our Customer Care Department within the United States at (800) 762-2974, outside the United States at (317) 572-3993 or fax (317) 572-4002.

Wiley also publishes its books in a variety of electronic formats. Some content that appears in print may not be available in electronic books. For more information about Wiley products, visit our web site at www.wiley.com.

Library of Congress Cataloging-in-Publication Data:

Biegelman, Martin T.
    Executive roadmap to fraud prevention and internal control : creating a culture of compliance / Martin T. Biegelman, Joel T. Bartow. – 2nd ed.
        p. cm.
    Includes index.
    ISBN 978-1-118-00458-6 (hardback); 978-1-118-22179-2 (ebk.); 978-1-118-23551-5 (ebk.); 978-1-118-26035-7 (ebk.)
    1. Corporations–Accounting–Corrupt practices–United States.   2. Corporations–Corrupt practices–United States.   3. Accounting fraud–United States.   I. Bartow, Joel T., 1958–   II. Title.
    HF5686.C7B52 2012
    658.4'73–dc23
                                                                              2011042677

Printed in the United States of America

10   9   8   7   6   5   4   3   2   1

This book is dedicated to our families, who have supported and encouraged us throughout our careers. Without them, we would not be where we are today.

Contents

Foreword to the Second Edition

In the aftermath of the worst financial crisis since the Great Depression, companies both in the United States and around the globe struggle to meet investor expectations and remain competitive on the international stage. Faced with challenging financial conditions, companies have focused efforts on essential cost-cutting measures, while also exploring opportunities in emerging markets and developing new products and services for this decade and beyond. With these challenges come tremendous opportunities, and out of the ashes of the financial crisis will rise stronger, more resilient companies. Unfortunately during challenging times, some employees become tempted to cut corners and engage in fraud.

At the same time, regulators, faced with increased scrutiny for their apparent shortcomings prior to and during the financial crisis, have increased investigative and enforcement efforts to combat a perceived growth in corporate fraud. Armed with new enforcement powers such as the Dodd-Frank Wall Street Reform and Consumer Protection Act and the UK Bribery Act, regulators have increased their efforts to investigate and prosecute corporate fraud.

Against this backdrop, companies must remain focused on building and maintaining a strong fraud prevention and compliance program. The best global companies of today and the future must make corporate integrity and ethics the centerpiece of their culture—permeating every level of the organization, from the board and senior management down to entry-level employees in foreign subsidiaries. Focus must be placed not only on compliance with the law but compliance with the tenets of honesty, ethics, and highest levels of integrity. Creating such a culture is not easy, but must become a reality for any organization that hopes to compete on the global stage.

A strong antifraud program is not only an essential business requirement in today's modern world, it is a crucial factor for regulators when determining sanctions after problems arise. The United States Department of Justice and the Securities and Exchange Commission have written policies that allow for leniency when sanctioning companies that have established and maintained robust compliance programs and internal controls.

Having spent their careers investigating and preventing fraud and corruption, Messrs. Biegelman and Bartow have unique insights in helping organizations develop best-in-class compliance programs and internal controls. Following a distinguished career in federal law enforcement, Mr. Biegelman entered the private sector and became a senior compliance official at a Fortune 25 company. In that role, Mr. Biegelman designed and oversaw a financial integrity unit that remains the model for corporations around the globe. A prolific writer and speaker, Mr. Biegelman has assisted corporations worldwide in crafting and improving fraud prevention programs. Mr. Bartow followed a similar path with leadership roles in law enforcement, consulting, and the corporate sector. He also has designed and implemented fraud prevention programs for corporations and is an accomplished speaker and author.

Martin Biegelman and Joel Bartow understand both regulators and corporations; they have conducted law enforcement investigations and internal investigations; and they have interacted with companies at the preventative stage and following a scandal. The two men have spent their careers with a singular, unwavering focus on improving organizations through fraud prevention and deterrence. Always searching for new and innovative methods, Messrs. Biegelman and Bartow remain thought-leaders and driving forces in the field.

In this second edition of the acclaimed *Executive Roadmap to Fraud Prevention and Internal Control: Creating a Culture of Compliance*, Martin Biegelman and Joel Bartow convert their lifelong experiences and unparalleled knowledge into a concise, well-written book. They provide the essential tools to take aspirational goals for fraud prevention and compliance and build them into concrete and effective programs. The authors offer subject matter expertise on fraud risk assessments, internal investigations, hotlines, whistleblowers, training, and much more. This second edition also discusses the significant regulatory changes that have transpired since their last edition. Through engaging and thought-provoking examples and case studies, the authors provide practical advice for all types and sizes of organizations. As with the prior edition, this book will prove to be essential reading for compliance professionals.

—BRADLEY J. BONDI
Partner, Cadwalader, Wickersham & Taft LLP

Foreword to the First Edition

Today's business leaders operate in an environment of unprecedented opportunity and complexity. The globalization of business grows apace in nearly every industry. The most competitive companies and best business leaders are seizing this opportunity with new products and services that are developed, manufactured, and sold in every country of our planet. Partnerships between companies from different regions of the world are commonplace today; in fact, they are expected. The workforces of the best companies reflect the brightest minds from a multitude of cultures and backgrounds. Technological advances have facilitated the advances of global business practices and in many ways have accelerated the speed of change. Capital markets operate around the clock, rewarding the successful and punishing those who fall short. Media and press coverage and scrutiny have never been as pervasive as today. News made in Cairo, Illinois, reaches a world audience as quickly as news from Cairo, Egypt. Legal and regulatory regimes vary dramatically from both a regional and national perspective. The largest market, the United States, recently enacted the most sweeping reform of public companies since the 1933 and 1934 Securities Acts. It is accurate to characterize this period as one of the most complex and exciting in the history of capitalism. There is unprecedented opportunity and complexity.

To seize the opportunity and manage the complexity, business leaders are elevating their leadership and improving their management practices. This heightened performance is evident in every facet of the best companies' operations, from R&D and Sales and Marketing all the way through to the Board and the governance of the extended organization. The rewards of global markets for the best companies are unprecedented. However, companies that fail to improve or have lapses in performance face swift and negative consequences to their financial results and company brands.

Nowhere are the negative consequences of inadequate leadership and performance more glaring than when fraud has been perpetrated or internal controls have been compromised. Unfortunately, too many companies have failed to establish a well-architected system of controls and governance. The Sarbanes-Oxley Act is providing a catalyst for change, but in too many instances it is a checklist exercise.

The best global companies today and those of the future will have well-defined and disciplined business practices that are executed uniformly on a global basis. This includes systems of accountability and compliance, regardless of different customs and laws. The Board of Directors and senior management establish codes of conduct and a tone that is well understood and a core part of the company culture. Business processes are defined and established to ensure that accounts are correct, disclosures are complete, and policies are followed. Management does the job of ensuring that prevention and detection systems are established. In short, the best leaders and companies ensure that compliance systems are an integral component of their business. Surprisingly, fraud is often overlooked as a key component of an ongoing compliance environment. The best companies assume that they hire the top people. They set the right tone at the top. They have well-understood and articulated codes of conduct. They are often surprised when individuals in their organizations commit fraud.

The leading companies of the world are taking their compliance programs to the next level by building and staffing fraud units to prevent compliance problems. Having been a senior executive at one of the world's premier companies, I can speak first hand about the value and importance of establishing a preventative fraud program as part of a comprehensive compliance environment. Establishing this unit allowed Microsoft to detect and address problems we would not have seen. In addition, the fraud unit leadership became an important part of a management training program to ensure consistent and disciplined business practices worldwide. From a CFO perspective, I was most pleased to see a unit and a program that helped to ensure compliance, but also more than paid for itself!

In this book, the reader will be given a delightful roadmap to fraud prevention and internal controls. Illustrative stories and tips along with practical managerial advice on establishing the right organization, objectives, and practices make this book a must read.

There is important contextual information on current practices and requirements from regulatory regimes. Finally, the 14-point management antifraud program will allow every reader to meet challenges and complexities in a global business environment.

Enjoy!

—JOHN CONNORS

Preface

Welcome to the second edition of *Executive Roadmap to Fraud Prevention and Internal Control*. The first edition was very well-received with excellent feedback from readers, and for that we are most appreciative. Nothing pleases authors more than to know their writing labor is providing educational value. This book is being used as a textbook at colleges and universities. It has been translated into Chinese and used in compliance programs as a reference source. Yet time and fraud march on. There have been events and changes since the original publication that require updating this book. For this second edition, we have kept what is still timeless and relevant while adding new material.

We continue to see fraud and corporate misdeeds with the inevitable impact and enforcement response. Dozens of companies were caught up in the government probes of backdating of stock options. The United States Department of Justice and the Securities and Exchange Commission ramped up investigations of corruption and bribery, bringing more and more prosecutions for violations of the Foreign Corrupt Practices Act. A huge accounting fraud occurred at a once highly regarded technology powerhouse in India. We witnessed the worst financial crisis since the Great Depression and the collapse of once-venerable financial institutions. As a result, new laws were enacted, including the Fraud Enforcement and Recovery Act and the Dodd-Frank Wall Street Reform and Consumer Protection Act (Dodd-Frank).

In a perfect world, this book would not be needed. All corporate employees, from the Chief Executive Officer, the Chief Financial Officer, and the Board of Directors to the entry-level workers, would have the highest degrees of honesty and integrity. Fraud and abuse would be nonexistent. There would be no financial statement fraud, asset misappropriation, kickbacks, or bribery. Unfortunately, we live in an imperfect world in which noncompliance, misconduct, fraud, and corruption exist. One only needs to read the daily papers or watch the evening news to learn of the latest corporate scandal, government investigation, or shareholder litigation. Once respected corporate titans continue to face the prospect of "perp walks" and prison because of financial impropriety.

Common sense tells us that a business executive or manager only needs to hear: "Never commit fraud of any kind." However, fraud prevention always involves further measures: a zero tolerance of fraud in any shape or form, providing fraud awareness and prevention training for all employees, instituting strong internal controls, and limiting exposure to fraud through a robust fraud detection, investigation, and prevention program. Nevertheless, it is naïve to expect that these steps alone can stop all forms of fraud and abuse from occurring. It is a given that corporate crime will always be with us. What is really needed is an ongoing culture of compliance that takes years to build but only a moment to collapse. Corporate executives who are charged with protecting their companies from fraud need a guide to establish an effective program. The passage of the Sarbanes-Oxley Act of 2002, the Amendments to the Federal Sentencing Guidelines for Organizational Crime, the enactment of Dodd-Frank, and other related compliance enhancements have required CEOs, CFOs, and boards to understand the protections that need to be in place to prevent corporate fraud.

Fraud is nothing new. History has shown that fraud has long been a part of our society and will continue to be. As Judge Edwin R. Holmes said in the case of *Weiss v. United States* in 1941, "The law does not define fraud; it needs no definition; it is as old as falsehood and as versatile as human ingenuity."[1] We continue to see corporate scandals and the strong enforcement response of the government. Gone are the days of a slap on the wrist to the wrongdoer and all is forgotten. Today, corporate fraud results in shareholder lawsuits, the implosion of companies, executive prison sentences, and an investor outcry for reform.

In addition, there is a greater focus than ever before on uncovering and preventing fraud as a result of the loss of billions of dollars in equity and greatly diminished investor confidence in the markets. Financial statement fraud and other internal fraud schemes provide considerable risk to a corporation. The enactment of enhanced reporting requirements and greater public scrutiny of companies have contributed to this new age of enforcement. However, internal fraud is not the only risk that businesses face. External fraud schemes also attack companies and can do significant damage to both finances and reputations.

Although no one expects CEOs, CFOs, and other corporate executives and managers to be experts in fraud prevention, the current climate requires a thorough understanding of the principles of fraud examination and state-of-the art compliance programs. This book is a roadmap to help executives understand fraud and reduce its impact. George Santayana once said that those who do not remember the past are condemned to repeat it. This book looks to the past to gain a better understanding of the nature of fraud and how to prevent it. It relates lessons that can be applied now and in the future to prevent fraud, and it also reviews theories and models that explain how and why fraud happens inside an organization. It then describes the current climate as well as the critical importance of fraud prevention and culminates by providing a roadmap to establishing a culture of compliance. Creating this culture is the only way businesses can position themselves to meet the new environment of tighter regulations, transparency, and accountability. It is a proactive method for actually preventing fraud. Simply reacting to fraud issues as they occur is no longer acceptable.

The authors bring a unique perspective to corporate fraud prevention. We are life-long practitioners in the field, with a combined 60-plus years of experience in both the public and private sectors detecting and investigating fraud and white-collar crime. Our careers parallel each other. As federal agents with the United States Postal Inspection Service and the Federal Bureau of Investigation, we investigated fraud and corruption, including corporate crime, investment fraud, kickback schemes, international fraud scams, insurance and healthcare fraud, organized crime, and violations of the Racketeering and Corrupt Organizations Act (RICO). We were involved in the prosecutions of hundreds of fraudsters.

We then went into the private sector to conduct investigations on behalf of corporate clients that were victims of fraud and other crimes. We worked cases all over the world for companies large and small, public and private, and we helped business executives understand the importance of fraud prevention. We were subsequently recruited by corporations and given the responsibility of creating and managing worldwide fraud prevention and anti-corruption programs using our knowledge, skills, and experience. We are both Certified Fraud Examiners (CFEs) who are still doing this work today.

After spending our careers with victims and perpetrators, investigators and prosecutors, in courtrooms and boardrooms, we have great insight into all kinds of fraud and the reasons people commit them. We have many lessons to share as well as numerous case studies and experiences about how to detect, investigate, and prevent fraud. This book is intended to be a primer for corporate executives at both public and private companies who are expected to protect their organizations from fraud and inappropriate behavior. This book will provide special insights to executives at medium and smaller size companies who may falsely believe that they are not facing fraud issues or who may not fully understand the relationship between fraud prevention and good corporate compliance. In addition to senior executives, this book will be beneficial for middle and lower-level executives and managers to help them understand their roles in fraud prevention. It will also be of value to fraud investigators, prosecutors, academics, students, and anyone with an interest in the world of fraud. Each chapter starts with an Executive Summary detailing the key points and takeaways from each chapter. Executive Insights and exhibits are used in various chapters to emphasize important concepts and provide case studies. We have designed the book to be user friendly—the reader does not have to be a CFE to understand the concepts and procedures described. By setting out the generally accepted standards for fraud prevention along with new recommendations, this book helps executives establish a world-class fraud investigation and prevention program. A discussion of the enforcement landscape helps the reader understand the implications of fraud and the need for compliance at every turn.

In all the years we have been investigating fraud and corruption, we have yet to see a decrease in the problem. We probably never will. However, there have been changes in how fraud is addressed. Tougher laws against corporate wrongdoing have been enacted with greatly increased prison sentences for those convicted. It is not the best of times for fraudsters; it is definitely a good time for guardians and gatekeepers. There has never been a better time to be a fraud investigator. Any corporate executive, manager, or employee contemplating a journey to the "dark side" should keep in mind that fraud and noncompliance will be met with the strong arm of the law.

This book will be your roadmap to an understanding of corporate fraud, the implementation of fraud prevention, and the creation of a culture of compliance. Lastly, it is our honor and privilege to be your guides on this journey.

Acknowledgments

Writing a book such as this is never an easy task, and we could not have completed it without the wisdom, assistance, and encouragement of others. First, to our friend and mentor, Joe Wells, founder and Chairman of the Association of Certified Fraud Examiners (ACFE), a true fraud prevention visionary: He encouraged us to write this book and helped us along the way.

Daniel Biegelman again provided extraordinary assistance in contributing ideas, research, and content while helping with editing and proofing. Martin Biegelman's wife, Lynn, reviewed the manuscript, providing valuable feedback and suggestions.

A special note of thanks to our executive editor, Timothy Burgard. Tim gave us the original opportunity to write this book and then guided us through the writing and publishing process. He did it again with this second edition, and we are especially grateful. We also want to acknowledge Helen Cho, Stacey Rivera, and Todd Tedesco at John Wiley & Sons, who were invaluable in helping us successfully navigate through the production process.

We acknowledge those who provided ideas, content, and assistance: Jim Ratley, John Gill, Dick Carozza, Brock Phillips, Tammi Johnson, Jerry Bamel, Gaurav Ajmani, Karen Popp, Frank Goldman, Walt Pavlo, John McDermott, George Stamboulidis, Mark Kirsch, Anthony Migliaccio, Patricia Sweeney, and Aaron Beam. Dr. Richard Hurley provided rich feedback on our first edition that helped us make this book even better, and for that, we owe him a debt of gratitude.

Our deep appreciation to Bob Tenczar who provided guidance and content for the enterprise risk management (ERM) section in Chapter 5. As Senior Director of Enterprise Risk Management at Microsoft Corporation, Bob's unique subject matter expertise in building a world-class risk management program has made him a much-sought-after thought leader in the field.

A special thank you to Barbara Thompson for sharing her rich knowledge and experience in conducting background checks discussed in Chapter 13. Her wisdom and contribution are much appreciated.

When we wanted someone to read our second edition manuscript, we again turned to a dear friend, DeWayn Marzagalli. DeWayn, a former federal agent extraordinaire, provided a keen eye and constructive comments.

Our special appreciation to Bradley Bondi for writing the Foreword to our second edition. Brad is an exceptional litigator, prolific author, and a respected speaker. Thank you again to John Connors for the Foreword to our first edition. As the CFO of Microsoft Corporation, he built a world-class finance organization and led by example in creating a culture of compliance and integrity.

To those dedicated law enforcement professionals and CFEs who fight fraud and corruption on a daily basis, we salute you. It is their work that we recognize in this book. They are the ones whose unflagging efforts hold corporate fraudsters accountable while protecting the common good.

Executive Roadmap to Fraud Prevention and Internal Control

Fraud's Feeding Frenzy

EXECUTIVE SUMMARY

In the first decade of this century, the ongoing "feeding frenzy" of corporate fraud proves that we fail to learn from history. Respected and trusted corporate executives have been revealed to be morally corrupt fraudsters. They became rogue employees: too busy stealing from the corporate "piggy bank" to think of the consequences for their employees, shareholders, customers, or themselves. Corporate powerhouses such as Enron and World-Com and their executives were swept up in fraudulent financial accounting and a multitude of other frauds. The government reacted strongly in response to the public outcry after billions of dollars in investments evaporated. The President promoted the need for corporate responsibility and promised to arrest any corporate executive with a hand in the corporate coffers. Some indicted CEOs tried to use the "Chutzpah Defense," claiming they were deaf, dumb, and blind when the frauds were going on at their companies. The outcome has been indictments, followed by "perp walks" as well as convictions, and a change in how the government views corporate fraud prevention. Yet, fraud still rears its ugly head.

FRAUD'S FEEDING FRENZY STILL GOING STRONG

In the late 1980s, a federal agent investigated a $95 million swindle in New York City involving mail fraud, bank fraud, money laundering, and a host of other crimes. He and his team made arrest after arrest of the many fraudsters involved in this massive scheme. After the arrest of yet another major player in the fraud, this federal agent commented on the defendants' criminal behavior. He likened it to hungry sharks feeding on their helpless prey and called it a "feeding frenzy of fraud." Through the years, the expression has often been used to describe various fraud schemes that made the headlines. This snappy, off-the-cuff description of fraud and the people who commit it tells volumes about the damaging effect it can have. Like unrelenting sharks constantly searching for their next meals, fraudsters never stop their search for new opportunities to commit fraud and economic crime.

Fraud has always been a thorn in the side of honest citizens and businesses. The enactment of strong laws and the empowerment of enforcement agents are helpful but certainly do not guarantee an end to fraud, a crime of opportunity that has been with us through the ages. Uninformed people who think that the corporate wrongdoings in recent years comprised the first such instances of large-scale fraud have much to learn. "Thus, all through the country, thousands of innocent and unsophisticated people, knowing nothing about the ways of these city thieves and robbers, are continuously fleeced and robbed."[1] Does this sound like a description of the many victims of Enron, WorldCom, and other corporate frauds? It was said by a congressional sponsor of the United States Mail Fraud Statute[2] well over a century ago. The Mail Fraud Statute, the nation's oldest and premier fraud-fighting mandate, was enacted in 1872 after an epidemic of consumer mail-order frauds. Today, consumer frauds of all types are still prosecuted with the Mail Fraud Statute, as are many corporate frauds, large and small. The Mail Fraud Statute is a weapon of choice in prosecuting fraud because it covers any scheme or artifice to defraud as long as the mails are used in some way to further the crime. If e-mail, social media or other electronic communications are used to perpetuate the scam, the Wire Fraud Statute is available.

WHAT A DIFFERENCE A FEW YEARS MAKE

Fraud has had a tremendous impact on the corporate landscape of the early 21st century. Enron, WorldCom, Tyco, Adelphia, Health-South, and other companies dominated the headlines with allegations of accounting and other financial crimes. Chief executives were convicted after high-profile trials and sent to prison. Millions of investors lost billions of dollars, millions more lost confidence in Wall Street, and corporate crime remains in the news. In 2002, the government created the Corporate Fraud Task Force "to hold wrongdoers responsible and to restore an atmosphere of accountability and integrity within corporations across the country."[3] Besides prosecuting corporations and their executives for accounting fraud, the task force brought charges for options backdating, insider trading, securities fraud, market manipulation, revenue and earnings management schemes, Foreign Corrupt Practices Act violations, and hedge fund and tax shelter frauds. The Corporate Fraud Task Force has been successful because it brings the full weight of the federal government down on corporate fraudsters by combining "the talents and experience of thousands of investigators, attorneys, accountants, and regulatory experts" from across ten departments.[4]

The many corporate executives who have faced criminal prosecutions worked for both well-known and lesser known companies. Although the major players have dominated the headlines, defendants came from all types and sizes of business (e.g., a bagel business in New Jersey that created fake sales to fraudulently inflate revenue).[5] When it comes to corporate fraud, anyone can be a player. Exhibit 1.1 lists some of the many corporate defendants prosecuted by the Corporate Fraud Task Force.

PERSONAL PIGGY BANK CONCEPT OF LEADERSHIP

The corporate scandals in recent years had a common recipe: corporate executives with no integrity, total arrogance, and huge greed, combined with weak boards and accounting firms that failed to fulfill their responsibility for independent auditing. Executives showed

EXHIBIT 1.1   Significant Criminal Cases Prosecuted by the Corporate Fraud Task Force

Adelphia
Allfirst
Allou Healthcare
American Tissue
Arthur Andersen
Biocontrol
Cendant
Charter Communications
Computer Associates
Comverse Technology
Credit Suisse First Boston
Dynegy
eConnect
Enron
Financial Advisory Consultants
GenesisIntermedia, Inc.
Golden Bear Golf
HealthSouth
Homestore
ImClone
Informix
Just for Feet
Katun Corporation
L90, Inc.
Leslie Fay
Manhattan Bagel
McKesson
Merrill Lynch
MonsterWorldwide
Network Associates
NextCard, Inc.
Nicor Energy
Peregrine Systems
PurchasePro
Quintus
Qwest
Refco
Reliant Energy Services, Inc.
Rite Aid
SafeNet
Symbol Technologies
Targus Group
U.S. Technologies
Vari-L Company, Inc.
Waste Management
WorldCom
Zurich Payroll

Source: U.S. Department of Justice, Corporate Fraud Task Force, *Significant Criminal Cases and Charging Documents*, www.justice.gov/archive/dag/cftf/cases.htm.

complete disregard for shareholders with a belief they could steal huge amounts of money from their respective companies. In the case of former Tyco CEO Dennis Kozlowski, there were multiple reports of his excessive spending of corporate funds for extravagant parties and personal purchases.[6] Kozlowski received from Tyco a $19 million no-interest loan and $11 million for art, antiques, and furniture for his New York City apartment, including the now infamous $6,000 floral patterned shower curtain. To top it off, Tyco paid half the cost for a $2.1 million junket for friends and family to the Italian island of Sardinia to celebrate the birthday of Kozlowski's wife.[7] Because Kozlowski was the CEO, it was easy for him to take as much money out of the company as he wanted. However, he did not escape justice and was subsequently convicted and sent to prison for his criminal behavior.

Kozlowski was not the only corporate titan to take freely from the corporate coffers. Those executives who allow greed to overcome them can easily abuse the power that comes from absolute control. It is a given that former Adelphia CEO John Rigas never thought he would be arrested and convicted for stealing from the corporate piggy bank. Rigas and other Adelphia executives were accused of looting the company of more than $1 billion. They didn't care that the company's assets belonged to shareholders. Even though they felt they were accountable to no one, their accounting fraud was discovered, and federal authorities arrested them.

Former WorldCom CFO Scott Sullivan also thought he had a personal piggy bank to freely tap. This once well-respected CFO of a telecom powerhouse never believed he would be paraded before the media like a common criminal, but there he was doing the "perp walk" with FBI agents in Manhattan following his arrest for a massive accounting fraud. Soon after, he was helping the government prosecute and convict his boss, former WorldCom CEO Bernard Ebbers.

A culture of noncompliance combined with a lack of accountability and transparency contributed to the wholesale looting of once respected companies by their fraudster CEOs, CFOs, and others. People who commit fraud never think about the consequences, or they believe there will be no consequences because they are above the law. They think the piggy bank is theirs to crack open and spend, not caring or understanding that shareholders are the true owners of the funds. These executives forgot who they really worked for.

EXECUTIVE INSIGHT 1.1: A MILLIONAIRE CEO GETS GREEDY

Rocky Aoki was the founder of the successful Benihana Asian restaurant chain. Aoki started the company in 1964 by introducing the Japanese steakhouse experience with entertaining chefs preparing meals in front of the dining guests. He created outlets all over the United States, and eventually Benihana became a publicly traded company on the NASDAQ, with Aoki as both CEO and Chairman of the Board. The company's slogan of "An Experience at Every Table" says it all about dining at Benihana.[i]

Unfortunately, Aoki had another kind of experience that was anything but positive. In 1993, Aoki participated in an insider trading scheme that would eventually result in his indictment and conviction.[ii] Aoki received insider information from a stock promoter who was also a public relations consultant for Spectrum Information Technologies. Spectrum was a publicly held corporation in Manhasset, New York.[iii] Spectrum and its corporate officers would later make the headlines with other issues including allegations of "defrauding investors by artificially boosting its stock price" and other frauds.[iv] The Spectrum case is further profiled in Executive Insight 13.1 in Chapter 13.

According to the June 1998 federal indictment of Aoki, in September and October 1993, Spectrum held secret negotiations with John Sculley, former CEO and Chairman of the Board of Apple Computer, to get him to join Spectrum in a similar executive capacity. During this period, Aoki solicited and received "non-public information concerning Spectrum's negotiations" with Sculley. On October 18, 1993, Spectrum publicly announced that Sculley had accepted the executive positions and would be joining the company. As expected, Spectrum's stock rose from $7.63 to $11.13, a 46 percent jump. Between September 29 and October 15, 1993, Aoki purchased 200,000 shares of Spectrum through three different brokerage accounts. On November 2, 1993, Aoki sold the 200,000 shares for a profit of approximately $590,000.[v]

Aoki then opened a brokerage account for the tipster on or about November 8, 1993, and instructed that 1,000 shares of

Spectrum be purchased for that account. Shortly thereafter, Aoki instructed his personal brokerage account to transfer $10,000 to the tipster's account to pay for the 1,000 shares purchased. The tipster then sold the stock.[vi] After the investigation of Aoki became public in May 1998, he resigned as chairman and CEO in the hopes that the impact on Benihana would be lessened by his departure.[vii]

Postal Inspectors on Long Island, New York, conducted the investigation that resulted in the June 1998 federal indictment of Aoki for one count of conspiracy and five counts of trading with insider information.[viii] In announcing the indictment, Zachary Carter, then United States Attorney for the Eastern District of New York, stated that "insider trading undermines the public's confidence in the fair operation of our nation's securities markets."[ix]

Although Aoki made a major transgression affecting his life and his company, he realized the error of his ways and took responsibility. He pled guilty on August 23, 1999, to four counts of insider trading and on March 8, 2000, was sentenced to three years of probation and a $500,000 fine.[x] The judge was lenient on Aoki because the plea agreement had mandated a $1 million fine and eight months of home detention.[xi]

John McDermott, the Postal Inspector who conducted the investigation, commented that Aoki could not resist making a relatively small amount of money compared with his probable net worth. Aoki used the insider information but got caught because he foolishly paid the tipster by wire transfer of the funds from his brokerage account. The wire transfer led right back to Aoki.

---

[i] Benihana, Inc., www.benihana.com.

[ii] Alan Wax and Patricia Hurtado, "Benihana Founder Gets Probation, Reduced Fine," *Newsday*, March 8, 2000, A54.

[iii] *United States v. Rocky Aoki*, Indictment, United States District Court, Eastern District of New York, CR 98–593.

[iv] James Bernstein, "Feds Charge 3 in Spectrum Fraud, SEC Says Execs Artificially Boosted Stock Price," *Newsday*, December 5, 1997, A77.

[v] *United States v. Rocky Aoki*, Indictment.

[vi] Ibid.

[vii] Combined news services, "Benihana Founder Resigns," *Newsday*, May 20, 1998, A47.

[viii] Robert E. Kessler, "Aoki Indicted in Stock Deal, Benihana Founder Allegedly Paid for Insider Information about Spectrum Development," *Newsday*, June 10, 1998, A51.

[ix] Ibid.

[x] Wax and Hurtado, "Benihana Founder Gets Probation, Reduced Fine."

[xi] Ibid.

THE ROGUE EMPLOYEE

A "rogue employee" is any employee, no matter the level, who deviates from hired duties and perpetrates fraud by attacking the company from within, causing financial and reputational damage.[8] Rogue employees have their own agendas, and their interests are not aligned with those of their employers. In fact, they are not really employees of the company. True employees are committed to the company's mission and are part of the team in helping the company to grow to even greater heights and results. Rogue employees are not out for the common good and betterment of the business. They are out to steal, defraud, and line their pockets to the detriment of their employers. The rogue employee typically portrayed in the media has been the CEO, CFO, or other senior executive. Although these positions attract the most media attention, rogue employees can be anywhere in the organization. In many cases, a long-time, lower level employee who stays "below the radar screen" is the culprit. No matter where the rogue employee may be in a company, greater attention to internal controls and fraud prevention is essential in lessening the damaging effects of employee fraud.

THE CEO'S CHUTZPAH DEFENSE

The significant corporate frauds and resulting prosecutions of responsible corporate executives have provided a new defense posture appropriately named the "Chutzpah Defense." *Chutzpah* is a Yiddish term meaning unbelievable gall, audacity, arrogance, or utter nerve. Corporate executives are taking this word to a new level and it can be applied to their criminal defense strategies as they attempt to escape criminal convictions and lengthy prison time. You can call this defense what you like—The Deaf, Dumb, and Blind Defense; The Dog Ate My Homework Defense; The Hey, I'm Just the CEO, What Do I Know about What's Going On? Defense—but the Chutzpah Defense is the best description. This troubling defense strategy is a last-ditch effort to extricate the corporate fraudster from appropriate punishment.

As former federal agents in the pursuit of justice, the authors know full well what capable, professional defense attorneys are obliged to do when representing clients facing criminal charges. However, it is hardly believable that CEOs, CFOs, or other high-level corporate officers would not know what is going on at their companies. If they are so unaware of what is happening, they should not be in those roles. Boiler room scam artists are fond of saying "put some lipstick on this pig and sell it" when trying to push fraudulent securities on unsuspecting investors. That is what some indicted corporate defendants are trying to do with this Chutzpah Defense. Although the deception may work on some, it is generally not working on juries. Recent experience has shown that juries will just not accept the Chutzpah Defense. Corporate executives on trial who have tried this approach to avoid conviction have lost.[9] Juries will just not believe the CEO who claims ignorance of large-scale fraud occurring right under their nose. Pigs, even with lots of lipstick, don't fly.

Bernard Ebbers tried the Chutzpah Defense and lost. During closing arguments the prosecutor called it the "Aw Shucks Defense": Ebbers claimed he had no expert knowledge of accounting and no idea that any fraud was going on at WorldCom. He was just a "good ol' boy," a cheerleader for the company, who left the details to others. Justice prevailed because pleading ignorance about massive fraud when one is the CEO or CFO just does not work. The basic principles of the changes in corporate governance are all about accountability, especially for the corporate executive.

Although it can be argued that acceptance of responsibility for one's actions is on a societal decline of late, judging from the lawsuits filed against McDonald's Corporation blaming their burgers for weight-related problems or their hot coffee for burns, at least there have been changes for the better. Sarbanes-Oxley and improved corporate governance have increased corporate responsibility and accountability. A word to the wise: "The Buck Stops Here" should be written in big letters and displayed on every corporate executive's desk as a reminder to all that the Chutzpah Defense is not an option.

A SAMPLING OF CORPORATE FRAUDS

Enron's collapse was the first of many publicized corporate scandals and started Congress on the path to enact legislation intended to stop corporate fraud. More transgressions and revelations followed. The biotech firm ImClone Systems was probed by congressional investigators for failing to tell investors that one of its drugs had not been approved by the Food and Drug Administration. Adelphia failed to disclose that it paid billions of dollars in secret loans to its CEO and his family. Arthur Andersen was indicted and convicted on charges of obstruction of justice in the Enron investigation. In May 2005, the U.S. Supreme Court overturned the conviction on improper jury instructions, but the damage was done as the company went out of business. Merrill Lynch agreed to pay a $100 million fine to settle charges that the firm's stock research misled investors. These disclosures and others that followed forced Congress to take a new look at corporate reform. There are many similarities in the lessons that can be learned from the fall of these major corporations.

Enron

More than any other company facing scandal in recent years, Enron stands out as the poster child for corporate greed and fraud. Beginning with Enron's reporting of $638 million in losses on October 16, 2001, the revelations of fraud were nonstop. The resignation of former CEO Jeffrey Skilling in August 2001 was probably more than a coincidence and a harbinger of things to come. As stated in Skilling's indictment of February 18, 2004, the resignation came with "no forewarning to the public."[10] The reading of the criminal charges tells why he would want to leave as quickly as possible. The indictment of Skilling and other co-conspirators details the feeding frenzy of fraud at Enron. In describing the scheme to defraud, the indictment stated that:

> *From 1999 through late 2001, defendants Jeffrey K. Skilling and Richard A. Causey (former Enron Chief Accounting Officer and Executive Vice-President) and their co-conspirators engaged in a wide-ranging scheme to deceive the investing public, the SEC, credit rating agencies, and others about the true performance of Enron's businesses by (1) manipulating Enron's finances so that Enron's publicly reported financial results would falsely appear to meet or exceed analysts' expectations; and (2) making public statements and representations about Enron's financial performance and results that were false and misleading in that they did not fairly and accurately in all material aspects represent Enron's actual financial condition and performance, and omitted to disclose facts necessary to make those statements and representations truthful and accurate.[11]*

Early on, there was much criticism of the Enron Task Force for not moving faster in bringing the company's corporate crooks to justice. There was a constant complaint that the prosecutors were dragging their feet and getting nowhere fast. How wrong the critics were. Complex white-collar crime investigations can often take many months and even years to complete before any indictments are brought. A slow and steady but exhaustive collection of evidence cannot be confused with inactivity. Corporate executives need to remember that federal investigators and prosecutors are working behind the scenes interviewing witnesses, subpoenaing documents, quietly "flipping" targets into cooperators, corroborating information, and building a case. This is what happened with the Enron investigation. As then U.S. Assistant Attorney General Christopher Wray said at the time of Skilling's indictment, "the indictment of Enron's CEO shows that we will follow the evidence wherever it leads—even to the top of the corporate ladder."[12]

The late Kenneth Lay, former Enron Chairman and CEO, subscribed to the Chutzpah Defense by using his own variation, the "Mr. Magoo Defense." Mr. Magoo is the bumbling and nearsighted cartoon character who has no clue what is happening around him. Comedian and television commentator Dennis Miller made a joke about Ken Lay, who was telling everyone who would listen how he was a corporate and financial genius with the ear of presidents—that is, until "the feds" started investigating Enron. Suddenly he became a bumbling Mr. Magoo, who had no idea what was going on inside his own company. He was blind beyond belief to the massive fraud permeating the company he led as founder, chairman, and CEO. Lay repeatedly appeared on television to defend himself and said he knew nothing of Enron's "cooking the books" or other frauds at the company. While the company was heading for bankruptcy, he was publicly encouraging his employees to buy more stock in Enron, claiming it was a great value at the beaten-down price. Although convicted after jury trial, Lay died before sentencing so his conviction was set aside.

Creating a culture of compliance is a common theme of this book. Truly great leaders inspire and mentor their employees to higher standards of accomplishment and integrity. That was clearly missing at Enron. More than two dozen company executives were eventually charged with numerous financial crimes including Skilling, Lay, and former CFO Andrew Fastow. There is no doubt that the "tone at the top" was one of noncompliance and lawlessness that fostered an environment of fraud and corruption at all levels of the company.

Tyco

Dennis Kozlowski, Tyco's former CEO, was accused with other Tyco executives of looting $600 million from the company and defrauding investors through unauthorized loans and bonuses, loans improperly forgiven, and sales of stock that were inflated by fraudulent corporate accounting. Kozlowski joined Tyco in 1975 and rose through the ranks to President, Chief Operating Officer, and then CEO. Over time, he came to typify the corporate lifestyle of excess at every turn. It all came tumbling down when in late May 2002, he learned he was about to be indicted by the Manhattan District Attorney's Office. Kozlowski resigned from Tyco on June 3, 2002, and on June 4, he was arrested.

Tyco's new management commissioned an internal accounting and corporate governance review of the allegations of fraud and abuse by Kozlowski and other former Tyco executives. The review was conducted by New York attorney David Boies with assistance from numerous forensic accountants. The scope of the internal accounting review included 1999 to 2002 reported revenues, profits, cash flow, internal auditing, control procedures (or lack of them), the use of corporate assets to pay personal expenses, employee loans and loan forgiveness, and other corporate governance issues. The subsequent report found the company "engaged in a pattern of aggressive accounting which, even when in accordance with Generally Accepted Accounting Principles (GAAP), was intended to increase reported earnings above what they would have been if more conservative accounting had been employed."[13]

Tyco was successful to a degree in playing the numbers through accounting manipulations. For one, it abused goodwill. *Goodwill* in accounting terms is a financial advantage that a business gains from the purchase price over fair market value of assets acquired. When a company is purchased, goodwill is the difference between the amount paid over the net asset value. Tyco had a "staggering $26 billion worth of goodwill on its balance sheet."[14] This maneuver greatly increased earnings and cash flow because it allowed Tyco to book additional revenue without associated costs of acquisition. Tyco also did not report acquisitions that it stated were small enough to be considered "immaterial" under GAAP. "From 1991 through 2001, Tyco spent $8 billion on more than 700 acquisitions that it said were not material. But taken as a group, these 700 deals clearly had a huge impact on Tyco's results."[15] There is no doubt that these accounting moves had a material impact on the revenue and expenses of the company and should have been disclosed.

An important lesson to remember is that no matter how strong the evidence appears to be in a case, there is no such thing as a guaranteed conviction. Dennis Kozlowski's first trial in state court in Manhattan in April 2004 ended in a mistrial. The evidence seemed to be overwhelming, but still the jury could not come to a decision after 12 days of deliberations. After the mistrial, one of the jurors called the case against the defendants "a slam dunk" and stated, "Those guys [Kozlowski and Mark Schwartz, Tyco's former CFO] are never going to get acquitted, no matter what they do. The best they can hope for is a hung jury."[16] Despite this juror's view, the jury could not come to an agreement to convict, forcing a retrial of the defendants. At the second trial in June 2005, Kozlowski and Schwartz were found guilty of looting $600 million from the company. They were each sentenced to between $8^{1}/_{2}$ and 25 years in prison and immediately began serving their sentences. Kozlowski and Schwartz were also hit with fines and restitution totaling $239 million. It was one of the biggest wins for prosecutors fighting corporate fraud.

WorldCom

WorldCom was once the second largest long-distance telecommunications company. It was a Wall Street darling that in reality had a culture of noncompliance and criminality at the highest levels of leadership. Former CEO Bernard Ebbers was convicted after trial in March 2005. Former CFO Scott Sullivan pled guilty, as did several other executives who agreed to cooperate against Ebbers. The downfall began in March 2002, when then Vice-President of Internal Audit Cynthia Cooper went to Sullivan with her concerns about the company's accounting. He angrily told her to mind her own business and that everything was fine. Her instincts told her there were big problems, and she kept digging. Ebbers resigned in April 2002 amid questions regarding $408 million in personal loans. A $7.2 billion accounting fraud eventually became a $107 billion bankruptcy filing, the largest in corporate history.

In late May 2002, Cooper and her staff uncovered $500 million in fraudulent computer expenses. Arthur Andersen, WorldCom's auditors, refused to respond to some of Cooper's questions about the auditing. On June 20, 2002, Cooper told WorldCom's Audit Committee that the company was falsifying its accounting. The Audit Committee and Board of Directors are credited with acting quickly. A few days later Sullivan was fired, and WorldCom admitted it hid $3.85 billion in expenses, allowing it to post a profit in 2001 instead of a loss. In 1998, *CFO* magazine named Sullivan one of the country's best CFOs. What the magazine did not know was that Sullivan had instructed his people to cook the books. WorldCom hid billions of dollars in expenses by transferring them throughout the company's capital expenditures accounts. Cooper exposed this massive fraud and became a famous whistleblower, recognized as one of *Time* magazine's Persons of the Year for 2002.

Federal prosecutors moved swiftly to prosecute Sullivan and former controller David Myers on 17 criminal counts including conspiracy to commit securities fraud. They were arrested on August 1, 2002, just two days after President Bush signed the Sarbanes-Oxley Act into law. At a Washington, D.C., news conference after the arrests, then Attorney General John Ashcroft stated, "With each arrest, indictment and prosecution, we send this clear, unmistakable message: corrupt corporate executives are no better than common thieves."[17]

The subsequent federal indictment issued by a Grand Jury in the Southern District of New York alleged that Sullivan and his co-conspirators "engaged in an illegal scheme to inflate artificially WorldCom's publicly reported earnings by falsely and fraudulently reducing reported line cost expenses."[18] Furthermore, the indictment stated that the "co-conspirators made these false and fraudulent journal entries in WorldCom's general ledger knowing, and intending (1) that such journal entries would ultimately be reflected in WorldCom's financial statements and public filings with the SEC; (2) that World-Com's financial statements and public filings would falsely overstate WorldCom's earnings; and (3) that the investing public would rely upon such overstated earnings."[19] As often happens, federal prosecutors convinced Sullivan, Myers, and several other executives to testify against an even bigger catch, CEO Ebbers. Ebbers, who steadfastly maintained his innocence and demanded a jury trial, got his wish.

Sullivan was the star government witness against Ebbers at trial. The jury spent eight exhausting days deliberating. It came back on March 15, 2005, with a conviction on all counts, including conspiracy to commit fraud by falsifying WorldCom's financial results; securities fraud by misleading investors and the public about WorldCom's true financial condition; and making false filings that misrepresented WorldCom's financial state with the SEC. Although Ebbers took the stand and claimed he was unaware of the fraud and that Sullivan alone was the mastermind behind it, the jury did not believe him. Leslie Caldwell, the former head of the Enron Task Force, who is knowledgeable about the CEO ignorance defense, stated after the conviction, "There's inherently a lot of suspicion when a highly paid CEO says there were significant things he wasn't aware of. There's a certain cynicism among jurors, who ask, 'How'd you get to be CEO?'" On July 13, 2005, Ebbers was sentenced to 25 years in prison for masterminding the fraud at WorldCom. The trial judge rejected his plea for leniency and gave him the harshest sentence yet for corporate fraud.

Adelphia

John Rigas had it all. At 78 years of age, he was the founder of one of the nation's largest cable companies. He was a son of Greek immigrants who became an entrepreneur and eventually got into the cable subscription business by starting Adelphia Communications Corporation. He built it from the ground up into a public company worth billions of dollars. His two sons were executives in the company. Rigas and his family lived the good life that mega millions in corporate earnings can provide. They had mansions, their own personal golf course, a fleet of luxury cars, and power. Unfortunately, Rigas had a secret that would soon be exposed. He was a corporate fraudster, and Adelphia had become his personal piggy bank.

All came crashing down for Rigas on July 24, 2002, when United States Postal Inspectors arrested Rigas, his two sons, and two other Adelphia executives and charged them with multiple counts of conspiracy to commit mail fraud, wire fraud, bank fraud, and securities fraud. Rigas and his sons did their obligatory "perp walk" in Manhattan just days before the Sarbanes-Oxley Act was signed into law. Rigas and his sons knew they were about to be arrested and offered to surrender, to avoid the perp walk. The government refused because they wanted the spectacle of a very public arrest to send a strong message to other corporate crooks. As stated in the criminal complaint, "the defendants and their co-conspirators perpetrated an elaborate and multifaceted scheme to defraud stockholders and creditors of Adelphia, and the public." Another statement found in the criminal complaint describing the defendants' behavior was unusual: "The investigation has revealed probable cause to believe that John J. Rigas, the defendant, together with members of his family, has looted Adelphia on a massive scale, using the company as the Rigas family's *personal piggy bank* [emphasis added], at the expense of public investors and creditors."[20] The United States Attorney for the Southern District of New York called the crime "one of the most elaborate and extensive frauds ever."

The scheme ran from 1999 through May 2002, but the criminal investigation only began in March 2002, resulting in prosecution by July 2002. When Adelphia filed for bankruptcy protection on June 25, 2002, it listed $18.6 billion in debt. The investigation found that Rigas and his sons had looted the company of more than $1 billion. Among the many financial transgressions they were alleged to have committed are the following:

- Received a million dollars a month in secret cash payments
- Built a $13 million private golf course using Adelphia funds that were not disclosed to the non-Rigas family members of the board of directors or to the public
- Borrowed $2.3 billion from banks with Adelphia guaranteeing loans that were not recorded in the company's books
- Used $252 million to pay margin calls against loans that the family received from various brokerage firms
- Personal use of corporate aircraft and New York City apartments by Rigas family members (Adelphia employees were allegedly instructed not to record personal use of the aircraft in the usage logs.)

Rigas, his sons, and one other co-defendant went to trial in New York on March 1, 2004. On July 8, 2004, Rigas and one son, Timothy Rigas, were convicted on all 15 counts. The jury deadlocked on another son, Michael Rigas, who later pled guilty to making a false entry in a company record to avoid a retrial. A fourth defendant, Adelphia's assistant treasurer, was acquitted. One of the government's star witnesses at trial was cooperating defendant James R. Brown, once Adelphia's Vice-President of Finance. He testified that Adelphia developed a culture of lies. They had kept two sets of books for more than 10 years. One book contained the falsified numbers, and one had the actual numbers, so they would know which ones they had manipulated and by how much. As Brown testified, "We don't want to fool ourselves."[21] Brown was a critical insider witness for the government, and although he spent 18 years at the company and was a loyal employee, the threat of a long prison term turned him into a government cooperator. There are no bonds of loyalty when prison is a reality.

At his sentencing hearing on June 20, 2005, Rigas told the judge, "In my heart and in my conscience, I'll go to my grave really and truly believing that I did nothing but try to improve the conditions of my employees."[22] The judge did not buy Rigas' story and sentenced him to a "life sentence" of 15 years in prison since Rigas was 80 years old when originally sentenced. Rigas' son, Timothy, received 20 years in prison.[23] In 2008, a federal judge reduced the elder Rigas' sentence by three years and his new release date is scheduled for 2018.

THE DRIVE FOR CORPORATE RESPONSIBILITY

In 2002, President George W. Bush saw corporate fraud as such an enormous problem that he made corporate responsibility a core element of his administration, along with the war on terrorism. Early on in the emerging corporate scandals, President Bush set out an aggressive agenda to fight corporate fraud including:

- Exposing and punishing acts of corruption
- Holding corporate officers and directors accountable
- Protecting small investors, pension holders, and workers
- Moving corporate accounting out of the shadows
- Developing a stronger, more independent corporate audit system
- Providing better information to investors[24]

On March 7, 2002, the President announced his "Ten-Point Plan to Improve Corporate Responsibility and Protect America's Shareholders." It was based on three principles: information accuracy and accessibility, management accountability, and auditor independence. The Ten-Point Plan declared that:

1. Each investor should have quarterly access to the information needed to judge a firm's financial performance, condition, and risks.
2. Each investor should have prompt access to critical information.
3. CEOs should personally vouch for the veracity, timeliness, and fairness of their companies' disclosures, including their financial statements.

4. CEOs or other officers should not be allowed to profit from erroneous financial statements.
5. CEOs or other officers who clearly abuse their power should lose their right to serve in any corporate leadership positions.
6. Corporate leaders should be required to tell the public promptly whenever they buy or sell company stock for personal gain.
7. Investors should have complete confidence in the independence and integrity of companies' auditors.
8. An independent regulatory board should ensure that the accounting profession is held to the highest ethical standards.
9. The authors of accounting standards must be responsive to the needs of investors.
10. Firms' accounting systems should be compared with best practices, not simply against the minimum standards.[25]

These tenets were to form the basis of the Sarbanes-Oxley Act of 2002.

President Bush went further to demonstrate to the investing public that he meant business. On July 6, 2002, he called on Congress to legislate new powers and statutes to stop corporate fraud and bring to justice those wrongdoers who violated the public and corporate trust. On the same date, he created the Corporate Fraud Task Force, headed by then Deputy Attorney General Larry Thompson, to coordinate the investigation and prosecution of financial accounting fraud and other corporate frauds. The full force of federal law enforcement would be brought to bear on corporate wrongdoers. Although some may argue that it should not have taken massive corporate implosions and billions of dollars in losses to get the government to act, "better late than never" was the refrain of the day.

Congress and the President did act. On July 30, 2002, President Bush signed the Sarbanes-Oxley Act into law. This law has had significant implications for public companies. Sarbanes-Oxley will not make fraud disappear, but its strong language and stiff penalties could deter corporate executives who are tempted to stray. Sarbanes-Oxley has become a household name with corporate America, accounting firms, and government prosecutors and regulators. In corporate suites and boardrooms of public companies, Sarbanes-Oxley and its requirements, safeguards, and sanctions are discussed daily. Sarbanes-Oxley has had a major impact on corporate crooks and enhanced corporate compliance and governance in the process.

In November 2009, President Barack Obama established the Financial Fraud Enforcement Task Force to replace the Corporate Fraud Task Force. The new task force builds upon the work of the Corporate Fraud Task Force with an added emphasis on financial fraud that resulted in the financial crisis of 2008 and those economic recovery efforts that came in its wake. "The task force's mission," according to U.S. Attorney General Eric Holder, "is not to just hold accountable those who helped bring about the last financial meltdown, but to prevent another meltdown from happening."[26] The task force investigates a variety of frauds, including bank, mortgage, loan and lending fraud, securities and commodities fraud, retirement plan fraud, mail and wire fraud, tax crimes, money laundering, False Claims Act violations, and other financial crimes.

FIGHTING FRAUD IS GUARANTEED EMPLOYMENT

Investigators beginning a career or assignment in fraud detection are commonly told never to worry about being out of a job because investigating fraud provides job security. The message is that fraud is an evil that will always be present in our society and that anyone smart enough to enter the field of fraud detection and prevention will find full and long-term employment. Sad as it may seem, fraud will always occur wherever there is opportunity. The feeding frenzy of fraud will not abate unless fraud prevention is embraced and instituted at all levels of a company, especially in the executive suite.

NOTES

1. Attributed to an unnamed Congressional sponsor of the *Mail Fraud Statute*, enacted in 1872.
2. *Mail Fraud Statute,* U.S. Code Title 18, Section 1341.
3. U.S. Department of Justice Archives, *The President's Corporate Fraud Task Force*, www.justice.gov/archive/dag/cftf/.

4. Ibid.

5. *United States v. Allan Boren and Eric Cano*, First Superseding Indictment filed February 2001, Cr. No. 01–730(A)-GAF, United States District Court for the Central District of California, 5–6.

6. Mark Maremont and Colleen DeBaise, "Prosecutor Says Two Executives Used Tyco as 'Piggy Bank,'" *Wall Street Journal*, March 17, 2004, C1.

7. Colleen DeBaise, "Newest 'Tyco Gone Wild' Video Is Out, and Jurors See $6,000 Shower Curtain," *Wall Street Journal*, November 26, 2003, C1.

8. Timothy L. Mohr, "Employee Fraud and Rogue Employees-Prevention and Detection," a professional project submitted to the faculty of Utica College, Utica, N.Y., December 2002.

9. The acquittal of former HealthSouth CEO Richard Scrushy in June 2005 is an exception. Although the evidence against Scrushy appeared to be formidable, the jury felt otherwise. There are some who attribute the acquittal to the "homefield advantage" of having the case tried in Birmingham, AL, where Scrushy was very popular, as well as the excellent work of the defense team in impeaching many of the prosecution witnesses.

10. *United States v. Jeffrey K. Skilling and Richard A. Causey*, Superseding Indictment filed February 18, 2004, Cr. No. H-04–25, United States District Court, Southern District of Texas, Houston Division at 3.

11. Ibid., 5.

12. "Ex-Enron CEO Named in 42-Count Indictment," *MSNBC .com*, February 19, 2004, www.msnbc.msn.com/id/4311642.

13. Summary of Findings of Accounting and Governance Review prepared for Tyco International, Ltd. by Boies, Schiller & Flexner, December 30, 2002.

14. Anthony Bianco, William Symonds, Nanette Byrnes, and David Polek, "The Rise and Fall of Dennis Kozlowski," *Business Week*, December 23, 2002, 64–77.

15. Ibid.

16. Christopher Mumma and Thomas Becker, "Jurors Expect Conviction in Tyco Retrial," *Seattle Times*, April 7, 2004, E4.

17. Carrie Johnson and Ben White, "WorldCom Arrests Made," *Washington Post*, August 2, 2002, A1.

18. *United States v. Scott D. Sullivan*, First Superseding Indictment, S1 02 Cr. 114 (BSJ), United States District Court for the Southern District of New York, 9.

19. Ibid., 10.

20. *United States v. John J. Rigas, Timothy J. Rigas, Michael J. Rigas, James R. Brown, and Michael C. Mulcahey*, criminal complaint unsealed on July 24, 2002, United States District Court, Southern District of New York, sworn to by United States Postal Inspector Thomas F.X. Feeney.

21. Peter Grant, "Adelphia Insider Tells of Culture of Lies at Firm," *Wall Street Journal*, May 19, 2003, C1.

22. "Adelphia Founder Gets 15-Year Term; Son Gets 20," *MSNBC .com*, June 20, 2005, www.msnbc.msn.com/id/8291040/.

23. Ibid.

24. The White House, "The President's Leadership in Combating Corporate Fraud," *Corporate Responsibility*, http://georgewbush-whitehouse.archives.gov/infocus/corporateresponsibility/.

25. Ibid.

26. U.S. Securities and Exchange Commission, "President Obama Establishes Interagency Financial Fraud Enforcement Task Force," press release (November 17, 2009), www.sec.gov/news/press/2009/2009–249.htm.

CHAPTER 2

Fraud Theory and Prevention

EXECUTIVE SUMMARY

The Association of Certified Fraud Examiners (ACFE) reports that the average organization loses 5 percent of its annual revenue to fraud. This statistic alone should be reason enough to embrace fraud prevention. Even if this number is off slightly, the cumulative losses to businesses are staggering. Why do people commit fraud? There are many theories. One centers on the elements of motive, opportunity, and rationalization. Can fraud be prevented? Lessening or removing opportunity is one way to fight fraud. This can be accomplished by improved internal controls and accountability. If people know they will be held responsible for acts of fraud, then likely perpetrators will often not commit the crime. Understanding the importance of fraud prevention is critical for a business organization in this new era of improved corporate governance.

FRAUD 101

What is fraud? Before one can completely understand fraud prevention, one must know what fraud is. Webster's dictionary defines fraud as "an instance or act of trickery or deceit especially when involving misrepresentation; an intentional misrepresentation, concealment, or nondisclosure for the purpose of inducing another in reliance upon it to part with some valuable thing belonging to him or to surrender a legal right."[1] *Black's Law Dictionary* defines fraud as "the knowing misrepresentation of the truth or concealment of a material fact to induce another to act to his or her detriment and a misrepresentation made recklessly without belief in its truth to induce another to act."[2] The Mail Fraud Statute defines fraud as "any scheme or artifice to defraud, or for obtaining money or property by means of false or fraudulent pretenses, representations, or promises."[3] The word *artifice* was included in the original wording of the Mail Fraud Statute in 1872 and means trickery or guile, both of which are very descriptive of fraud.

The Association of Certified Fraud Examiners (ACFE) uses the term *occupational fraud and abuse* and defines it as "the use of one's occupation for personal enrichment through the deliberate misuse or misapplication of the employing organization's resources or assets."[4] When boiled down to its essence, fraud is all about stealing, cheating, lying, and lack of integrity. However, the best definition might be something fraudster Barry Minkow once said, "Fraud is nothing more than the skin of a truth stuffed with a lie."[5] Proving that it takes one to know one, his definition says it all about fraud. Minkow was a teenager in Southern California in the 1980s when he founded and built a multimillion-dollar carpet cleaning business. Unfortunately, he succumbed to the "dark side." He decided to take his company public and conspired to defraud investors in a $26 million initial public offering (IPO) fraud. He went to jail for seven years. After serving his sentence, Minkow began to lecture and write about the consequences of fraud as well as starting a fraud detection consulting business. Unfortunately, Minkow once again succumbed to the evil allure of fraud and his old ways and was charged with insider trading in 2011.

CORPORATE FRAUD

The term *corporate fraud* has been defined by the Department of Justice to include the following illegal conduct:

1. *Falsification of corporate financial information (including, for example, false/fraudulent accounting entries, bogus trades, and other transactions designed to artificially inflate revenue, fraudulently overstating assets, earnings and profits or understating/concealing liabilities and losses, and false transactions designed to evade regulatory oversight);*
2. *Self-dealing by corporate insiders (including, for example, insider trading, kickbacks, misuse of corporate property for personal gain, and individual tax violations related to any such self-dealing);*
3. *Fraud in connection with an otherwise legitimately operated mutual or hedge fund (including, for example, late trading, certain market-timing schemes, falsification of net asset values, and other fraudulent or abusive trading practices by, within, or involving a mutual or hedge fund); and*
4. *Obstruction of justice, perjury, witness tampering, or other obstructive behavior relating to categories 1 to 3 above.*[6]

Whether it is a boiler room scam promising a luxurious, seven-day, all-expenses-paid cruise to the Bahamas that turns out to be a cruise to nowhere, or a "cooking the books" accounting scheme at a major corporation, fraud is the skin of a truth, stuffed with a lie. All fraud appears on the surface to be forthright, but as one peels away the layers, the inner deceit, corruption, and lies are exposed.

As young federal agents, the authors wanted to arrest every fraudster they could find. Although a fair number of them were arrested, it was easy to see that there were not enough law enforcement officers to arrest all the criminals out there. Even if there were enough resources to put every schemer in jail, the damaging effects of fraud would not be reversed, nor would lost assets or reputations be restored. It became apparent that detecting fraud early, or, better yet, stopping it from occurring, was far more effective. However, stopping fraud's feeding frenzy is easier said than done.

Preventing fraud is often much harder than it would appear. Human nature and greed guarantee that society and corporations will always face the issue of fraud. It may be noble to try to stop all fraud, but the reality is that it will always be present, although much can be done to limit its effects. The key to preventing fraud is first to understand that fraud exists and then limit its potential for harm. To do this, the detection of fraud is paramount, along with exceptional fraud prevention programs.

THE ACFE 2010 REPORT TO THE NATIONS ON OCCUPATIONAL FRAUD AND ABUSE

The ACFE is the world's premier provider of antifraud training and education. The organization has over 60,000 members worldwide who fight and prevent fraud in the public and private sectors. A number of them are Certified Fraud Examiners (CFE). CFEs are certified specialists in the detection, investigation, and prevention of fraud. They have a unique set of skills and experiences to resolve allegations of fraud. The ACFE's goal is to reduce business fraud worldwide and inspire public confidence in the value and integrity of the fraud detection and prevention profession. The ACFE also conducts studies and issues reports on occupational fraud to examine the effects of occupational fraud and abuse on individuals and organizations.

The ACFE's *2010 Report to the Nations*[7] covers 1,843 cases of occupational fraud in the United States and more than 100 other countries with a total of over $18 billion in losses. Participants in the study included CFEs with direct involvement in the actual detection and investigation of the fraud. The study found some very interesting and ominous trends for fraud:

- The typical organization loses 5 percent of its annual revenues to fraud. Applied to the Gross World Product for 2009, that equates to more than $2.9 trillion in total losses. Although this number may seem high, even a loss of 1 percent translates into a significant shortfall for a company. Thus, any reduction in the amount of fraud and abuse that occurs in a business will result in additional gains for the bottom line.
- The study found that occupational frauds are more likely to be detected through an employee tip than through internal audits or internal controls. This finding clearly supports the key Sarbanes-Oxley requirement for audit committees to establish confidential reporting mechanisms. This requirement will be covered in more detail in Chapters 3 and 12.
- The establishment of confidential reporting mechanisms can dramatically reduce fraud losses. The median loss for organizations

that had a confidential and/or anonymous reporting hotline was $100,000. The study further found that organizations without established reporting processes had median losses that were more than double those with established reporting procedures.

■ Tips about fraud are reported not only by employees but also by those outside the company with connections and knowledge. The study found that 49.2 percent of tips came from employees of the subject company, 17.8 percent came from customers, and 12.1 percent came from vendors. Thus, it is imperative to publicize the existence of a hotline and other confidential reporting mechanisms to ensure that all possible allegations are investigated.

■ The initial detection of occupational frauds came from tips in 40.2 percent of cases. Management review and internal audit accounted for a total of 29.3 percent of cases. Although internal controls have long been established as an effective way to reduce fraud and abuse, all too often they are not robust enough to be effective in detecting and stopping fraud. The study found that a lack of internal controls, such as segregation of duties, contributed to fraud in 37.8 percent of cases. The override of existing controls was second with 19.2 percent.

■ There is a false impression that small companies are better protected from fraud than larger companies. In reality, they suffer disproportionately greater fraud losses although the 2010 study found less than in previous studies. Small companies generally have fewer fraud prevention controls in place than larger organizations. Small companies are defined as those with fewer than 100 employees. The median loss experienced by small companies was $150,000. That was higher than the median loss suffered by the largest businesses. A small company may not survive a large fraud loss and needs to be at least as proactive in fraud prevention as larger companies. The key message is that all companies, no matter the size, need to have effective fraud detection and prevention programs in place.

■ The fraud loss amount is directly related to the position of the perpetrator. Common sense and history tell us that a CFO can do far more financial damage to a company than someone in the mailroom. The study found that frauds perpetrated by owners and executives resulted in a median loss of $723,000. This was more than three times higher than the losses resulting from managers and nine times higher than losses caused by lower-level employees.

- ■ The study also found that most occupational fraudsters (85 percent) were first-time offenders. (The authors of this book had the same experience—the vast majority of the people they arrested were first-time fraud offenders.) Only 7 percent of the subjects in the study had a previous conviction for fraud. Instituting a process for conducting background checks will eliminate some offenders from an organization but clearly will not be enough to stop all fraud and abuse. An important point to remember is that just because fraudsters have not been arrested before does not mean they have not been committing fraud for some time. Fraud is often hard to expose, so it is common for fraudsters to be involved in long-term schemes without being detected.

- ■ Frauds lasted a median of 18 months before being detected. Since fraud is often hard to detect, the longer a fraud runs, the more damage can be done to an organization. Fraudsters often display warning signs or red flags that can aid in early detection. Exhibit 2.2 lists many of the behavioral red flags of a fraudster. Fraud examiners and compliance professionals need to be trained to recognize these behavioral signs.

The *2010 Report to the Nations*, like its predecessor reports in 1996, 2002, 2004, 2006, and 2008, shows that the 5 percent figure for loss of total revenue to occupational fraud has generally remained the same; the actual losses have increased, however. The report classified occupational fraud into three major categories:

1. Asset misappropriation, which involves theft or misuse of an organization's assets such as billing schemes, payroll schemes, and expense reimbursement schemes. These types of fraud are discussed in Chapter 7.
2. Corruption, including conflicts of interest in which the employee's motivations may not be aligned with the best interests of the employer. Typical examples include kickbacks, bid-rigging, and hidden business interests in vendors. These types of fraud are also discussed in Chapter 7.

3. Fraudulent financial statements, including overstating revenues and understating liabilities and expenses. These types of fraud are discussed in Chapter 6.

Although asset misappropriation schemes were by far the most common (more than 86 percent), they had the lowest median loss, of just $135,000. Fraudulent financial statement schemes occurred only 4.8 percent of the time but had the highest median losses, of $4,100,000. Typically, companies can recover from asset misappropriation schemes, but financial statement frauds can have devastating effects on an organization, as was seen with Enron, WorldCom, and others. Corruption schemes occurred in 32.8 percent of cases with a median loss of $250,000. The sum of percentages exceeds 100 percent because several cases involved schemes from more than one category.[8]

FRAUD PREVENTION

The ACFE's *Fraud Examiners Manual* states that "Fraud prevention requires a system of rules, which, in their aggregate, minimize the likelihood of fraud occurring while maximizing the possibility of detecting any fraudulent activity that may transpire. The potential of being caught most often persuades likely perpetrators not to commit the fraud. Because of this principle, the existence of a thorough control system is essential to fraud prevention."[9] The key words here are in the last two sentences. The "potential of being caught" and "the existence of a thorough control system" are critical to any effective fraud prevention program. It is about being proactive rather than reactive. As the important elements of a fraud prevention program are discussed within a company, repetition and reinforcement are necessary because they are so critical to the success of a program.

Fraud prevention is much more than just a good business practice; it is a requirement today. Companies face numerous risks, some of which are potentially devastating. Among these risks, the issue of vicarious liability stands out. Corporations and other organizations can be held liable for criminal acts committed as a matter of organizational policy. They may also be held liable for the criminal acts of their employees if those acts are performed in the course and scope of their employment for the purpose of benefiting the corporation. An organization can be held liable for something an employee does on behalf of the organization even if the employee is not authorized to perform that act.

The financial risks from fraud losses, shareholders' lawsuits, federal prosecution, fines, and convictions for fraud are all good reasons to institute a strong fraud prevention program. Risk to reputations and the emotional toll of fraud should also be considered. As hard as it is to believe now, Arthur Andersen once had a sterling reputation among accounting firms. If Arthur Andersen, the founder, were alive today, he would be devastated to see what happened to the company that he spent the better part of his life building into an accounting and consulting powerhouse. The sad fact is that it takes just a handful of employees to destroy a company of many thousand innocent individuals. The emotional toll of fraud is the impact on the employees and families who had nothing to do with their company's fraud but who suffer the consequences. The personal devastation to the Enron employees who believed in their company and were deceived like all the other shareholders is but one example. These employees saw their jobs, life savings, and retirement plans disappear, all because of corporate fraud and executives with no integrity.

PERP WALKS AS A FORM OF FRAUD PREVENTION

We have seen numerous perp—that is, *perpetrator*—walks as corporate executives are arrested for fraud. Perp walks have come to be expected in high-profile cases. They are the very public parading of a high-profile person charged with a serious crime before television cameras by law enforcement officers for the express purpose of publicizing the defendant's arrest and sending a strong message to other such criminals that this is what will soon happen to them.

Perp walks are nothing new. They have long been used by law enforcement to publicize arrests. They were often called "conga lines" because they resembled the rhythmic line dance with defendants handcuffed and led by law enforcement officers in a twisting formation from the street to the courthouse. By the early 1990s, law enforcement officers in some jurisdictions were being criticized by judges and prosecutors for conducting perp walks, as the defendants had only been charged with a crime and were deemed innocent until proven guilty. The belief was that the very public displays could prejudice potential jurors. Federal judges, United States Attorneys' offices, and federal law enforcement agencies issued edicts against them.

In reality, perp walks were a simplistic form of fraud prevention. The public display of fraudsters was thought to send a strong message. It was hoped that parading fraudsters to court and plastering their faces all over newspapers and television would deter others from committing such crimes. It was also used to turn co-conspirators into informants and witnesses in order to avoid being perp-walked themselves. The authors remember suspects in cases saying that they would cooperate in criminal investigations as long as there was a promise not to expose them to the media. Perp walks are back with a vengeance as the government is using old as well as new weapons to prosecute and prevent corporate crime. Perp walks show defendants that although they were once captains of industry with billions of dollars, now the whole world can see they are just common criminals. Although perp walks are useful for publicizing and sending a strong message about committing fraud, they are only a small piece of the business of fraud prevention.

In the mind of federal agents and prosecutors, nothing stops fraud better than the arrest of corporate fraudsters resulting in criminal prosecutions. Law enforcement knows all too well the damaging effects of corporate fraud in recent years. The pursuit of justice requires that corporate crooks be held accountable for their criminal acts. The knock on the front door at six o'clock in the morning by two beefy federal agents in suits with an arrest warrant in one hand and handcuffs in the other will bring even the most powerful and arrogant corporate executive to tears. Getting arrested, cuffed, being read one's constitutional rights, fingerprinted, photographed, and taken to court are traumatic experiences. Federal authorities know this and use it to their advantage.

EDWIN SUTHERLAND AND WHITE-COLLAR CRIME

The term *white-collar crime* was coined in 1949 by Indiana University criminologist Edwin H. Sutherland. He defined white collar crime as "a crime committed by a person of respectability and high social status in the course of his occupation."[10] Sutherland rejected the common belief at the time that attributed theft and fraud to either abject poverty or genetics. Sutherland's white-collar criminal was described as a person who learned how to commit crimes, much like a person learns other things. The longer the person committed crimes, the better they got at it. Sutherland attributed the reason for the theft to criminal rationalizations, motives, and other learned attitudes.

DR. DONALD CRESSEY AND THE FRAUD TRIANGLE

Although it is common knowledge that people and corporations commit fraud, what is often not understood is why they do it. Understanding the motive behind fraud is important in preventing it. Dr. Donald Cressey, a renowned teacher and pioneer in fraud research and an important fraud expert developed the Fraud Triangle Theory (Exhibit 2.1) to explain why people commit fraud. Dr. Cressey came to the conclusion that the propensity for fraud occurred when three critical elements came together: motive, opportunity, and rationalization. Each of these three elements is necessary and interrelated in order for a person to actually commit a fraud. The absence of any one of them would not allow a person to commit a fraud. Every corporate executive needs to understand the Fraud Triangle and why employees commit various kinds of fraud.

EXHIBIT 2.1 The Fraud Triangle
Source: Reprinted with permission from the Association of Certified Fraud Examiners, Austin, Texas © 2011.

FINANCIAL PRESSURE AND OTHER MOTIVES

Financial pressure is often the motive for people who commit fraud. It is the element that causes a person to act or react and typically implies an emotion or desire.[11] It is the driving force behind a person changing from a law-abiding citizen to one who commits a felony. There are many motivations to commit fraud; most of them are greed related. They include living beyond one's means, an immediate financial need, debts, poor credit, a drug or gambling addiction, and family pressure, to name a few. In the movie *Wall Street*, the character Gordon Gekko said, "Greed, for lack of a better word, is good. Greed is right. Greed works."[12] Greed epitomized Wall Street in the 1980s. Just as greed led many down the path to insider trading and other financial crimes, it is a motivating force in all kinds of frauds, especially the corporate frauds seen over the last few years. The recent housing bubble and the associated subprime meltdown, mortgage and securitization frauds, and the resulting devastating impact on the economy prove once again that greed and fraud are ever-present.

Although greed is the usual motive, sometimes revenge and ego play a role. An employee may feel anger and hostility against a company for some perceived wrong and may try to get back at the company by defrauding it. Although the argument goes that this is revenge, when this behavior results in money in the pocket, it boils down to greed, pure and simple. Sometimes the motive is a desire to beat the system. People may think they are smarter than anyone else, and they believe that no one can stop them. Pressure to perform is often a motive for fraud. Sometimes the perpetrator has committed fraud to help improve the bottom-line financial results. Emotional instability is also a motivating factor, but this is seen far less than the other motives for fraud.

An excellent example of greed as a motive is a case involving a multimillionaire industrialist from New York. He owned businesses all over the country. He lived in a mansion in one of Long Island's most exclusive communities. He gave large donations and endowments to universities, museums, hospitals, and other charitable organizations. Most amazing of all, he served several presidents in a variety of diplomatic and economic assignments in his lifetime. He was well respected, and reference materials include pages of his accolades and achievements. Compared with all the good this man did throughout a lifetime, the one stain on his career is his conviction for fraud. Unfortunately, he conspired with others to submit a fraudulent insurance claim on one of his many businesses.

Why would this otherwise good man do something that was so contrary to the rest of his life? What was his motive? The answer that comes to mind is simply greed. His path to a courtroom and a sentencing before a federal judge started with an insurance claim for damage at a factory. The problem was that the type of damage that occurred was not covered by the policy. The damage was in the hundreds of thousands of dollars. Rather than just let it go and view it as a business loss, this industrialist decided to take the advice of his public adjuster and falsify the claim by changing the cause of damage to one that was covered by the policy. Payoffs were made to insurance adjusters to go along with the fraudulent claim. The kickbacks that were paid took almost half of the proceeds from the insurance claim.

This insurance fraud might have gone undiscovered if not for the fact that greed overtook the insurance adjusters involved. They continued to engage in staged and inflated insurance claims with dozens of other insureds and insurance adjusters in settling bogus insurance claims. When federal agents eventually discovered their crimes, the adjusters admitted their long involvement in insurance fraud, the many phony claims they had submitted to numerous insurance companies, and the many co-conspirators with whom they had worked. Again proving that there is no honor among thieves, they gave up the name of the industrialist. After a short investigation, the industrialist admitted his involvement and pled guilty to charges of fraud.

OPPORTUNITY

Opportunity is the favorable circumstance that allows a fraud to occur. The degree of opportunity that a person has to commit fraud is usually determined by his or her position of authority in the company and access to assets and records. Poor internal controls contribute to opportunity and fraud. An employee who can both open a new vendor account and also pay that vendor provides an example of weak internal controls and a good opportunity for fraud. Blank check stock that is not properly inventoried and locked is another example of opportunity. Strong separation of duties along with oversight lessens the opportunity to commit and succeed at fraud. Of the three Fraud

Triangle elements, opportunity is the one area in which fraud prevention can excel. Removing or lessening the opportunity to commit fraud and abuse is important in any fraud prevention program but is absolutely critical for a corporate fraud prevention program.

Scammers commit the frauds they do because they have the opportunity. A mailroom employee may not be able to conspire with a vendor to create a contract that provides no service but yields a kickback to the employee. Yet, a mail clerk could steal incoming mail containing highly confidential proprietary information and sell it to a competitor in a foreign country. It all depends on the opportunity and how it is limited.

RATIONALIZATION

The Fraud Triangle's third element is rationalization. Rationalization is how the fraudster justifies inappropriate actions. It is "the provision of reasons to explain to oneself or others behavior for which one's real motives are different and unknown or unconscious."[13] When the elements of need and opportunity come together, the fraudster is convinced that what occurred is not bad or wrong. Fraudsters often think of themselves as honest. Rather than consider themselves as criminals who just defrauded their company, they make themselves into victims. They may say: *I was only borrowing the money, I'll pay it back someday; This is not much money, the company is rich and won't really miss it; Everybody does it; They owe it to me; I'll stop once I get over this financial hump; It's for a good purpose; The company mistreats me.* Rationalization is another way of saying the end justifies the means.

In our careers as federal agents, we arrested hundreds of fraudsters. None of these criminals ever expected to get caught. They all thought that they would get away with their crimes. They rationalized what they did and came to believe they were invulnerable. If they did not rationalize their actions, their consciences would take over.

DR. W. STEVE ALBRECHT'S FRAUD SCALE

In the 1980s, Dr. W. Steve Albrecht of Brigham Young University studied and analyzed frauds. His findings showed that the persons most likely to commit fraud in the workplace were living beyond their means and had personal or gambling debts, a desire to have personal status, or pressure to have status from family or peers. Those employees who believed they were underpaid or underappreciated were also more likely to steal from their workplace. The desire to give free merchandise and gifts to friends and family was also mentioned as a motivator.

Dr. Albrecht explained the motivations to commit fraud by creating a Fraud Scale. Similar to Cressey's Fraud Triangle, Albrecht's Fraud Scale theorizes that even if opportunity and situational needs are present, some employees will never commit fraud. According to Albrecht, the motivation to commit fraud depends on how strong each of the three factors is in each particular employee. It is a complex combination of the degrees to which the three factors of opportunity, motive, and rationalization exist in each situation. Thus, Albrecht believes that fraud is much harder to predict than Cressey believed.

FRAUD DIAMOND

As further research has been conducted into fraud and the fraudster's motivation, a variation of the Fraud Triangle has been advanced. The Fraud Diamond adds the fourth element of *capability* to the existing elements of motive, opportunity, and rationalization. A person may be in a job function where he or she can commit fraud but their capability to actually carry out the fraud may be limited. Capability includes the fraudster's personality and traits, including knowledge, creativity, and ego that differentiate from opportunity. While opportunity refers to the person's role and access to commit fraud, the fourth element takes this one step further. The fraudster "must be intelligent enough to understand and exploit internal control weaknesses and to use position, function, or authorized access to the greatest advantage."[14] Another aspect of capability is self-confidence and being able to handle the stress that occurs when perpetrating fraud.[15]

FRAUD THEORIES

In addition to the traditional theories of fraud just described, the authors have designed some theories of their own. Over their many years as fraud investigators, they have seen more than their share of schemes, scams, cons, and frauds. Some were simple, such as credit card fraud and loan scams. Others were complex financial crimes such as insider trading, securities fraud, and RICO cases. Some were so well thought out and successful that they were repeated time after time. Although some of these new theories may seem light-hearted and even whimsical at first, they speak volumes about how and why fraud is perpetrated and is all too often successful.

Tip of the Iceberg Theory

When first discovered, very few frauds yield their true extent, along with the actual amount of the loss. Often the fraud first seen is just a small part of the actual deceit, much the same way most of an iceberg is hidden below the surface of the water. As an investigator conducts the investigation, interviews people, reviews supporting documentation, and takes other related steps in the process, a much larger fraud is usually revealed. Corporate fraud is no different.

An excellent example of the "Tip of the Iceberg Theory" of fraud is an insurance fraud case investigated by the Postal Inspection Service, the IRS, and the FBI in the 1990s in the New York metropolitan area. The case started with an anonymous tip to an insurance company that homeowner property claims were fraudulently inflated. One of the first claims investigated was for $8,000, rather small in terms of insurance fraud that would be authorized for federal prosecution. The federal agents on the case believed that multiple fraudulent claims were involved and kept digging. Their hard work paid off. By the end of the case several years later, more than 200 defendants had been arrested and convicted, and more than $500 million in staged and inflated commercial and homeowner property claims were uncovered.

Potato Chip Theory

Committing fraud and getting away with it can become addictive. Once one succeeds at an embezzlement scheme or payment of a bribe to a foreign government official to secure a contract and gets away with it, it gets harder and harder to stop that activity. This may be characterized as the "Potato Chip Theory" of fraud. Just as a person is unable to eat only one potato chip, once employees start committing fraud, they cannot stop. Assuming they do not get caught, they will commit fraud after fraud, even branching out to new frauds to obtain money and other things of value. An excellent example is a long-time employee of a corporation who was investigated for allegedly receiving kickbacks from a vendor. Applying the Potato Chip Theory, other avenues of possible fraud were investigated. Knowing that expense reporting fraud is very common, a review of this employee's travel and entertainment reports found personal expenses fraudulently claimed as business expenses. Thus, two different frauds against the company were discovered.

Greed and the successful perpetration of fraud become addictive, yet if fraudulent behavior continues, the perpetrator will eventually be found out. Criminals make mistakes no matter how smart they think they are. They can get bolder and bolder each time they are not discovered. Experience has taught us that they eventually make fatal mistakes leading to detection. However, employees involved in fraud can do great damage until they are caught. The longer a fraud continues, no matter the employee level, the greater the potential financial and reputational damage. Exhibit 2.2 is a list of many of the behavioral red flags of fraudsters.

Rotten Apple Theory

It has often been said that one rotten apple can ruin the whole basket. This can be applied to unchecked fraud in an organization or group. True leaders can inspire their employees to reach new heights of personal growth and career development. They can be role models who help create a new generation of corporate leaders. Employees want to emulate the leaders they see at their companies. Executives and managers who lead by example in compliance and integrity lessen the risk of fraud by their employees.

Unfortunately, the opposite also applies. Poor leaders who lack character and integrity, and who turn to fraud and abuse, can damage the people they lead. In a twist on imitation being the sincerest form of flattery, there are examples of employees who turn to fraud because their managers were doing it and getting away with it. This

EXHIBIT 2.2   Behavioral Red Flags of Fraudsters

- Living beyond means
- Financial difficulties
- Control issues, unwillingness to share duties
- Unusually close association with vendor/customer
- Wheeler-dealer attitude
- Divorce/family problems
- Irritability, suspiciousness, or defensiveness
- Addiction problems
- Refusal to take vacations
- Past employment-related problems
- Complaints about inadequate pay
- Excessive pressure from within organization
- Past legal problems
- Instability in life circumstances
- Excessive family/peer pressure for success
- Complaints about lack of authority

Source: Association of Certified Fraud Examiners, *2010 Report to the Nations on Occupational Fraud and Abuse* (Austin, TX: ACFE, 2010), 70.

is also called the "Culture of Noncompliance Theory" because when there is no culture of compliance, a breakdown of rules, policies, and accountability occurs.

A manager committed thousands of dollars of fraud by charging personal expenses on his corporate credit card. He did this on a continuing basis, and his subordinate saw that he did it. The employee copied the fraudulent behavior of his boss. When discovered, the subordinate unsuccessfully claimed that he was just doing what his superior did and should not be fired. This strategy did not work, and both were fired.

Another variation of the "Rotten Apple Theory" of fraud is seen when a manager fails to provide adequate supervision of a team, leaving the team members with no direction. When oversight is lacking, successful fraud is easier to commit. Expense reporting fraud is much more common in groups in which it is known that managers do not thoroughly review the submitted payment requests. Although these kinds of managers do not personally commit the fraud, they promote it by not being alert and fully engaged. "Trust but verify" should be an ongoing policy.

Low-Hanging Fruit Theory

Although priority attention should be given to high-risk fraud such as financial misstatement and accounting issues, one must not forget about the lower risk but high occurrence frauds such as procurement frauds. It is often thought that fraudsters are cunning, imaginative, and brilliant in devising and executing their many schemes, but this presumption is often a misconception. Investigators, at times, give these violators too much credit for thoroughly thinking through their fraudulent activity and subsequent actions.

The reason that so much fraud is eventually discovered is simply that most fraudsters make mistakes that lead to their discovery. If the "low-hanging frauds" are not given appropriate attention, the fraudster employees will continue their crimes until discovered. This could be months or years, and by that time, more damage will have been done. Executives should ensure that their fraud investigation units do not overlook these low-hanging frauds, as they will solve several problems. First, they are usually simple frauds that do not take a significant amount of investigative time. Second, by stopping this fraudulent activity, there is an immediate benefit by removing a bad employee while sending a strong message about the company's commitment to fraud prevention. Third, the fraudster employee is removed before he or she is able to commit much more complex and serious frauds.

Addition by Subtraction Theory

One of the best ways to reduce fraud is by removing the source of the problem. When a company terminates an employee who has committed fraud, a risk is removed and that improves the company. This theory refers to the benefits that an organization receives when it takes a proactive approach to fraud detection and investigation. As simple as that may sound in theory, it is often hard to do in practice. It requires a business to take a zero-tolerance and hard-core approach to fraudulent behavior by its employees, partners, and vendors. In a case involving embezzlement by a relatively low-level employee, the evidence was overwhelming that the fraud did indeed occur. In addition, the employee admitted his involvement when confronted with the evidence found by investigators.

When the manager was provided with the evidence, he commented that he was sorry he had to terminate the employee because that worker had the potential to be a high-level executive one day. What the manager failed to realize was the "Addition by Subtraction Theory" of fraud. The company is best served when a dishonest employee is removed before he or she moves up the corporate ladder, where far more damage can be done. If a business is going to have a zero tolerance for fraud, it must apply to all employees. As soon as a high-level executive who commits any kind of fraud is not held accountable, the entire program has lost credibility.

Fraudster as Employee Theory

The employee who turns to the "dark side" and commits fraud against the company should not be considered an employee. Good employees are critical to the operation of a business. As stated previously, they are ideally concerned about the future of the business, working hard to ensure its growth and future, maintaining integrity, and bettering the company. Fraudsters masquerading as employees use their positions to find weaknesses in the internal controls and exploit them to commit fraud. These people are not out to better the company, other employees, shareholders, customers, or partners. They are only out to line their pockets with ill-gotten gains and have ceased to be employees. They have, in effect, gone into business for themselves. Executives need to understand this concept when dealing with employees who commit fraud.

THE SHORT MEMORY SYNDROME

As a society, we have a poor memory. We fail to study and remember history and because of that, we are condemned to repeat it as George Santayana opined. This is especially true when it comes to fraud. Charles Ponzi created the Ponzi scheme almost 100 years ago and it has generated untold news stories of deception and shock year after year. Through various iterations and untold millions of victims and financial losses, the Ponzi scheme is still going strong. Why is that?

Are we incapable of learning from the misfortunes of others when they fall victim to tricks, cons, and fraud? Are fraudsters smarter than honest citizens? Are greed and naiveté too powerful to resist? The investment fraud scheme of Bernie Madoff—discussed in Chapter 9—proves that we suffer from a "Short Memory Syndrome."

In a memorable cartoon strip on the first Earth Day in 1971, the title character of the Walt Kelly comic strip *Pogo* uttered the famous quote, "We have met the enemy, and he is us." Pogo was reflecting on the sad state of the environment and the growing problem of pollution when he made this comment. Yet, Pogo's timeless quote is just as relevant to our victimization by fraud and how often we enable the fraudsters in committing their crimes. We need to resist the lure of scammers. No one makes huge investment returns every year and when the markets are in a downward cycle. We need to take responsibility for fraud prevention, whether on the individual consumer or business level. We need to constantly repeat and remember that if something sounds too good to be true, it usually is.

RECIDIVIST FRAUDSTER

It would be unfair to say that fraudsters are incapable of reforming their criminal ways. Many of them have served their sentences and become productive members of society. Frank Abagnale, portrayed in the movie *Catch Me If You Can* and an author, lecturer, and consultant in fraud detection and prevention for 35 years, may be the best example of one who truly left his past behind. Walt Pavlo, profiled in Chapter 8, is another example of a former fraudster who learned that honesty, integrity, and character really count. Still, there are some who on the surface seem reformed but never really get it. Their arrogance, manipulative abilities, sense of being smarter than others, and contempt eventually return them to fraud. These recidivists claim, as reformed fraudsters, that they can best embrace fraud detection and prevention using the French proverb to "Set a thief to catch a thief." Barry Webne and Steve Comisar are examples of supposedly reformed fraudsters who became fraud prevention speakers and consultants but continued their recidivist fraudster ways. Barry Minkow's egregious behavior may be the most blatant example of the recidivist.

After serving seven and a half years in prison for orchestrating the ZZZZ Best $100 million securities fraud in the late 1980s, Minkow left prison claiming that he had turned over a new leaf in his life. He was an outspoken proponent of holding fraudsters accountable and hosted a national radio talk show. He founded a fraud investigation firm whose intent was to expose corporate fraudsters. He even became a minister at a church in San Diego. It certainly seemed that Minkow had found a purpose to his life and had put his fraudster ways behind for good. Unfortunately, his fall from grace makes him a poster child for the recidivist fraudster.

In 2009, his investigative report on Lennar Corp. alleged a massive fraud and Ponzi scheme perpetrated by the homebuilder company. Lennar's stock dropped more than 30 percent as a result of the report, causing investors to lose more than $583 million.[16] In reality, Minkow's investigation of Lennar was a sham intended to "artificially manipulate and depress Lennar's stock" and extort money from the builder.[17] His criminal conduct resulted in criminal charges and, on March 30, 2011, he pled guilty in federal court in Miami, Florida, to conspiracy to commit securities fraud. In an example of ultimate betrayal, the criminal complaint alleged that Minkow used his close relationship with the FBI to get them to "open up an investigation into Lennar, and then used his knowledge of the investigation to bet against Lennar's stock."[18]

Like most successful fraudsters, Minkow was charismatic and used his silver tongue to charm and con victims. The federal judge who sentenced him in 1989 recognized Minkow's way with words. "You're dangerous because you have this gift of gab, this ability to communicate, you don't have a conscience," stated District Court Judge Dikran Tevrizian.[19] Apparently, the conscience issue was a challenge for Minkow. One reporter wrote that "Minkow's dealings as a fraud investigator seemed ethically challenged" by shorting "the companies he targeted as a fraud investigator."[20] When fraudsters become fraud investigators, it can become a case of the fox guarding the henhouse. The temptation and power—without ethics and character—make a recipe for disaster. At his guilty plea in the Lennar case, an uncharacteristic Minkow explained to the judge why he committed the fraud. "I'm not too wise, ma'am."[21] Watch out for the supposedly reformed fraudster who retains the slickness and arrogance, as well as the "gift of gab." They are red flags of a recidivist fraudster. On July 22, 2011, Minkow was sentenced to five years in prison and $583 million in court-ordered restitution.

NOTES

1. *Webster's Third New International Dictionary*, 1986 ed., s.v. "fraud."
2. Bryan Garner, ed., *Black's Law Dictionary*, 7th ed., s.v. "fraud."
3. *Mail Fraud Statute*, U.S. Code Title 18, § 1341.
4. Association of Certified Fraud Examiners, *2010 Report to the Nations on Occupational Fraud and Abuse* (Austin, TX: ACFE, 2010), 6.
5. Adam Zagorin, "Scambuster, Inc.," *Time*, January 31, 2005, 47.
6. U.S. Department of Justice, Corporate Fraud Task Force, *Second Year Report to the President*, July 20, 2004, 3.2, www.usdoj.gov/dag/cftf/2nd_yr_ fraud_report.pdf.
7. Association of Certified Fraud Examiners, *2010 Report to the Nations on Occupational Fraud and Abuse* (Austin, TX: ACFE, 2010).
8. Ibid., 11.
9. Association of Certified Fraud Examiners, *Fraud Examiners Manual* (Austin, TX: ACFE, 2006), 4.601.
10. Edwin H. Sutherland, *White Collar Crime* (New York: Holt, Rinehart and Winston, 1949), 9.
11. *Webster's Third New International Dictionary*, 1986 ed., s.v. "motive."
12. *Wall Street*, directed by Oliver Stone (1987; Beverly Hills, CA: Twentieth Century Fox, 2003), DVD.
13. *Webster's Third New International Dictionary*, 1986 ed., s.v. "rationalization."
14. Jack W. Dorminey, Aaron Scott Fleming, Mary-Jo Kranacher, and Richard A. Riley, Jr., "Beyond the Fraud Triangle: Enhancing Deterrence of Economic Crimes," *CPA Journal*, July 2010, 16.
15. Ibid.
16. Rose Whelan, "Minkow Pleads Guilty in Fraud Case," *Wall Street Journal*, March 31, 2011, C3.
17. Rose Whelan, "U.S. Charges Fraud Sleuth in Fraud," *Wall Street Journal*, March 24, 2011, C3.

18. Rose Whelan, "Minkow Pleads Guilty."
19. Al Lewis, "Barry Minkow Backslides," *Dow Jones Newswires*, March 22, 2011, www.denverpost.com/breakingnews/ci_17675964.
20. Ibid.
21. Curt Anderson, "Guilty Plea for Conman-Turned-FBI Informant," *Miami Herald*, March 30, 2011, www.signonsandiego.biz/news/2011/mar/30/ guilty-plea-for-conman-turned-fbi-informant/.

The Path to Greater Corporate Compliance, Accountability, and Ethical Conduct

COSO to Sarbanes-Oxley

EXECUTIVE SUMMARY

The path to greater corporate compliance, accountability, and ethical conduct has been evolving and improving over the last 25 years. It began in 1985 with the Committee of Sponsoring Organizations (COSO) and a framework of compliance, continued in 1991 with the Federal Sentencing Guidelines for Organizations, and then exploded into corporate suites and boardrooms with the enactment of the Sarbanes-Oxley Act of 2002. The enhancement of corporate compliance and ethics programs continues today. Transparency and accountability became keywords for corporate governance, government oversight, and investor protection. If corporate executives could not be trusted to protect employees and shareholders, then government would step in. New laws and compliance requirements resulted from the many corporate scandals, and although some are onerous to businesses, they are the result of fraudulent conduct of the highest magnitude and impact.

WHAT IS CORPORATE GOVERNANCE?

Corporate governance is a system of checks and balances between management and all other connected parties with the aim of producing an effective, efficient, and law-abiding corporation. It is how a company defines itself to its shareholders, employees, partners, customers, government regulators, and others in terms of compliance and accountability. Corporate governance involves all aspects of a company's operations, including the roles of management and the board of directors, the qualifications and independence of the board, ethics, conflicts of interest and enforced codes of conduct, reporting of fraud and other business practice issues, corporate citizenship, succession planning, and shareholder rights. These words, or those very similar, can be seen on the Web sites and in the annual reports of companies large and small because of the many changes in corporate accountability and responsibility.

Corporate governance is about promoting fairness, honesty, and transparency. Transparency has become a keyword in improved corporate governance and is reflected throughout Sarbanes-Oxley as well as other important compliance initiatives. It is a term "that has been adopted by the business community to describe the obligation to disclose basic financial information."[1] Transparency is the quality or state of being open, easily detected, or seen through. *Black's Law Dictionary* defines it as a "lack of guile in attempts to hide damaging information especially in financial disclosures where organizations interact with the public."[2] Transparency is a critical element in allowing investors and government regulators to know exactly what is going on behind the corporate veil. If investors knew about the off-book transactions, the self-dealings, the hidden loans, and the looting at Enron and Adelphia, there is no doubt that most people would never have invested their hard-earned money there. It is imperative that all financial transactions be transparent, with no possibility of financial shenanigans, undisclosed deals, or conflicts of interest. Transparency reassures shareholders, corporate employees, and the public that they have a level playing field in which to invest and hopefully makes it harder for corporate crooks to "cook the books."

A CULTURE OF COMPLIANCE

A culture of compliance takes time to develop. It can be a long journey to reach the highest levels of ethical standards and compliance requirements. All the positive changes in legislation, initiatives, and policies have taken years to unfold with the purpose of improving corporate governance. It can be argued that this journey to greater compliance started with the creation of COSO in 1985, continued with the United States Sentencing Guidelines for Organizational Crime in 1991, and became widely embraced with the enactment of the Sarbanes-Oxley Act of 2002 and the subsequent enhanced accounting and auditing standards.

As William H. Donaldson, former Chairman of the Securities and Exchange Commission (SEC), stated in a speech to the National Press Club on July 30, 2003, "If companies view the new laws as opportunities—opportunities to improve internal controls, improve the performance of the board, and improve their public reporting—they will ultimately be better run, more transparent, and therefore more attractive to investors."[3] The laws and compliance requirements have changed the way businesses operate. Today's informed executives and, in fact, all employees must be aware of them and their impact on a culture of compliance. Executive Insight 3.1 provides a timeline of the various corporate compliance initiatives and milestones since 1985.

EXECUTIVE INSIGHT 3.1: TIMELINE OF KEY CORPORATE COMPLIANCE INITIATIVES & MILESTONES SINCE 1985

Year	Compliance Initiatives and Milestones	Impact
1985	Committee of Sponsoring Organizations (COSO)	"Voluntary private sector organization dedicated to improving the quality of financial reporting through business ethics, effective internal controls and corporate governance."[i]

Year	Compliance Initiatives and Milestones	Impact
1986	Defense Industry Initiative on Business Ethics and Conduct	Established by 32 major defense contractors to improve corporate compliance after widespread reports of waste, fraud, and abuse by government contractors in the procurement process.[ii]
1987	Report of the National Commission on Fraudulent Financial Reporting ("The Treadway Commission")	"Studied the financial reporting system in the U.S. to identify causal factors that can lead to fraudulent financial reporting and steps to reduce its incidence."[iii]
1991	United States Sentencing Guidelines for Organizational Crime	Guidelines to hold organizations accountable by applying "just punishment" for criminal actions and "deterrence" incentives to detect and prevent crime.[iv]
1992	Internal Controls—Integrated Framework (COSO Report)	"Established a common definition for internal controls and a standard against which businesses can assess their control systems and how to improve them."[v]
1996	Statement on Auditing Standards (SAS) 82, "Consideration of Fraud in a Financial Statement Audit"	Provided guidance to auditors for detecting fraud when conducting audits. Replaced the previously used term of "errors and irregularities" with "fraud" for the first time.[vi]

Year	Compliance Initiatives and Milestones	Impact
1998	Arthur Levitt's "The Numbers Game" Speech	Prophetic speech by former SEC chairman foretelling the coming doom in the financial markets by exposing the deception being played with earnings management.
1999	National Commission on Fraudulent Financial Reporting, 1987–1997	"Research project to guide efforts to combat the problem of financial statement fraud and to provide a better understanding of financial statement fraud cases."[vii]
2002	Sarbanes-Oxley Act	"Public Company Accounting Reform and Investor Protection Act of 2002"—landmark legislation with the most significant changes to U.S. securities laws in 70 years.
2002	Statement on Auditing Standards (SAS) 99, "Consideration of Fraud in a Financial Statement Audit"	Auditing standard that superseded earlier SAS 82 and gave auditors the "responsibility to plan and perform the audit to obtain reasonable assurance about whether the financial statements are free of material misstatement, whether caused by error or fraud."[viii]
2003	"Principles of Federal Prosecution of Business Organizations" (The "Thompson Memo")	Provided Department of Justice prosecutors with ground-breaking guidance when deciding to seek charges against a business organization.

Year	Compliance Initiatives and Milestones	Impact
2003	SECs Final Rule for Section 404 of Sarbanes-Oxley	SECs adoption of rules for Section 404 requiring management's assessment and reporting of internal controls over financial reporting and attestation by external auditor.
2003	New York Stock Exchange & NASDAQ Listing Requirements	New listing requirements for issuers of securities including independence of directors and enhanced corporate governance.
2004	PCAOB Auditing Standard No. 2: An Audit of Internal Control over Financial Reporting Performed in Conjunction with an Audit of Financial Statements	Provides increased responsibilities for external auditors beyond those required by SAS 99 including requiring auditors to evaluate antifraud programs and controls as part of the audit of internal control over financial reporting.
2004	Stephen Cutler's "Gatekeepers" Speech	Seminal speech by former SEC director of enforcement where he reinforced the critical role of gatekeepers—those people who are responsible for monitoring and oversight of others in the financial markets.
2004	Enterprise Risk Management— Integrated Framework	Groundbreaking guidance on enterprise risk management (ERM) that is now universally used by organizations.

Year	Compliance Initiatives and Milestones	Impact
2004	United States Sentencing Commission's Amendments to the Federal Sentencing Guidelines for Organizations	Introduced seven amendments to strengthen corporate compliance and ethics programs of business organizations to mitigate punishment for a criminal offense.
2006	Internal Control over Financial Reporting—Guidance for Smaller Public Companies	Building upon the 1992 ICFR report, this guidance helps smaller public companies institute internal controls for improved financial reporting using a principles-based approach.[ix]
2007	PCAOB Auditing Standard No. 5: An Audit of Internal Control over Financial Reporting Performed in Conjunction with an Audit of Financial Statements	Replaced Auditing Standard No. 2 with "new management guidance" that is "more risk-based and scalable to company size and complexity" while increasing the accuracy of financial reporting.[x]
2010	Fraudulent Financial Reporting: 1998–2007—An Analysis of U.S. Public Companies	Updates 1999 report on fraudulent financial reporting with results of new research from 347 cases involving U.S. public companies over a 10-year period between 1998 and 2007.[xi]
2010	Dodd-Frank Wall Street Reform and Consumer Protection Act Whistleblower Provisions	New legislation that provides whistleblowers with huge financial incentives for reporting to the SEC violations of federal

Year	Compliance Initiatives and Milestones	Impact
		securities laws while providing strong protection from retaliation to those who report.
2010	United States Sentencing Commission's Amendments to the Federal Sentencing Guidelines for Organizations	Updates the 2004 amendments with new guidelines for effective compliance programs including a direct reporting structure for compliance officers as well as taking steps to remedy the harm caused to victims and making appropriate restitution.
2011	UK Bribery Act	Strong UK anti-corruption legislation, often called the "FCPA on steroids," as it criminalized both governmental corruption and commercial bribery. A corporate offense of failure of a commercial organization to detect and prevent bribery is also included in the Act that took effect on July 1, 2011.

---

[i]Committee of Sponsoring Organizations of the Treadway Commission, www.coso.org.

[ii]Defense Industry Initiative on Business Ethics and Conduct, www.dii.org.

[iii]Committee of Sponsoring Organizations of the Treadway Commission, *Report of the National Commission on Fraudulent Financial Reporting*, October, 1987, www.coso.org/Publications/NCFFR.pdf.

[iv]Supplemental Report on Sentencing Guidelines for Organizations, (August 30, 1991), 6.

[v]Committee of Sponsoring Organizations of the Treadway Commission, *Internal Control-Integrated Framework*, 1992, www.cpa2biz.com/AST/Main/CPA2BIZ_Primary/InternalControls/COSO/PRDOVR~PC-990009/PC-990009.jsp.

[vi]Association of Certified Fraud Examiners, *Fraud Examiners Manual*, 3rd ed., (Austin, TX: 2001), 1.203.

[vii]Committee of Sponsoring Organizations of the Treadway Commission, *Fraudulent Financial Reporting: 1987–1997—An Analysis of U.S. Public Companies*, March, 1999, www.coso.org/publications/ffr_1987_1997.pdf.

[viii]Statement on Auditing Standards 99, "Consideration of Fraud in a Financial Statement Audit," American Institute of Certified Public Accountants, www.aicpa.org.

[ix]Committee of Sponsoring Organizations of the Treadway Commission, *Internal Control over Financial Reporting—Guidance for Smaller Public Companies*, 2006, www.cpa2biz.com/AST/Main/CPA2BIZ_Primary/InternalControls/COSO/PRDOVR~PC-990017/PC-990017.jsp.

[x]Public Company Accounting Oversight Board, Auditing Standard No. 5, pcaobus.org/Standards/Auditing/Pages/Auditing_Standard_5.aspx.

[xi]Committee of Sponsoring Organizations of the Treadway Commission, *Fraudulent Financial Reporting: 1998–2007—An Analysis of U.S. Public Companies,* May, 2010, www.coso.org/documents/COSOFRAUD STUDY2010_001.pdf.

COSO

COSO is the Committee of Sponsoring Organizations, a voluntary, private sector organization dedicated to improving the quality of financial reporting through business ethics, effective internal controls, and corporate governance. COSO's extensive studies and intuitive recommendations over the years provide great insight into the problem and prevention of corporate fraud. In today's compliance-driven environment, a thorough understanding of a COSO framework is a prerequisite to an effective culture of fraud prevention.

COSO was formed in 1985 by the major accounting and finance professional organizations including the American Accounting Association, the American Institute of Certified Public Accountants, Financial Executives International, The Institute of Internal Auditors, and the Institute of Management Accountants. COSO sponsored the National Commission on Fraudulent Financial Reporting that studied the financial reporting system in the United States "to identify causal factors that can lead to fraudulent financial reporting and steps to reduce its incidence."[4] The first Chairman of the National Commission was James C. Treadway, Jr., Executive Vice-President and General Counsel, Paine Webber, Incorporated, and a former SEC Commissioner. Thus, the National Commission is commonly referred to as the Treadway Commission (the Commission).

The Commission reviewed numerous instances of fraudulent financial reporting, including 119 enforcement actions against public companies or associated individuals, and 42 cases against independent public accountants or their firms brought by the SEC from 1981 to 1986.[5] The Commission defined fraudulent reporting as "intentional or reckless conduct, whether by act or omission, that results in materially misleading financial statements."[6] Many different factors were considered including the distortion of corporate records, falsified transactions, misapplication of accounting principles, and other related intentional misconduct. The Commission did not include in its study other internal frauds such as asset misappropriation or corruption schemes. The study found that opportunities for fraudulent financial reporting exist when certain circumstances are present including:

- The absence of a strong and engaged board of directors or audit committee that vigilantly oversees the financial reporting process
- Weak or nonexistent internal accounting controls
- Unusual or complex financial transactions
- Accounting estimates requiring subjective judgment by company management
- Ineffective internal audit staffs resulting from inadequate staff size, staff expertise or limited audit scope[7]

The Commission's key recommendations fall into several categories including the tone at the top as set by senior management; the quality of internal accounting and audit functions; the roles of the board of directors and the audit committee; the independence of external auditors; and enforcement enhancements. The findings and recommendations of the Commission are as relevant today as when the study was released in 1987. Some of the key recommendations are as follows:

- The top management of a public company must "identify, understand, and assess the factors" that may result in financial statement fraud.
- Internal controls must provide a "reasonable assurance" that fraudulent financial reporting will in the best case be prevented or in the worst case be quickly detected.
- "Public companies should develop and enforce written codes of corporate conduct" to "foster a strong and ethical climate" and ensure compliance with the code.
- An effective and objective internal audit function "staffed with an adequate number of qualified personnel" must be in place.
- The audit committee should be "composed solely of independent directors" and "have adequate resources and authority to discharge their responsibilities."
- The audit committee should provide "vigilant and effective" oversight of the company's financial reporting process and internal controls.
- There should be an evaluation of the independence of the company's public accountant by the audit committee.
- The SEC should require the CEO and/or the CFO to include signed management reports in annual reports to shareholders.
- The SEC should require the chairperson of the audit committee to provide a signed letter in the company's annual report detailing the "committee's responsibilities and activities" in the past year.
- "Public accounting firms should recognize" and address the inherent pressures that can potentially affect audit quality and independence.
- The SEC should seek new "statutory authority to bar or suspend corporate officers and directors involved in fraudulent financial reporting."
- There should be an increased emphasis on criminal prosecutions and the SEC should devote greater resources to detecting and preventing fraudulent financial reporting.[8]

COSO believes that internal controls are an important component of a robust fraud prevention program. However, internal controls can only provide reasonable, not absolute, assurance and should be geared to the achievement of objectives. In 1992, COSO issued a landmark report on internal controls entitled *Internal*

Control—Integrated Framework that is the basis for establishing an effective internal control system. If adopted by a company, this system would promote (1) efficient and effective operations, (2) accurate financial reporting, and (3) compliance with laws and regulations. The report outlined the five essential elements of an effective internal control program:

1. **The control environment,** which is the basis for the system by providing fundamental discipline and structure
2. **Risk assessment,** which involves the identification and analysis by management of risks to achieving predetermined objectives
3. **Control activities** or policies, procedures, and practices to ensure that management objectives and risk mitigation are achieved
4. **Information and communication** by management so that all employees are aware of their control responsibilities and their requirement to support them
5. **Monitoring,** which encompasses external oversight of internal controls by management and independent auditors outside the process to determine the quality of the program and compliance[9]

A COSO framework is the standard for many corporations in the United States, and there is no reason the same framework could not be universally used worldwide. However, the voluntary COSO framework didn't stop many corporations from collapsing. Enron had controls in place, but they were overridden by senior management. Arthur Andersen, its auditor, developed Enron's risk assessment framework, but Enron did not follow it. Enron's "push the envelope" environment, emanating from the highest levels of the company, contributed to its demise.

As a follow-up to the original 1987 report, the Treadway Commission studied financial statement fraud occurring during the period 1987 to 1997. The result was a research report entitled *Fraudulent Financial Reporting 1987–1997: An Analysis of U.S. Public Companies*. One concern was whether there had been any lessening of the problem of fraudulent financial reporting in the years since the previous report. Nearly 300 companies facing allegations of fraudulent financial reporting were identified, and from that number, 200 companies were randomly selected for detailed analysis. The Summary of Findings from the report includes the following:

- Most companies that committed financial statement fraud were relatively small, with most well below $100 million in total assets, and most were not listed on the New York or American Stock Exchanges.
- Senior executives were frequently involved in the fraud, with 83 percent of CEOs and CFOs associated in some way.
- Financial pressures were in play in the period before the occurrence of the financial statement fraud that may have contributed to the fraud.
- Most audit committees met only once a year, some companies had no audit committees, and most had no accounting or finance expertise.
- Insiders and "gray" directors (nonindependent outsiders with special ties to the company) dominated boards.
- The dollar amounts of the frauds were high in comparison with the relatively small size of the companies involved.
- The average fraud continued for almost two years before discovery.
- Overstating revenues and assets was the most common technique involved.
- Both large and small audit firms were associated with the companies committing the frauds, with no significance as to size.
- External auditors were implicated in 29 percent of the frauds as being either complicit or negligent.
- There were severe consequences for the companies committing fraud, including bankruptcy, delisting, and SEC actions. Few executives either admitted wrongdoing or ever served any prison time.[10]

In 2010, COSO issued a new study of fraudulent financial reporting entitled *Fraudulent Financial Reporting: 1998–2007—An Analysis of U.S. Public Companies* that updates the 1999 research. Not surprisingly, the study found that "companies engaged in fraud often experienced bankruptcy, delisting from a stock exchange, or asset sale, and in nine out of ten cases, the SEC named the CEO and/or CFO for alleged involvement."[11] The key findings of the report include:

- Fraudulent financial reporting cases increased from 294 in the 1987 to 1997 period to 347 in the 1998 to 2007 period. The corporate accounting frauds at Enron, WorldCom, and other companies contributed to the increase in both number of cases and loss amounts. The cumulative loss was $120 billion with an average loss of about $400 million per case.

- The CEO and/or CFO were inculpated in 89 percent of the fraud cases. This was an increase from 83 percent in the 1999 study. Of those chief executives indicted, 60 percent were later convicted.
- Revenue recognition fraud was the most common technique employed by the fraudsters and accounted for 60 percent of all cases.
- Twenty-six percent of firms that had fraud subsequently changed audit firms.
- There was an average stock price drop of 16.7 percent in the two days after disclosure of the fraud.
- Companies involved in fraud experienced an increased incidence of bankruptcy, delisting or material asset sales than firms without fraud.[12]

FEDERAL SENTENCING GUIDELINES FOR ORGANIZATIONAL CRIME

The disparity in federal sentencing of defendants for all crimes was an issue among prosecutors, defendants, defense attorneys, judges, and the public. The prison term, or lack of one, that a defendant received in one federal jurisdiction would vary greatly for a similar act by a different defendant in another. After years of complaints about the system, the Sentencing Reform Act of 1984 changed the way federal sentencing was conducted. The Act created the United States Sentencing Commission (USSC) as an independent agency of the Judicial Branch. The USSC was directed to develop guidelines and policy for federal courts to follow when sentencing offenders convicted of federal crimes. The Sentencing Guidelines for individuals who committed any type of federal crime was enacted and made effective as of November 1, 1987.[13]

The next step for the USSC was dealing with organizational crime. Organizations, like individuals, can commit crimes and also be charged with and convicted of criminal conduct. Although organizations cannot be sentenced to prison for their crimes, there are penalties if a guilty verdict is delivered. The resulting convictions and fines can put a company out of business. In 1991, the USSC issued guidelines for the criminal sentencing of corporations as well as recommended guidelines for corporate compliance programs. The guidelines were an attempt to lessen the harshest aspects of federal sentencing for crimes if an organization could demonstrate that it instituted an appropriate compliance program prior to being charged. There was a substantial reduction in fines for corporations that have vigorous fraud prevention and detection programs in place prior to the offense and that self-report the crimes. To receive any mitigating credit under the guidelines, the organization must have reported the criminal activity promptly to appropriate authorities.

A robust fraud prevention program at the time had to consider and implement the following seven steps for compliance with the Federal Sentencing Guidelines for Organizational Crimes:

- **Established compliance standards:** policies and procedures reasonably capable of reducing the prospect of criminal activity that must be followed by all employees
- **Setting the tone at the top:** oversight by high-level management to ensure compliance
- **Use of due care not to delegate to individuals who might engage in illegal activities:** instituting background checks and management oversight to lessen the chance that employees who either have criminal histories or a propensity to engage in illegal activities will be placed in positions of authority
- **Effective communication of standards to all employees:** requiring participation in training programs and creating and communicating codes of conduct through employee handbooks and in new employee orientation
- **Reasonable steps to achieve compliance:** utilizing monitoring and auditing systems to detect criminal and other improper activity, as well as creating reporting systems for whistleblowers to report such conduct
- **Consistent enforcement and discipline:** the creation of an appropriate disciplinary mechanism, consistent and fair, incremental to the conduct alleged and made known to all employees
- **Reasonable steps in response to reports of compliance concerns:** identifying internal control lapses and deficiencies and taking all reasonable steps to respond to the offense appropriately,

including making modifications to the program to prevent and detect violation of law[14]

The Sentencing Guidelines for Organizational Crime were a good beginning, but it would take many more years before they would be dramatically improved as a result of the changing landscape of corporate fraud.

SAS 82

For too long, accountants and auditors felt no responsibility to uncover fraud. Their excuse was that it was not their job. With the growing importance of effective compliance stemming from COSO and the United States Sentencing Guidelines, fraud mitigation became a consideration but not always a priority. By the mid-1990s, the accounting and auditing profession determined that it needed to take stronger measures to detect and prevent fraud in business in the wake of growing criticism that it was not doing enough to stop fraud. In November 1996, the Auditing Standards Board of the American Institute of Certified Public Accountants (AICPA) issued SAS 82, "Consideration of Fraud in a Financial Statement Audit." SAS 82 provided new guidance to auditors for detecting fraud when conducting audits. In previously issued guidance for auditors, fraud had not been defined, and instead the term "errors and irregularities" was used. Moreover, auditors were not responsible for finding "intentional misstatements concealed by collusion."[15]

The new standard stated that an auditor "has a responsibility to plan and perform the audit to obtain reasonable assurance about whether the financial statements are free of material misstatement, whether caused by error or *fraud* [emphasis added]."[16] SAS 82 stated that "The primary factor that distinguishes fraud from error is whether the underlying action in financial statements is intentional or unintentional."[17] Under SAS 82, financial statement fraud includes the falsification, manipulation, or alteration of accounting records and supporting documents; deliberate misapplication of accounting principles to defraud; and submission or omission of misleading financial transactions or other significant information.

SAS 82 required the auditor to plan and perform an audit in order to determine whether the financial statements are free of material misstatements. The auditor was required to assess 41 risk factors related to fraudulent financial reporting and misappropriation of assets. The risk factors fell into three main categories; some of the more important ones are as follows:

- Risk Factors Relating to Management's Characteristics and Influence
  - Performance-related compensation plans
  - Management's desire to keep the stock price high
  - Need for credit and financing
  - Management's desire to reduce tax liability
  - Corporate values or ethics not being effectively communicated
  - Domination of one person or small group of people in management
  - Lack of control monitoring
  - Ineffective accounting, information technology, or internal auditing staff
  - Nonfinancial management's excessive involvement in accounting and finance activities
  - High turnover of management
  - Strained relations between management and employees
  - History of fraudulent behavior
- Risk Factors Relating to Industry Conditions
  - New accounting or statutory regulations
  - High degree of market competition with declining margins
  - Rapidly changing industry, such as technology
- Risk Factors Relating to Operational Characteristics and Financial Stability
  - Cash flow problems while also reporting earnings or growth in earnings
  - Pressure or need to obtain additional capital financing
  - Assets, liabilities, revenues, or expenses based largely on estimates
  - Significant related-party transactions not in the ordinary course of business
  - Significant, unusual, or highly complex transactions
  - Significant bank accounts or a subsidiary branch in tax-haven jurisdictions
  - Overly complex operational structure or unusual legal entities

- Difficulty in determining the individual(s) who controls the entity
- Especially high vulnerability to changes in interest rates
- Unusually high dependence on debt or marginal ability to meet payment requirements
- Unrealistically aggressive sales or profitability incentive programs
- Threat of imminent bankruptcy
- Poor, deteriorating financial position when management has personally guaranteed significant debts of the entity[18]

Auditors needed to assess the total risk from fraud facing a company and design the audit to encompass the fraud risk among other business risks. Risks involving the misappropriation of assets related to their susceptibility to such fraud and whether appropriate controls were in place to mitigate the risk were now considered. SAS 82 only required that when a material fraud was discovered, the auditor should consider the implications and discuss with appropriate management. Although evidence that a fraud may exist would be communicated, the presence of a fraud risk that did not meet the evidence of fraud threshold might not be communicated. SAS 82 did prescribe that the audit committee or its equivalent be advised of any fraud involving senior management, but it would have been rare for an auditor under SAS 82 to go above the management structure to report serious fraud issues to either the audit committee or outside counsel. The problem was that senior management was often involved in financial statement fraud and other misconduct. SAS 82 was meant to provide guidance to auditors on how to consider the possibility of fraud when conducting an audit and evaluating the results when conducting financial statement audits; it was not a guide to the many other frauds affecting companies.[19] It was never meant to make auditors into fraud examiners. In fact, there was no requirement that auditors be trained in fraud examination and detection.

ARTHUR LEVITT AND THE "NUMBERS GAME"

Although July 30, 2002, may mark the birth of the new age of corporate enlightenment and governance, with the signing of the

Sarbanes-Oxley Act into law, September 28, 1998, may very well be its conception. On that day, Arthur Levitt, the former Chairman of the SEC, gave a powerful and prophetic speech at the New York University Center for Law and Business in New York City. The speech was aptly called the "Numbers Game," and Levitt spoke like a modern-day Nostradamus foretelling the coming doom in the financial markets. Levitt used this speech as a forum to discuss what he felt was a deception being played with earnings management. He called it "a game that, if not addressed soon, will have adverse consequences for America's financial reporting system," and "a game that runs counter to the very principles behind our market's strength and success."[20] Coming three years before the Enron collapse, few listened to Levitt as the bubble continued to grow.

Levitt warned that there was "erosion in the quality of earnings, and therefore the quality of financial reporting." He saw fraud as a possible end result because of pressure from management to meet or beat the numbers expected by Wall Street. The audience was told that there was a distinct possibility of executives who would cross into the "gray area" by "cutting corners" rather than be totally honest to investors about financial performance. Although he did not use the "F" word of fraud or the term "cooking the books," Levitt implied that the integrity of the markets was being called into question. He stated, "Managing may be giving way to manipulation; integrity may be losing out to illusion."[21] He was telling us about the future, but not all in the corporate suites were listening.

Levitt gave a brief history lesson on how financial shenanigans result in investor panic and financial ruin. He expressed his concern about the need for improving accounting and disclosure rules, the need for independence and oversight of external auditors, and the importance of a company's board of directors and audit committee. He mentioned the critical importance of transparency and accurate reporting. All these issues became core elements of the Sarbanes-Oxley legislation. There is no doubt that when the congressional framers of Sarbanes-Oxley sat down to build the act's content, they read what Levitt had said. He also made a point of saying that the serious issues he was discussing would not be solved by government alone and that it would take the dedicated involvement of investors, financial analysts, and, of course, corporate executives. Of the three, investors were the most naïve and the least concerned at the time to have any impact on financial reporting.

Levitt said the SEC was seeing five accounting "gimmicks" or "accounting hocus-pocus" that were proving problematic:

- "Big Bath Restructuring Charges": when companies overstate restructuring charges or make other large charges that have a tendency to "clean up" the balance sheets with a "big bath." Restructuring involves significant changes in the financial structure, ownership, or operations of a company to ultimately increase value through various practices such as mergers and acquisitions, leveraged buyouts, divestitures, and recapitalization.[22] Inappropriate one-time charges for restructuring can inflate earnings going forward. Levitt cautioned that all involved parties including management, employees, investors, vendors, and others need to fully understand the effects of any restructuring and ensure accurate and transparent financial reporting.

- "Creative Acquisition Accounting": classification of acquisition costs as "in-process research and development" so they can be "written off as one-time charges removing any future earnings drag."

- "Cookie Jar Reserves": unrealistic estimates of liabilities such as sales returns, loan losses, or warranty costs that tend to stockpile accruals in "cookie jars" to be used in times of financial instability. Large, one-time losses to earnings can be problematic for financial reporting and can lead to scandal and prison.

- "Immaterial Misapplication of Accounting Principles": Levitt said that materiality helps build flexibility into financial reporting and that "some items may be so insignificant that they are not worth measuring and reporting with exact precision." However, he argued that some companies "fib" (again, as close to using the F-word that he would say in this speech) by intentionally including errors that pump up the bottom line. He added, "In markets where missing an earnings projection by a penny can result in a loss of millions of dollars in market capitalization, I have a hard time accepting that some of these so-called nonevents simply don't matter."

- "Premature Recognition of Revenue": the manipulation of revenue is one of the most serious accounting issues faced today. Recognizing revenue before the contract is signed, sealed, and delivered, when the customer still has the option to return the goods or refuse the services, is an easy way to commit fraud and abuse. Levitt recognized it as a problem in 1998 and maintained that some unnamed companies recognized revenue before a transaction was complete or a product had been delivered. He stated that this attempt to "boost earnings" was like a "bottle of fine wine" that one "wouldn't pop the cork before it was ready."[23]

Levitt ended his visionary speech by outlining an action plan to improve the transparency of financial statements and reporting. The program included recommendations for an improved accounting framework, improved outside auditing of the financial reporting process, strengthening the audit committee process, and the need for a culture change. Levitt stated that, "For corporate managers, remember, the integrity of the numbers in the financial reporting system is directly related to the long-term interests of a corporation. While the temptations are great, and the pressure strong, illusions in numbers are only that—ephemeral, and ultimately self-destructive."[24] Few were listening in 1998.

THE SARBANES-OXLEY ACT OF 2002

The fall of the stock market in 2000 was quickly followed by daily revelations of corporate fraud and indiscretions. The constant reporting of corporate scandals reinforced the belief that some corporate titans personified greed and lack of accountability, while lining their pockets at the expense of the average investor. Investors lost faith in the financial markets. They came to believe the market was rigged and no one was there to protect their interests and their hard-earned money. Something needed to be done to restore faith and trust in Wall Street and punish the many corporate fraudsters.

Congress responded in July 2002 by passing landmark legislation, the Public Company Accounting Reform and Investor Protection Act of 2002, commonly called the Sarbanes-Oxley Act (the "Act"). Sarbanes-Oxley is named for its Congressional sponsors, Senator Paul Sarbanes (D-Maryland) and Representative Michael Oxley (R-Ohio). In support of his measure, Senator Sarbanes said "the problems originally laid bare by the collapse of Enron are by no means unique to one company, one industry, or even one profession." He added that "something needs to be done to restore confidence in the world's greatest marketplace."[25]

Many were uncertain the bill would become law. Previous efforts to curb corporate crime had languished in Congress because of opposition from the accounting profession and from politicians. But WorldCom's $3.8 billion accounting fraud and collapse in June 2002 spurred Congress to pass the Sarbanes-Oxley Act with overwhelming bipartisan support in the House and Senate. President Bush signed the Act into law on July 30, 2002. "Every corporate official," he said at the signing, "who has chosen to commit a crime can expect to face the consequences."[26]

The legislation strengthens corporate accountability and governance of public companies; affects their officers and directors; improves auditor integrity and independence; greatly empowers audit committees; addresses conflicts of interest by stock analysts; and most importantly, protects employees, pension holders, and investors from fraud.

The Act is comprehensive and ground-breaking. It consists of 11 titles covering the public company accounting oversight board, auditor independence, corporate responsibility, enhanced financial disclosures, and analyst conflicts of interest. It also includes the Corporate and Criminal Fraud Accountability Act (Title VIII), the White-Collar Crime Penalty Enhancements Act of 2002 (Title IX), and the Corporate Fraud Accountability Act of 2002 (Title XI). The Act covers areas of great importance to companies, shareholders, and the government, including concerns that had not been addressed before.

This section covers the salient points of the Act but is by no means an exhaustive overview of all its aspects. For such an overview, the reader is invited to read the text of the Sarbanes-Oxley Act of 2002 (www.sec.gov/about/laws.shtml#sox2002) to gain a detailed understanding.

Implications for Independent Auditors

The Sarbanes-Oxley Act creates a strong and independent Public Company Accounting Oversight Board (PCAOB) to oversee the audit of public companies that are subject to securities laws. More information on the formation of the PCAOB and its implications can be found in Chapter 4. The PCAOB protects the interests of investors in the preparation of accurate and independent audit reports. The Act requires that the PCAOB have five members appointed from among prominent individuals of integrity and reputation who have a demonstrated commitment to the interests of investors and the public. The members cannot currently be connected with any public accounting firm. Each member must have financial expertise and understand generally accepted accounting principles, internal controls, financial statements, and audit committee functions. Two of the members must be or have been Certified Public Accountants (CPAs), and the remaining three must not be and cannot have been CPAs. The chair may be held by one of the CPA members, provided that the person was not engaged as a practicing CPA for five years.

The PCAOB oversees the accounting industry, subject to SEC supervision through a number of actions including:

- Registering public accounting firms that prepare audit reports for issuers
- Establishing or adopting, or both, by rule, auditing, quality control, ethics, independence, and other standards relating to the preparation of audit reports for issuers
- Conducting inspections of public accounting firms
- Conducting investigations and disciplinary proceedings and imposing appropriate sanctions on public accounting firms
- Performing such other duties or functions as the PCAOB (or the SEC, by rule or order) determines are necessary or appropriate to promote high professional standards and improve the quality of audit services offered by public accounting firms
- Enforcing compliance with the Act, the rules of PCAOB, professional standards, and the securities laws relating to the preparation and issuance of audit reports

Auditor Independence

The Act promotes auditor independence by prohibiting an auditor from providing a number of nonaudit services when performing an audit for a public company audit client including the following:

- Bookkeeping or other services related to the accounting records or financial statements of the audit client
- Financial information systems design and implementation

- Appraisal or valuation services, fairness opinions, or contribution-in-kind reports
- Actuarial services
- Internal audit outsourcing services
- Management functions or human resources
- Broker or dealer, investment advisor, or investment banking services
- Legal services and expert services unrelated to the audit
- Any other service that PCAOB determines, by regulation, is not permissible

Corporate Responsibility: Implications for Audit Committees

The Sarbanes-Oxley Act improves corporate responsibility by increasing the independence of the audit committee. Audit committee members cannot be affiliated with the issuers except in this oversight role and cannot accept any consulting or advisory work or any other compensation from the issuer. Each member of the audit committee shall be a member of the board of directors of the issuer and shall be independent. Auditors must report to the audit committee of a client and not to management. The audit committee will be responsible for the appointment, compensation, and oversight of the work of the auditor, as well as resolution of any disagreements or disputes between the company and the auditor.

The company must also disclose whether the audit committee has at least one member who is a "financial expert." The Act defines a financial expert as a person who, through education and experience as a public accountant or auditor, or from serving as a principal financial officer, comptroller, or principal accounting officer of an issuer, or from a position involving the performance of similar functions, has:

- An understanding of generally accepted accounting principles and financial statements
- Experience in the preparation or auditing of financial statements for generally comparable companies
- Experience with internal accounting controls
- An understanding of audit committee functions

Previously, many audit committees did not have "financial experts" among the members. The belief is that by having individuals who are knowledgeable and experienced in financial matters, corporate indiscretions and deceptions will be discovered and reported. The SEC has ruled that the expert's name must be disclosed and whether the expert is independent of management. A company that does not have such an expert will be required to disclose this and must explain why it has no such expert.

Each public accounting firm is required to report, on a timely basis, to the audit committee on all critical accounting policies and practices used in the financial statements. This report must include all alternative treatments of financial information within generally accepted accounting principles that have been discussed with management, the ramifications of the use of such treatments, and the treatments preferred by the accounting firm. In addition, the auditors must provide any material written communications between the firm and company management, such as management letters or schedules of unadjusted differences.

Complaints and Whistleblower Protection

The Sarbanes-Oxley Act requires each publicly traded company to create a reporting system for employees to report misconduct. Although the Act does not specifically mention whistleblowers, the implication is clear. Thanks to Sherron Watkins, formerly of Enron, and Cynthia Cooper, formerly of WorldCom, whistleblowers have gained new respectability and the gratitude of the investing public. *Time* magazine recognized these women as the 2002 Persons of the Year for their commitment to disclosing corporate fraud.

Each audit committee must establish procedures for receiving, retaining, and responding to complaints received by the issuers including the confidential, anonymous submission of questionable accounting, internal accounting controls, or auditing matters. Generally, these will be in the form of hotlines to receive confidential calls and provide the information to the company for appropriate action. Hotlines can help employees feel safe from retaliation.

The Act provides enhanced whistleblower protection for employees of publicly traded companies who are discharged, demoted, suspended, threatened, harassed, or discriminated against after disclosing evidence of fraud and assisting in investigations to stop fraud. A whistleblower who has been retaliated against may seek relief through the U.S. Department of Labor and the district courts. What many people do not realize is that there is now a criminal consequence for someone who retaliates against a whistleblower. The Act makes retaliation a federal offense punishable by up to 10 years in prison.

Improving Corporate Governance: Implications for Public Companies

CEO and CFO Certifications   The Sarbanes-Oxley Act enhances corporate governance and accountability by requiring both the CEO and CFO of a public company to certify the disclosures they make in periodic reports. This puts the responsibility directly onto the key officers of a company to ensure that their financial statements and other disclosures filed with the SEC are truthful. Executives can no longer ask, "Who, me?" or say, "I didn't know."

In required certifications, CEOs and CFOs must certify that:

- They have reviewed the report.
- To the best of their knowledge, the report contains no untrue material fact and does not omit a material fact that would make the statements misleading.
- To the best of their knowledge, the financial statements and other financial information in the report fairly presents, in all material respects, the financial condition and results of operations of the company.
- They are responsible for establishing and maintaining internal controls.
- They have designed internal controls to ensure that material information relating to the company is made known to other officers in the company.
- They have evaluated the effectiveness of the internal controls within their company prior to the issuance of the report.
- They have presented in the report their conclusions about the effectiveness of their internal controls.
- They have disclosed to their auditors and the audit committee all significant deficiencies in the design or operation of internal

controls that could adversely affect the company's ability to record, process, and report financial data, and they have identified any material weaknesses in internal controls.

- They have disclosed whether or not there were significant changes in internal controls or other factors that might significantly affect internal controls subsequent to the date of their evaluation, including any corrective actions taken.
- They have disclosed any fraud, whether material or not, that involves management or other employees who have a significant role in the company's internal controls.

Ignorance of the law is no excuse. Certifying officers who violate this section of the act will face criminal prosecution and be guaranteed a perp walk. A violation of this certification process is a felony punishable by up to 20 years in prison if the violation is knowing and willful.

Insider Trading   A common concern is that corporate executives under investigation will falsely reassure investors and employees about the health of the company while quietly dumping large amounts of their stock. Sarbanes-Oxley addresses this by dramatically shortening the deadline for insiders to report any trading in their company's securities. Officers and directors of a publicly traded company previously had up to 40 days to report their trades of company stock, but they now have two business days. The trades must also be posted on the company's Web site. There is also a prohibition on insider trades during pension fund blackout periods. Any profits realized by an officer or director in violation of this section may be recovered by the company.

Disgorgement   Under the Act, if a company is required to restate its financial statement as a result of misconduct, the CEO and CFO must reimburse the company for any bonuses or other compensation received during the 12-month period following the first public issuance or filing with the SEC of the financial document. This is a new concept for chief executives but one that should have occurred long ago. Having to surrender ill-gotten gains or even legally permissible gains that were not obtained with transparency is a new phenomenon in corporate America.

Ban on Personal Loans to Officers and Directors   The Act bans personal loans from public companies to their executive officers and directors that they do not make in the ordinary course of business. John Rigas, former CEO of Adelphia, Dennis Kozlowski, former CEO of Tyco, and others took large personal loans without the knowledge or approval of their company boards. Corrupt executives who use their companies as personal piggy banks will now face civil and criminal penalties.

Code of Ethics   The cornerstone of an effective fraud prevention program and a culture of compliance is a strong value system based on integrity. These values can best be reflected in a code of ethics or conduct to ensure that employees know what is expected of them and then make the right decisions. This is especially true for executives and officers. Sarbanes-Oxley requires that public companies have a code of ethics for its senior financial officers. It must then disclose whether it has adopted a code of ethics; if it has not, it must disclose the reasons for not doing so.

Enhanced Financial Disclosures   The Act enhances financial disclosures in a number of other ways. A company must file a report on its internal controls with its annual reports. The report must confirm management's responsibility for establishing and maintaining adequate internal control structures and procedures for reporting, as well as evaluating the effectiveness of these controls and procedures. The issuer's public accountants must attest to and report on the management assessment as part of the audit engagement. These are the requirements of Section 404.

The Act also improves on the timely reporting of potentially derogatory information. Each annual report filed with the SEC containing financial statements will be required to include all material correcting adjustments. Each annual and quarterly financial report shall disclose all material off-balance sheet transactions and other relationships that may have a material effect on the financial condition of the company. Enron used off-balance sheet transactions to hide debt that contributed to the massive fraud at the Houston energy company.

Civil and Criminal Penalties

The Act creates a number of new criminal statutes and amends others to add some strong teeth to enforcement actions. These include the following:

Destruction, Alteration, or Falsification of Records in Federal Investigations and Bankruptcy. The destruction, alteration, or falsification of records or documents with the intent to impede, obstruct, or influence a federal investigation is a new statute punishable by a fine, imprisonment of up to 20 years, or both. An accountant who conducts an audit of an issuer of securities is required to maintain all audit or review work papers for a period of five years from the end of the fiscal period in which the audit or review was concluded. This new statute provides a fine, a maximum term of imprisonment of 10 years, or both, for anyone who knowingly and willfully violates it.

Securities Fraud. This statute provides criminal penalties for defrauding shareholders of a publicly traded company. It complements existing securities law and provides a fine, a maximum term of imprisonment of 25 years, or both. The statute of limitations for securities fraud is increased to two years after the discovery of the facts constituting the violation or five years after such violation.

White-Collar Crime Penalty Enhancements. Criminal penalties are increased under Title IX of the Act, which is called the "White-Collar Crime Penalty Enhancement Act of 2002." There is increased jail time for a number of existing criminal statutes including the workhorse of fraud prosecution, the Mail Fraud Statute. Sarbanes-Oxley increases the criminal penalties for mail fraud as well as wire fraud to 20 years in prison. There are also increased penalties for tampering with or impeding an official investigation and retaliation against informants and whistleblowers.

Failure of Corporate Officers to Certify Financial Reports. There is also a new criminal statute relating to the certification of periodic financial reports filed by a company with the SEC. If the CEO or CFO falsely certifies any statement regarding the financial condition and results of operations of the company, he or she can face up to 20 years in prison and/or a $5 million fine.

Amendment to the Federal Sentencing Guidelines. The Act required the U.S. Sentencing Commission (USSC) to review and amend its sentencing guidelines for securities fraud, obstruction of justice, and extensive criminal fraud. As a result of Sarbanes-Oxley, there are harsher sentences in fraud cases with large numbers of victims and large dollar losses, cases involving officers and directors of public companies, destruction of evidence, and falsely certifying financial statements.[27]

The USSC has increased penalties for corporate crimes that affect a large number of victims or endanger the financial viability of publicly traded companies.

Sarbanes-Oxley Today

Given the many years that have passed since Sarbanes-Oxley's enactment, there is still much debate about whether it has reduced fraud in the corporate suites. The Act's authors, former Senator Paul Sarbanes and former Representative Michael Oxley, reaffirmed their support for it. Oxley points out that the Sarbanes-Oxley Act has resulted in greater confidence among investors, pointing to the tremendous increase in the Dow Jones industrial average, for instance, since the bill was passed.[28] Sarbanes echoed these comments about improved investor confidence. In his view, the Act markedly improves corporate accountability, and by removing many conflicts of interests, "[c]hecks and balances are working again and the watchdogs are functioning as watchdogs."[29] To further counter the argument that the Act has inhibited U.S. markets relative to foreign ones, he points out that other countries are moving in a similar direction, with higher standards and other provisions similar to the Act. He sees the money spent on compliance as a capital investment: expensive at first, particularly for a very good system, but something that will pay off and cost less in subsequent years. Sarbanes-Oxley is a necessary burden, a cost that must be paid to ensure that companies are held to a high standard and that people can invest their money with confidence.[30]

Overall, the law has done far more good than harm and should not be weakened by legislative reforms. Even those who criticize its cost and burdensome aspects acknowledge the greater boardroom accountability it produced and how it has helped to spur further changes within companies to help them avoid future scandals. Boards can now address and solve internal problems "before they fester and explode."[31] Institutional shareholders have benefited as disclosure and certification requirements have helped to reassure investors and restore their confidence in the integrity of companies' financial statements. Even though many companies had to restate financial results in the years immediately following the law's passage, that practice is much less common now as companies have fixed old problems and avoided new ones. Many more companies immediately escalate discovered financial issues.[32] Thanks to the reforms put into place, these usually minor issues can be handled quickly. Companies can constantly fine-tune their procedures to ensure their compliance efforts are as robust as they can be.[33]

NOTES

1. Don Tapscott, "Transparency as a Business Imperative," *Association Management*, April 2005, 17.
2. Bryan Garner, ed. *Black's Law Dictionary*, 8th ed., s.v. "transparency."
3. William H. Donaldson, "Speech by SEC Chairman: Remarks to the National Press Club" (speech, Washington, D.C., July 30, 2003), *U.S. Securities and Exchange Commission,* www.sec.gov/news/speech/spch073003whd.htm.
4. National Commission on Fraudulent Financial Reporting, *Report of the National Commission on Fraudulent Financial Reporting*, October 1987, 1, www.coso.org/publications/NCFFR_Part_1.htm.
5. Ibid., 23.
6. Ibid., 1.
7. Ibid., 24.
8. Ibid., 17–78.

9. The Committee of Sponsoring Organizations of the Treadway Commission, *Internal Control—Integrated Framework,* 1992, www.coso.org/publications/executive_summary_integrated_framework.htm.

10. Mark S. Beasley, Joseph V. Carcello, and Dana R. Hermanson, *Fraudulent Financial Reporting 1987–1997, An Analysis of U.S. Public Companies* (Committee of Sponsoring Organizations of the Treadway Commission, 1999), www.coso.org/publications/ffr_1987_1997.pdf.

11. "Financial Fraud at U.S. Public Companies Often Results in Bankruptcy or Failure with Significant Immediate Losses for Shareholders and Penalties for Executives," COSO News Release, May 20, 2010, www.coso.org/documents/cosoreleaseonfraudulentreporting2010pdf_002.pdf.

12. Committee of Sponsoring Organizations of the Treadway Commission, *Fraudulent Financial Reporting: 1998–2007: An Analysis of U.S. Public Companies,* May 2010, www.coso.org/fraudreport.htm.

13. *Sentencing Reform Act,* U.S. Code 28 (2003) § 991.

14. *United States Sentencing Commission Guidelines Manual,* Ch. 8, Sentencing of Organizations, November 1, 1991.

15. Association of Certified Fraud Examiners, *Fraud Examiners Manual,* 3rd ed. (Austin, TX: 2001), 1.203.

16. Ibid, 1.204.

17. Donald Fogel, "SAS 82: Providing Guidance in the Hunt for Fraud," *The White Paper* (September–October 1998), 28.

18. Association of Certified Fraud Examiners, *Fraud Examiners Manual,* 3rd ed. (Austin, TX: ACFE, 2001), 1.205–1.206.

19. SAS 82 content reprinted from the *Fraud Examiners Manual,* 3rd ed. (Austin, TX: ACFE, 2001), 1.203–1.207 with permission of the Association of Certified Fraud Examiners, Austin, Texas © 2005.

20. Arthur Levitt, "The 'Numbers Game'" (speech, NYU Center for Law and Business, New York, September 28, 1998), *U.S. Securities and Exchange Commission,* http://www.sec.gov/news/speech/speecharchive/1998/spch220.txt.

21. Ibid.

22. Ian Giddy, *Corporate Financial Restructuring* (course description), www.stern.nyu.edu/~igiddy/restructuring.html.

23. Levitt, "The 'Numbers Game.'"
24. Ibid.
25. Eric Winig, "Government Meddling Won't Stop Cheats," *Washington Business Journal*, July 12, 2002.
26. Elisabeth Bumiller, "Bush Signs Bill Aimed at Fraud in Corporations," *New York Times*, July 31, 2002. A2.
27. Martin T. Biegelman, "Sarbanes-Oxley Act: Stopping U.S. Corporate Crooks from Cooking the Books," *The White Paper*, March–April 2003, reprinted with permission from the Association of Certified Fraud Examiners, Austin, Texas © 2005.
28. Alison Grant, "Corporate Reforms Working, Says Law's Co-Author," Newhouse News Service, *Seattle Times*, April 22, 2007, F1. The Dow Jones was a little over 7,000 when the bill was passed and was over 12,500 in 2007 when the interview took place.
29. Dick Carozza, "Sarbanes-Oxley Act Revisited: An Interview with Sen. Paul S. Sarbanes," *Fraud Magazine*, May–June 2007, 36.
30. Ibid.
31. Joann S. Lublin and Kara Scannell, "Critics See Some Good from Sarbanes-Oxley," *Wall Street Journal*, July 30, 2007, B1.
32. Ibid.
33. Material in this last section is reproduced from *Building a World-Class Compliance Program: Best Practices and Strategies for Success,* by Martin T. Biegelman with Daniel R. Biegelman, published by John Wiley & Sons, 2008.

The Path to Greater Corporate Compliance, Accountability, and Ethical Conduct

SAS 99 to the 2010 Amendments to the Federal Sentencing Guidelines for Organizations

EXECUTIVE SUMMARY

Improved corporate compliance and stricter enforcement did not end with the enactment of Sarbanes-Oxley in 2002. The American Institute of Certified Public Accountants released their Statement on Auditing Standards 99, an auditing standard that now requires greater involvement of external auditors in developing reasonable assurance that an entity's financial statements are free of material misstatements whether by fraud or error. The government gave strong guidance to federal prosecutors in its historic "Thompson Memo" of how and when to bring criminal charges against an organization. In the process, the government sent a chilling message to corporations that cross the line. The Securities and Exchange Commission drove home the important role of "gate-keepers" in protecting the interests of the investing public and the government. The government greatly enhanced prison sentences for fraud so that a fraud conviction could now bring a life sentence. Other compliance enhancements followed, all leading the way toward the creation of a culture of compliance.

THE SAS 99 FIX

After several tries and the inability to detect massive financial statement frauds, the accounting industry may have finally gotten it right. In December 2002, the new Statement on Auditing Standards (SAS) 99, Consideration of Fraud in a Financial Statement Audit, superseded the earlier SAS 82 and gave auditors better tools and guidance for effectiveness in uncovering fraud. Auditors now had "a responsibility to plan and perform the audit to obtain reasonable assurance about whether the financial statements are free of material misstatement, whether caused by error or fraud."[1] Quite simply, SAS 99 requires auditors to look for fraud throughout the audit process. SAS 99 provides auditors with guidance on detecting fraud through the following content:

- Description and characteristics of fraud
- Importance of exercising professional skepticism
- Discussion among engagement personnel regarding risk of material misstatement due to fraud
- Obtaining information to identify risks of material misstatement due to fraud
- Identifying risks that may result in a material misstatement due to fraud
- Assessing the identified risks after taking into account an evaluation of the entity's programs and controls
- Responding to the results of the assessment
- Evaluating audit evidence
- Communicating about fraud to management, the audit committee, and others
- Documenting the auditor's consideration of fraud[2]

Fraud According to SAS 99

SAS 99 incorporates fraud theory and practice in developing reasonable assurance that an entity's financial statements are free of material misstatements whether by fraud or error. SAS 99 defines fraud as "an intentional act that results in a material misstatement in financial statements that are the subject of an audit."[3] Cressey's Fraud Triangle is incorporated into SAS 99 with a discussion of the three conditions that are generally present for fraud to occur: incentive or pressure (motive), opportunity, and rationalization or attitude. Furthermore, two types of financial misstatements are defined under SAS 99, misstatements arising from fraudulent financial reporting and misstatements arising from misappropriation of assets, often referred to as defalcation or theft.

Misstatements arising from fraudulent financial reporting are considered intentional misstatements or omissions of information from financial statements with the intent to deceive. SAS 99 explains that fraudulent financial reporting can be accomplished by:

- Manipulation, falsification, or alteration of accounting records or supporting documents
- Misrepresenting or intentionally omitting events, transactions, or other significant information
- Intentionally misapplying accounting principles relating to amounts, classification, manner of presentation, or disclosure

SAS 99 takes into consideration that financial schemes, such as manipulating accounting records and management override, are often perpetrated by a company's management. As a result, auditors are urged to be aware of this possibility in addition to collusion among employees engaging in a fraud and the falsification of documentation that is presented for review. As an example, SAS 99 details how the common management override of internal controls can be accomplished by:

- Recording fictitious journal entries, particularly those recorded close to the end of an accounting period in order to manipulate operating results

- Intentionally biasing assumptions and judgments used to estimate account balances
- Altering records and terms related to significant and unusual transactions

Exercising Professional Skepticism

SAS 99 requires auditors to apply professional skepticism when doing their audits to ensure that the truth is found. This requires a questioning mind at all times and critical assessments of the statements and documentation provided by the entity. The auditor must also conduct the audit with the idea in mind that a fraud may be present and without bias by past experiences or beliefs in the honesty and integrity of management. Some of the auditors involved in auditing companies caught up in corporate frauds failed to exercise the due care or skepticism that might have detected the accounting deception.

Discussion among Engagement Personnel

SAS 99 requires that auditors exchange ideas or "brainstorm" during an audit about how an entity's financial statements might be fraudulently misstated, how fraud may be concealed, and how assets could be misappropriated. The various elements of the Fraud Triangle should be discussed as to the fraud risks that might be in play at the company. The key members of the audit team must be involved in this brainstorming with consideration given to involving other experts in fraud detection as the need arises. Communication among team members is critical throughout the audit to ensure that all fraud risks are considered in evaluating the existence of material misstatements.

Obtaining, Identifying, and Assessing Fraud Risks

When beginning an engagement, auditors must make inquiries of management to learn about the organization's business and the potential risks of material misstatement because of fraud. This inquiry should include questioning whether:

- Management has an understanding of fraud and fraud risks facing the entity
- Management has knowledge of allegations of fraud either through identified parties or whistleblower hotlines
- The organization has implemented programs and controls to detect, deter, and prevent fraud and how it monitors the programs and controls
- Organizations with multiple locations and business segments are appropriately monitoring the fraud risk at each location or business segment and whether, as a result, there is significantly more risk involved
- Management communicates to employees its policies on ethical standards and business practices

Auditors should inquire of management whether the audit committee has been briefed on how the entity's internal controls help detect and prevent fraud. In addition to discussions with management, auditors should also speak with the audit committee about their understanding of fraud risks and whether the audit committee has any knowledge of allegations of fraud. Auditors should also ask the entity's internal audit function about their views on fraud risk and whether there have been instances of fraud. If so, auditors should inquire about the response to these allegations by the internal audit group and management's response to any findings emanating from a fraud investigation. In addition, inquiries should be made of any other appropriate employees such as fraud investigators and legal compliance personnel who might have knowledge of fraud within the entity. Auditors must always remember that fraudsters within a company will not willingly reveal their involvement in fraudulent activities and thus, there is the need for independent verification and corroboration.

In determining the entity's fraud risk, the motive/incentive/pressure to commit fraud, the opportunity that exists to commit fraud, and the rationalization/attitude to justify the fraudulent actions must all be considered by the auditors. Analytical procedures to identify unusual or suspect transactions must also be considered. Examples of such analytical procedures might include reviewing sales volume over production capacity for fictitious sales. Trend analysis of revenues and sales returns may disclose channel stuffing and side agreements for customers to return merchandise, resulting in revenue recognition issues. Channel stuffing is an illegal practice by a company to inflate its sales and earnings numbers at the end of a fiscal year by offering distributors and other channel partners more products than they might be able to reasonably sell.

SAS 99 requires auditors to consider a number of issues involving fraud risk, including the following:

- The *type* of risk that may exist and whether it involves fraudulent financial reporting or misappropriation of assets
- The *significance* of the risk identified and whether it could lead to a material misstatement
- The *likelihood* that the risk will result in a material misstatement
- The *pervasiveness* of risk as to whether it permeates the entire financial statement or is confined to a particular transaction or account

To assess any identified fraud risks, auditors must have a thorough understanding of an entity's internal controls that have been designed and are in place. The program and controls must be evaluated to determine whether they are sufficient to mitigate the risk of material misstatement fraud.

The auditors must recognize the possibility of other fraud risks for misstatement being present in the entity, including the following:

- *Revenue recognition.* Material misstatements are common because of premature revenue recognition, recording fictitious revenues, and improperly shifting revenues to a later period.
- *Management overrides.* Overrides by management are also common and should be considered a potential risk. Today there is greater scrutiny of management overrides such as phony journal entries. Fraudsters have favored manual entries, and now auditors are looking closely at them.
- *Inventory quantities.* Falsifying inventory numbers is another fraud risk. Auditors should consider identifying the location of inventory and conducting a physical inventory count if there is an indication of manipulation. The examination may include the contents of boxes, the manner in which the goods are stacked, and the quality of the contents. Fraudsters have been known

to stack empty boxes, as well as boxes containing damaged or discontinued stock to deceive auditors checking inventory.

■ *Management estimates.* The fraud risk may involve specific transactions including acquisitions, restructurings, or disposals of business segments or significant accrued liabilities such as pension and other postretirement benefit obligations.

■ *Manipulation of journal entries.* Material misstatements often involve recording inappropriate or unauthorized journal entries throughout the year or at year-end, as well as making adjustments to financial statements that are not reflected in formal journal entries.

Evaluating Audit Evidence

Under SAS 99, auditors may identify risks that need further examination in order to determine the full extent of a possible fraud, including the following:

■ Discrepancies in Accounting Records
  ● Transactions that are not recorded in a complete or timely manner or are improperly recorded as to amount, accounting period, classification, or entity policy
  ● Unsupported or unauthorized balances or transactions
  ● Last-minute adjustments that significantly affect financial results
  ● Evidence of employees' access to systems and records inconsistent with that necessary to perform their authorized duties
  ● Tips or complaints to the auditor about alleged fraud
■ Conflicting or Missing Evidential Matter
  ● Missing documents
  ● Documents that appear to have been altered
  ● Unavailability of photocopied or electronically transmitted documents when documents in original form are expected to exist
  ● Significant unexplained items on reconciliations
  ● Inconsistent, vague, or implausible responses from management or employees arising from inquiries or analytical procedures

- Unusual discrepancies between the entity's records and confirmation replies
- Missing inventory or physical assets of significant magnitude
- Unavailable or missing electronic evidence, inconsistent with the entity's record retention practices or policies
- Inability to produce evidence of key systems development and program change testing and implementation activities for current-year system changes and deployments

■ Problematic or Unusual Relationships between the Auditor and Management
  - Denial of access to records, facilities, certain employees, customers, vendors, or others from whom audit evidence might be sought
  - Undue time pressures imposed by management to resolve complex or contentious issues
  - Complaints by management about the conduct of the audit or management intimidation of audit team members, particularly in connection with the auditor's critical assessment of audit evidence or in the resolution of potential disagreements with management
  - Unusual delays by the entity in providing requested information
  - Unwillingness to facilitate auditor access to key electronic files for testing
  - Denial of access to key IT operations staff and facilities, including security, operations, and systems development personnel
  - An unwillingness to add or revise disclosures in the financial statements to make them more complete and transparent

If, after conducting a thorough audit, the auditor believes there is the likelihood of misstatements that could be material to the entity's financial statements, the auditor should:

■ Attempt to obtain additional evidence to determine whether material fraud has occurred or is likely to have occurred, and if so, the effect on the financial statements
■ Consider the implications for other aspects of the audit that may require additional testing

- Discuss the matter with an appropriate level of management that is at least one level above those involved, as well as with senior management and the audit committee
- If appropriate, suggest that the entity consult with legal counsel

Communicating and Documenting the Risk of Fraud

As an element of SAS 99, when auditors find evidence of fraud, they must communicate it to the appropriate level of management. Any fraud that is discovered involving senior management or relating to material misstatements must be disclosed to the audit committee. Risks of fraud should also be communicated to other appropriate parties because of their potential to result in fraud at some future time. For a record of the auditor's consideration of fraud, the following should be documented:

- The discussion(s) among engagement personnel when planning the audit as to the susceptibility of the organization's financial statements to material misstatements resulting from fraud, how and when the discussion(s) took place, the audit team members who participated, and what was discussed
- The specific procedures performed to identify and assess the risks of material misstatement because of fraud as well as a description of the auditor's response to those risks
- The specific risks of material misstatement that were identified and the auditor's response to those risks
- The results of procedures performed to address the risk of management override of controls
- Any other conditions or analytical relationships that caused the auditor to believe that additional audit procedures were required
- The nature of the communications about fraud made to management, the audit committee, and others[4]

PRINCIPLES OF FEDERAL PROSECUTION OF BUSINESS ORGANIZATIONS

On January 20, 2003, then Deputy Attorney General Larry Thompson took the fight against corporate fraud to a higher level. On that date, he issued a landmark memorandum entitled "Principles of Federal Prosecution of Business Organizations" and sent it to all United States Attorneys' Offices. It contained a revised set of principles to guide Department of Justice prosecutors when they were deciding to seek charges against a business organization.

The "Thompson Memo" and its subsequent revisions are a roadmap for federal prosecutors in the investigation and prosecution of corporate fraud. The principles provide a unique window into the government's strategy on corporate fraud prosecution and every vigilant executive must be aware of its contents. The memo should help businesses focus on protection of their employees and investors from fraud, and themselves from prosecution. Additionally, by understanding how the government thinks about prosecuting businesses, organizations can implement robust compliance and fraud prevention programs to lessen their culpability.

These guidelines for federal prosecutions of business organizations apply not only to public companies but also to other types of businesses including partnerships, sole proprietorships, government entities, and unincorporated associations. Every corporate executive and general counsel should be familiar with this government strategy memo. In fact, it should be read and reread by every CEO and CFO as a reminder of the consequences for a culture of noncompliance.

THE FINAL RULE OF THE SEC FOR SECTION 404 OF SARBANES-OXLEY

Sarbanes-Oxley's Section 404 requires that the SEC adopt rules requiring companies subject to the reporting requirements under the Securities Exchange Act of 1934 to include in the company's annual reports a report from management on the company's internal control over financial reporting. Section 404 requires an annual evaluation and report by management on the effectiveness of internal controls and procedures for financial reporting, as well as a report by the independent auditor attesting to management's assertions.[5] In August 2003, the SEC issued its final rule entitled *Management's Report on Internal Control over Financial Reporting and Certification of Disclosure in Exchange Act Periodic Reports.* The SEC's rule defines internal controls and procedures for financial reporting to mean "controls that pertain to the preparation of financial statements for external purposes that are fairly presented in conformity with generally accepted accounting principles."[6]

As stated in the rule, "The assessment of a company's internal control over financial reporting must be based on procedures sufficient both to evaluate its design and to test its operating effectiveness. Controls subject to such assessment include...controls related to the prevention, identification, and detection of fraud." The final SEC rules require that a company's annual report contain an internal control report from management that includes the following:

- A statement of management's responsibility for establishing and maintaining adequate internal control over the company's financial reporting.
- A statement identifying the framework used by management to conduct the required evaluation of the effectiveness of the company's internal control over financial reporting (ICFR).
- Management's assessment of the effectiveness of the company's ICFR as of the end of the company's most recent fiscal year, including a statement as to whether or not the company's ICFR is effective. The assessment must include a disclosure of any "material weaknesses" in the company's ICFR identified by management. A "material weakness" is defined as "a reportable condition in which the design or operation of one or more of the internal control components does not reduce to a relatively low level the risk that misstatements caused by errors or fraud in amounts that would be material in relation to the financial statements being audited may occur and not be detected within a timely period by employees in the normal course of performing their assigned function."[7] Management is not permitted to conclude that the company's ICFR is effective if there are one or more material weaknesses in the company's ICFR.
- A statement that the registered public accounting firm that audited the financial statements included in the annual report has issued an attestation report on management's assessment of the company's ICFR reporting as well as the actual attestation report of the accounting firm that audited the company's financial statements.[8]

THE PCAOB AND AUDITING STANDARD NO. 2

The Public Company Accounting Oversight Board (PCAOB) was created by the Sarbanes-Oxley legislation to be a strong and independent oversight body of the auditing of public companies by external auditors. The PCAOB is a private sector, nonprofit corporation set up to protect the interests of investors and ensure the preparation and release of accurate and independent audit reports. Several sections of Sarbanes-Oxley pertain to the PCAOB including the following:

- Section 102: prohibits accounting firms that are not registered with the PCAOB from preparing or issuing audit reports on United States public companies and from participating in such audits.
- Section 103: directs the PCAOB to establish auditing and related attestation, quality control, ethics, and independence standards and rules to be used by registered public accounting companies in the preparation and issuance of audit reports.
- Section 104: requires the PCAOB to conduct a continuing program of inspections of registered public accounting firms.
- Section 105: grants the PCAOB broad investigative and disciplinary authority over registered public accounting firms and persons associated with such firms.

The PCAOB has a strong enforcement role to prevent violations of Sarbanes-Oxley. To assist its mission, the board has established the PCAOB Center for Enforcement Tips, Complaints and Other Information. Individuals can file a complaint or provide tips on potential violations by a public accounting firm, its employees or others, or provide any information that might be relevant to the work of the PCAOB. There are several ways to contact the PCAOB hotline, including their Web site at www.pcaobus.org/Enforcement/Tips/Pages/default.aspx, via e-mail, by letter, or by telephone. This hotline will take action on any information received including the referral of other violations out of their jurisdiction to appropriate law enforcement agencies.

On March 9, 2004, the PCAOB adopted Auditing Standard No. 2 (AS No. 2), *An Audit of Internal Control over Financial Reporting*

Performed in Conjunction with an Audit of Financial Statements. At the time, No. 2 provided increased responsibilities for external auditors beyond those required by SAS 99. Although SAS 99 provides detailed guidance on a fraud risk assessment, it only requires an auditor to gain an understanding of management's fraud prevention and detection programs and controls. AS No. 2 requires auditors to evaluate antifraud programs and controls as part of the audit of internal control over financial reporting. It requires an integrated audit of the financial statements and an audit of internal control over financial reporting. Under AS No. 2, external auditors must test a company's internal controls and not rely on work performed by the company. AS No. 2 states that the costs of internal control must be appropriate to the expected benefits reaped from improved controls. It also requires auditors to evaluate the fraud-related activities of the internal audit department. Some of the key provisions of AS No. 2 are as follows:

- Evaluating management's assessment
- Obtaining an understanding of internal control over financial reporting including performing walkthroughs
- Identifying significant account and relevant assertions
- Testing and evaluating the effectiveness of the design of controls
- Testing operating effectiveness
- Timing of testing
- Using the work of others
- Evaluating the results of testing
- Identifying significant deficiencies
- Forming an opinion and reporting
- No disclosure of significant deficiencies
- Material weaknesses resulting in adverse opinion on internal control
- Testing controls intended to prevent or detect fraud[9]

Fraud Considerations in an Audit of Internal Control over Financial Reporting

AS No. 2 advises, "Strong internal controls also provide better opportunities to detect and deter fraud. For example, many frauds resulting in financial statement restatement relied upon the ability of management to exploit weaknesses in internal control."[10] It goes on to say, "For this reason, Auditing Standard No. 2 specifically addresses and emphasizes the importance of controls over possible fraud and requires the auditor to test controls specifically intended to prevent or detect fraud that is reasonably possible to result in material misstatement of financial statements."[11]

Auditors need to evaluate all controls specifically intended to address fraud risks that may have a likelihood of having a material impact on the company's financial statements. Some of the controls that must be evaluated included the following:

- Poor or lack of controls over misappropriation of assets that could result in a material misstatement
- The company's risk assessment processes
- Code of ethics and conduct provisions, especially those related to conflicts of interest, related party transactions, illegal acts, and the monitoring of the code by management and the board
- Adequacy of the internal audit function and whether internal audit reports directly to the audit committee, as well as the audit committee's involvement and interaction with internal audit
- Adequacy of the company's procedures for responding to complaints and accepting confidential submissions of questionable accounting and auditing matters

Auditors were required to identify, inquire about, and evaluate fraud of any magnitude on the part of senior management of a company. While Auditing Standard No 2 was comprehensive, it was costly to implement and subject to criticism.

Auditing Standard No. 5

Although Auditing Standard No. 2 resulted in a greater focus on corporate governance, internal controls, and the quality of financial reporting, the costs and resources necessary for compliance have resulted in unnecessary inefficiencies. As a result, the PCAOB and the SEC studied the implementation of Section 404 to make it more effective and efficient. Subsequently, *Auditing Standard No. 5, Audits of Internal Control Over Financial Reporting* was approved on July

25, 2007, to replace AS No. 2. While there are many similarities between the old and new standards, Auditing Standard No. 5 (AS No. 5) differs in the following ways:

- AS No. 5 is less prescriptive, removing the many "shoulds" and allowing the external auditor to use his or her judgment using a principles-based focus. As a result, there is a greater focus on risk and materiality including entity-level controls.
- Reducing the audit costs for small or less complex public companies is another focus. Control systems do not have to be designed to fit the audit standard but rather to achieve the objective of enhancing the quality of financial statements.
- A top-down risk assessment now must be performed by both management and the external auditor with an emphasis on the risk of fraud, fraud prevention and awareness. Deficiencies that are not material weaknesses are less important and the focus should be on the highest risk areas. Evaluating and communicating deficiencies that are found is an important element of the new standard.
- Using the work of others is now encouraged resulting in applying professional judgment and a more integrated approach. Auditors can use the work product of others with the consideration of the objectivity and competence of those who performed the prior work.

STEPHEN CUTLER'S "GATEKEEPERS SPEECH"

In September 2004, Stephen M. Cutler, then SEC Director of Enforcement, delivered a landmark speech entitled "The Themes of Sarbanes-Oxley as Reflected in the Commission's Enforcement Program." The speech was presented to the UCLA School of Law in Los Angeles and has become known as the "Gatekeepers Speech." Cutler tackled the importance of gatekeepers, those people who are responsible for monitoring and oversight of others in the financial markets. They are the people in important positions to whom the investing public, the government, and others look for truth and honesty in financial reporting. They must be beyond reproach and accountable for their actions.

Cutler started the speech with an interesting quote regarding the impact of fraud and corruption on corporations. He said, "The public corporation is currently under severe attack because of the many revelations of improper corporate activity. It is not simple to assess the cause of this misconduct. Since it has taken so many forms, the one-dimensional explanation that... such conduct is a way of life, is simply not acceptable."[12] Although the quote sounded like a reference to the current corporate scandals, Cutler surprised the audience when he told them it was actually said in 1974 by then SEC Enforcement Director Stanley Sporkin, who was describing the many disclosures of bribes paid to foreign government officials that led to enactment of the Foreign Corrupt Practices Act. Cutler warned that history repeats itself time and again unless a culture change occurs in the securities markets.

Cutler outlined three ongoing themes that he believed were needed in order to prevent history from repeating itself:

- The critical role of gatekeepers in maintaining fair and honest markets
- The requirement for integrity in the investigative process to detect, investigate, and prosecute securities law violations
- The need for greater personal responsibility and accountability from corporate executives and strong civil and criminal penalties when they cross the line

Cutler defined gatekeepers as "[t]he sentries of the marketplace: the auditors who sign off on companies' financial data; the lawyers who advise companies on disclosure standards and other securities law requirements; the research analysts who warn investors away from unsound companies; and the boards of directors responsible for oversight of company management. They're paramount in ensuring that our markets are clean. And Congress recognized that when it enacted Sarbanes-Oxley."[13]

Cutler recalled the many criminal prosecutions and civil enforcement actions taken against corporations and corporate executives, independent directors, in-house counsel gone astray, research analysts, financial services firms, and others who failed in their important roles as gatekeepers. He stressed that holding gatekeepers responsible for their actions was key to preventing continued corporate fraud and abuse.

ENHANCED SENTENCING GUIDELINES: LESS CARROT AND MORE STICK

With the continuous tweaking of compliance programs, it only makes sense that the Federal Sentencing Guidelines for Organizations would be reworked and strengthened. Previously, the United States Sentencing Commission (USSC) recommended seven minimum requirements for an effective program to prevent and deter violations of law that encompassed self-reporting and acceptance of responsibility. Effective November 1, 2004, the USSC enhanced the guidelines by emphasizing effective compliance and ethics programs in order to mitigate punishment for a criminal offense. Now organizations must promote an organizational culture that encourages ethical conduct and a commitment to compliance with the law. It places the responsibility directly on the chief executives and directors to ensure compliance. Organizations must now have adequate resources, authority, training programs, reporting mechanisms, risk assessment, and periodic evaluation to ensure that fraud prevention and compliance are paramount.

The guidelines have seven requirements, significantly enhanced as follows:

- Standards and Procedures
  - The organization shall establish standards and procedures to prevent and detect criminal conduct and ensure compliance with the law. In other words, an organization's code of conduct must be robust and incorporate ethical conduct as an integral component of the ethics and compliance program.
- Organizational Leadership and a Culture of Compliance
  - The organization's governing authority shall be knowledgeable about the content and operation of the compliance and ethics program. This would normally be the CEO, CFO, and the Board of Directors.

- They shall exercise reasonable oversight with respect to the implementation and effectiveness of the compliance and ethics program.
- Specific individual(s) within the highest levels of the organization shall be assigned overall responsibility for the compliance and ethics program.
- Specific individual(s) within the organization shall be delegated day-to-day operational responsibility for the compliance and ethics program. The individual(s) with operational responsibility shall report periodically to high-level personnel and, as appropriate, to the governing authority on the effectiveness of the compliance and ethics program.
- To carry out such operational responsibility, such individual(s) shall be given adequate resources, appropriate authority, and direct access to the governing authority of the organization.

- Reasonable Efforts to Exclude Prohibited Persons
  - The organization shall use reasonable efforts not to include within the substantial authority personnel whom the organization knew, or should have known through the exercise of due diligence, have engaged in illegal activities or other conduct inconsistent with an effective compliance and ethics program.
- Training and Communication
  - The organization shall take reasonable steps to communicate periodically and in a practical manner its standards and procedures, and other aspects of the compliance and ethics program by conducting effective training programs and otherwise disseminating information appropriate to such individuals' respective roles and responsibilities.
  - Training shall be provided to members of the governing authority, other high-level leadership, employees, and, as appropriate, the organization's agents.
- Monitoring, Auditing, and Evaluating Program Effectiveness
  - The organization shall take reasonable steps to ensure that the organization's compliance and ethics program is followed, including monitoring and auditing to detect criminal conduct.
  - The organization shall take reasonable steps to evaluate the effectiveness of the organization's compliance and ethics program.

- The organization shall take reasonable steps to have and publicize a system, which may include mechanisms that allow for anonymity or confidentiality, where the organization's employees and agents may report or seek guidance regarding potential or actual criminal conduct without fear of retaliation, such as hotlines.
- Performance Incentives and Disciplinary Action
  - The organization's compliance and ethics program shall be promoted and enforced consistently within the organization through appropriate incentives to perform in accordance with the compliance and ethics program.
  - The organization's compliance and ethics program shall be promoted and enforced consistently within the organization through appropriate disciplinary measures for engaging in criminal conduct and for failing to take reasonable steps to prevent or detect criminal conduct.
- Remedial Action
  - After criminal conduct has been detected, the organization shall take reasonable steps to respond appropriately to the criminal conduct and to prevent further similar conduct, including making any necessary modifications to the organization's compliance and ethics program.
  - The organization shall periodically assess the risk of criminal conduct and shall take appropriate steps to design, implement, or modify each compliance requirement to reduce the risk of criminal conduct identified through this process.[14]

In addition to the preceding seven requirements, there are others that must be implemented by an organization. An organization must incorporate and adhere to industry practices and standards of compliance as required by government regulation. Unless this is followed, an organization is not considered to have an effective compliance and ethics program. Waivers of attorney–client privilege and work–product protections are not a prerequisite to a reduction in culpability score. Courts are required to order probation if the organization failed to have an effective compliance program in place when one was required and can upwardly depart from the guidelines if a compliance program is not in place. Organizations must remember that the only way to avoid or at least lessen the impact of prosecution is through self-reporting, cooperation with the government, acceptance of responsibility, and an effective compliance and ethics program.

FILIP MEMORANDUM

The Department of Justice's (DOJ) Filip Memorandum ("Filip Memo"), which sets forth the current guidance, lays out the standard for corporate federal prosecution and updates the government's stance on requests for privileged material. The Filip Memo, released in August 2008 and now integrated into the DOJ's charging guidelines, supersedes the previous Thompson Memo and its successor, known as the "McNulty Memo." The Filip Memo retains much of its predecessors' principles. The factors used to decide whether to criminally charge a company have not changed significantly. The major changes have come with respect to the use of privileged materials and the requests for the same.

Under this guidance, the DOJ will not ask a company in the course of an investigation to waive the attorney–client privilege and disclose privileged material to the government. Instead, the government will seek the underlying facts of the putative misconduct under review. Information prepared by counsel, in form of notes, memoranda, reports, and other documents created in the course of an internal investigation is protected by the attorney–client privilege, but the underlying facts are not privileged. These underlying facts, should they be relevant to the government's investigation and are not core work product—the attorney's mental impressions and legal theories—would need to be disclosed under the cooperation standard.

A company is free to waive the privilege in whole or in part as it sees fit, but the decision to do so should be the company's and the company's alone. Prosecutors should not ask for waivers. The critical factor in the government's analysis will be whether the corporation has timely disclosed the relevant facts about the events. This is the standard for receiving credit for cooperation. Failure to cooperate does not mean in and of itself that the company will be indicted; it merely means if charges are brought it will not receive cooperation credit. In addition to the company itself, the DOJ will also strongly pursue charging individually culpable defendants. In fact, the Memo specifically states that charging only the company and not seeking charges against individuals should happen only in very rare circumstances.[15]

The Filip Memo includes the standards used to hold a company liable for individual action, the legal concept of *respondeat superior*. *Respondeat superior* is the doctrine holding an employer or principal liable for the wrongful acts of an employee or agent committed within the scope of their duties. To hold a corporation liable for the illegal acts of its directors, officers, employees, and agents, the government must establish that the individual's actions (1) were within the scope of his duties and (2) were intended, at least in part, to benefit the corporation. The existence of an actual benefit to the company does not matter; all that matters was whether there was some intent to benefit.

The Filip Memo lists nine factors specifically to be considered by prosecutors when assessing the criminal culpability of corporations, in addition to the typical considerations, such as the strength of the evidence and the likelihood of conviction. In conducting an investigation, determining whether to bring charges, and negotiating plea agreements, prosecutors must consider:

- The nature and seriousness of the offense, including the risk of harm to the public, and applicable policies and priorities, if any, governing the prosecution of corporations for particular categories of crime
- The pervasiveness of wrongdoing within the corporation, including the complicity in, or condoning of, the wrongdoing by corporate management
- The corporation's history of similar conduct, including prior criminal, civil, and regulatory enforcement actions against it
- The corporation's timely and voluntary disclosure of wrongdoing and its willingness to cooperate in the investigation of its agents
- The existence and effectiveness of the corporation's pre-existing compliance program
- The corporation's remedial actions, including any efforts to implement an effective corporate compliance program or to improve an existing one, to replace responsible management, to discipline or terminate wrongdoers, to pay restitution, and to cooperate with the relevant government agencies

- The collateral consequences, including whether there is disproportionate harm to shareholders, pension holders and employees, and others not personally proven culpable, as well as impact on the public arising from the prosecution
- The adequacy of the prosecution of individuals responsible for the corporation's malfeasance
- The adequacy of remedies such as civil or regulatory enforcement actions[16]

2010 AMENDMENTS TO FEDERAL SENTENCING GUIDELINES FOR ORGANIZATIONS

On November 1, 2010, the United States Sentencing Commission's amendments to the Federal Sentencing Guidelines for Organizations took effect. The amendments provide new rules for corporate compliance programs while reinforcing existing guidance. The amendments continue the requirement for effective compliance and ethics programs to "exercise due diligence to prevent and detect criminal conduct" and "promote an organizational culture that encourages ethical conduct and a commitment to compliance to the law."[17]

The 2010 amendments leave intact the seven steps for an effective compliance and ethics program from the 2004 amendments. The most significant of the 2010 amendments provide credit for an organization in sentencing even if high-level personnel were involved in the criminal conduct at question if the following four conditions are met:

- The individual or individuals with operational responsibility for the compliance and ethics program have direct reporting obligations to the government authority or an appropriate subgroup (e.g., an audit committee of the board of directors).
- The compliance and ethics program detected the offense before discovery outside the organization or before such discovery was reasonably likely.
- The organization promptly reported the offense to appropriate governmental authorities.
- No individual with operational responsibility for the compliance and ethics program participated in, condoned, or was willfully ignorant of the offense.[18]

The 2010 amendments also require organizations to remedy the harm from criminal conduct including providing appropriate restitution to victims and self-reporting. To prevent further criminal conduct, organizations must continually reassess their existing programs and make necessary modifications to improve effectiveness. Another recommended step from the 2010 amendments is to use "an outside professional advisor to ensure adequate assessment and implementation of any modification."[19] In today's complex world, an effective compliance and ethics program may not be enough. Depending on an organization's global business operations, industry, geography, and other risk factors, a gold or platinum standard compliance program may be required.

NOTES

1. Statement on Auditing Standards 99, "Consideration of Fraud in a Financial Statement Audit," American Institute of Certified Public Accountants, www.aicpa.org. Copyright 2012 by the American Institute of Certified Public Accountants, Inc. All rights reserved. Used with permission.
2. Ibid.
3. Ibid.
4. Ibid. SAS 99 content reprinted with permission from the American Institute of Certified Public Accountants. Copyright 2012 by the American Institute of Certified Public Accountants, Inc. All rights reserved. Used with permission.
5. *Sarbanes-Oxley Act,* U.S. Code Title 15 Section 7262.
6. Securities and Exchange Commission, "Final Rule: Management's Reports on Internal Control over Financial Reporting and Certification of Disclosure in Exchange Act Periodic Reports," www.sec.gov/rules/final/33–8238.htm.
7. Codification of Statements on Auditing Standards (AU § 325), "Communication of Internal Control Related Matters Noted in an Audit," American Institute of Certified Public Accountants, 434, www.aicpa.org/download/members/div/auditstd/AU-00325.pdf.
8. Securities and Exchange Commission, "Final Rule: Management's Reports on Internal Control over Financial Reporting and

Certification of Disclosure in Exchange Act Periodic Reports," www.sec.gov/rules/final/33–8238.htm.

9. Public Company Accounting Oversight Board, "Auditing Standard No. 2—An Audit of Internal Control over Financial Reporting Performed in Conjunction with an Audit of Financial Statements," March 9, 2004, 11–24, www.pcaobus.org/Rules_of_the_Board/Documents/Rules_of_the_Board/Auditing_Standard_2.pdf.

10. Ibid., 4.

11. Ibid., 24.

12. Stephen M. Cutler, "The Themes of Sarbanes-Oxley as Reflected in the Commission's Enforcement Program" (speech, UCLA School of Law, Los Angeles, CA, September 20, 2004), www.sec.gov/news/speech/spch092004smc.htm.

13. Ibid.

14. United States Sentencing Commission, *2010 Federal Sentencing Guidelines Manual*, www.ussc.gov/Guidelines/2010_guidelines/Manual_HTML/8b2_1.htm.

15. Mark Filip, "Principles of Federal Prosecution of Business Organizations," 2 (memorandum, United States Department of Justice, August 28, 2008), www.justice.gov/dag/readingroom/dag-memo-08282008.pdf.

16. Filip, "Principles of Federal Prosecution," 3–4.

17. United States Sentencing Commission, *2010 Federal Sentencing Guidelines Manual*, www.ussc.gov/Guidelines/2010_guidelines/Manual_HTML/8b2_1.htm.

18. United States Sentencing Commission, *2010 Federal Sentencing Guidelines Manual*, Supplement to Appendix C, www.ussc.gov/guidelines/2010_guidelines/Manual_PDF/Appendix_C_Supplement.pdf.

19. Ibid.

Internal Controls and Antifraud Programs

EXECUTIVE SUMMARY

The best way to ensure a culture of compliance is through an appropriately designed internal control and antifraud program. The American Institute of Certified Public Accountants' Management Antifraud Programs and Controls is an exceptional 14-step program that any organization can implement to detect and prevent fraud. The steps include creating a culture of honesty and high ethics, evaluating antifraud processes and controls, and developing an appropriate oversight process. A key component of any program is a proper code of conduct or ethics policy that can help set a tone of honesty and integrity in an organization. The code must be well communicated to all employees. Before fraud risks can be mitigated, the risks must be identified and properly quantified as to their likelihood and potential financial impact. These two factors help determine the method of risk mitigation. There are several methods in use to conduct a risk assessment. Some methods for charting the likelihood and impact of fraud are more effective than others.

MANAGEMENT ANTIFRAUD PROGRAMS
AND CONTROLS: THE 14-POINT PROGRAM

In 2002, the Fraud Task Force of the American Institute of Certified Public Accountants (AICPA) commissioned a study to provide guidance to help prevent and detect fraud. The AICPA, the Association of Certified Fraud Examiners, the Institute of Internal Auditors, and other professional organizations sponsored the study. The result, *Management Antifraud Programs and Controls*, was released in November 2002 as an exhibit to SAS 99.[1] The overall message of this document is those organizations that take proactive steps to prevent and deter fraud will preserve their financial integrity, their reputation, and their future.

The study found that an organization must take three fundamental actions to mitigate fraud. They include creating a culture of honesty and high ethics, evaluating antifraud processes and controls, and developing an appropriate oversight process. The following are some of the highlights from the document, which should be the cornerstone of any fraud prevention program. There are three main headings and 14 subheadings.

Creating a Culture of Honesty and High Ethics

It is the organization's responsibility to create a culture of honesty and high ethics and to communicate clearly acceptable behavior and expectations for each employee. Creating a culture of honesty and high ethics should include the following:

1. Setting the Tone at the Top Directors and officers of corporations set the "tone at the top" for ethical behavior within any organization. Research in moral development strongly suggests that honesty can best be reinforced when a proper example is set (the tone at the top). The management of an entity cannot act one way and expect others in the entity to behave differently.

2. Creating a Positive Workplace Environment Research indicates that less wrongdoing occurs when employees have positive feelings about work. Factors that detract from a positive work environment and that may increase the risk of fraud include the following:

- Top management that does not seem to care about or wish to reward appropriate behavior
- Negative feedback and lack of recognition for job performance
- Perceived inequities in the organization
- Autocratic rather than participative management
- Low organizational loyalty or feelings of ownership
- Unreasonable budget expectations or other financial targets
- Fear of delivering "bad news" to supervisors and/or management
- Less-than-competitive compensation
- Poor training and promotion opportunities
- Lack of clear organizational responsibilities
- Poor communication practices or methods within the organization

3. Hiring and Promoting Appropriate Employees   The threshold at which dishonest behavior starts will vary among individuals. If an entity is to be successful in preventing fraud, it must have effective policies that minimize the chance of hiring or promoting individuals with low levels of honesty, especially for positions of trust. Proactive hiring and promotion procedures may include:

- Conducting background investigations on individuals being considered for employment or for promotion to a position of trust. Some organizations also have considered follow-up investigations, particularly for employees in positions of trust, on a periodic basis (for example, every five years) or as circumstances dictate.
- Thoroughly checking a candidate's education, employment history, and personal references.
- Periodic training of all employees about the entity's values and code of conduct.
- Incorporating into regular performance reviews an evaluation of how each individual has contributed to the creation of an appropriate workplace environment in line with the entity's values and code of conduct.

4. Training   New employees should be given training at the time of hiring covering the entity's values and its code of conduct. This training should explicitly cover expectations of all employees regarding

(1) their duty to communicate certain matters; (2) a list of the types of matters, including actual or suspected fraud, to be communicated along with specific examples; and (3) information on how to communicate those matters. Such training should include an element of "fraud awareness," the tone of which should be positive but nonetheless stress that fraud can be costly (and detrimental in other ways) to the entity and its employees. In addition to training at the time of hiring, employees should receive refresher training periodically thereafter.

5. Confirmation   Management needs to articulate clearly that all employees will be held accountable to act within the entity's code of conduct. All employees within senior management and the finance function, as well as other employees in areas that might be exposed to unethical behavior (for example, procurement, sales, and marketing) should be required to sign a code of conduct statement annually, at a minimum.

6. Discipline   The way an entity reacts to incidents of alleged or suspected fraud sends a strong deterrent message throughout the entity, helping to reduce the number of future occurrences. The following actions should be taken in response to an alleged incident of fraud:

- A thorough investigation of the incident should be conducted.
- Appropriate and consistent actions should be taken against violators.
- Relevant controls should be assessed and improved.
- Communication and training should occur to reinforce the entity's values, code of conduct, and expectations.

Expectations about the consequences of committing fraud must be clearly communicated throughout the entity. If a violation occurs and an employee is disciplined, it can be helpful to communicate that fact, on a no-name basis. Seeing that other people have been disciplined for wrongdoing can be an effective deterrent, increasing the perceived likelihood of violators being caught and punished. It can also demonstrate that the entity is committed to an environment of high ethical standards and integrity.

Evaluating Antifraud Processes and Controls

Neither fraudulent financial reporting nor misappropriation of assets can occur without a perceived opportunity to commit and conceal the act. Organizations should be proactive in reducing fraud opportunities by (1) identifying and measuring for fraud risks, (2) taking steps to mitigate identified risks, and (3) implementing and monitoring appropriate preventive and detective internal controls and other deterrent measures.

7. Identifying and Measuring Fraud Risks   Management has the primary responsibility for establishing and monitoring all aspects of the entity's fraud risk assessment and prevention activities. Fraud risks are often considered part of an enterprise-wide risk management program, although they may be addressed separately. The fraud risk assessment process should consider the vulnerability of the entity to fraudulent activity (fraudulent financial reporting, misappropriation of assets, and corruption) and whether any of those exposures could result in a material misstatement of the financial statements or material loss to the organization. In identifying fraud risks, organizations should consider the organizational, industry, and country-specific characteristics that influence the risk of fraud. The topic of fraud risk assessment is addressed in more detail later in this chapter.

8. Mitigating Fraud Risks   It may be possible to reduce or eliminate certain fraud risks by making changes to the entity's activities and processes. An entity may choose to sell certain segments of its operations, cease doing business in certain locations, or reorganize its business processes to eliminate unacceptable risks. For example, the risk of misappropriation of funds may be reduced by implementing a central lockbox at a bank to receive payments instead of receiving money at the entity's various locations. The risk of corruption may be reduced by closely monitoring the entity's procurement process. The risk of financial statement fraud may be reduced by implementing shared services centers to provide accounting services to multiple segments, affiliates, or geographic locations of an entity's operations. A shared services center may be less vulnerable to influence by local operations managers and can implement more extensive fraud detection measures cost effectively.

9. Implementing and Monitoring Appropriate Internal Controls   Once a fraud risk assessment has taken place, the entity can identify the processes, controls, and other procedures that are needed to mitigate the identified risks. Effective internal controls include a secure information system and appropriate monitoring activities. In particular, management should evaluate whether appropriate internal controls have been implemented in any areas management has identified as posing a higher risk of fraudulent activity, as well as controls over the entity's financial reporting process.

Developing an Appropriate Oversight Process

Oversight can take many forms and can be performed by many individuals within and outside the entity, under the overall oversight of the Audit Committee (or Board of Directors when no Audit Committee exists).

10. Audit Committee   The Audit Committee should evaluate management's identification of fraud risks, implementation of antifraud measures, and creation of the appropriate tone at the top. Active oversight by the audit committee can help reinforce management's commitment to creating the proper antifraud culture. The Audit Committee has the responsibility to oversee the activities of senior management and to consider the risk of fraudulent financial reporting involving the override of internal controls or collusion.

11. Management   Management is responsible for overseeing the activities carried out by employees, and typically does so by implementing and monitoring processes and controls, such as those discussed previously. However, management also may initiate, participate in, or direct the commission and concealment of a fraudulent act. Accordingly, the Audit Committee (or the Board of Directors when no Audit Committee exists) has the responsibility to oversee the activities of senior management and to consider the risk of fraudulent financial reporting involving the override of internal controls or collusion.

12. Internal Auditors   An effective internal audit team can be extremely helpful in performing aspects of the oversight function. Their knowledge about the entity may enable them to identify indicators that suggest fraud has been committed. Internal auditors also have the opportunity to evaluate fraud risks and controls and to recommend action to mitigate risks and improve controls. Internal audit should have a reporting line to the audit committee in addition to the CFO or other executive leadership.

Internal audit can be both a detection and a deterrence measure. Internal auditors can assist in the deterrence of fraud by examining and evaluating the adequacy and the effectiveness of the system of internal control, commensurate with the extent of the potential exposure or risk in the various segments of the organization's operations. In carrying out this responsibility, internal auditors should, for example, determine whether:

- The organizational environment fosters control consciousness.
- Realistic organizational goals and objectives are set.
- Written policies (for example, a code of conduct) exist that describe prohibited activities and the action required whenever violations are discovered.
- Appropriate authorization policies for transactions are established and maintained.
- Policies, practices, procedures, reports, and other mechanisms are developed to monitor activities and safeguard assets, particularly in high-risk areas.
- Communication channels provide management with adequate and reliable information.
- Recommendations need to be made for the establishment or enhancement of cost-effective controls to deter fraud.

13. Independent Auditors Independent auditors can assist management and the Board of Directors (or Audit Committee) by providing an assessment of the entity's process for identifying, assessing, and responding to the risks of fraud. The Board of Directors (or the Audit Committee) should have an open and candid dialogue with the independent auditors regarding management's risk assessment process and the system of internal control. Such a dialogue should include a discussion of the susceptibility of the entity to fraudulent financial reporting and the entity's exposure to misappropriation of assets.

14. Certified Fraud Examiners   Certified Fraud Examiners may assist the Audit Committee and Board of Directors with aspects of the oversight process either directly or as part of a team of internal auditors or independent auditors. Certified Fraud Examiners can provide extensive knowledge and experience about fraud that may not be available elsewhere within a corporation. They can provide more objective input into management's evaluation of the risk of fraud (especially fraud involving senior management, such as financial statement fraud) and the development of appropriate antifraud controls that are less vulnerable to management override. They can assist the Audit Committee and Board of Directors in evaluating the fraud risk assessment and fraud prevention measures implemented by management. Certified Fraud Examiners also conduct examinations to resolve allegations or suspicions of fraud, reporting either to an appropriate level of management or to the Audit Committee or Board of Directors, depending on the nature of the issue and the level of personnel involved.[2]

EXECUTIVE INSIGHT 5.1: ACFE FRAUD PREVENTION CHECK-UP

The Association of Certified Fraud Examiners (ACFE), to which we both belong, has developed a *Fraud Prevention Check-Up*, which is a good place to start a fraud risk assessment.[i] It is a series of questions about processes that may or may not be in place at a particular company. The answers are awarded points. Beware! Only a score of 100 is passing. The idea is to get leaders thinking about what processes need to be in place.

How vulnerable is your company to fraud? Do you have adequate controls in place to prevent it? Find out by using the *Fraud Prevention Check-Up*, a simple yet powerful test of your company's fraud health. Test fraud prevention processes designed to help you identify major gaps and fix them before it is too late. The ACFE *Fraud Prevention Check-Up* can pinpoint opportunities to save an organization from financial and reputational risk.

Before You Take the ACFE Fraud Prevention Check-Up

- Let your organization's general counsel or outside legal counsel know you plan to take the test. Your counsel may want to direct taking the test in order to protect your legal rights.
- Do not take the check-up if you plan to ignore the results. If it shows you have poor fraud prevention processes, you need to fix them. Failing to act could cause legal problems.

Who Should Perform the ACFE Fraud Prevention Check-Up?

- The check-up should ideally be a collaboration between objective, independent fraud specialists (such as Certified Fraud Examiners) and people within the organization who have extensive knowledge about its operations.
- Internal auditors bring extensive knowledge and a valuable perspective to such an evaluation. At the same time, the perspective of an independent and objective outsider is also important, as are the deep knowledge and experience of fraud that full-time fraud specialists provide.
- It is helpful to interview senior members of management as part of the evaluation process. But it is also valuable to interview employees at other levels of the organization, since they may sometimes provide a "reality check" that challenges the rosier view management might present, such as management's commitment to ethical business practices.

How Many Points Should Be Awarded for Each Answer?

- The number of points available is given at the bottom of each question. You can award zero points if your entity has not implemented the recommended processes for that area. You can give the maximum number of points if you have implemented those processes and have had them tested in the past year and found them to be operating effectively. Award no more than half the available points if the recommended process is in place but has not been tested in the past year.

- The purpose of the check-up is to identify major gaps in your fraud prevention processes, as indicated by low point scores in particular areas. Even if you score 80 points out of 100, the missing 20 could be crucial in fraud prevention measures that leave you exposed to major fraud. So there is no passing grade other than 100 points.

The ACFE Fraud Prevention Check-Up

Organization: _____

Date of Check-Up:_____

RESULTS

1. *Fraud risk oversight*
   - To what extent has the organization established a process for oversight of fraud risks by the board of directors or others charged with governance (e.g., an audit committee)?
   Score: From 0 (process not in place) to 20 points (process fully implemented, tested within the past year, and working effectively).

2. *Fraud risk ownership*
   - To what extent has the organization created "ownership" of fraud risks by identifying a member of senior management as having responsibility for managing all fraud risks within the organization and by explicitly communicating to business unit managers

that they are responsible for managing fraud risks within their area?
Score: From 0 (process not in place) to 10 points (process fully implemented, tested within the past year, and working effectively).

3. **Fraud risk assessment**
   - To what extent has the organization implemented an ongoing process for regular identification of the significant fraud risks to which it is exposed?
   Score: From 0 (process not in place) to 10 points (process fully implemented, tested within the past year, and working effectively).

4. **Fraud risk tolerance and risk management policy**
   - To what extent has the organization identified and had approved by the board of directors its tolerance for different types of fraud risks? For example, some fraud risks may constitute a tolerable cost of doing business, while others may pose a catastrophic risk of financial or reputational damage.
   - To what extent has the organization identified and had approved by the board of directors a policy on how the entity will manage its fraud risks? Such a policy should identify the risk owner responsible for managing fraud risks, what risks will be rejected (e.g., by declining certain business opportunities), what risks will be transferred to others through insurance or by contract, and what steps will be taken

to manage the fraud risks that are retained.

Score: From 0 (process not in place) to 10 points (process fully implemented, tested within the past year, and working effectively).

5. *Process level antifraud controls/reengineering*

   ▪ To what extent has the organization implemented measures, where possible, to eliminate or reduce through process reengineering each of the significant fraud risks identified in its risk assessment? Basic controls include segregation of duties relating to authorization, custody of assets, and recording or reporting of transactions. In some cases it may be more cost effective to reengineer business processes to reduce fraud risks rather than layer on additional controls over existing processes. For example, some fraud risks relating to receipt of funds can be eliminated or greatly reduced by centralizing that function or outsourcing it to a bank's lockbox processing facility, where stronger controls can be more affordable.

   ▪ To what extent has the organization implemented measures at the process level designed to prevent, deter, and detect each of the significant fraud risks identified in its risk assessment? For example, the risk of sales representatives falsifying sales to earn sales commissions can be reduced through effective monitoring by their

RESULTS

sales manager, with approval required for
sales above a certain threshold.
*Score: From 0 (process not in place) to 10
points (process fully implemented, tested
within the past year, and working
effectively).*

6. *Environmental level antifraud controls*
   - Major frauds usually involve senior
     members of management who are able to
     override process-level controls through
     their high level of authority. Preventing
     major frauds therefore requires a very
     strong emphasis on creating a workplace
     environment that promotes ethical
     behavior, deters wrongdoing, and
     encourages all employees to communicate
     any known or suspected wrongdoing to
     the appropriate person. Senior managers
     may be unable to perpetrate certain fraud
     schemes if employees decline to aid and
     abet them in committing a crime.
     Although "soft" controls to promote
     appropriate workplace behavior are more
     difficult to implement and evaluate than
     traditional "hard" controls, they appear
     to be the best defense against fraud
     involving senior management.
   - To what extent has the organization
     implemented a process to promote ethical
     behavior, deter wrongdoing, and facilitate
     two-way communication on difficult
     issues? Such a process typically includes:
   - Having a senior member of management
     who is responsible for the entity's
     processes to promote ethical behavior,

deter wrongdoing, and communicate appropriately on difficult issues. In large public companies, this may be a full-time position as ethics officer or compliance officer. In smaller companies, this will be an additional responsibility held by an existing member of management.

- A code of conduct for employees at all levels, based on the entity's core values, which gives clear guidance on what behavior and actions are permitted and which ones are prohibited. The code should identify how employees should seek additional advice when faced with uncertain ethical decisions and how they should communicate concerns about known or potential wrongdoing.

- Training for all personnel upon hiring and regularly thereafter concerning the code of conduct, seeking advice, and communicating potential wrongdoing.

- Communication systems to enable employees to seek advice where necessary prior to making difficult ethical decisions and to express concern about known or potential wrongdoing affecting the entity. Advice systems may include an ethics or compliance telephone help line or e-mail to an ethics or compliance office/officer. The same or similar systems may be used to enable employees (and sometimes vendors, customers, and others) to communicate concerns about known or potential wrongdoing. Provisions should be made to enable such communications to be made anonymously, though strenuous efforts should be made to create an environment in which callers feel sufficiently confident to express their concerns openly. Open communication makes it easier for the entity to resolve the issues raised, but protecting callers from retribution is an important concern.

- A process for promptly investigating where appropriate and resolving expressions of concern regarding known or potential wrongdoing, then communicating the resolution to those who expressed the concern. The organization should have a plan that sets out what actions will be taken and by whom to investigate and resolve different types of concerns. Some issues will be best addressed by human resources personnel, some by general counsel, some by internal auditors, and some may require investigation by fraud specialists. Having a prearranged plan will greatly speed and ease the response and will ensure appropriate persons are notified where significant potential issues are involved (e.g., legal counsel, board of directors, audit committee, independent auditors, regulators, etc.).

- Monitoring of compliance with the code of conduct and participation in the related training. Monitoring may include requiring at least annual confirmation of compliance and auditing of such confirmations to test their completeness and accuracy.

- Regular measurement of the extent to which the organization's ethics/compliance and fraud prevention goals are being achieved. Such measurement typically includes surveys of a statistically meaningful sample of employees. Surveys of employees' attitudes towards the company's ethics/compliance activities and the extent to which employees believe management acts in accordance with the code of conduct provide valuable insight into how well those items are functioning.
- Incorporation of ethics/compliance and fraud prevention goals into the performance measures against which managers are evaluated and that are used to determine performance related compensation.
  Score: From 0 (process not in place) to 30 points (process fully implemented, tested within the past year, and working effectively).

7. *Proactive fraud detection*
   - To what extent has the organization established a process to detect, investigate, and resolve potentially significant fraud? Such a process should typically include proactive fraud detection tests that are specially designed to detect the significant potential frauds identified in the organization's fraud risk assessment. Other measures can include audit "hooks" embedded in the transaction processing systems that can

RESULTS

flag suspicious transactions for investigation and/or approval prior to completion of processing. Leading edge fraud detection methods include computerized e-mail monitoring (where legally permitted) to identify use of certain phrases that might indicate planned or ongoing wrong-doing.
Score: From 0 (process not in place) to 10 points (process fully implemented, tested within the past year, and working effectively).

TOTAL SCORE (out of a possible 100 points)

Interpreting the Organization's Score

A brief fraud prevention check-up provides a broad idea of your organization's performance with respect to fraud prevention. The scoring necessarily involves broad judgments, while more extensive evaluations would have greater measurement data to draw upon. The important information to take from the check-up is the identification of particular areas for improvement in the company's fraud prevention processes. The precise numerical score is less important and is only presented to help communicate an overall impression.

The desirable score for an entity of any size is 100 points, since the recommended processes are scalable to the size of the entity. Most companies should expect to fall significantly short of 100 points in an initial fraud prevention check-up. That is not currently considered to be a material weakness in internal controls that represents a reportable condition under securities regulations. However, significant gaps in fraud prevention measures should be closed promptly in order to reduce fraud losses and reduce the risk of future disaster.

[i]Association of Certified Fraud Examiners, *Fraud Prevention Check-Up*, www.acfe.com/documents/Fraud_Prev_Checkup_IA.pdf.
Source: Reprinted with permission from the Association of Certified Fraud Examiners, Austin, Texas © 2011.

MANAGING THE BUSINESS RISK OF FRAUD

In April 2008, the Institute of Internal Auditors (IIA) along with the Association of Certified Fraud Examiners (ACFE) and the American Institute of Certified Public Accountants (AICPA) released new guidance to help organizations enhance their fraud risk management capabilities. The report is entitled *Managing the Business Risk of Fraud: A Practical Guide* and provides key guidance in preventing fraud in an organization, including guidance on effective fraud risk management. The guide introduced a new definition of fraud that proclaims, "Fraud is any intentional act or omission designed to deceive others, resulting in the victim suffering a loss and/or the perpetrator achieving a gain."[3]

The guidance outlines five key principles of a fraud risk management process and recommends ways in which boards, senior management and internal auditors can enhance fraud risk management effectiveness. The five principles are as follows:

Principle 1: As part of an organization's governance structure, a fraud risk management program should be in place, including a written policy (or policies) to convey the expectations of the board of directors and senior management regarding managing fraud risk.

Principle 2: Fraud risk exposure should be periodically assessed by the organization to identify specific potential schemes and events that the organization needs to mitigate.

Principle 3: Prevention techniques to avoid potential key fraud risk events should be established, where feasible, to mitigate possible impacts on the organization.

Principle 4: Detection techniques should be established to uncover fraud events when preventive measures fail or unmitigated risks are realized.

Principle 5: A reporting process should be in place to solicit inputs on potential fraud and a coordinated approach to investigation and corrective action should be used to help ensure potential fraud is appropriately dealt with in a timely manner.[4]

The guide contains sample polices, a risk management framework, scorecards, and other excellent reference materials for enhanced fraud prevention. The guide should be another tool to use in developing and maintaining a robust fraud prevention program. The Appendix contains a checklist from the Association of Certified Fraud Examiners to help organizations test the effectiveness of their fraud prevention measures.

FRAUD RISK ASSESSMENT

Management must conduct periodic assessments of the risk of fraud at all levels and document the results. In most cases, companies predict the risk of fraud based on past events and current conditions. Although an outside audit can identify control gaps, only an honest inside assessment can truly gauge a company's risk of fraud. The decision of what control activities should be implemented means little if the decision is not based on a complete assessment of risk. There are three types of risk to consider when one is conducting risk assessments:

1. **Financial Reporting Risk** is the risk that there could be fraud on the financial statement or misconduct by senior management. Although this is a relatively low-occurrence fraud, it is devastating for a company. The Board of Directors, Audit Committee, and the Internal Audit Department are responsible for reducing the financial reporting risk at their company in conjunction with the CEO and CFO.

2. **Operational Risk** is the risk that the organization itself will commit fraud by action or omission, such as not paying taxes or cheating customers. Again, this is fraud that involves senior

management, so the Board, Audit Committee, and Internal Auditor are responsible for controlling Operational Risk.

3. **Compliance Risk** is the risk of corruption, internal asset misappropriation, and external fraud anywhere in the company. This is where the job of assessment becomes complicated. There are multiple ways for a company or organization to be defrauded by its own employees or outsiders. The response to compliance risk is much more complex than the other types of risk since there are many more factors to be considered and many more ways a company can experience a loss.

The fraud risk assessment is the process through which management identifies the risks of fraud it faces as an organization. The exercise involves identifying the fraud risks, analyzing their likelihood, and determining the impact. This assessment looks at frauds that have affected the business in the recent past, that are common to their industry, and that are located in specific geographic locations (countries, cities) that may increase the risk of fraud.

Fraud risk assessments are not compliance audits, rather they look for areas in which the company could be exposed to criminal activity that could result in a financial loss, a loss of reputation, or any other liability. The fraud risk assessment looks at all business units, departments, and geographic areas of the company to determine the risk of specific frauds. This process can be as formal as a company wishes, but it is usually best to keep things simple. There has been a long debate between scientists and social scientists as to whether risk can actually be measured objectively.

The use of a cigar box as a petty cash drawer is a theft risk. Theft is very likely from this unsecured box, but the impact is limited to the amount of petty cash in the box at any one time (usually less than $100). The risk management solution would be to use a lock box, which is inexpensive and simple. The fraud risk posed by payroll accounts is much greater, and the risk management will be more complicated and expensive.[5] The goal is to determine:

- The areas where fraud is possible (risks)
- The probability of a fraud (likelihood)
- The cost of the fraud (impact)
- The proper countermeasure and its cost (risk management)

ENTERPRISE RISK MANAGEMENT

Enterprise Risk Management (ERM) has become a hot topic among companies across all industries. Boards and senior management rely on the ERM program to help them understand and manage their company's most important risks. At its core, ERM is a management practice that can provide tremendous value to a company. While entire books have been written about ERM, we've boiled it down to its essential ingredients and have highlighted some leading practices.

A good ERM program will help a company understand and articulate its most important risks and risk management options across several dimensions, including:

- Its inherent level of risk
- Its residual level of risk, also called its managed level of risk
- Its appetite for the risk and, therefore, a realization of whether the risk is within or outside of the company's appetite[6]
- Its risk management plan, considering the deviation from risk appetite and costs to manage

Every ERM program has three foundational steps. First, a company identifies risks. Second, it assesses the risks. Third, it manages the risks. A company can choose different frameworks and methods to guide each step. One size does not necessarily fit all. Arguably, the most important consideration is to adopt a framework and methods that leverage existing business processes and consider the industry and organizational structure of the company.

We have seen some leading ERM practices emerge. The following sections discuss the key elements of these leading practices.

Inherent Risk Identification

An enterprise risk is an uncertain event that, if it happened, would impact the achievement of an enterprise objective, strategy, or initiative. In the process of identifying a company's most critical inherent risks, it is important to establish and agree on the objectives, strategies, or initiatives against which risk is being assessed. This is different from, and more relevant than, the approach of asking, "What keeps us up at night?"

Sometimes the biggest risks are related to unstated assumptions that management makes and that might go unquestioned (e.g., everyone assumes that a key partner that has been in business for 30 years will stay in business, or, more to the point of this book, assumes that a wealthy well-known CEO of a key partner would never commit fraud).

Applying these ideas to uncover fraud risks might take the approach of (1) including, as company objectives, accurate financial reporting and compliance with laws, and then (2) asking "what if" questions to reveal the biggest inherent risks related to these objectives, many of which would likely highlight potential fraud risks. A great exercise is to do a theoretical fast forward and ask, "If we are sitting here in three years, and discussing how we failed to meet this objective (e.g., compliance with laws), what scenarios and causes might we be discussing?"

Risk Assessment

While identifying inherent risks helps a company to understand its business vulnerability, assessing the inherent risks identifies those that are most critical. Further assessing the effectiveness of the controls that are used to manage the inherent risks helps a company to understand its current level of risk exposure. This actual exposure, taking into account all current controls, is called *residual risk*. Armed with the understanding of residual risk, management can prioritize risks and make prudent risk management decisions.

A proper risk assessment requires an accepted language in which to characterize, express, and interpret the level of inherent and residual risk. Typically, two dimensions of risk, impact and likelihood, are used to measure risk. Management should determine what scales it wishes to use to rate the different levels of impact and likelihood and assign its own meaning to those scales.

A company's value can be impacted in a number of ways other than just financially. Reputation, the ability to compete in certain markets, customer satisfaction, and other intangibles can suffer and affect whether a company achieves its short- and long-term goals.

Therefore, it is important to calibrate levels across different areas of impact, so that a "10" in the area of reputation means the same to a company as a "10" in any other area. Doing this will also help highlight fraud risks that might be more damaging to a company because of their hit to its reputation than to immediate profit loss.

What is a "high" risk? A company must establish a consistent way of interpreting the results of a risk assessment in order to answer this. It also should consider its risk appetite. We present two alternative and leading practices for measuring risk levels and identifying the highest priority risks.

The First Method (Control Effectiveness)

1. Measure inherent risk by rating impact and likelihood on some scale.
2. Combine the impact and likelihood scores to come up with a single inherent risk level (e.g., could be as simple as impact times likelihood).
3. Set a threshold above which inherent risk level would be considered "high." These are the ones to track.
4. Identify the set of controls for each "high" risk.
5. On a scale of 1 to 5, where 1 means that controls are perfectly effective and 5 means that controls are ineffective or absent, rate the effectiveness of the set of controls for each risk.
6. If controls do not meet a minimum level of effectiveness (e.g., 1 or 2 on the scale of 1 to 5), then the organization should improve them, otherwise it should monitor them on a regular basis.

For this example, imagine that two risks, A and B, have been identified. Inherent risk was assessed and we assigned scores of 8 on the impact scale and 7 on likelihood scale. Risk B was scored 10 on impact and 9 on likelihood. Plotting would look like Exhibit 5.1.

Both A and B are pretty high inherent risks. We could assign an overall inherent risk score to each by multiplying impact times likelihood (again, a company can assign its own scales and determine its own formula for inherent risk score, which could weight impact and likelihood differently). So risk A would have an inherent risk score of 56 (8 times 7) and risk B would have an inherent risk score of 90 (10 times 9).

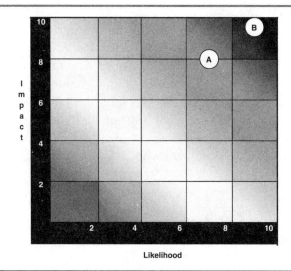

Likelihood

EXHIBIT 5.1 Plotting Inherent Risk by Impact and Likelihood

These numbers represent inherent risk and not residual, or managed, risk. Next, the controls should be identified and assessed for each risk. Assigning scores of 1 for controls that are perfectly effective and 5 for controls that are not effective (2, 3, 4 would be somewhere between), we can rate the controls for each risk. Imagine for our example that risk A's controls were determined to be poor and given a score of 4. Risk B's controls were strong and given a score of 1. Further, imagine that our company's appetite is that no risk with an inherent score of 40 or greater should have controls worse than a 2 in effectiveness.

Plotting inherent risk score versus control effectiveness, shown in Exhibit 5.2, reveals visually those risks that need control improvement and those that need continued monitoring. Risks with inherent risk levels less than 40 are deemed to be low priority and there could be an opportunity to reduce resources spent on controls.

We can now prioritize these risks and discuss an appropriate risk management plan for each.

The Second Method (Residual Risk and Risk Appetite)

1. Measure inherent risk by rating impact and likelihood on some scale. Plot this point. This is the inherent risk level.

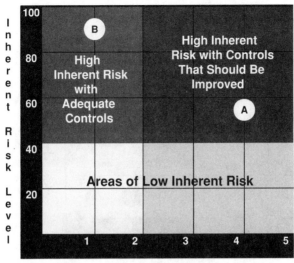

Control Effectiveness (1 is best / 5 is worst)

EXHIBIT 5.2 Inherent Risk versus Control Effectiveness

2. Set an appetite for impact and likelihood for this risk, by asking, "Where do we want the impact and likelihood of this risk to be?" Plot this point.
3. For each risk where the inherent risk is outside of the company's appetite, identify the set of controls.
4. Taking into account the set of controls, assess the actual impact and likelihood of the risk. Plot this point. This is the residual risk level.
5. For each risk, its inherent risk level, residual risk level, and risk appetite can be compared to see which risks need further improvement controls. Risks with the highest residual exposure to the company are also revealed.

Imagine that we are dealing with the same two risks, A and B, as above, with the same inherent impact and inherent likelihood levels as before. Risk A's inherent impact was 8 and inherent likelihood was 7. Risk B's inherent impact was 10 and likelihood was 9.

Next, we need to discuss where, in the space of impact and likelihood, our company's appetite for each risk sits. This discussion can be very valuable in itself. Imagine that we determine that our appetite

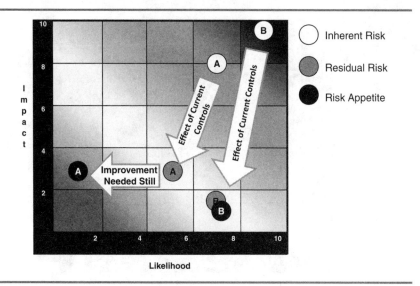

EXHIBIT 5.3   Inherent Risk, Residual Risk, and Risk Appetite

for risk A is for the impact to be 3 and the likelihood to be 1. We have a pretty low tolerance for this (fraud risk, maybe?). Let's say that for risk B, our appetite is an impact of 1 but a likelihood of 7. Why might this be? Maybe it's a risk that would be cost prohibitive to prevent, or something that we don't think we can prevent, so we think that we should focus on mitigating the impact.

Last, we need to identify our current controls and then assess, given the controls, the potential impact and likelihood of the risk. This is risk A's residual risk level. In our example, imagine that we think our controls for risk A have knocked the potential impact down, but that the risk event is still fairly likely to happen. Plotting these three points on Exhibit 5.3 reveals that risk A is still outside of our appetite, so we should consider a management plan in place to lower the likelihood. Similarly, imagine that for risk B, our residual risk level is right on top of our risk appetite. That risk is under control and should be monitored going forward.

Risk Management

Once risks are understood, a company can prioritize risks and put appropriate risk management plans into place. Companies can manage risks by avoiding, accepting, transferring, or mitigating risk. Companies can mitigate by addressing a risk's impact or likelihood, or both. The right management plan must take into account the cost or benefit of the risk to the company as well as resource and other constraints. Armed with a good ERM program, management can make more informed decisions.

Summary

A good ERM program will identify and make transparent the exposure to risks that affect the company's ability to achieve its objectives. It will enable the company to determine its appetite for certain risks and whether the current set of controls are effective at keeping the risk within its appetite. Further, it will provide a way to determine what types of controls (i.e., those that affect likelihood and those that affect impact) are appropriate given the company's risk appetite. Last, it will allow for the company to estimate the cost–benefit tradeoff of investing in different levels of controls.

Implementing an ERM program can be complex. The program should consider and leverage the company's existing business processes to the extent possible. Given the strategic nature of ERM, the most effective programs have senior level executive sponsorship and involvement.

NOTES

1. American Institute of Certified Public Accountants, "Consideration of Fraud in a Financial Statement Audit" (statement on Auditing Standard 99, December 15, 2002), www.aicpa.org/ Research/Standards/AuditAttest/Pages/SAS.aspx.
2. "Management Antifraud Programs and Controls" is reprinted with permission from the AICPA; Copyright 2012 by the American Institute of Certified Public Accountants, Inc. All rights reserved. Used with permission.
3. Institute of Internal Auditors, American Institute of Certified Public Accountants, and Association of Certified Fraud Examiners, *Managing the Business Risk of Fraud: A Practical Guide*, 5, www.acfe.com/documents/managing-business-risk.pdf.

4. Ibid., 6.

5. Charles A. Sennewald, *Effective Security Management*, 3rd ed. (Boston: Butterworth-Heinemann, 1988), 180.

6. In the context of an individual risk, what we call *risk appetite* is sometimes also referred to as *risk tolerance*. Whatever the name, the important point is that for different risks, an organization should set and communicate how much uncertainty in likelihood and impact it would like to take in order to achieve its objectives. Assuming that there are both costs and benefits to taking risks, an organization could be taking too little risk in some areas while taking too much in others.

Financial Statement Fraud

EXECUTIVE SUMMARY

Financial statement fraud can be fatal to a company. One way to prevent it is to understand what motivates executives to do it. Barry Minkow, who was convicted of fraud as CEO of ZZZZ Best, said that he began to feel that his worth as a person was tied to the performance of his stock. Joseph Wells, founder of the Association of Certified Fraud Examiners, has said that the only thing that will deter fraudsters is the real perception that they will be caught if they commit the crime. Personal accountability along with strong gatekeeper oversight and government enforcement will lessen corporate fraud. Numerous red flags and elements of financial statement fraud need to be understood to lessen the possibility of its occurrence. It is always important to remember the corruption equation in preventing fraud: Power without sufficient accountability leads to corruption.

RECURRING THEMES IN FINANCIAL STATEMENT FRAUD

Financial statement fraud cases contain the following recurring themes:

- Pressure on senior management to meet financial goals
- Autocratic senior management
- Aggressive accounting practices
- Weak internal controls
- No whistleblowers

Sarbanes-Oxley was enacted as a result of a flood of financial statement scandals, but any fraud prevention program in a company has to include efforts to prevent all types of fraud. This chapter addresses financial statement fraud, with the succeeding chapters addressing asset misappropriations, corruption, bribery, and external frauds.

COOKING THE BOOKS

In financial statement fraud cases, the CEO, CFO, Controller, or others may engage in any of several manipulations to improve the financial statement (case examples shown in parentheses):

- Overstatement of inventory, which is the most frequent area of fraudulent asset valuation (Warnaco, 2004)
- Overstating assets and income by using timing differences (Computer Associates, 2004)
  - Holding the books open to record January sales as December sales
  - Holding December liabilities until January
  - Shifting future expenses to the current period as a special charge
- Failure to record write-offs as required—reversing bad debt into income (Signal Technology, 2002)
- Not reducing the value of assets that have declined in value using "mark to market" (Lehman Brothers, 2008)
- Capitalizing expenses (WorldCom, 2002)
- Concealing liabilities—it is difficult for an auditor to audit something that is not listed on the books (Enron, 2001)

- Boosting income with one-time gains (Krispy Kreme, 2005)
- Recording revenue before it is realized or revenue that may never be collected (Gemstar, 2002)
- Creating fictitious revenues, that is, bogus sales with phony invoices, which result in a boost to assets and income (Satyam Computer, 2009) or premature recognition of revenue or using "boomerang" deals (MicroStrategy, 2000). (A boomerang might be an agreement for company A to invest in company B if company B agrees to purchase products from company A.[1])

There are obvious risks to a company when the choice is made to manipulate the figures in order to achieve earnings estimates, including:

- Loss of a stock's market value
- Lawsuits
- Loss of reputation
- Criminal prosecution
- Bankruptcy

RED FLAGS OF FINANCIAL STATEMENT FRAUD

ACFE founder and Chairman Joseph Wells provides some questions to ask when one is looking for red flags that may signal financial statement fraud:

- Does management display significant disregard for regulations or controls?
- Has management restricted the auditor's access to documents or personnel?
- Has management set unrealistic financial goals?
- Does one person or small group dominate management?[2]

Scott Green, in his *Manager's Guide to the Sarbanes-Oxley Act*, lists more red flags for financial statement fraud:

- Aggressive revenue recognition policies
- Frequent changes in accounting policies regarding bad debt reserves, depreciation, and amortization expenses or comprehensive income

- Unsupported topside entries affecting income
- Underfunded defined pension plans
- Management compensation that is seriously out of line with company performance[3]

Michael Young's Six Elements of Financial Statement Fraud

Michael Young, in his book *Accounting Irregularities and Financial Fraud*, explains financial statement fraud as a symptom of our real-time world. There is an insatiable desire for financial information. Multiple cable television stations dedicate themselves entirely to financial news. Real-time data is the norm—people expect the latest financial statistics to be available at all times on their television or computer screen.

Young goes on to point out that the financial reporting system used by U.S. companies today originated in the 1930s. Financial information then was designed to be communicated on paper. Speed was not a concern. Financial information was a periodic report to the public so they could make their investments accordingly. Then, according to Young, analysts began to make projections to fill the void of financial news. Analysts' projections and expectations are the result of the real-time world's demand for up-to-the-minute financial information. These projections are up to the minute, but they might not be right![4]

These analysts' projections can have a huge impact on the stock price of companies. Because investors expect companies to meet projected earnings, companies face great pressure to meet these estimates. Every division of the company knows what it must bring in.

The market volatility during "earnings season" shows what potential for disaster this system has created. Some executives see failure to meet projections as unfathomable because much of their personal earnings are tied to the stock price of their companies.

Picture a fictitious, publicly traded manufacturing company called Willoughby Manufacturing. Profits have been good for the past four years and are growing steadily. As its stock price has grown, several Wall Street analysts have begun reporting on Willoughby. The publicity on television and in the newspapers has caused the stock to rise even higher. There are projections that this quarter will be a record profit.

Unbeknownst to the investment community, there is a problem. The market for the goods manufactured by this company has begun to level off. The Wall Street projections are not realistic, but the price of the company's stock is now tied to this projection. Investors are "counting their chickens" in shares of Willoughby that will never hatch.

The managers at Willoughby can either accept the bad news or put the pressure on all managers to meet sales projections. Willoughby's CEO chooses pressure. Each division is expected to meet unrealistic sales quotas. One division president, "Peter," already fears for his job. Peter knows that he can never get to the quota by the end of the quarter. Rather than risk his job by failing to meet quota, Peter books sales in this quarter that will not really be earned until next quarter. By then, sales will probably be better, he hopes.

Thanks to creative accounting in several divisions, Willoughby Manufacturing meets market projections for the quarter and sets a record. The projections for the next quarter are for continued growth; however, three divisions have already booked sales that are in the pipeline to the last quarter. Three divisions are now already behind on meeting an unrealistic projection for the next quarter. There is no way out. Eventually someone higher up will find out, the auditor or the CFO. Some CFOs might choose a cover-up rather than public disclosure of the irregularity in the timing of transactions, which could kill the stock price. Michael Young cites six elements in our story:

1. It doesn't start out as dishonesty.
2. It starts with pressure.
3. It starts small.
4. It starts in gray areas of accounting.
5. The fraud grows over time.
6. There is no way out.[5]

Lessons Learned

The lessons for corporations regarding financial reporting are simple:

- Book profits for real transactions that have been completed.
- Profit is what a company earns for taking a risk, not what a company gets by taking advantage.
- Booking profits too soon is building a pyramid scheme on sand; it cannot last.[6]

EXECUTIVE INSIGHT 6.1: A $300 MILLION FRAUD IS NOTHING TO SNEEZE AT

Fortune 500 companies are not the only ones that commit massive accounting frauds. American Tissue may not be well known by name, but many consumers use American Tissue products on a daily basis. This public company was once the fourth largest United States manufacturer of toilet paper, paper towels, napkins, pulp, and office paper products. It had almost 5,000 employees in offices and mills in the United States and Mexico.

In March 2003, the United States Attorney in Brooklyn, New York charged seven former executives including the CEO and CFO of American Tissue, Inc. for defrauding investors and creditors of over $300 million. American Tissue filed for bankruptcy protection in September 2001 as a result of the wholesale looting of the company. The defendants recorded fraudulent sales and created phony documentation to inflate American Tissue's revenues and ensure a continuing line of credit from banks and other lenders. The CEO also diverted tens of millions of dollars to two other corporations he controlled. The charges filed by the government included securities fraud, bank fraud, and obstruction of justice.[i]

The SEC also charged the company and three former executives with fraudulently overstating revenue, earnings, and assets in 2000 and 2001. The diversion of money and equipment had probably been going on for many years. American Tissue's external auditor, Arthur Andersen, also assisted in the conspiracy as American Tissue was about to collapse in the bankruptcy filing. A senior Andersen auditor ordered other Andersen employees to shred incriminating American Tissue documents and delete e-mails.[ii]

In a related civil suit, the former American Tissue executives were alleged to have used their public company as if it was a personal piggy bank. They received almost $24 million in loans with no interest or repayment schedule. Another $2.3 million was provided to family and friends, and fraudulent transactions were hidden by using more than 4,000 phony checks and invoices. The CEO and another executive at first blamed the CFO and Arthur Andersen for the sloppy record keeping.[iii] The federal investigation by Postal Inspectors and the FBI in New York proved that was not the case.

The former CEO was convicted on all counts after a ten-week trial in 2005. The company's former CFO pled guilty and testified for the government, as did other former employees. Then Brooklyn United States Attorney Roslyn Mauskoff commented on the conviction by stating, "This massive corporate fraud was a classic case of greed, lies, and obstruction. Today's conviction demonstrates our commitment, as part of the President's Corporate Fraud Task Force, to investigating and prosecuting corporate fraud to the full extent of the law."[iv] The fraudster CEO was sentenced to 15 years in prison.

As in other trials of CEOs, the defendant used the "Mr. Magoo Defense." His defense attorneys contended that the CEO "was essentially a talented technician who knew little about business finances, and that the frauds were created by others in the company, who were interested in profits."[v] One defense attorney further added that his client was a refugee from Iran and "didn't understand our business ways; he's from another country . . . He doesn't have a college degree in accounting or an MBA."[vi] The prosecutor said it best by telling the jury that the CEO controlled every aspect of the operation and "oversaw a sinkhole of fraud."[vii] The prosecutor then added, "Sometimes you have to wonder, with all the fraudulent activity going at that time, how they had any time to make tissue."[viii]

American Tissue was also alleged to have defrauded its employees by "deducting money from workers' salaries for medical insurance and 401(k) retirement plans but never making the required payments."[ix] A union president in northern New

Hampshire, where one of American Tissue's mills was once located, blamed the CEO for "destroying people's lives, their retirements, their savings plans" and said that the government needs "to deal with him like the criminal he is."[x]

[i]Corporate Fraud Task Force, *First Year Report to the President*, July 22, 2003, www.usdoj.gov/dag/cftf/first_year_report.pdf; and Corporate Fraud Task Force, *Second Year Report to the President*, July 20, 2004, www.usdoj.gov/dag/cftf/2nd_yr_fraud_report.pdf.

[ii]"Former Andersen Auditor Arrested, Charged with Obstruction of Justice," *Accountingweb.com*, March 11, 2003, www.accountingweb.com/item/97276.

[iii]"Suit Targets American Tissue's Memphis Mill," *Memphis Business Journal*, September 18, 2002, //memphis.bizjournals.com/memphis/stories/2002/09/16/daily28.html.

[iv]United States Attorney's Office, Eastern District of New York "Press Release: Former President and CEO of American Tissue Corporation Convicted of Conspiring to Commit $300 million Bank and Securities Fraud after Ten-week Trial," April 13, 2005, //www.justice.gov/usao/nye/pr/2005/2005apr13.html.

[v]Robert E. Kessler, "Convicted on All Counts," *Newsday*, April 14, 2005, A46.

[vi]Ibid.

[vii]Frank Eltman, "Former CEO Convicted of Fraud Scheme in American Tissue Case," *Newsday*, April 13, 2005, //library.newsday.com.

[viii]Ibid.

[ix]James T. Madore, "Hurt Paper-Mill Towns See Rays of Justice in Indictments," *Newsday*, March 18, 2003, A63.

[x]Ibid.

WHY DO THEY TAKE THE RISK?

The potential results of financial statement fraud are disastrous, so why do so many companies take the risk? The motive is often in the incentives. When huge bonuses are tied to meeting projections, the manager who would receive that bonus may make the determination that the risk is worth the reward. At the point that an executive is considering fudging the numbers to ensure a bonus, the primary question in the executive's mind is, "What is the likelihood that anyone will catch this?" Pressure to meet high estimates could put executives in fear of their jobs if projections are not met. The emphasis on results in the short term creates an environment in which failure is seen as unforgivable. This pressure, combined with a low perception of detection, can make the idea of fraud a viable option in the mind of the executive.

Some CEOs run their companies in a highly autocratic manner and manage by fear. If such a CEO is reasonably sure that no one will ask questions, there is a low likelihood that anyone will catch questionable practices. Autocratic and arrogant CEOs often feel like they are deserving of perks and luxuries. CEOs that make millions of dollars a year can begin to feel superhuman and think they can get away with anything. No one seemed to be able to say no to Dennis Kozlowski. When he turned around some poorly performing operations, Kozlowski moved into the limelight. As the CEO of Tyco International in 1997, he was making over $8 million a year, but it wasn't enough. By 1999, Kozlowski was making $170 million a year, but it wasn't enough. He allegedly stole another $430 million through illicit stock sales.[7] These are the actions of a man who thought he was above question, above detection.

After several years in jail, Kozlowski realized the error of his ways. He said, "There is a saying that the only whale that gets harpooned is the one that comes up to the surface. I should have been content with far more modest growth in the company..."[8]

Since many companies offer bonuses and stock options based on company performance, executives and managers are motivated to report more favorable financial results. This creates an environment that encourages financial shenanigans.[9] Convicted fraudster Barry Minkow explained it best:

> I would get letters from people telling me how great I was and what a business genius I was... What people thought about me became the prize and an end in itself... my worth as a person was tied up in the performance of my stock.[10]

Minkow went on to say that he cared more about what other people thought of him than he did about what was right.[11]

The reduction of average CEO salary from 2001 to 2007 in the United States resulted from the drop of the stock market. This would be an indicator that pay-for-performance functions on the whole. Nevertheless, plenty of examples can be cited when it comes to high incentive pay for poor performance. Bear Stearns chairman, Jimmy

Cayne, received $60 million when he was replaced and J.P. Morgan was buying the remnants of Bear for $10 per share, or Merrill Lynch CEO Stan O'Neal who received $160 million after "the thundering herd" stampeded off a cliff.[12]

The high pay to CEOs in comparison to the average worker began to show itself in the late 1970s. This is when the stock option award not only became more valuable, but more common. Throughout the 1950s, only about 16 percent of the executives were awarded an option in any given year. The frequency of stock option grants has increased steadily since then. By the 1990s, executives receiving an option had reached 82 percent.[13]

A corporate board of directors has the responsibility to be independent from the CEO. If a company's board was truly independent, CEO pay would be representative of how well the company did each year. However, senior executives appear to get ever higher salaries and bonuses, even for substandard performance with excuses provided by the board to justify the higher pay. If a board cannot reduce a CEO's pay for bad years, it is probably a rubberstamp board. This is a red flag for investors.

One particularly interesting turn of events with the bankruptcy of Lehman Brothers was that all of the bonuses that the managers earned came in the form of company stock, which was vested after five years. When the company went bankrupt, the prize they had sought at all costs became worthless. CEO Dick Fuld's shares that once made him worth over a billion dollars dropped to $65,486.72.[14]

GEITHNER'S 5 PRINCIPLES ON COMPENSATION

In a statement on June 10, 2009, Treasury Secretary Timothy Geithner proposed five principles that he intended to better align compensation practices with the interests of shareholders, and promote the stability of firms and the financial system:

- Compensation plans should properly measure and reward performance.
- Compensation should be structured to account for the time horizon of risks.

- Compensation practices should be aligned with sound risk management.
- Golden parachutes and supplemental retirement packages should be reexamined to determine whether they align the interests of executives and shareholders.
- Transparency and accountability are encouraged in the process of setting compensation.[15]

Unfortunately, many companies have not heeded these lessons as executive pay has continued to rise in spite of economic impact of the Great Recession.

THE PERCEPTION OF DETECTION

In almost every instance of creative corporate accounting, one or more persons in the organization see signs of trouble. The misdeeds can take on a life their own, with the cover up becoming more of a job than the initial misdeed.

It has been said that the only thing that will deter potential fraudsters is the perception that their actions will be detected. Simply put, people who think they will get caught don't commit fraud.[16] Those who do not understand this principle think that Sarbanes-Oxley is too strict, government regulation is not the answer or that the system doesn't apply to them.

Karpov and Lott's Enforcement Effect of Reputation

Jonathan Karpov, a finance professor at the University of Washington School of Business, believes that recognizing the financial value of a law-abiding reputation is the best way to prevent future financial reporting scandals, not tighter government controls.

Karpov and John Lott, from the University of Pennsylvania's Wharton Business School, cite the "enforcement effect" of reputation, which will do more than expensive and possibly harmful government regulation to encourage companies to audit themselves honestly.

Karpov and Lott studied 132 cases of actual and alleged corporate fraud from 1978 to 1987 and found that the average company involved in the frauds lost over $60 million in stock valuation drop.

EXHIBIT 6.1   The PAC Formula

$$P - A = C$$

Power − Accountability = Corruption

This was 20 times any fines, penalties, restitution, and legal costs. Karpov argues that this research shows that reputational costs far outweigh legal penalties.[17]

Although one would hope that all companies would strive to be honest in their financial reporting for the sake of their corporate reputation, this does not appear to be the case. Fear of financial scandal did not prevent Enron executives from choosing to "cook their books." Nor did Enron's fraud-induced collapse and aftermath discourage future irresponsible uses of securitization by other firms like Bear Stearns, Lehman Brothers, and Merrill Lynch.

Accountability Is the Word

Actually, there is a formula for corruption: Power without Accountability breeds Corruption. We call it the PAC formula, as shown in Exhibit 6.1.

Clinard and Yeager

This idea that fear of sanctions is not a deterrent is supported by the research on corporate crime conducted by Marshall Clinard and Peter Yeager, which is appropriately titled *Corporate Crime* (published in 1980). Clinard and Yeager's work is required reading for the Certified Fraud Examiner or anyone interested in why corporate fraud occurs. In their research, Clinard and Yeager analyzed 477 corporations that had engaged in illegal behavior of all kinds, finding that only 10 percent of corporations even received sanctions for their behavior.[18]

According to Clinard and Yeager's findings, the discipline of the market is not a sufficient force to dissuade corporate crime. Consumers are often unaware that corporations have engaged in illegal activity. Therefore, the illegal activity rarely results in decreased patronage, significant reputational damage, or organized boycotts. Not all firms suffer the way Enron and Arthur Andersen did. Some firms are able to control the damage and survive, at least until another event befalls them.

A prime example of such a company is Citigroup. It had record quarterly profits in 2004 at the same time regulators were considering charges against top Citi officials for failure to supervise analysts and investment bankers. The SEC and the Justice Department were examining whether Citigroup Asset Management overcharged mutual fund investors for record keeping. British authorities were investigating Citi's government bond desk in London for selling European debt in August and then quickly buying it back at a much lower price. Enron creditors were suing Citi for failure to say what they knew about the state of Enron's finances, and the SEC was looking at Citi's accounting in Argentina, where it wrote off $2 billion in bad loans.[19] Bad headlines and questionable accounting did not result in sufficient damage to Citi's reputation to impact its stock price or profits. That is until the financial crisis hit.

Of those companies who are caught and exposed for committing financial fraud, the financial impact of the negative publicity can be devastating, but how many more companies would continue to get away with or attempt financial statement fraud in the future without the regulations imposed by Sarbanes-Oxley?

IS SARBANES-OXLEY WORKING?

While there was hope that Sarbanes-Oxley would have its intended regulatory effect in reducing fraud, abuse, and willful blindness, corporate and individual misconduct continue. Although ethical companies comply with Sarbanes-Oxley, there are some that practice lies and deception. Sarbanes-Oxley was supposed to foster transparency and due diligence but there are always exceptions and noncompliance, as we learned from the financial crisis. We witnessed the following:

- Financial institutions made loans without proper documentation on the borrowers, which the borrowers would never pay back, and they didn't seem to care.
- Firms selling credit default swaps on mortgage-backed securities did not have the capital to pay if the mortgages defaulted, and they didn't seem to care.

- When collateralized debt obligations lost value, firms did not mark them down to market value on their books.
- Lehman Brothers pulled a page out of the Enron play book with Repo 105.

Senator Paul Sarbanes said in 2007, "The act is not an absolute guarantee. You will always have some sharp operators trying to get away with something. But hopefully the act will screen a lot of that out and they will be punished if they're caught. Much of the act is designed to strengthen the system to keep the bad apples from developing in the first place."[20]

THE GREED FACTOR

Perhaps all this greed is the result of the increasing emphasis that began to be placed on practical arts like finance, marketing, and business management in the past 25 years. In the 1980s, the "me" generation scoffed at a liberal arts education as outdated. The glory was in big business, high finance, and material gain. CEOs were heroes to be emulated. Today, CEOs are depicted in the media as less than heroic.

In 2003, Diane L. Coutu, Senior Editor of the *Harvard Business Review* from 1998 to 2009, argued that the backlash against corporate executives was just another form of pandering to the public by the media. The pandering allowed many to see themselves as victims of greedy corporate America. Coutu argued that strong egotists were needed to make their companies grow. Replacing them with modest men might soothe the rage, but the economy could suffer for it.[21] Well the economy suffered in 2008, but not because companies were being run by modest, risk-averse people. The stock market crashed, real estate bottomed out, and the government had to bailout the financial system with billions of dollars. This resulted from corporate leaders who took on far too much risk without paying proper attention to the consequences. The activities that led to this disaster are discussed in more detail in Chapter 10. As Scott Green points out in his *Manager's Guide to the Sarbanes-Oxley Act*, it would be wise for any CEO to avoid any hint of unfair dealing. The board should adopt a policy to automatically investigate any sale of company stock by management if it preceded the release of bad news. Such a policy, according to Green, would cause senior managers to ensure that they consider all legal and ethical requirements before they sell stock.[22]

EXECUTIVE INSIGHT 6.2: SATYAM COMPUTER SERVICES: THE ENRON OF INDIA

The United States does not have a monopoly on massive financial statement frauds. The Satyam Computer Services (Satyam) $1.1 billion accounting fraud that was disclosed in 2009 made international headlines and rocked the business community in India. The fraud involved numerous accounting shenanigans, including overstated revenue income, and operating margins, understated liability, inflated cash and bank balances and more.

This fraud's impact came not just from its enormity, but how it caught investors and government regulators completely off guard. Satyam had a stellar reputation as a corporate powerhouse in India. In September 2008, Satyam received the "Golden Peacock award from the World Council for Corporate Governance for excellence in corporate governance" and had received praise for its corporate governance practices in 2006 and 2007.[xi] Unfortunately, the scandal exposed the suspect governance model of Satyam and other companies in India as well as red flags that were ignored. In the end, Satyam became India's Enron.

Byrraju Ramalinga Raju, founder and Chairman of Satyam, disclosed the accounting scandal to Satyam's Board of Directors in a letter dated January 7, 2009, in which he admitted to wrongdoing. "It is with deep regret," he began, "and tremendous burden that I am carrying on my conscience, that I would like to bring the following facts to your notice," and then proceeded to detail how the company's books were cooked over many years. He admitted that he knew this was wrong but was unable to stop it once it started. "It was like riding a tiger, not knowing how to get off without being eaten," he wrote. Raju concluded the letter by stating: "I am now prepared to subject myself to the laws of the land and face consequences thereof."[xii]

Satyam was the proverbial rags to riches saga. From a farming family background, through education and entrepreneurship, Raju founded Satyam in June 1987 with 20 employees. It went public in India in 1991 and grew to become the fourth largest IT company in India, providing consulting, system integration, and outsourcing services. It was listed on NASDAQ in 1999 and then on the New York Stock Exchange in 2001. Over the years, Satyam developed operations in 67 countries with 53,000 claimed employees, although 13,000 were nonexistent with that compensation siphoned off as part of the fraud by Raju. Satyam had revenues of over $2 billion a year and had 185 out of the Fortune 500 companies as clients. All that could not stop Satyam's share price from falling 82 percent on the day the fraud was disclosed.

Within days of the disclosure of the fraud, Raju and other Satyam executives were arrested by India's Central Bureau of Investigation. The arrests continued with other senior management, including the CFO. The government investigation also snared employees of the Satyam's independent auditor, PricewaterhouseCoopers (PwC). Two partners from the Indian office of PwC were arrested and charged with "dishonesty, cheating, falsification of accounts and using forged documents."[xiii]

The extent and length of the accounting fraud made it inevitable that the house of cards would eventually topple. Starting in 2001, Raju and his co-conspirators perpetrated their crimes by inflating the balance sheet with fictitious assets as well as employing other accounting trickery:

- Sales figures were inflated every quarter to make it appear that business volume was growing.

- Forged invoices for fake customers were generated to falsely report revenue.

- Nonexistent cash and bank balances. Forged bank account documents supposedly from major banks supported a claim of over a $1 billion in various accounts.

- The company overstated revenues by $120 million and understated liabilities by $240 million.

- The company overstated operating margins by $120 million.
- There was nonexistent accrued interest of $100 million.
- Company headcount was inflated by 13,000 to match the fictitious revenue claimed.
- The debtor position was inflated to show money was owed the company.

Numerous red flags and rumors of irregularities went unheeded. Had they been thoroughly vetted, the fraud might have been discovered much earlier. These red flags included:

- Rumors of financial shenanigans by Satyam in the Indian financial community that no one followed up on.
- Family members and friends of the founder involved in senior management overseeing corporate governance.
- Board members, including some supposed corporate governance experts, "who should have been asking questions did not."[xiv]
- Related-party transactions. Raju looted the company and "attempted to saddle Satyam with debt-ridden companies owned by his sons, persuading his board to approve the deal."[xv]
- Belief by a global organization of corrupt activity by Satyam. In 2006, the World Bank reported to the Department of Justice that "it suspected Satyam may have been involved in bribery" of a World Bank senior official.[xvi] Yet the World Bank failed to make any public notifications of its concern, even after an internal investigation in 2007 "found that Satyam had acted improperly."[xvii]

Even with red flags, Satyam's accounting firm signed off on the company's financial records for eight years with no clue as to the fraud. Similarly, regulators in the United States, Europe, and India had no indication of wrongdoing. In a statement issued shortly after the disclosure of the financial fraud, PricewaterhouseCoopers commented, "We placed reliance on management controls over financial reporting and the information and explanations provided by management and also the verbal and written representations made to us during the course of our audits."[xviii] Warning signs the PwC auditing team should have acted on included being told by a partner from another PwC international firm that Satyam's "cash confirmation procedures appeared substantially deficient but the Indian firm did nothing to correct the procedures."[xix] In April 2011, Price India, the Indian affiliate of PricewaterhouseCoopers, was fined $7.5 million by the Securities and Exchange Commission. "PW India violated its most fundamental duty as a public watchdog by failing to comply with some of the most elementary auditing standards and procedures in conducting the Satyam audits," commented Robert Khuzami, the SEC's Director of Enforcement.[xx]

Satyam completely changed it corporate leadership and is working to reclaim its reputation and its business while the prosecution of former Satyam executives continues. In April 2009, Indian conglomerate Tech Mahindra purchased 31 percent of Satyam and rebranded it as Mahindra Satyam. The company also took steps to resolve pending litigation and investigations. In February 2011, Mahindra Satyam paid $125 million to settle class action suits filed by investors in the United States. In April 2011, Mahindra Satyam paid $10 million to settle charges filed by the SEC related to fraudulently overstating the company's revenue for over five years.

In an ironic footnote to this scandalous episode, Satyam means truth in Sanskrit.

[xi] Andrew Ross Sorkin, "Talk of 'India's Enron' as Satyam Shares Plunge," *New York Times*, January 7, 2009, //dealbook.nytimes.com/2009/01/07/talk-of-indias-enron-as-satyam-shares-plunge/.

[xii] Letter of confession and disclosure of the financial accounting fraud from B. Ramalinga Raju, Chairman, Satyam Computer Services, to the Satyam Board, January 7, 2009.

[xiii] Heather Timmons, "2 Auditors Held in India Fault System," *New York Times*, May 28, 2009, B1.

[xiv] Salil Tripathi, "India Faces an 'Enron Moment,'" *Wall Street Journal*, January 9, 2009, A11.

xvManjeet Kripalani, "Corporate India's Governance Crisis," *BusinessWeek*, January 26, 2009, 78.
xviBob Davis, "World Bank Had Cited Concerns About Firm," *New York Times*, January 8, 2009, A9.
xviiIbid.
xviiiRomit Guma, "Satyam Seeks Leaders, Names Auditors," *New York Times*, January 15, 2009, B3.
xixFloyd Norris, "Indian Accounting Firm Is Fined $7.5 Million over Fraud at Satyam," *New York Times*, April 5, 2011, B3.
xxIbid.

MICROSTRATEGY BECOMES MICROTRAGEDY

Few auditors want to be the messenger breaking the news to a client that earnings will have to be restated. Such an event can be disastrous. Take the example of MicroStrategy, a data mining software maker. In 2000, MicroStrategy became "MicroTragedy" when it had to restate its 1998 and 1999 earnings. The first problem was that rather than spreading earnings out over the length of multi-year consulting contracts, MicroStrategy booked the profits right away. Another problem was the October 1999 announcement of a $52 million licensing agreement with NCR Corporation, whereby MicroStrategy "invested" in NCR, and NCR would purchase products from MicroStrategy—a "boomerang!"[23]

The restatement of MicroStrategy earnings turned a reported $12 million profit into a $34 million loss. The shares of MicroStrategy plummeted from $333 per share in March 2000 to $22 in May 2000 and MicroStrategy was hit with three lawsuits.[24] Avoiding such immediate adverse consequences is a human defense mechanism that can lead to an auditor deciding to "go with the flow."

WHERE WERE THE STOCK ANALYSTS?

In 2008, when the stock of the large Wall Street firms started dropping, the stock analysts worked at many of those Wall Street firms: Merrill Lynch, Bear Stearns, and Citigroup. They knew better than anyone the true state of financial affairs. According to Joseph Wells, fraud is very difficult to find in many audit situations because it is often committed by insiders who are more familiar with the accounting system(s) than the auditors are.[25] Because of the limited time auditors spend looking at the records, they just see a snapshot in time. They do not monitor the books on a day-to-day basis.

Some of the burden belongs with the stock analysts. Analysts took WorldCom's reported income as proof of its success. If those analysts had analyzed the free cash flows of WorldCom, they would have seen that capital expenditures were false, designed to hide the operating costs.[26]

Other questions that analysts should ask include:

- Is the company negotiating financing based on its receivables?
- Have receivables increased significantly but not sales?
- Has cash decreased compared with sales and receivables?
- Are shipping costs consistent with sales?[27]

Perhaps a question that is as valid as "Where were the auditors?" is "Where were the investment analysts?" Here are some more instances that might signal the need for closer review:

- High-growth companies entering a low-growth phase; there may be a temptation to mask the decline.
- Companies that are always under the Wall Street microscope; any bad news could tank the stock.
- Many companies that are not followed by most analysts.
- New businesses have to decide how to measure key transactions.
- Complex ownerships or financial structures can make related-party transactions less transparent.[28]

There have been numerous instances in which analysts have been not just sloppy or negligent, but downright corrupt. Several investigations since 2000 have shown that the stock analysis done by several large firms was neither independent nor unbiased.

In 2002, then investment giant Merrill Lynch paid a $100 million fine after an internal e-mail was discovered showing that analysts were publicly recommending stocks that they knew were not good investments. These were, of course, the stocks of companies from which Merrill wanted to win investment business.[29]

Conflict of interest cases also surfaced at the investment firms Goldman Sachs, Morgan Stanley, and Citigroup Global Markets. In October 2002, then New York State Attorney General Eliot Spitzer filed suit against five clients of Citigroup for granting investment business to Citibank in exchange for favorable stock ratings by Citigroup analysts.[30]

How is it that bias invaded the advice of stock analysts? In 1975, Congress removed the fixed rate on commissions for analysts, allowing the market to dictate commission rates. Of course, competition for the business of middle-class Americans entering the stock market for the first time drove commissions lower. Lower commissions forced many Wall Street brokerage companies to rely more and more on investment banking deals to maintain themselves in the manner to which they had become accustomed.

Jack Grubman from Salomon Smith Barney, the investment banking arm of Citigroup, had become one of the top dealmakers. Grubman generated tens of millions of dollars in fees from companies that benefited from Grubman's market research. In 1998, Citi rewarded Grubman with a contract that would pay him $20 million over a five-year period.[31]

In 2000, Grubman was pushing the stocks of WorldCom and Global Crossing, which were expanding with billions of dollars of bonds issued by Citigroup. These telecom giants made money from broadband and cable lines, the rates for which were in free fall. With the rates dropping, someone should have questioned whether WorldCom and Global Crossing would still be able to pay their debts. Grubman did not seem to be concerned.[32] This is the perfect example of why Karpov and Lott's Enforcement Effect of [a good] Reputation is so hard to accept. When business executives and star analysts lose touch with reality, they cannot be thinking of their company's good reputation.

It was just this kind of greed for fees and commissions that contributed to a financial disaster of epic proportions in 2008 as managers stopped seeing the good of the customer, or even the good of their own firms, and chased their bonus triggers. In the rush for profits, risks (however remote they seemed at the time) that could bring down the whole company were accepted at major firms.

NOTES

1. Joseph T. Wells, "So That's Why It's Called a Pyramid Scheme," *Journal of Accountancy*, 190 (October 2000), 91; and Howard Schilit, *Financial Shenanigans*, 2nd ed. (New York: McGraw Hill, 2002), 62.
2. Joseph T. Wells, "Why Employees Commit Fraud," *Journal of Accountancy* 191 (February 2001): 89.
3. Scott Green, *Manager's Guide to the Sarbanes-Oxley Act* (New York: John Wiley & Sons, 2004), 123.
4. Michael R. Young, *Accounting Irregularities and Financial Fraud*, 2nd ed. (New York: Aspen Publishers, 2002), 306–309.
5. Ibid., 11–13.
6. Jerry Fleming, *Profit at Any Cost?* (Grand Rapids, MI: Baker Books, 2003), 28, 52.
7. Green, *Manager's Guide.*
8. Michael Medved, *The 5 Big Lies About American Business* (New York: Crown Forum, 2009), 139.
9. Howard Schilit, *Financial Shenanigans*, 2nd ed. (New York: McGraw Hill, 2002), 29.
10. Barry Minkow, *Cleaning Up* (Nashville: Nelson Current, 2005), 155.
11. Ibid., 215.
12. Barry Ritholtz, *Bailout Nation* (Hoboken, NJ: Wiley, 2009), 200.
13. Carola Frydman and Raven E. Saks, *Executive Compensation: A New View From a Long-Term Perspective, 1936–2005*, Federal Reserve Board Technical Report No. 2007–35 (2007).
14. Andrew Ross Sorkin, *Too Big To Fail* (New York: Penguin, 2009), 487.
15. John E. Core and Wayne R. Guay, "Is There a Case for Regulating Executive Pay in the Financial Services Industry?" *Social Science Research Network*, January 25, 2010, ssrn.com/abstract=1544104.
16. Joseph T. Wells, "The S&L Scandal, the Biggest Crime of All Time?" *The White Paper* (May–June 1990), 2.
17. Robyn Eifertsen, "Regulations Not Best Prevention against Fraud," *University Week* (University of Washington) March 14, 2002, //depts.washington.edu/uweek/archives/2002.03.MAR_14/news_i.html.

18. Marshall Clinard and Peter Yeager, *Corporate Crime* (New York: Free Press, 1980).
19. Mara Der Hovanesian, Paula Dwyer, and Stanley Reed, "Can Chuck Prince Clean Up Citi?" *BusinessWeek*, October 2, 2004, 11.
20. Dick Carozza, "Sarbanes-Oxley Act Revisited," *Fraud Magazine*, May–June, 2007, 63.
21. Diane L. Coutu, "I Was Greedy Too," *Harvard Business Review* 81 (February 2003): 38–44.
22. Green, *Manager's Guide.*
23. Howard Schilit, *Financial Shenanigans*, 2nd ed. (New York: McGraw Hill, 2002), 44.
24. H. David Sherman and S. David Young, "Tread Lightly through These Accounting Minefields," *Harvard Business Review* 79 (July–August 2001): 129–35.
25. Joseph T. Wells, "Follow the Likely Perp," *Journal of Accountancy* 191 (March 2001): 91.
26. William A. Sahlman, "Expensing Options Solves Nothing," *Harvard Business Review* 80 (December 2002): 91–96.
27. Wells, "Follow the Likely Perp."
28. Sherman and Young, "Tread Lightly."
29. Joshua Kurlantzick, "Word on the Street," *Entrepreneur*, January 2005, 55.
30. Ibid.
31. Charles Gasparino, *Blood on the Street* (New York: Free Press, 2005), 96.
32. Ibid., 7.

CHAPTER 7

Internal Fraud

Protecting a Company

EXECUTIVE SUMMARY

Financial statement fraud is not the only kind of fraud that can damage a company. According to the Association of Certified Fraud Examiners' *2010 Report to the Nations on Occupational Fraud and Abuse*, 86 percent of all frauds perpetrated against companies are asset misappropriation. The three types of cash misappropriation are larceny, skimming, and fraudulent disbursements. These are frauds committed by employees and those outside the organization, such as contractors. Check fraud, although still a concern, is not the problem it used to be, because of technological advances that have improved prevention. Corruption schemes involving bribery, kickbacks, and bid-rigging continue to be a problem and are more common than most people realize.

FRAUDULENT DISBURSEMENTS AND ASSET MISAPPROPRIATION

After Sarbanes-Oxley, many internal audit departments increased their testing aimed at finding financial statement fraud, but one cannot ignore another type of occupational fraud and abuse, asset misappropriation involving employee fraud.

There are various schemes and methods to misappropriate assets, and some tend to show up more frequently than others. In its *2010 Report to the Nations*, the Association of Certified Fraud Examiners classifies the different types of asset misappropriations, which are involved in about 86 percent of all internal frauds. These frauds are also the lowest in median loss, at about $135,000 per incident. Exhibit 7.1 lists the many types of asset misappropriation as well as the various corruption and fraudulent statement schemes.

Fraudulent disbursements constitute an important area in which to conduct a fraud risk assessment. Employees may attempt fraudulent disbursements in various ways, so there are numerous controls to be considered. Of all fraudulent disbursements, more than half are billing schemes.[1]

FALSE BILLING SCHEMES

Invoicing through Shell Companies

Although sometimes a legitimate business need exists for shell companies, they are often created for the sole purpose of committing fraud or masking the true owner of funds. Shells can be incorporated in the United States. Delaware and Nevada are popular because of low cost and ease of incorporation. Shell companies are also incorporated offshore to take advantage of privacy laws. The shell can be nothing more than a fake name and a post office box used to collect proceeds from false billings, or it can be as elaborate as multiple companies in several different countries. It is a good idea to check out any vendor thoroughly, especially one using a post office box address.

Not all fraudsters are street smart. Some employees submit fake invoices for nonexistent companies and use their home addresses or the maiden names of wives and mothers. A comparison of employee

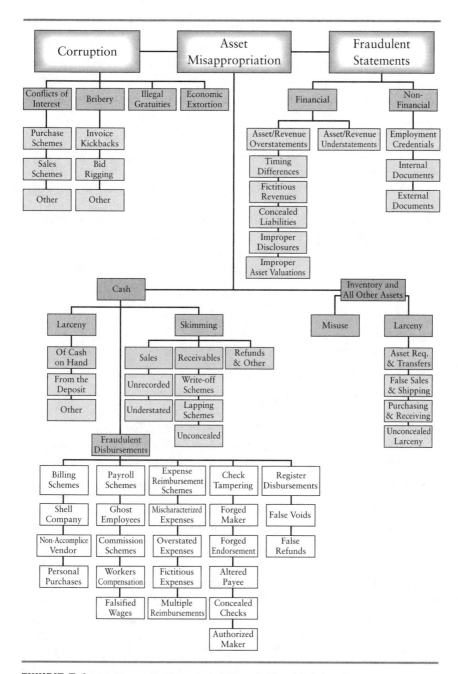

EXHIBIT 7.1 Uniform Occupational Fraud Classification System
Source: Reprinted with permission from the Association of Certified Fraud
Examiners, Austin, Texas ©2005.

addresses with a list of vendor addresses will catch these novice fraud-sters.

Once a shell company has been established and the fraudster has opened a bank account in the name of the shell, invoices are created by various means. The invoices are usually for services, as these are harder to track than goods. Often the fraudster has approval power, or a supervisor who simply rubberstamps everything. Invoices that have not been folded may not have been mailed, but rather placed into the system from someone inside. Accounts payable staff should be on the lookout for unfolded invoices and for the following:

- Vendors that have received payments at two different addresses
- More than one vendor with the same address
- Vendors that have the same address as an employee
- Vendors using post office box addresses or commercial mail re-ceiving agencies

The Pass-Through Scheme

More ingenious fraudsters do not invoice for nonexistent goods or services. Instead, they use the shell company to purchase actual goods at regular prices. They then resell these goods to their companies at inflated prices. This is known as a pass-through scheme. The fraudster is usually someone in charge of purchasing for the victim company. A practice of putting big-ticket items out for bid can stop this, as competitive bids will be lower than the pass-through company's price.

Personal Purchases with Company Money

This fraud can easily start when a manager purchases software as an example. The manager asks how to get a certain software program and is told to put in a formal request under the office supply budget. The manager is able to approve the purchase, as the amount is only a few hundred dollars. The software arrives and a clerk brings it directly to the manager. The manager has ordered, approved, and received goods. There is no separation of duties. At this point the manager realizes that anything can be purchased within reason, be it for personal or business use. Only conscience and the fear of being caught control the manager's actions. This is how most internal frauds start. An employee finds an area without strong controls and takes advantage of it. This is the "opportunity" mentioned in Cressey's Fraud Triangle Theory.

EXECUTIVE INSIGHT 7.1: EXPENSE REPORTING FRAUD: DO WHAT I SAY, NOT WHAT I DO

Expense reporting fraud is one of the most common asset misappropriation frauds, and experience has shown that employees at all levels of an organization can be involved. It is particularly embarrassing when the victim is a corporate governance center at a respected institution of higher learning. This story involves Florencio López-de-Silanes, who was a renowned professor of finance and economics as well as the Director of the International Institute of Corporate Governance at the prestigious Yale School of Management. López-de-Silanes advised organizations and governments around the world on corporate governance best practices. He was a founding member of the Blue Ribbon Panel on Corporate Governance in Russia and the Committee on Best Corporate Practices in Mexico. He received his undergraduate degree and a doctorate from Harvard University as well as numerous achievements and honors throughout his career.[i]

Officials at Yale started an investigation in September 2004 and "uncovered alleged evidence that he double-billed for hotels, flights and similar travel expenses" that totaled almost $150,000 since 2001.[ii] In December 2004, Yale's senior faculty was told that the investigation "found a pattern of financial impropriety and was negotiating with Mr. López-de-Silanes' attorney to avoid the messy process of removing his tenure."[iii] In January 2005, it was decided that López-de-Silanes would leave Yale because of "financial misconduct and irregularities."[iv] In a statement issued by López-de-Silanes' attorney, the professor said, "I deeply regret any unintended harm. I can offer no excuse except the intensity of my focus on work. I am leaving Yale because it is the right thing to do for the Institute and all concerned."[v] Subsequently, the Yale School of Management Web site advised that López-de-Silanes was on a leave of absence for Spring 2005 and had resigned effective June 30, 2005.

Jack Siegel, author of *Avoiding Trouble While Doing Good: A Guide for the Non-Profit Director and Officer,* commented on his Web blog that Yale set a very bad example in handling the situation and in the process undermined the university's credibility as a provider of corporate governance training. Siegel said with respect to corporate governance, "The talisman is transparency" and that was not the case here. He added, "As a consequence, we don't know the facts, including the exact amount involved, the amount of intentional behavior on Mr. López-de-Silanes' part, or the extent of the weaknesses in Yale's accounting system. If there was blatant wrongdoing, there should not have been negotiation." Siegel also questioned what kind of example this would provide to Yale students who may find themselves in fiduciary roles later in life.[vi]

There are a few lessons to be learned here. One, travel and expense reporting fraud and abuse are widespread and can be found in any organization. Proactive detection and prevention are always required. Second, any organization, especially a high-profile one, must always remember that its actions will be scrutinized. Any decisions that are suspect will open the organization to adverse publicity. A good rule to remember is how the final action will look if it is published on page one of the *Wall Street Journal.* As an ironic touch to this story, the Yale School of Management's Web site at the time advised that López-de-Silanes had been working on a research paper entitled "Theft Technologies."

[i]Yale School of Management faculty page. López-de-Silanes' Yale biography at mba.yale.edu/faculty/professors/lopez.shtml (This link is no longer active).
[ii]Joann S. Lublin, "Travel Expenses Prompt Yale to Force Out Institute Chief," *Wall Street Journal*, January 10, 2005, B1.
[iii]Ibid.
[iv]The Associated Press, "Governance Expert Resigns over Finances," *MSNBC.com*, January 10, 2005, www.msnbc.msn.com/id/6809368.
[v]Ibid.
[vi]Jack Siegel, "Tunneling through Expense Account Reimbursements at Yale: "Do What I Say, Not What I Do," Charity Governance Consulting LLC, charitygovernance.blogs.com/charity_governance/2005/01/tunneling_throu_1.html.

PAYROLL SCHEMES

These schemes can take many forms, from a person lying on a time card to entering nonexistent or ghost employees on the payroll. The company cuts the ghost employee a paycheck, which is intercepted by the fraudster and cashed. Use of direct deposit only makes the fraudster's work easier. The best way to discover ghost employees is to check periodically to determine whether more than one check is going to a particular address or bank account. Looking for two employees with the same Social Security number is also a way to find ghosts. Lack of segregation of duties or the absence of review makes it easier for the fraudster to slip ghosts into the system. Ghost employees will often have no withholding for insurance or taxes.

Check Tampering

This fraud scheme could be internal or external. Anyone who has seen the movie *Catch Me If You Can* starring Tom Hanks and Leonardo Di Caprio, about the life and crimes of Frank Abagnale, has an idea of how the world of check fraud used to be. With the onset of wire transfers and Positive Pay, the check forger or "paperhanger" is a dying threat to the corporate world, unless one is in the business of cashing checks. Positive Pay is a service provided by a bank to its commercial customers, whereby the customer company provides an electronic file to the bank that lists the date, payee, and amount of all checks written each period. If a check that is not on the list is presented for payment, the bank must get approval before honoring the check.

Positive Pay is highly regarded, as more than 50 percent of all check tampering schemes are "forged maker" schemes.[2] This means that a fraudster has obtained a blank check and forged the signature of the official signatory. It includes the use of photocopy forgeries. The fraudster often presents these checks for cashing at casinos or check cashing services. Positive Pay prevents the funds from being withdrawn from a company's bank account because these checks will not be on the list prepared for the bank. In his book *The Art of the Steal*, Frank Abagnale writes, "I feel that positive pay is the greatest concept available to deal with the problems of forgery or

EXHIBIT 7.2 Types of Check Tampering Schemes by Occurrence

Forged Maker	50%
Alteration to Payee	20%
Authorized Maker	15%
Forged Endorsement	11%
Concealed Checks	4%

Source: Joseph T. Wells, *Occupational Fraud and Abuse* (Austin, TX: Obsidian Publishing, 1997), 159.

fraud."[3] That is a high-level endorsement. (See Exhibit 7.2 for the different check tampering schemes and occurrence percentages.)

There are two types of check fraud that occur when a valid check is intercepted by an internal fraudster. Alteration to payee occurs when the fraudster changes the payee and then converts the check to his or her own use. The other type of check fraud occurs when the check is intercepted and the endorsement forged. The fraudster poses as the payee and converts the check.

Authorized maker schemes take place when those with signature authority write checks to themselves. Concealed checks are bogus checks slipped in with valid checks for the official signatory to sign.

To prevent check interception schemes, checks should be mailed directly to the payee as soon as they are prepared. Employees and contractors should not be allowed to collect checks in person. Electronic funds transfers are good in that they reduce the number of persons with access to negotiable documents.

For a fraudster, checks have some very big drawbacks; they leave behind an audit trail, handwriting evidence, and fingerprints that can be detected for months or even years after a transaction. Passing counterfeit checks may involve face-to-face transactions and false identification, which are more risky and difficult than making long-distance orders with stolen credit card numbers. Credit card fraud has become a more popular, easier, and safer way to make a dishonest living. Some paperhangers still use the "Bust Out" strategy (described in Chapter 9), which involves becoming a trusted customer by placing small orders before eventually placing a very large one, paying with a bad check, and absconding. This "one-time hit" strategy is the norm in this type of scheme.

Another type of employee check fraud is the "stop payment scam." This usually occurs when an employee is leaving a company, and the last paycheck is being mailed. The employee will wait until the paycheck has been mailed, ask that payment be stopped, and then request that a new check be issued and mailed to a new address. The former employee will then attempt to cash both checks and move on.

Payroll Debit Cards

Along with Positive Pay, payroll debit cards are an excellent way to curb check fraud. Controllers or treasurers never have to sign checks again. Once an employee has been issued a card, payday is as easy as electronic payments into the accounts. The employee does not have to have a checking account. The payroll debit card is like a prepaid credit card. The American love affair with plastic is well documented. Employees without bank accounts who were used to cashing paychecks will save the check cashing fee imposed by check cashing services, plus employees do not have to walk around with large amounts of cash. According to *INC.* magazine, some 30 million American workers do not have checking accounts.[4]

The Association of Certified Fraud Examiners (ACFE) *Fraud Examiners Manual* lists some red flags that may signal check tampering in a company:

- Voided checks: These should be verified against the physical copies of the checks.
- Missing checks: They indicate lax control over check stock. Stop payment on all missing checks.
- Checks, other than paychecks, payable to any employee: These should be reviewed.
- Altered or dual endorsements: These may mean fraud.[5]

BRIBERY, KICKBACKS, AND BID-RIGGING

In many parts of the world, a bribe is a normal business transaction. The bribe buys influence and is the unfortunate cost of doing business where the rule of law is weak. When a bribe is paid to a foreign government official with the intent to influence an official act, that may lead to violations of the Foreign Corrupt Practices Act or the UK Bribery Act as detailed in Chapter 15. Commercial bribery involves payments to influence a person in a position to make business decisions that are not government-facing.

Corruption schemes include:

1. Commercial Bribery: Company A makes a payment to a particular person at company B (with or without the knowledge or consent of company B) to influence the decision of that person in a way favorable to company A. Company A is willing to pay, and the bribe-taker pockets the money. An example is a bank that bribes the decision-maker at a company to steer the company's banking business to that bank.

2. Kickbacks: Company A overcharges or submits bogus invoices to company B. There is an accomplice inside company B who helps cover the fraud in exchange for part of the proceeds being kicked back to the accomplice on a continuing basis. An example is a procurement officer who approves inflated invoices from a vendor in return for a cut of the profits.

3. Bid-Rigging: Company A is bidding on a large contract with company B. The person at company B in charge of the bid solicitation offers to help company A win the contract in exchange for a percentage of the profit from the contract. Once the agreement has been made, the fraudster can specify items in the contract that only company A can provide, or make sure that company A's bid is the lowest by passing on inside information. One fraudster even went as far as submitting bogus bids from nonexistent companies, all higher than the company that had agreed to pay him a bribe. Once the contract is awarded to company A, the fraudster protects the relationship and continues to receive a portion of the profit on a continuing basis. An example is a company bribing the bid solicitor to overlook the fact that the company has no references, work history, or other required qualifications. The bid solicitor helps the company falsify the proper documents in exchange for a cut of the contract.

Red flags for corruption include the following:

- A company paying more than the best price available
- Very specific requirements that tend to favor one bidder

- Projects that are broken into two contracts to keep them under a review limit or approval authority
- Very narrow time window for companies to submit bids
- A too-successful bidder who is consistently winning bids
- Social contact between the bid solicitors and bidders
- Lower quality goods from a new vendor
- A company procurement officer living beyond his/her means

There are various ways to make a bribe payment to avoid detection. Many bribes take the form of expensive gifts, trips, drugs, or sexual favors. Of course the most preferred bribe or kickback is cash. When very large sums are involved, cash is not always practical. Cash transactions of more than $10,000 should generate government reporting requirement through a Suspicious Activity Report. One of the favored methods to get cash to the bribe recipient is to apply for a loan. The company paying the bribe then makes the loan payments for the bribe recipient. A variation on this idea would be for the bribe-payer making payments to the recipient's credit card(s). In some cases, the bribe-payer simply hands over a credit card as the bribe and then pays the bills, which are sent directly to the bribe-payer. A bribe might take the form of a house sold at a fraction of market value, or the spouse of the bribe-taker being employed by the bribe-paying company at a high salary or no-show job.

Every industry has its rotten apples. At Home Box Office (HBO), the director of print services was sentenced in 2004 to five years of probation for soliciting more than $400,000 in kickbacks from vendors in exchange for awarding them HBO ad business. She used some of that money to pay for a lavish wedding at the Plaza Hotel in Manhattan.[6]

EXECUTIVE INSIGHT 7.2: FRANK GRUTTADAURIA: THE ROGUE EMPLOYEE

Rogue employees can cause great financial and reputational damage to an organization. It is unusual for a rogue employee to disclose a fraud personally through pangs of guilt and a change in his/her rationalization. However, this is exactly what happened in the case of rogue employee Frank Gruttadauria. In January 2002, Gruttadauria sent a letter to the Cleveland office of the FBI identifying himself as Managing Director of the brokerage firm Lehman Brothers in Cleveland. In the confession letter, Gruttadauria stated, "During the course of the past 15 years, I have caused misappropriation through various methods, which resulted in other violations. It has occurred at brokerage firms Lehman Brothers, SG Cowen Securities Corp., Cowen & Co., Hambrecht & Quist, Inc. and LF Rothschild, Inc."[vii]

The FBI started an investigation, as did Lehman Brothers. It was discovered that Gruttadauria maintained a "stand-alone" computer that was not connected to Lehman's computer network. This computer allowed Gruttadauria to create phony customer account statements that he caused to be mailed to customers. A comparison of Lehman's actual client statements and the doctored statements in Gruttadauria's computer found 110 instances in which statements that were "mailed to said customers contained grossly inflated values totaling approximately $289 million, while the actual account values of the same Lehman Brothers' customer accounts on the same date were only approximately $12 million."[viii]

Gruttadauria had stolen millions of dollars for years, and no one was the wiser. He worked at SG Cowen prior to working at Lehman Brothers and committed the same fraud there. The FBI initially estimated that he cooked his client's books by as much as $300 million.[ix] An arrest warrant was issued for Gruttadauria, and after a nationwide search, he surrendered to authorities on February 9, 2002. The continuing investigation found that Gruttadauria was operating a Ponzi scheme, taking money from one investor and paying it to another. He moved money out of the accounts of his richest investors without their knowledge to cover withdrawal requests from other clients.[x] He did this to avoid detection while he was cleaning out his clients' accounts. He diverted client statements to a post office box he opened and then sent clients phony statements showing inflated balances. When he fled, he created phony identities to avoid detection by law enforcement.

On February 21, 2002, the Securities and Exchange Commission (SEC) charged Gruttadauria and two companies he controlled, DH Strategic Partners and JYM Trading Trust, with a massive fraud against more than 50 customers over a 15-year period. In August 2002, Gruttadauria pled guilty to securities fraud, mail fraud, identity theft, and making false statements to a bank. He was subsequently sentenced to seven years in prison.

Gruttadauria's last employer, Lehman Brothers, may have missed the red flags. He produced almost $6 million in commissions in 1999 compared with the industry average of $485,500. He also earned almost $3 million in compensation.[xi] In his letter to the FBI, Gruttadauria said, "The various firms' greed and lack of attention on a senior level contributed greatly" to his committing the fraud and "I hardly believe that I could have done this without detection for so long."[xii]

Defrauded investors also felt that Gruttadauria was not the only one to blame for the fraud. They blamed the brokerage firms that employed Gruttadauria for not doing enough to detect and stop the fraud. Greater attention to internal controls, compliance, and fraud prevention programs may have caught this fraud earlier. Gruttadauria's free reign at the brokerage firms where he worked may have contributed to the fraud going undetected for so long. He created phony account statements, used post office boxes to send out client statements, and had a personal computer not connected to the company network, but no compliance programs ever detected this as possible fraud.

Defrauded investors sued Lehman Brothers and SG Cowen for the return of their defrauded investments. A prosecutor in Cuyahoga County, Ohio, threatened to hold Lehman Brothers and SG Cowen criminally liable under a theory of "willful blindness" for not discovering and stopping the fraud. As a result, Lehman Brothers and SG Cowen agreed in January 2004 to pay $1.74 million and $4.5 million, respectively, to the county prosecutor to settle the case and avoid criminal charges.[xiii] Both companies also settled civil proceedings with the SEC but did not admit to any wrongdoing. Lehman Brothers agreed to pay $2.5 million to the SEC, and SG Cowen agreed to pay $5 million.[xiv]

[vii]United States Securities and Exchange Commission, Plaintiff, v. Frank D. Gruttadauria, DH Strategic Partners Inc., JYM Trading Trust, United States District Court, Northern District of Ohio, filed February 21, 2002, 1:02CV324, 6.

[viii]United States v. Frank D. Gruttadauria, criminal complaint, United States District Court, Northern District of Ohio, January 2, 2002, 3.

[ix]Susanne Craig and Charles Gasparino, "Lehman's Gruttadauria Planned Run With Aliases, French Francs," *Wall Street Journal*, February 12, 2002, C8.

[x]Teresa Dixon Murray, John Caniglia, and Bill Lubinger, "Mr. Coffee Co-Founder, Forbes Lose Millions," *Cleveland Plain Dealer*, February 7, 2002, A1.

[xi]Charles Gasparino and Susanne Craig, "Disappearing Act: A Lehman Broker Vanishes, Leaving Losses and Questions," *Wall Street Journal*, February 8, 2002, A1.

[xii]Ibid.

[xiii]"Firms Agree to Pay for Broker's Fund," *Wall Street Journal*, January 8, 2004, C7.

[xiv]Ann Davis and Susanne Clark, "Cowen, Lehman Are to Settle Case of Broker's Fraud," *Wall Street Journal*, January 6, 2004, C6.

NOTES

1. Association of Certified Fraud Examiners, *2010 Report to the Nations on Occupational Fraud and Abuse* (Austin, TX: ACFE, 2010), 15.
2. Joseph T. Wells, *Occupational Fraud and Abuse* (Austin, TX: Obsidian Publishing, 1997), 159.
3. Frank Abagnale, *The Art of the Steal* (New York: Broadway Books, 2001), 57.
4. Nicole Gull, "Taking the Pain out of Payday," INC., January 2005, 36.
5. Association of Certified Fraud Examiners, *Fraud Examiners Manual*, (Austin, TX: ACFE, 2006), Section 1.530.
6. Jim Edwards, "Taken for a Ride," *Brandweek*, November 1, 2004, 24.

CHAPTER 8

Former Fraudster and New Man

EXECUTIVE SUMMARY

There is much to be learned when one hears from one who perpetrated a corporate fraud and paid the price with a prison term, personal and professional disgrace, but ultimately found redemption. Corporate fraudster Walt Pavlo, who "cooked the books" and in the process defrauded a company out of almost $6 million, believes that employees are basically good but get corrupted by the system. A mixture of temptation, greed, and opportunity turned him to the dark side, and he paid a heavy price. Fraud prevention and internal controls were almost nonexistent at Pavlo's former company, with many temporary employees and manual transactions. The tone at the top was "meet the numbers."

CONVERSATION WITH WALT PAVLO

Much of what has been discussed in this book involves the criminal actions of corporate fraudsters. When the fraud is discovered, some deny any wrongdoing and, as is their legal and constitutional right, fight the government charges in court. Others take responsibility for their criminal acts, plead guilty, and face the consequences. The very act of admitting to oneself that the actions were wrong is but the first step in the redemption process.

Walt Pavlo is an example of such a person. He was a senior manager of credit and collections for telecom giant MCI in the mid-1990s before the company was bought by WorldCom. Pavlo directed the billing and collections process in their reseller division. His division was having a hard time collecting fees from resellers, but Pavlo came up with a devious approach to the problem. He turned to "cooking the books" and between April 1996 and January 1997, he and others defrauded MCI of almost $6 million.

When the company became aware of the fraud, it launched an internal investigation that eventually involved the FBI and the IRS. As the pressure increased to a near breaking point, Pavlo turned himself in to the FBI and admitted his crimes. He pled guilty to wire fraud, money laundering, and obstruction of justice and received a nearly three-and-a-half-year prison term in March 2001. He completed a drug and alcohol abuse program while in prison that reduced his sentence, as did good behavior. He was subsequently transferred to a half-way house for six months and was released in March 2003. Pavlo now travels the country lecturing at major university business schools, professional societies, corporations, and law enforcement agencies concerning the mistakes he made in his business career.

After graduating from West Virginia University in 1985, where he received an engineering degree, Pavlo joined Goodyear Aerospace as an estimator in its military defense division. There he designed and implemented computer estimating systems for complex military contracts. He left Goodyear in 1988 to work at GEC Avionics, Ltd. Pavlo was a senior contract administrator responsible for pricing and negotiations for military avionics equipment sold to countries around the world. While working at GEC Avionics, Pavlo completed an executive MBA program at Mercer University. After graduation in 1991, he began searching for a job more suited to his new degree in finance and accepted employment at MCI Telecommunications,

Inc. in Atlanta, Georgia. He was given the title of manager of credit and collections and within three years was named senior manager of a $1 billion per month portfolio of clients. These clients represented wholesale carrier customers that bought long distance from MCI and resold it under their own brand name. Some of the clients were household names like Sprint and AT&T; many others were start-up long distance companies in the new world of deregulation.

When Pavlo was asked by the authors to submit to an interview for this book, he readily agreed and replied, "I truly appreciate the opportunity to express my opinions on the important subject of white-collar crime and its negative impacts to society, the victims, the convicted felon, and his/her family." The words in this interview are Pavlo's and whether one agrees with him, he provides much to think about.

Q: Explain the fraud scheme you were involved in.

A: A number of customers in MCI's reseller division began to default on payments during 1995. Frustrated by the fact that everybody (resellers of long distance service) seemed to be cheating, a person outside the company and I developed a scheme to enrich ourselves.

I would apply pressure to MCI's customers to pay up or be disconnected. I would institute a deadline with the customer that, if violated, would result in disconnection of service. The customer would then start a desperate search for funds to meet the demand for payment. These amounts were often in the millions of dollars. With what seemed like a stroke of good luck, my accomplice would show up at the MCI customer's doorstep within a day or two and portray himself as an investor looking to purchase telecommunications companies. The timing could not have been better.

My accomplice would send in accountants to scour the customer's finances. In the end, the angel investor would recommend that he pay off the debt to MCI for the customer so that they could begin their financial relationship. In return for paying off this debt, the angel investor would require a substantial fee, usually about $250,000, for putting the investment together and aggressive repayment of the loan amount in weekly payments to Cayman Island accounts.

The customer, desperate for money, quickly accepted. However, no money was ever sent by the angel investor to pay off the debt owed to MCI. Instead, I cooked the books at MCI to give the customer the impression that the outstanding balances had been paid by the angel investor. The customer believed the debt had been paid and began sending money to the Caymans. My accomplice and I did this with seven MCI customers and had $6 million in the Caymans within six months.

Q: **Were there internal controls in place that should have prevented your fraud?**

A: The biggest reason that my crime was not detected earlier is the simple fact that nobody questions good news. MCI had a number of customers that were not paying their invoices, so whenever I had a customer that suddenly paid $2 million as a result of my scheme, it was good news that nobody questioned. Everyone wanted to believe in the good news. My bosses believed, the internal auditors believed, and the customers even believed that an angel investor could come up with a few million dollars in a matter of days to pay off its debt to MCI. Good news is rarely criticized and rarely investigated. Had my bosses or an internal audit group asked me a simple question, Where's the check? I could not have provided one and was not prepared to invent one.

Q: **How did the internal controls at MCI break down to allow you and your co-conspirators to commit this fraud for so many months without detection?**

A: The first area of breakdown was the lack of control we had over temporary contractors. Of the 120 people in the department, nearly 50 percent were temporary contractors performing full-time roles for MCI. MCI, like many fast-growing companies, hired temporary help to not only meet demand for increases in work load but to also reduce costs associated with the overhead of full-time, permanent employees. In this environment, turnover of employees exceeded 100 percent each year. With new employees came challenges of controlling passwords, training, and still having to meet the month-end results with whatever staff was available. The results were that passwords were routinely shared between employees, training was on the fly, and naïve staffers could be shown any transaction and would ask few questions about the legitimacy of the transaction.

There were also multiple billing platforms at MCI as a result of acquisitions over the years. This was common among many long distance carriers who consolidated with mergers and acquisitions in the late 1990s. To accommodate these different billing platforms, revenue was combined from them onto a personal computer. On a personal computer, an analyst would calculate the contractual rates and then manually post the appropriate credits, or debits, back to the main accounts receivable system. For some companies this may be manageable, but at MCI we had tens of millions of dollars each month that were being credited off of accounts by manual billing systems. Many companies face the challenge of auditing off-line billing systems to accommodate special pricing situations, and most use a manual database or spreadsheet program to accomplish their desired goal. There were just very few checks on the manual billing systems, and there were also major holes in the audit controls as a result.

If one were to combine high employee turnover, loose audit controls, and aggressive financial goals for the department, it may create a unique situation in which fraud could occur. While the conditions of loose controls was convenient to get the work of our staff in a quick, and seemingly efficient manner, it created a growing opportunity to commit fraud later even though we were not aware of it at the beginning. MCI's goals for collections were very aggressive and measured in the amounts of bad debt written off each month as well as Days Sales Outstanding (days between invoice being sent to customer and invoice being paid). These absolute goals were measured, but the means by which they were attained were governed by weak internal controls. As was mentioned earlier, many of the staff were contractors, and they knew that the best way to get hired was to do a good job. A good job was measured in minimal amounts of bad debt and Days Sales Outstanding. This mentality was not unique to temporary employees but was merely a reflection of management and executives over them.

Q: Did MCI have a formal fraud prevention program in place? If not, would that have made a difference?

A: I assume that MCI had a fraud prevention program in place though I never heard of it. Being a Fortune 100 company, I would think that such a program was in place, but I had never attended a class on the program nor received any indoctrination on a fraud prevention or ethics program.

It is hard to say whether it would have made a difference in my crime or not. I think having a program would have been important, but if there was management that was more concerned with the result rather than the means of obtaining the result, I am not sure that any fraud prevention program would ever prevail in such an environment. With that said, the best fraud prevention is having management that is engaged and asks questions that provide clear answers as to how objectives are being met. The lack of questioning by management provides a veil of secrecy under which individual decisions are made without management input.

Q: **Can you explain your thoughts about the importance of appropriate internal controls and robust fraud prevention programs?**

A: Many who get involved in white-collar crime represent first-time offenders who were in a position of responsibility and abused it. Had the person known that the controls in place within the company would have detected his or her behavior, they most likely would not have attempted the crime. White-collar felons commit crimes because they do not believe they will get caught.

Management needs to understand that their staff is willing to do whatever it takes to meet the goals set. When those goals conflict with the reality that there may be no legitimate way to meet them, staff will search for solutions, even when those solutions include fraud. The desire to please senior management is great among the staff, and even more so when the staff is young and less experienced. This should not be misunderstood as saying management is responsible for all actions of staff, or the rogue employee, just realize that the desire to please is a real pressure that can affect good decision making.

Q: **If you had been in charge at MCI, knowing what you now know, what kind of internal controls and prevention efforts would you have installed?**

A: The first would be to split the responsibility of collections activity with accounts receivable management. Being in charge of both put me in a position where I was in charge of meeting collection goals while at the same time assuring those postings were accurate. When times got difficult, the more dominant goal of meeting the numbers trumped accuracy. After I left MCI, they split those responsibilities.

Audit should have concentrated on automation of billing systems and accounts receivable posting systems. The manual transactions that were being generated by over one hundred analysts were being manually audited by only a few. In this way the auditors were outnumbered and were never going to catch up. In this environment, finding a few million dollars in a pile of over a billion (MCI's monthly accounts receivable balance for the carrier division) is likened to the needle in the haystack.

Q: Our understanding is that you had never committed fraud before the crimes that you were charged with. What made you turn to fraud?

A: While I take full responsibility for my crime and have paid a significant price for it as well, I was frustrated by the unethical behavior of MCI's customers (resellers of long distance) and MCI executives who provided extreme performance measures for my department. In retrospect, it was my desire to try to please my management that drove me hard to provide results that were expected. For a while, even crossing the line to meet financial objectives made me feel better about my job as I hoped it would stop at some point. However, as time went on, and I did more and more financial transactions that were bogus that made me feel like I was being taken advantage of. That rationale pushed me further to act even more out of line.

At the height of my frustration, I met with someone who worked outside of MCI in order to look for a new job. However, when I told him of my frustration, the MCI customer behavior, and the creative bookkeeping that I was doing, he had an idea. After a number of meetings I was convinced that the only way to get ahead in telecommunications was to learn how to cheat. Clearly I was wrong, but the scorecard of now defunct telecommunications companies and exorbitant financial fraud in the industry illustrates the environment in which I found myself. Remember, my customers were the likes of Global Crossing, Winstar, Qwest, and WorldCom, all of whom went on to infamy for their creative business practices.

Q: **When you were doing the fraud, did you ever worry you would get caught?**

A: I worried but I did not feel that I would get caught. My own conscience was more of a problem than any internal controls. The ease with which we were able to move money internally at MCI to cover our fraud and the ease of convincing an MCI customer to go with the angel investor was remarkable. We stayed within the guidelines of our crime to keep the news good, and nobody would question how we were accomplishing what we did.

Having never committed a fraud before made for a new experience. It was exciting and not in a good way . . . exciting as in I want to throw up. Once the money started to flow, there were times that I felt that I deserved the money and the temporary excitement that it brought to my life. However, when I went to bed at night I found myself alone and felt sick at the person that I had become. Within eight months of committing the first act of fraud, I was near a nervous breakdown and could no longer function. I had not even been caught, but I wanted the madness of the crime to end.

Q: **Did a presence or absence of "tone at the top" at MCI impact what you did?**

A: MCI's tone was "meet the numbers." When numbers were met, there were few questions, accolades, and then quickly move to the next problem . . . then repeat. We were a fast-growing company and there was little time for reflection or to set a tone for anything other than "keep on going." Training and reflection of how business was being done was mostly left to the individual.

Q: **All the money that you embezzled did not make your life better. Can you explain your descent into despair?**

A: I think that many may view participation in a white-collar crime as it is portrayed in a John Grisham novel. However, clarity of thought and self-control are not normal for someone who is in the midst of a complex crime involving millions of dollars in offshore accounts. It is frightening. Purchases at expensive stores and travel did little to erase guilt and fear. Someone once had asked me why I did not flee the country once I was found out, as if running would solve this problem. I did not have the mental wherewithal to comprehend a life on some secluded island. Neither the crime nor the money did anything for me except destroy my ability to think clearly. After speaking with other white-collar offenders in prison, it was clear that none of us were prepared for the pressure of being involved in a crime. The pressure of the job itself was nothing compared to what I experienced during the diversion of funds from the company.

Q: Can you detail what went through your mind when you realized that the fraud had been discovered?

A: I was tired of running, so when I knew that they (the authorities) knew, it was a relief that I was not going to go on committing a crime that was driving me insane. Then I was sick at the thought of facing a punishment and being sought after for my actions. I don't want to sound like a coward, but I was frightened and not able to face the wrong that I had done or the associated punishment. More than anything, I started to realize the impact that this was going to have on my family (wife and two young kids). In the midst of all of my illegal activities I always was thinking about myself and how not to get caught. Then once caught, and looking beyond my own punishment, I saw my family as a victim. Anyone who has gone to prison will tell you that the real punishment is not prison, but the impact to the family. It's devastating.

Q: What was the hardest part about admitting your crimes, pleading guilty, and going to prison?

A: The hardest part, by far, is the impact that this has had on my family. While I prefer to not go into details, one can only imagine the pain shared by all when visiting someone that they love in prison. We have all made mistakes in our lives, but, thankfully, those who know of them are few. My mistake was most public and most tragic. Prison was easy if you knew you went by yourself. But the truth is that you take along a number of loved ones in the process, and lives are changed forever. I am two years out of prison as I write this now, and the sorrow that I feel in writing these lines is overwhelming. I can only hope that two years from now it will be better, but the impact of the prison experience on all of my family will never go away. In that way, I received a life sentence.

Q: When you were in prison, you met other corporate fraudsters. Was there anything that struck you from your interactions with them?

A: I only hung out with the guys who could face their own failures and understood why they were in prison. There were a number of inmates who could not come to grips with their actions and felt that they were wrongly incarcerated. I had no time for these guys. However, I met with a few guys who genuinely regretted their actions and were trying, even in prison, to begin their recovery. We prayed together, cried together, provided each other support, and discussed current events. I was in prison while Enron, World-Com, and the rest of the large corporate frauds were being uncovered, and it made for great talk around the dinner table. We did not condone the behavior of those involved, but we all certainly understood the pressure that may have led to their undoing.

Q: How would you characterize prison life?

A: The media has done an injustice to society by portraying prison for white-collar felons as a type of club fed, where there are swimming pools, golf courses, conjugal visits, and a life of relaxation. Nothing could be further from the truth. White-collar felons are housed with general population inmates in the same conditions. In the facility where I was located, Edgefield, South Carolina, there were roughly 500 inmates, and about 50 of those were white-collar offenders. The others were primarily drug offenders and counterfeiters who had either short sentences or had worked their way down through the prison system to end up in a prison camp with minimum security.

It is a difficult existence of missing home, family, and freedom. There is not one day from the prison experience that I would call a good day. They were all lonely and miserable, but somehow you learn to cope and survive. To do this, you must live a life that keeps you out of trouble, so I found comfort in writing, books, and meditation.

I hated prison, which is exactly what you are supposed to do. It is an unkind place with no love and none of the conveniences that make life worth living. Prison is meant as a punishment, and the media needs to get that fact out to the public, but that doesn't make for a good story.

Q: You committed your fraud scheme in the years before the enactment of Sarbanes-Oxley. Would it have stopped you?

A: I think that the unique thing about Sarbanes-Oxley is that it makes everyone responsible for ethical behavior. In the past, executives ignored unethical or illegal activities but no longer. Executives' treatment of offenders within the company is just as important as their own offenses. There is a punishment now if the watcher doesn't watch or react to violations. The chances of being caught for unethical behavior in this type of environment are very high, and with that the chances of testing the financial systems of the company would have been reduced. Would it have stopped me? I would like to think so, but even if it had not stopped me, it would have caught me sooner. With that said, I do not know if we can legislate our way as a country to act ethically all the time. In the end, good, engaged management will deter fraud better than any new reporting legislation.

Q: Do you think that Sarbanes-Oxley's increased criminal penalties for fraud acts as a deterrent?

A: I don't think that increased prison sentences are the answer. While I do believe that prison is a punishment and can be effective in changing behavior, especially for white-collar criminals, there is no need for these long sentences. I think the answer lies in the area of addressing economic crimes with economic solutions. White-collar criminals should have their assets taken away. My approach would be that they would give up ALL of their assets and start life over again after a few years reflecting on their actions. The government allows a person to go to prison with millions still in the bank. It is a reflection that money is more important than a human life and that seems excessive for a society that values life as we do in America. For the record, I went into prison with no assets and came out the same way. My life is much different today with few material things, and it will remain that way. Keeping a low overhead (costs) has freed me from some of the pressures I had once put on myself.

If prison sentences alone deterred crime, we would not need the procedures that are a part of the Sarbanes-Oxley legislation. Sarbanes-Oxley will not eliminate white-collar crime, but it does raise the bar for internal controls and oversight. Both of these should lead to an executive considering that the likelihood of being caught is high and therefore not worth the risk.

Sarbanes-Oxley and various internal controls should be viewed as a way to protect employees as much as they protect shareholders. Employees are constantly under pressure both professionally and personally. Under these pressures, employees must be provided a safe and ethical environment in which to work where temptations are limited and they can concentrate on the issues at hand. An unethical or loosely managed organization may provide what seems like an easy solution to the employee's problems or a quick way to feed the ego. Such an environment, I believe, can turn a good employee into a fraudster. I've seen it happen.

Q: **What message would you send to corporate executives and others in business to convince them to never commit fraud?**

A: Just as your family enjoys the riches associated with good and ethical decisions that you make, so they will also share in the pain of your unethical decisions. Many times those involved in white-collar crimes were thinking that their actions would only impact themselves, but this is far from the truth. It affects family, coworkers, subordinates, superiors (and we all have superiors, even CEOs), and friends. In the isolation of making a decision that may be unethical, let the pictures on your desk speak to you. How will your decision affect their lives? Will you sacrifice your integrity to meet financial goals at work? Would you do something that would also punish your family?

Q: **You are now a speaker on corporate fraud and conduct numerous presentations all over the world. How do audiences react to you when they learn what you did?**

A: I have never considered myself an expert on anything other than my own crime. I truly respect the many professionals that I have met over my years of speaking, and I do not pretend to be something I am not. Even in this exchange here, I answer based on my own perspectives from my own experience. This approach not only made me a better speaker, but gave me credibility with audiences. Audiences that I address want to hear a story that makes them smarter than before they came.

What is most important for me to get across to audiences is that I view them as victims of my crime. In some ways my crime represented greed and the loss of trust in our financial markets. As victims, the audience deserves to hear these four things from me:

1. I'm sorry and deeply regret what I have done and the people that I have hurt.
2. I understand my crime and have learned from it.
3. I was punished and suffered dire consequences for my crime.
4. I have found a way to give back to society through lecturing and sharing my story.

In this way the audience can see that the justice system works. This is something that I think the media misses in its coverage of the high-profile cases where there seems to be no real punishment.

CHAPTER 9

External Schemes and Scams

The Rest of the Fraud Story

EXECUTIVE SUMMARY

To be fully protected, companies need to be concerned with more than just internal fraud schemes such as financial statement fraud and asset misappropriation. They can just as easily be victimized by external frauds such as the Ponzi and Bust-Out schemes. Credit card fraud is also a common fraud affecting consumers and companies. The losses from credit card fraud can be substantial. The potential impact from online frauds can damage both a business and its relationship of trust with its customers. Corporate fraud solutions must include proactive measures to be fully protected. The Address Verification Service (AVS) and Card Security Value (CSV), also called the Card Security Number (CSN), Cardholder Verification Value (CVV), or Card Security Code (CSC), are tools to prevent credit card fraud. These and other detection and prevention solutions must be used for a successful online fraud prevention program.

PONZI SCHEME

Charles Ponzi came to America from Italy in the early 20th century to pursue the American dream. By 1920, Ponzi convinced many victims in Boston to invest in his "too good to be true" investment deal. It was a "robbing Peter to pay Paul" scheme. Using the money of new investors to pay high rates of return to the early investors, Ponzi soon got plenty of word-of-mouth. Many of those who received 50 percent returns on their initial investments reinvested them with Ponzi. Soon, Ponzi was receiving hundreds of thousands of dollars per day from investors. Ponzi took in over $20 million and paid out $15 million in interest, spending the remaining $5 million on himself and his wife.

Authorities shut down the scheme and sent Ponzi to prison for 10 years. He died penniless in Brazil in 1949. Today, any fraudulent investment scheme that pays returns to the early investors with the money of later investors is called a Ponzi scheme. Unfortunately, we have not learned from the past as Ponzi schemes are still commonplace.

MADOFF FRAUD

One consequence of the 2008 financial crisis was how many Ponzi schemes it unearthed. Investors pulled out money from these schemes to cover market losses and other expenses and as a result, many of them collapsed, often in spectacular fashion. The victims varied wildly, as did the perpetrators, from PTA mothers[1] to a Park Avenue law firm[2] to a college football coach.[3]

Of course, one scam stood well above all others. That was the Madoff Ponzi fraud. A multibillion dollar scheme came to light in December 2008, but it received scant media attention at the time or afterward, and had to settle for being considered the second-largest such scheme of all time.[4] It could not compete with Bernard L. Madoff and Bernard L. Madoff Investment Services (BLMIS). Few could. Wall Street considered Madoff a giant in the industry, one of the innovators of electronic trading, and a former chairman of NASDAQ. He could achieve results for his investors that no one else could. Of course, the reason that no one else could replicate his results, or figure out how he achieved them, was that his financial empire rested entirely on lies.

In many ways, the scheme Bernie Madoff ran is the epitome of what Ponzi did. In short, it was the ultimate Ponzi scheme. It took all the elements that led to a successful con and perfected them. Madoff's genius lay in two things: the perceived exclusivity of his investment fund and the consistency of his returns. Yet, the scheme was simultaneously expansive and exclusive, offering modest returns and gargantuan ones. In total, the fraud caused unprecedented losses.

The Scheme

In terms of size, Madoff ranks as the largest Ponzi scheme. Investors lost a cash amount of nearly $20 million, with losses of approximately $65 million on paper. Several thousand people invested directly with Madoff, plus thousands more invested in "feeder funds," which routed money to Madoff, oftentimes without investors even being aware of it. Thousands lost their life savings, forcing them to sell their homes or borrow heavily from other family, who all too often suffered their own Madoff losses.

This was an affinity fraud. Madoff exploited the bonds of his social group to continually manipulate victims and acquire new funding. He was a pillar of the New York Jewish community, heavily involved in charities and considered an investment wizard from his success on Wall Street; victims trusted him completely. Even those who questioned his success and the improbability of his consistent returns thought Madoff was trustworthy and did not speak out against him.

He would often reject potential investors several times, before finally letting them in. It was perceived at the outset of the collapse, that the victims were millionaires and well-to-do. In fact, many ordinary people invested their life savings with him, often pooling their money with family and friends to reach minimum investments amounts, thus further magnifying the harm.

Madoff wanted to keep the number of BLMIS investors as small as possible, both to maintain his image and to minimize the fake account statements he would have to prepare for his purported investors. This should have been a red flag, as it is unusual for a hedge fund like BLMIS to turn away investments. However, even as he turned business away, he actively recruited new investments from funds across the world, from Europe to the Middle East. This brought him the much-needed capital without any of the pesky need for individual record-keeping.

The consistency of his returns should also have been a major red flag for investors. How could he maintain the same 10 to 15 percent rate of return through the bursting of the tech bubble, the market crash after September 11, and so forth? No matter the economic circumstances, "Bernie" was solid. The mindset of investors was to trade the potential for higher returns elsewhere for the safety and security of BLMIS. Or so they thought.

Paradoxically, his fraud did very well in down years. Investors saw his investments as a safe haven from other market turmoil. When the market did well, he was in trouble, as he couldn't replicate the high rates of return legitimate brokerages could, and people would shift their investments elsewhere. Many of his core investors were elderly, and thus were the type of people who would invest large amounts then slowly withdraw them. At the same time, Madoff offered very high rates of return to prominent clients, who would often help to recruit other elite investors.[5]

The Legacy

Since Madoff's conviction and 150-year prison sentence, prosecutors have charged a handful of employees, with two of his lieutenants pleading guilty. This fraud's legacy may very well be that in the future they won't call it a Ponzi scheme but a *Madoff scheme*.

The court-appointed trustee, Irving Picard, of the law firm Baker Hostetler, is the person charged with fully unraveling this mess and pursing stolen assets to return to Madoff's victims. As of this writing, Picard and his team have recovered close to $10 billion. They are seeking tens of billions more from banks and other financiers who they alleged facilitated and benefited from the scheme, on top of hundreds of millions in "clawback" proceedings, to recover false profits paid to various investors, in excess of their actual investments.[6] They have begun to distribute these proceeds to the victims, but this highly contentious litigation looks to continue for many more years before it will be resolved.

BUST-OUT SCAM

A *bust-out* refers to a fraud committed by a subject who establishes a pattern of prompt payment on small orders. After several small orders have been transacted with no problems, the mark is no longer suspicious. At this point, the large order is made. When the goods are delivered, the customer does not pay for the goods and moves away. This can also be done in reverse, with the subject being a supplier of goods. In these situations, the supplier offers a very good price but requires payment prior to delivery. After several small orders, the victim company gets comfortable with the idea that the supplier is legitimate. As soon as a large order is placed, the supplier takes the money and runs.

EXECUTIVE INSIGHT 9.1: WENDY'S "FINGER HOAX" PROVES COSTLY

External fraud schemes can impact an organization in a number of ways. The financial loss can pale in comparison with the reputational damage that occurs when fraud crosses the line and becomes a corporate and public relations nightmare. One example is the product tampering that Wendy's International, Inc. faced in 2005. Wendy's is one of the world's largest restaurant operating and franchising companies. Their brand loyalty and reputation for quality food has been a mainstay of their success over the years, yet an incident on March 22, 2005, brought all that success into question.

A woman dining at a San Jose, California, Wendy's restaurant claimed that she found a severed finger in a bowl of chili she had just purchased. The woman was repulsed by the experience. She hired an attorney, who promptly filed a claim against Wendy's and threatened a damaging lawsuit. The story made national headlines and focused on Wendy's food-handling practices. The incident spawned jokes from late-night talk show hosts and others. Negative publicity was having an impact. Fewer customers ate at Wendy's. Sales for the first quarter of 2005 fell $1.5 million, in part because of the woman's claim that she found a severed finger in her food. The western region of Wendy's was hit the hardest, with the largest decrease in same-store sales.[i]

Wendy's is to be applauded for what it did next. Rather than caving in and paying out millions of dollars just to make the troubling affair go away, Wendy's quickly started an internal investigation to learn the facts. It teamed with law enforcement officials in San Jose and elsewhere. Every restaurant employee was interviewed, as were food suppliers. A massive search was conducted for anyone who had lost a finger and who could have been the source. On April 7, 2005, Wendy's posted a $50,000 reward on their Web site "for the first person providing verifiable information leading to the positive identification of the origin of the foreign object found" at their San Jose restaurant. Wendy's President and Chief Operating Officer stated, "It's very important to our company to find out the truth in this incident."[ii] He also said, "Our brand reputation has been affected nationally." Wendy's then doubled the reward to $100,000, ran newspaper ads communicating the reward, and listed a toll-free information hotline for tips.[iii]

Authorities conducted an innovative "Ingredient Trace Back" investigation to determine whether "the finger specimen came from the production, transportation, and/or preparation of the Wendy's chili." The analysis found no evidence connecting the finger to the chili. The police were also able to disprove certain statements made by the woman. A search warrant was conducted at her residence. In addition, the police learned that the woman had a history of filing "nuisance" suits against corporations, and an unrelated criminal allegation surfaced. On April 21, 2005, the woman was arrested and charged with attempted grand theft.[iv]

As the police continued their investigation, they learned that the finger fragment allegedly in the chili was actually lost in an industrial accident by a friend of the woman's husband. The friend gave the severed finger to the woman's husband after the accident. Wendy's had always believed the woman's story was a hoax, and the investigation vindicated the company. On September 9, 2005, the woman and her husband pled guilty to the scheme to extort money from Wendy's. The woman was sentenced to nine years in prison but only served four years. Her husband was sentenced to 12 years in prison. As Wendy's president publicly stated at the time, "We strongly defended our brand and paid a severe price."[v]

Wendy's crisis management program stopped what may have started out as an attempt to defraud the company that could have done far worse damage. Although it is rare for a company to do what Wendy's did in this case, it is a testament to its integrity and strength as a good corporate citizen. It conducted a thorough internal investigation, teamed with law enforcement authorities, and took a very public stance that its products and reputation were beyond reproach. Wendy's approach to this incident should be a roadmap for every organization facing a similar event.

---

[i]"Chili Finger Hurt Wendy's Profit," *CNNMoney*, April 28, 2005, money.cnn.com/2005/04/28/news/midcaps/wendys/index.htm.

[ii]Wendy's International, "Wendy's Offers $50,000 Reward for Information in San Jose Incident," Wendy's Press Release (April 7, 2005).

[iii]Wendy's International, "Wendy's President Comments on San Jose Incident," Wendy's Press Release (April 15, 2005).

[iv]San Jose Police Department Press Release (April 22, 2005).

[v]"The Jig Is Up: Wendy's Finger-in-Chili Case Develops; Digit Belongs to Associate of Accuser's Husband," *MSNBC.com*, May 13, 2005, www.msnbc.msn.com/id/7844274.

CREDIT CARD FRAUD

Credit card fraud continues to be an impactful crime for consumers and businesses. It encompasses several different aspects:

- **Stolen Cards:** The card itself has been physically taken from the cardholder and used before it is reported stolen by the cardholder and deactivated by the credit card issuer.
- **Credit Card Identity Fraud:** The card is not stolen, but the card information is obtained through various methods (see the section Obtaining Credit Card Numbers below) and used by a fraudster to order items online or through the mail. However, clever fraudsters have learned that they have a better chance of successfully

completing the fraud if they use the real billing address of the cardholder and a different "ship to" address.

- **Random Number Generators:** Software programs guess card numbers that are valid. Only valid credit card numbers will work, as virtually all credit card order systems screen out credit card numbers that have not actually been assigned. The fraudster then places large numbers of orders, each with a different credit card number. Merchants using "velocity" tables easily catch multiple orders on the same credit card number. Velocity tables look for multiple orders to one address in a short period.

- **The False Credit or Return Scam:** This is an internal credit card fraud. Customer service is important to all companies. When a customer is not happy, the policy of the company is usually to try to make things right. This often means refunding the money to the customer. Dishonest employees can enter a bogus refund into the system even though no merchandise was returned. Because there is no real customer asking for a credit, the employee credits the refund to his or her own credit card. Credit card refunds should be analyzed periodically to look for multiple refunds to the same credit card number or an unusual number of credits processed by the same employee.

Obtaining Credit Card Numbers

Credit card fraudsters can obtain valid numbers in a variety of ways. One way is to buy these numbers from a "credit doctor." A credit doctor is well known in the criminal community as someone who can get stolen credit card numbers for those who are unable to get their own credit cards. The standard rates for purchasing stolen credit card data (a valid number and expiration date) vary from forty cents to $20 per card. There are those who offer numbers for much less, but these are sucker numbers, which have already been fraudulently used. Those who purchase and use the sucker numbers are much more likely to be caught by authorities, since the cardholder will already have reported fraud on the card. Devious fraudsters use cards for themselves and then sell them to secondary fraudsters. These secondary fraudsters then become the targets of investigators, taking the heat off the first fraudster.

A way that fraudsters obtain "good" numbers is to bribe hotel desk clerks, call center agents, and gas station attendants. Organized credit card gangs actually send people to apply for these jobs for the sole purpose of obtaining as many credit card numbers as possible.

Credit Card Risk

Any company that uses the Internet or telephones to take orders relies on credit card transactions, but these "card not present" transactions are risky. They require only a valid credit card number, the expiration date, and the name and address of the cardholder. The majority of all credit card transactions are in-person transactions, but a larger percentage of online credit card transactions are fraudulent. It has been estimated that 28 percent of online retail orders are fraud attempts.[7]

Although credit card companies have consistently maintained that credit card fraud is no more prevalent online than in traditional forms of commerce, a number of experts are disputing the notion. One estimate by Alvin Cameron of Digital River, says that as many as 40 percent of online purchases are fraud attempts. Accordingly, Cameron says, e-tailers are now facing a do-or-die proposition: merchants who cannot control the flood of fraudulent purchase attempts will soon be out of business. According to Cameron, doing business on the Internet is the equivalent of having someone walk into a store wearing a ski mask without any identification and offering a bank counter check to purchase a $2,000 stereo system. Whereas no bricks-and-mortar store would make such sale, Internet merchants do it all the time.[8]

Contrary to popular belief, it is the merchant, not the consumer, who has the most to lose from credit card fraud. Federal laws limit consumer liability to $50 for fraudulent use of a stolen credit card but in reality consumers are never assessed that penalty. Since bricks-and-mortar shop merchants employ card readers, which require the actual card to be present, and a signature, the credit card company absorbs any fraud losses. Internet and shop-by-phone merchants have no such protection. The credit card company accepts no responsibility for fraudulent transactions. The credit card company reimburses the cardholder for unauthorized purchases and deducts the amount from the merchant's credit card account. A fee is added, usually $15 per transaction. This process is called a *chargeback*.

Credit card companies like MasterCard also impose fines on merchants if chargeback orders make up 1 percent or more of total dollar sales transactions, or 2.5 percent or higher of the total number of sales for more than two consecutive months. These rules could well force smaller e-tailers off the Web. However, many observers believe that MasterCard is merely trying to punish those merchants, which it sees as having lax credit card authorization policies.

Online merchants have been forced to develop sophisticated security protections that go far beyond the normal security approval process by the credit card companies. Customers have become accustomed to being able to bill the order to one address and ship the goods to another address. This is the weakness that credit card fraudsters exploit.

Credit card fraudsters make an order as the cardholder, entering the cardholder's name and address in the "bill to" field. They then put a temporary address in the "ship to" field. By the time the charge appears on the cardholder's bill, the orders have already been received and the fraudster is gone. Not all fraudsters use temporary addresses. Some cocky fraudsters have been known to use the same address for years to receive orders. Therefore, companies have to protect themselves by tracking addresses used to receive fraudulent orders. Denial tables (lists of known fraud addresses) can prevent subsequent orders from being shipped to a known fraud address. Denial tables are used to screen for any new orders to known fraud addresses. These denial tables should never try to match by the name of the customer, as false names are almost always used and are changed often. Fraudsters also have been known to alter the last digit in the delivery ZIP Code to defeat denial tables. The local post office or the private delivery carrier will often correct the last digit.

A clever form of mail order credit card fraud has emerged thanks to eBay. Fraudsters can list an item for auction on eBay before the fraudster even has the item. When the winning bidder is determined, the fraudster orders the item using a stolen credit card number. If the stolen credit card is from John Smith in New York, that address is entered in the billing address; however, the winning bidder's home address is entered as the "ship to" address. This is why many mail order businesses will not ship to any address other than the billing address of record for the credit card being used.

Reshipping Scams

Beginning in 2003, many Internet vendors saw a steady increase in the number of fraud attempts. Much of the increase in credit card fraud on the Internet can be directly attributed to a credit card scam started in Nigeria known as the *forwarder scam* or the *reshipping scam*.

Professional fraudsters surf Internet chat rooms looking for young marks. They give the young victim a story of how unfair the trade tariffs are in Africa on computer items. They ask the victim to accept orders from several merchants at the victim's home, and they ask the victim to forward the items to an address in Lagos, Nigeria, or elsewhere. They offer to pay the forwarder $100 per package (which would be more than any tariff). The naïve victim agrees and begins to receive packages. All orders are on a different stolen credit card for an amount that is usually less than $500.00. This popular amount is frequently used as a limit for fraud screening on orders in the industry. Of course, the victim never gets paid for forwarding the goods.

Some victims have decided just to keep all the merchandise, which sometimes results in death threats over the telephone. The typical victim of the scam is a male between the ages of 15 and 24, and the fraudsters often pose as young women. Some have even sent a photo of a pretty young blonde, who is supposed to be the person with whom the mark is communicating. Police all over the United States have been finding these mail drop forwarders who have been duped into forwarding stolen merchandise. The more advanced scammers use accomplices in the United States who rent warehouse space to use as a staging area for sending stolen goods overseas. Many such warehouses have been raided in Atlanta, Houston, Miami, and other cities, and authorities have found computer equipment and office supplies stacked to the ceiling, all bound for Nigeria, or sometimes Russia, Ghana, or the Ukraine.

The U.S. Postal Inspection Service organized a national initiative on this particular fraud. They interviewed over 700 victims of the reshipping scam who had fallen for "work from home" ads on various Web sites for positions such as "home warehouse expeditor." One gentleman in a retirement community thought he was assisting "a nice girl from London who is starting a business in Nigeria." He had paid to ship more than 70 boxes to Nigeria. The scam is still going strong because it works. Fraudsters like high-tech items but also go for clothing and shoes, which they can sell quickly on the street.

TOOLS TO STOP ONLINE FRAUD

Many companies use a "denied party list" to stop mail order fraud. If a fraud is discovered, the address is blocked to prevent any future orders. Although it is a good tool, a denied party list is not an effective protection against fraud by itself. There are too many ways for a fraudster to create address variations for a company to use denied party lists as the sole strategy to prevent mail order fraud.

The use of denied party lists along with velocity screening, Address Verification System (AVS) code blocking, and Card Security Value (CSV) can greatly reduce fraud losses.

Velocity

Velocity refers to the number of orders to one address in a short period. The order management system should be set to flag addresses that have more than three orders per week. Forwarder scams usually employ the same address for a short period but use different credit card numbers. Most of the time, the billing address is not the one on file with the credit card company. Velocity checks will be discussed again later in this chapter.

AVS

An *address verification system* (AVS) involves an authorization to compare the address provided by the online customer with the address of record for the credit card holder of that credit card number. There are three levels of address matching: (1) street number, (2) the first five digits of the ZIP Code, and (3) the extra four digits of the ZIP Code. The extra four digits of the ZIP Code are not widely used, so there are only two levels that should be addressed, street number and five-digit ZIP Code.

Credit card orders that have a customer-provided billing address that does not match the street number on the billing address on file with the credit card provider would result in a certain AVS code. These AVS codes identify whether the street address matches, if the ZIP Code matches, if both match, or if neither match.

Paymentech is an example of a middleman company that handles credit card payment verification for merchants using credit card merchant accounts. It generates AVS codes based on the information contained in online credit card transactions. Another credit card processing and risk management solutions company is CyberSource. Many companies are setting their preset address verification programs to automatically cancel orders that are returned from the address authorization process with I-8 type AVS codes. An I-8 AVS code means that neither the street address number nor the ZIP Code the customer has provided match the billing address of record for the credit card being used.

Customers whose orders are coded as I-8 are notified by an e-mail message saying that the billing address provided on their recent order does not match the address of record with the credit card provider. Real customers, who may have moved without officially notifying the credit card provider, will simply reorder using the proper address of record, the address to which their credit card statement is mailed. Fraudsters are defeated unless they have the billing address of the person whose credit card number they stole. AVS blocking will not stop the small minority of fraudsters who know the actual billing address for the credit card number they are trying to use. Of course, all the fraudster needs is a credit card statement intercepted from the mailbox.

Many fraudsters still use randomly generated credit card numbers, hoping for a match to a valid card. Again, only valid card numbers will work, as virtually every order management system screens out credit card numbers that have not been assigned to a cardholder. See Exhibit 9.1 for sample AVS codes.

EXHIBIT 9.1   Address Verification System (AVS) Codes

I-2	Address no match, but 9-digit Zip Code matches
I-4	Address no match, but 5-digit Zip Code matches
I-6	Address no match, first 5 digits of Zip Code no match
I-8	Address no match, no part of Zip Code matches

Orders with the proper billing street address will have an odd-numbered AVS code (I-1, I-3, I-5, I-7). System changes to cancel orders with I-8 AVS codes can save the company 10 percent of its total Internet business orders each year. There are too many innocent circumstances that generate codes I-2 or I-4 codes for these codes to be summarily blocked. For example, addresses that do not begin with a number, like One Rockefeller Plaza, will result in an I-4 code on many systems. This is because the whole address is not verified, only the numbers. If an address is 100 Main Street, Any Town, NY 10012, the AVS will see the address as 10010012. If it were typed as 100 High Street, Any Town, NY 10012, the AVS would see it as a matching 10010012. If the address does not have numbers (as in One Rockefeller Plaza), the number is an automatic no match. In short, order systems cannot be set to block all orders in which the street address does not match the AVS. At best, AVS stops fraudsters from using the credit cards of victims who live in different ZIP Codes. AVS is not an exact science. It is a tool that is best used in a system with other tools when one is developing a solid fraud prevention plan.

Fraudsters who have the proper billing address for the card number they are using will provide the correct billing address and get a valid AVS code and then enter a shipping address that is different from the billing address. This is an area in which company policy must come into play. Each company must decide whether to place limits on their customers' capability to send orders to addresses other than the one on their credit cards. The shortcomings of AVS were one of the reasons why the *card security value* (CSV) was created.

CSV

On a system using CSV, customers are prompted for the three-digit number on the back of a Visa or MasterCard or the four-digit number on the front of an American Express card. The small black numbers are located on the signature strip on the back of Visa and MasterCard. Supposedly, only a person with the card in hand can provide this number, as it is not allowed to be stored in any system. Companies have been found storing these codes in violation of payment card industry policy.

Many companies simply limit the dollar amount of an order that can be shipped to an address other than the billing address of record, or they call back the billing address to verify the order. Although this might be a grandparent sending birthday presents, it could be a fraudster looking to get free merchandise. The problem with call-back verification is that the callers often dial the billing phone number that was provided by the fraudster. The fraudster then verifies his own order. This is why CSV is becoming so popular.

Order screens that use CSV can be attacked by random number generators. The fraudster will use a computer to randomly attempt orders using every one of the 1,000 possible three-digit CSV codes. However, there are easier ways for the fraudster to steal than to try to defeat order systems protected by CSV. The most complete CSV protection includes a variable key word known as a CAPTCHA (Completely Automated Public Turing Test to Tell Computers and Humans Apart)[9] in a small picture on the order screen. The customer must read the key word and retype it. Since the word is a photo (not text) with lines, texture, and/or waves added, computers can't read it. This prevents automated order attempts, so the fraudster would actually have to type the 1,000 possible CSV codes by hand one at a time.

CSV requires an additional field on the order screen that must be included in the data sent to a credit card verification company (like Paymentech and CyberSource). Although CSV is the best protection, most fraudulent online credit card order attempts can be stopped with AVS. Fraudsters are looking for companies that do not yet use the strategy of blocking invalid AVS and CSV codes. That being said, it is still recommended that all companies taking credit card orders over the Internet use the CSV technology.

CyberSource sponsors an annual Online Fraud Report, which is conducted by Mindwave Research. This survey of online merchants shows which credit card prevention methods are being used by the industry and their increased or decreased usage[10] (Exhibit 9.2).

In 2010, one in four online orders was still subject to some type of manual review. The most common methods for reviewing orders was calling the customer (67 percent), or performing a reverse telephone look up on the phone number provided (63 percent). Thirty-six percent used geolocation.[11]

EXHIBIT 9.2   Credit Card Prevention Methods Usage By Year

Prevention Methods	2004[a]	2010[b]
CVS	56%	75%
AVS	82%	78%
Geolocation	31%	36%
Denial Report	45%	39%

[a]CyberSource 2005 Annual Online Fraud Report.
[b]CyberSource 2011 Annual Online Fraud Report.
Source: Cybersource, forms.cybersource.com/.

Geolocation

Geolocation identifies the origin of an order based on the Internet protocol (IP) address of the computer that generated the order. If an order is coming from an IP address in California, and the billing address of the credit card is in New York, there might be a problem. However, clever fraudsters can defeat geolocation by using anonymous proxy servers. Geolocation has not been very popular because it only works if the cardholder is using his or her home computer to place the order. This does not take into consideration business travel, college-aged children, or jet setters, who do not stay in one place all the time. As noted in Exhibit 9.2, the use of geolocation as a fraud preventative measure is increasing.

Multi-Merchant Purchase History

Credit card service providers like CyberSource build databases that track purchase behavior across multiple vendors and help merchants determine risk based on this information. For example, customers are tied to multiple credit card numbers, but might use a different credit card with each individual merchant. This service looks for common elements across multiple transactions to help identify fraud.

Purchase Device Fingerprinting

Similar to geolocation, purchase device fingerprinting gathers identifiers from the particular device being used to make the order. These identifiers are visible when the device communicates with the Web site and do not include any personal information about the user. In 2010, 13 percent of all online merchants were using this tool, but 30 percent of merchants with over $25 million in online revenue used device fingerprinting.

Data Mining: Digging for Credit Card Fraud

There are many companies that take orders by mail, by phone, and online and ship goods to their customers. Most orders involve customers using checks or credit card numbers. Sometimes, however, a problem arises with an order, and the customer deserves a free replacement. This is one of the most abused functions in a mail order business. Some companies do not require the customer to return the defective product in order to receive a new one. The companies' employees can send a free or "no charge" order to anyone, including themselves. A data mining operation would periodically query for any orders shipped "no charge" to any address in the same town as a company's order processing center. This is done by looking for orders with the same ZIP Code as the business. The "no charge" orders are then sorted by which employee processed the orders. This process will identify all orders shipped to employees, their friends, or relatives who live in the same town.

Another data mining function looks at addresses with multiple no charge orders or with multiple paid orders where the credit card number is not the same on all orders. A company would establish a set policy of how many "no charge" orders a customer can receive before being flagged as a fraud suspect. Future orders to suspects can be placed on hold. This is known as a *velocity check*.

Velocity tables look for multiple orders to one address in a short period. The order system should have preset rules that flag any customer who has ordered at least twice in the same week using a different credit card number on the orders. Fraudsters often try random credit card numbers in an attempt to obtain an order. Many rules engines are set to catch only more than one order in one day. Fraudsters have adapted to this and will often wait one day between orders. Many fraudsters also know that large dollar amounts are more likely to be verified prior to shipment. Therefore, they will try to place numerous small orders using different aliases. In most cases, however, the same address is used. Some fraudsters will attempt hundreds of orders in the hope that some will get through. They have all day to try to obtain free merchandise, because to them it is a full-time job. Simple rules engines created by an IT department to catch high-velocity order addresses can save thousands of dollars per day. If a company uses AVS and CSV, it can run velocity checks outside the order management system every week or so to screen for fraud that might have been missed by AVS and CSV.

Useful Tips

- Use CSV.
- Review credit card orders going to or coming from Eastern Europe, Africa, or the Middle East (including Israel), as there is a particularly high rate of credit card fraud originating from these areas.
- Do not allow customers to make last-minute alterations to their shipping addresses (after the AVS code has already been received).
- Deliver only to permanent addresses. Avoid shipping to hotels or mail drops.
- Consider calling to verify orders for high dollar amounts, but make sure the phone number area code matches the billing address of record. If the billing address is different from the shipping address, a company has no protection using AVS. It will lose any chargeback action by the cardholder.

NOTES

1. Andrew Blankstein, "PTA Moms Who Allegedly Ran Ponzi Scheme Charged with Multiple Felonies," *LAtimes.com*, July 6, 2011, latimesblogs.latimes.com/lanow/2011/07/prosectors-charge-reputed-pta-ponzi-scheme-moms-with-multiple-felonies.html.
2. Benjamin Weiser, "Lawyer Pleads Guilty in $400 million Fraud," *New York Times*, May 12, 2009, A23.

3. John Barr, "Jim Donnan Accused in Ponzi Scheme," *ESPN.com*, July 28, 2011, espn.go.com/espn/otl/story/_/id/6774323/jim-donnan-former-georgia-bulldog-coach-accused-ponzi-scheme.

4. Minnesota businessman Tom Petters ran a $3.65 billion scheme where he purported to buy high-end electronics to sell to retailers. *See* Annalyn Censky, "Tom Petters Gets 50 Years for Ponzi Scheme," *CNNMoney*, April 8, 2010, money.cnn.com/2010/04/08/news/economy/Tom_Petters.

5. A lawsuit filed by the Madoff trustee alleged that the late financier Jeffry Picower was one such client. Picower's widow reached a $7.2 billion settlement, stating that her husband was in no way complicit with the fraud but wanted to return the money to help Madoff's victims. *See* Diana B. Henriques, "Deal Recovers $7.2 Billion for Madoff Fraud Victims," *New York Times*, December 18, 2010, B5.

6. *See*, for example, "Trustee's Fifth Interim Report for the Period Ending March 31, 2011," *Bernard L. Madoff Investment Securities LLC Liquidation Proceeding*, May 16, 2011, madofftrustee.com/TrusteeReports.aspx.

7. Guneet S. Paintal, "Fraud Management in the Online Retail Environment," Infosys Technologies White Paper, July 2008, www.infosys.com/supply-chain/white-papers/Documents/fraud-management.pdf.

8. Stephen Caswell, "Credit Card Fraud Crippling Online Merchants," *E-Commerce Times*, March 20, 2000, www.ecommercetimes.com/story/2771.html.

9. Luis von Ahn, Manuel Blum, Nicholas Hopper, and John Langford of Carnegie Mellon University coined the acronym in 2000. See www.captcha.net.

10. CyberSource, *2011 Annual Online Fraud Report*, 12th ed., forms.cybersource.com/forms/FraudReport2011NAANETwww2011.

11. Ibid.

Not Too Big to Fail

EXECUTIVE SUMMARY

There has not been a universal name given to the financial crisis that occurred in 2007–2008. It has been referred to as "the Great Recession," "the financial crash of 2008," as well as "the TARP bailout," short for Troubled Asset Relief Program. David Wessel, in his book *In Fed We Trust*, calls it "the Great Panic." This seems to describe it quite well. To be clear, the Great Panic refers to the economic events that led to the collapse of Lehman Brothers, the fire sale of Bear Stearns and Merrill Lynch, the near collapse of American International Group (AIG), and the conversion of Morgan Stanley and Goldman Sachs from investment banks into bank holding companies under the greater influence of the Federal Reserve. Accepting Wessel's terminology, we analyze the perfect storm of events that created the Great Panic. There was no single cause, rather there were multiple, interrelated causes that converged:

- The government's visible hand influencing the invisible hand of the market, creating a "moral hazard" with "Too Big to Fail" policy
- Deregulation of the banking industry
- The rise of securitization of debt into investment vehicles and Collateralized Debt Obligations (CDOs)

- Questionable conflicts of interest at the ratings agencies, which rated CDOs and mortgage-backed securities
- The rise of subprime mortgages
- The housing bubble bursts and falling home prices
- Misaligned incentives in the bonus structures at the investment banks, which encouraged risky activity for short-term gains
- Fraud
- Poor risk management

All of these causes are addressed in the journey toward the answer to a question, which was initially raised back in 1993 by George Akerlof and Paul Romer from the University of California in a paper called "Looting: The Economic Underworld of Bankruptcy for Profit." Akerlof and Romer, Nobel Prize winners, theorized that bankruptcy for profit would occur if poor accounting, lax regulation, or low penalties for abuse give owners an incentive to pay themselves more than their firms are worth and then default on their debt obligations, especially if there was a precedent for the government to pick up the tab.[1] The question: Is this criminal activity, or just greed?

IN THE BEGINNING

A huge energy company had set up complex holding companies and investment securities that no one could understand. The company borrowed against future profits. As long as the stock price kept rising and there was available credit, everything was fine. However, like a Ponzi scheme, this was an unsustainable model. When stock prices eventually dropped, credit dried up and investors lost millions. The government stepped in to prosecute the leader of this company. Enron springs to mind, but the company referred to here is Commonwealth Edison, led by businessman and investor Samuel Insull. The government prosecuted Insull for mail fraud and antitrust violations after stock losses destroyed his company in 1932, but he was acquitted after trial.[2]

What investors were doing in the 1920s was betting on stocks to keep going up. They were so sure that stocks were going to keep rising that they borrowed money to buy more stocks. Banks were happy to lend the money, and loans were easy to get. Banks assumed that those buying stocks on margin could sell the stocks to repay the loan. (This only works when there is a buyer for the stock.) Companies like Commonwealth Edison were also borrowing money on the assumption that their stock price was going to continue to rise. When stock prices started to fall, investors wanted out. Companies like Insull's were left short of funds to pay their lenders. Credit dried up, causing stocks to drop further. Eventually, Insull could not pay all his investors.

This overenthusiasm for stocks, or stock market bubble, is a common occurrence. It happened with junk bonds in the late 1980s, tech stocks in the late 1990s, and home mortgages in 2008. This is not just a 20th and 21st century phenomenon; the Dutch tulip mania of the 1630s was another famous bubble. With capitalism and free markets there will always be those who believe unrealistically that they cannot lose.

In reaction to the stock market crash of 1929, and the failure of one out of every five banks, the Glass-Steagall or Banking Act of 1933 was passed.[3] The thinking was that interest rate competition had contributed to the bank failures. Banks paying higher interest rates took more risk to pay those higher rates.[4] Glass-Steagall not only created the Federal Deposit Insurance Corporation (FDIC), but it also prohibited a bank or a bank holding company from owning other financial companies. Commercial banks were separated from investment banks. Banks would be allowed to fail in an orderly fashion. Individual depositors at commercial banks would be protected, investors at financial firms and investment banks would not be. Capitalism would still function, but with a buffer.

TOO BIG TO FAIL POLICY BEGINS

In the early 1980s, an Oklahoma bank, Penn Square, was making loans to the oil industry. While these loans were risky, Penn Square did not really care. It was one of the first banks to make loans in order to sell them to investors. When the oil industry had a downturn, Penn

Square went out of business. One of the best customers for buying the loans of Penn Square was Continental Illinois National Bank and Trust. As the bank's losses became known, its stock price dropped and depositors with accounts over the then $100,000 FDIC limit for insurance withdrew their money out of fear of losing it.[5]

In an unprecedented attempt to stabilize the banking system and to save Continental Illinois, the Federal Reserve and the FDIC pledged that no depositor would lose a penny, not even bond holders.[6] This new policy became known as "Too Big to Fail" during Congressional hearings on the failure of Continental Illinois. The comptroller of the currency testified that the United States would not let the largest eleven banks in the country fail.[7]

THE COMMITTEE TO SAVE THE WORLD

On February 15, 1999, the cover of *Time* featured Alan Greenspan, Robert Rubin, and Larry Summers as the Committee to Save the World for the bailout of Long-Term Capital Management (LTCM). LTCM was a hedge fund that had borrowed to make bets on small differences in price models. Since the price differences were small, LTCM had to put down lots of money to make a significant profit. LTCM used leverage, borrowing much more than the amount of capital it had. If you leverage 10 times more than your capital, a 10 percent loss wipes you out. LTCM was leveraged at 100 to 1.[8]

Since LTCM had borrowed money from the 14 largest banks, those banks (with the exception of Bear Stearns) were willing to step in and loan an additional $3.65 billion to rescue LTCM in a Fed sponsored bailout.[9] This was much less painful than if the fund failed naturally, but it sent a dangerous message. It eliminated the lesson that risk brings reward, but excessive risk brings ruin. Too Big to Fail was reinforced along with its moral hazard.

MORAL HAZARD

Under certain conditions, a bank with government guarantees has a strong incentive to take on significant risk.[10] Too Big to Fail erodes the discipline of the market. Creditors are not worried about a bank being weak if it is guaranteed not to fail. A bank in financial trouble in the past would have to slow its activities due to lack of capital. That is no longer the case with government guarantees. The bank continues to take excessive risk and make poor use of the financial capital that it would not have otherwise have continued to receive.[11]

REGULATION SEEN AS RESTRICTING MODERNIZATION

In 1971, investment banks were permitted to be publicly traded on the New York Stock Exchange. This allowed a huge influx of capital for investment. The firms were no longer risking their own money. Depositors at commercial banks, where interest was capped, were also moving their money to investment banks for a better return.

With the merger and acquisition mania of the 1990s, banks lobbied for the right to get bigger. There were several attempts to repeal the Glass-Steagall Act. In 1998, Citibank merged with The Travelers Group to form Citigroup. This merger was in violation of the Glass-Steagall Act, but regulators gave the new company a two-year exemption.[12]

In 1999, the Gramm-Leach-Bliley Act repealed Glass-Steagall restrictions and allowed banks, brokerage firms, and insurance companies to merge into huge financial networks. Once banks were freed from New Deal regulations, they "snapped up" financial services companies and became more aggressive in their investment strategies, betting on real estate and stock markets.[13]

Democratic Senator Byron Dorgan of North Dakota was one of eight votes against the bill. He said, "I think we will look back in ten years' time and say we should not have done this because we forgot the lessons of the past."[14]

MORE DEREGULATION

The second big step on the road to deregulation of the financial services industry happened in 2000 with the passage of the Commodity Futures Modernization Act. This act (also sponsored by Senator Phil Gramm) was tacked onto an 11,000-page budget bill the day before

Christmas recess. The Commodity Futures Modernization Act took deregulation of the finance industry even further by freeing credit default swaps and other derivatives from state and federal regulation.[15] This would allow the eventual creation of *collateralized debt obligations* (CDOs) as investment vehicles made from subprime mortgages.

In 2004, in another loosening of restrictions, the SEC waived leverage limits for five firms: Bear Stearns, Merrill Lynch, Lehman Brothers, Morgan Stanley, and Goldman Sachs.[16] The leverage limits had required these firms to have capital on hand at the rate of $1 for every $12 leveraged. By 2007, Bear Stearns was leveraged up to 33 to 1, Merrill Lynch 32 to 1, and Lehman Brothers 29 to 1.[17] These three firms would cease to exist or be acquired, and the other two granted the leverage exemption would be forced to become bank holding companies, subject to the supervision of the Federal Reserve, in order to survive.

FORESHADOWING

It was Enron's lobbying for an exemption for trading energy derivatives that ultimately led to the Commodity Futures Modernization Act in 2000. Enron spent $3.45 million lobbying for the deregulation of energy futures.[18] It is interesting that Texas Senator Phil Gramm was a key sponsor of the bill that was so beneficial to Enron since his wife was a member of the Enron board at the time and owned Enron stock.[19]

In 1998, Enron promoted a new CFO, Andrew Fastow. He had already been working at Enron for some time, setting up its complex financial creations, building credit out of thin air and the illusion of prosperity. Fastow had come a long way from his first job out of college at Continental Illinois National Bank and Trust, where he learned securitization. Although he started at Continental Illinois after the bailout, it was still doing deals the likes of which no one had ever seen before."[20]

Continental Illinois, allowed to keep doing business when it should have failed, taught Fastow its risky practices. He took them to Enron, where financial tools were not used to support business, but used in place of real business. Enron's high-profile failure was a foreshadowing of the problems to come in the financial industry, which was using many of the same financial strategies that brought down Enron.

THE RISE OF SECURITIZATION

Securitization is the creation of securities or investments out of loans or debt. The loans that became the most popular to securitize were mortgages, creating mortgage backed securities. The idea was to spread ownership of individual mortgages to multiple owners. Many investors owned pieces of groups of mortgages. Securitization had been around a long time, but it was not being used aggressively. By 2002, a mortgage borrower's ability to repay the loan had taken a back seat to the lender's ability to sell the debt for securitization purposes.[21] Subprime loans were three to five times more profitable than any other type of loan to securitize.[22] The reason banks were willing to issue so many risky home loans was they could pawn them off on Wall Street.[23]

According to Yves Smith, "Deregulation led to structural changes in the financial services industry that not only made it less stable, but also predatory, fixated on its own profits rather than serving customers."[24] When Fed Chairman Alan Greenspan dropped interest rates to 1 percent, the result was that most bonds could not keep up with the rate of inflation. Investors wanted a way to get a better return, but still have a triple-A-rated investment. Enter the CDO, the collateralized debt obligation. Because the CDO was sold as a bond, it had to be rated by a rating agency. According to Michael Lewis in his book *The Big Short,* "A CDO was a pile of 80% triple B rated mortgage bonds, which Wall Street firms had conspired with ratings agencies to rate higher than triple B."[25] Ratings agencies protected themselves by issuing disclaimers with their ratings, saying users should not rely on credit ratings to make investment decisions.[26]

WAS IT FRAUD?

There is always the question: When does the questionable behavior cross the line and become fraud? Was this behavior criminal, or were these just bad decisions by leaders with questionable motives? We will ask this question several times in this chapter.

Charley Ledley of Cornwall Capital Management, one of the subjects of *The Big Short*, had this to say about CDOs: "But the more we looked at what a CDO really was, the more we were like.... That's fraud. Maybe you can't prove it in a court of law. But it's fraud."[27] Barry Ritholtz in his book *Bailout Nation* asked how CDOs could be rated triple-A when U.S. treasuries were triple-A, but paid a much lower yield. Doesn't higher yield mean more risk? "Either this was brilliant heretofore unrealized insight or it was a massive fraud."[28]

Citigroup called it "the machine" It was the process Citigroup used to create mortgage-backed debt. Its traders contacted mortgage brokers for loans, put the loans into risk models and then into CDOs, then went to the ratings agencies for the triple-A rating. Soon Citigroup was making a billion dollars a year in profit.[29] "From the investment bank's point of view, the key to the deal was obtaining a triple-A rating, without which the deal wouldn't be profitable."[30]

MISALIGNED INCENTIVES AT THE RATINGS AGENCIES

In 2001, Moody's had revenues of $800.7 million. In 2005, thanks to fees from rating CDOs, their revenues had soared to $1.73 billion. In 2006, it was over $2 billion.[31] Lawrence G. McDonald, former vice president of distressed debt and convertible securities trading at Lehman Brothers, had this to say about the rating agencies: "Forgive me a harsh judgment, but I think those raters were a bunch of half-assed, dishonest villains who would do anything for a fast buck. I just don't believe they were that stupid. And anyway, I believe a plea of 'stupid' is probably the saddest of all defenses."[32]

THE GROWTH OF SUBPRIME LENDING

The Commodity Futures Modernization Act had already removed all federal and state oversight from credit default swaps. Other standards were relaxed in 2000 as well when Standard & Poor's (one of the ratings agencies along with Moody's) decided that a borrower with an 80/20 mortgage was no more likely to default than a person who received a traditional 80 percent loan. An 80/20 loan is actually two loans, an 80 percent primary loan and a 20 percent second loan. A person with an 80/20 loan is making no down payment and has no equity in the house. The other ratings agencies soon followed the lead of Standard & Poor's.[33] In 2001, 15 percent of borrowers financed with "no money down"; by 2006 the number of borrowers with "no money down" was 50 percent.[34]

Subprime loans are dominated by hybrid adjustable rate mortgages (ARMs) with fixed rates for just a short amount of time that then adjust upward either monthly or yearly thereafter. "These loans are made on the value of the property, not the ability of the borrower to repay. This is the fundamental definition of predatory lending."[35] James Surowiecki from *The New Yorker* magazine characterized subprime lenders as "predators in the same sense that Wile E. Coyote was" a predator, as many of the subprime lenders were themselves going bankrupt.[36] While this is humorous, many of the leading subprime lenders were using practices that took advantage of people. Perhaps the worst offender was Ameriquest Mortgage.[37]

Prior to 2002, lenders rarely approved loans to borrowers with low credit scores (below 660). Borrowers had to document their income and their employment, often placing 20 percent down. Fewer than $100 billion in subprime loans were made per year. That changed quickly with securitization. Since the repayment of the loan was no longer the main concern, subprime lending took off. By 2005, $600 billion in subprime loans were being made each year.[38] The loans became known as *NINJA loans*, for No Income, No Job or Assets.

By 2006, 75 percent of all subprime loans were feeding the securitization market, and they had grown from 7 percent to 14 percent of all loans.[39] The loans were made based on the value of the house, which everyone believed would be worth more in the near future. It was just like the investors in the 1920s who borrowed money to buy stock, believing that the stock market would continue to go up.

Lehman Brothers aligned itself with subprime lenders, actually owning several. It became a leader in funding subprime mortgage lenders. As their leverage ratio increased, Lehman Brothers was in a position that required real estate to perform favorably to grow

Lehman revenue and keep the company profitable. If the "securitiza-tion machine slowed down," the firm could be in trouble.[40]

WAS IT MORTGAGE FRAUD?

Ameriquest Mortgage was seen as the poster child for mortgage fraud and predatory lending practices. Although, there are some who would argue that Countrywide Mortgage is the more egregious poster child. In Michael W. Hudson's book, *The Monster*, Ameriquest's standard operating procedures are documented. The following is just a sam-pling of their questionable behavior:

1. Inaccurate disclosure statements
2. Failure to reveal that the interest rate was adjustable
3. Exaggerating borrowers' incomes
4. Inflating property appraisals
5. Blacklisting appraisers who would not cooperate
6. Altering documents like borrowers' W-2s
7. Loan salesmen approving their own loans[41]

In 2003, the California attorney general was investigating Ameriquest due to a large number of complaints. Their investigation found that on almost half of all the loan applications the occupa-tion of the borrower was one of three things: "consultant," "owner" (with no other information as to what was owned), or the line was left blank.[42] After 466 complaints to the Federal Trade Commission from 2000 to 2004 and lawsuits from several states, Ameriquest agreed to a settlement in early 2006 of $325 million.[43]

EVOLUTION OF COLLATERALIZED DEBT OBLIGATIONS

Lehman Brothers and other investment banks began to sell CDOs backed not with assets but with *credit default swaps* (CDS). A CDS was a guarantee of payment in the event of default. Their value was based on the credit rating of the firm selling the guarantee. No collateral was put up. Enter American International Group (AIG), the largest underwriter of commercial and industrial insurance in the

United States. To executives at AIG, this looked like easy money. The odds of a wave of defaults occurring simultaneously seemed remote. The millions in premiums seemed like free money. By 2005, AIG was a big player in credit default swaps. If all the CDOs went bad, AIG would be on the hook for hundreds of billions of dollars, which begs the question.... "Were they stupid—or were they just never intending to pay?"[44] Was this behavior the result of moral hazard created by Too Big to Fail policy?

One reason some people questioned the wisdom of AIG's credit default swaps was that the investment banks were buying the CDOs at the London Interbank Offered Rate (LIBOR) plus .50 percent or "LIBOR plus fifty." AIG was insuring them against default with credit default swaps for "LIBOR plus ten."[45] If the banks were getting .5 percent in interest and dumping all the risk to AIG for .1 percent, the investment banks were getting .4 percent free money on hundreds of millions of dollars, and AIG paid if there was a default. The investment bank couldn't lose, unless AIG couldn't pay.

AIG was making $300 million a year selling credit default swaps that insured pools of loans against default.[46] By late 2005, AIG had figured out that insuring against the default of hundreds of billions of dollars of subprime mortgages could have been a bad idea, so it stopped selling insurance for CDO debt.[47] People were starting to figure out that the models behind the CDOs had another flaw.... A 7 percent default rate in the home loans within a CDO was enough to wipe out the entire CDO.[48] This is not something you would expect in a triple–A-rated investment.

THE HOUSING BUBBLE BURSTS

The delinquency rates of subprime borrowers in 2006 had reached 7.5 percent.[49] This was enough to crash entire CDOs. AIG was called on to post collateral for its credit default swaps, which were now coming due. The big Wall Street firms had become dependent on rising real estate values and the fees from selling credit derivatives, but now they could not move the loans or CDOs. With housing prices collapsing, the subprime mortgage market could not continue to make loans. Many subprime lenders went out of business. The CDO market was blocked as investors stopped buying. People stopped getting home equity loans, as the value of their houses went down. Sales of appliances and building materials dropped. Orders from China decreased, so China bought fewer U.S. Treasuries. The whole economy slowed to a crawl in a "negative feedback loop."[50]

Like the larger economy, each financial entity was interconnected. Although securitization supposedly reduced risk and increased liquidity, what it really meant was that the fortunes of many institutions and investors were intertwined. Failure at one institution spilled over and contaminated other institutions.

MISALIGNED INCENTIVES IN THE BONUS STRUCTURES

Why did Lehman Brothers go out of business? One of the reasons was that after the real estate market had turned, it continued doing real estate deals for bonuses.[51] By the end of 2006, the market for subprime mortgages was perceptibly unraveling. Prices were falling and delinquencies were rising. AIG stopped selling credit default swaps on CDOs. But the CDOs kept moving to generate bonuses, even though the investment banks had nowhere to buy the credit default swaps.

What about Merrill Lynch? It had huge bonus triggers tied to the fees generated by creating and trading CDOs. In the first seven months of 2007, Merrill Lynch churned out $30 billion in additional CDOs.[52] However, Merrill Lynch had a problem. No one, not even the bank's own traders, wanted to buy the supposedly safe portions of the mortgage-backed securities Merrill Lynch was creating. It solved the problem by forming a new department to take these bad deals. The traders, who were able to make big bonuses as a result, shared their bonuses with the traders who bought the securities that were sure losers. It was called "A Million for a Billion," meaning $1 million in bonus money for every $1 billion in securities purchased.[53] Merrill Lynch's traders put individual bonuses ahead of the health of the firm. In October 2007, the firm was looking at a quarterly loss of close to $8 billion from plummeting CDO values.[54]

MARK TO MARKET

Most banks valued their illiquid investments simply at the price at which they paid for them. If they sold them for more at a later time, they recorded a profit; if they sold them for less, a loss. In 2007, this changed with a new accounting rule from the Financial Accounting Standards (FAS) Board, FAS 157. FAS 157 required the value of assets to be "written up" or "written down" even though no profit or loss had yet been realized. This was called "mark to market."[55] It is easy to determine the market value of an asset when there are buyers for similar assets. However, when everyone is treating the asset like toxic waste, what is the value?

One of the firms questioned as to whether it was appropriately marking down its real estate assets was Lehman Brothers. Specific to their CDOs in the first quarter of 2008, Lehman reported only a $200 million write down on $6.5 billion in toxic assets.[56]

WERE THEY MISLEADING THE MARKET?

Former SEC Chairman Harvey Pitt, speaking of investment banks during the Great Panic, said, "The level of accounting chicanery that is going on in these major institutions is stunning."[57] Pitt pointed out that investment banks took multiple marks on the same assets. Depending on the situation, they would give it a higher or lower mark (value). The assets were worth more when they were calculating fees and worth less when calculating margin calls. "That reflects more than carelessness," he said. "It reflects criminality."[58]

Lehman Brothers also employed off-balance sheet devices, known within Lehman Brothers as "Repo 105" transactions, to temporarily remove securities inventory from its balance sheet, usually for a period of 7 to 10 days, and to create a materially misleading picture of the firm's financial condition in late 2007 and 2008. Repo 105 transactions utilized fixed income securities and required a minimum 5 percent overcollateralization amount (i.e., a minimum of $105 worth of securities in exchange for $100 cash borrowed) Lehman Brothers' Repo 105 practice consisted of a two-step process: (1) undertaking Repo 105 transactions followed by (2) the use of Repo 105 cash borrowings to pay down liabilities, thereby reducing leverage. A few days after the new quarter began, Lehman Brothers would borrow the necessary funds to repay the cash borrowing plus interest, repurchase the securities, and restore the assets to its balance sheet.[59]

In December 2010, then New York Attorney General Andrew Cuomo filed a civil fraud lawsuit against Ernst & Young, the accounting firm for Lehman Brothers, over the practice of Repo 105 at Lehman Brothers. The 32-page lawsuit depicted a cozy relationship between the big accounting firm and its client. Ernst & Young collected over $150 million in fees from Lehman Brothers while allegedly helping it disguise its financial condition.[60]

RISK MANAGEMENT IS HARD

At a G7 Summit dinner in April 2008, Mervyn King, the governor of the Bank of England, admonished the leaders of the Wall Street firms, "... Risk management is hard. So the lesson is, we can't let you get as big as you were or do the damage that you have done."[61] What was the attitude toward risk management at the Wall Street firms?

> **Citigroup:** CEO Charles Prince seemed to believe Citigroup had no ability to control the amount of risk it would take. Prince is quoted asking then Treasury Secretary Hank Paulson, "Isn't there something you can do to order us not to take all of these risks?"[62]
>
> **Lehman Brothers:** CEO Dick Fuld left most of the management of the firm to president and COO, Joe Gregory. His motto was, "Do as much business as you can; take risk." He argued with risk officer Madelyn Antoncic, kept her out of meetings, or asked her to leave the room.[63]
>
> **Merrill Lynch:** CEO Stan O'Neal replaced risk manager Jeff Kronthal in July 2006. Kronthal was an experienced risk manager. His replacement, Osman Semerci, was a salesman with no experience in the American mortgage market.[64]

BEAR STEARNS

The beginning of the end for Bear Stearns came when it posted significant losses at the end of 2007. CEO Jimmy Cayne was forced to resign. Two of the company's hedge funds, which had been heavily invested in subprime mortgages, had failed. In March 2008, Moody's downgraded the mortgage backed debt issued by Bear Stearns.[65]

Other banks became hesitant to lend to Bear Stearns. Without cash, it could not operate. Investors began to bail out as rumors spread of liquidity problems, and the stock price plummeted.

JPMorgan Chase was interested in buying Bear Stearns to keep it from going under. However, JPMorgan Chase was getting cold feet after looking at the billions of dollars in mortgage-backed securities in the Bear Stearns portfolio. U.S. Treasury Secretary Timothy Geithner and Federal Reserve Chairman Ben Bernanke had three options:[66]

1. Let Bear Stearns go under
2. Buy time by infusing cash to finance Bear Stearns
3. Subsidize the JPMorgan Chase deal

The first option was the least attractive, as the web of relationships between banks and the vulnerability of the markets made the Fed hesitant to risk a large bankruptcy if there were other options. JPMorgan Chase eventually paid $10 a share for Bear Stearns and agreed to eat the first $1 billion in a $30 billion pool of mortgage-backed assets the Fed would take off their hands.[67]

FANNIE MAE AND FREDDIE MAC

Federal National Mortgage Association, which became known as Fannie Mae, and Federal Home Loan Mortgage, better known as Freddie Mac, were companies that guaranteed repayment of mortgages that were turned into securities. They also built massive portfolios of mortgages that they held. Fannie and Freddie were owned by shareholders and run for profit, but everyone assumed that they were backed by the U.S. government.

In the summer of 2008, losses on mortgage-backed securities the two companies had guaranteed grew and the share prices dropped by more than half.[68] Falling stock prices made it more difficult for the companies to borrow. Liquidity issues caused more problems. Foreign investors became worried and asked the Fed if it was going to stand behind Fannie and Freddie. In September 2008, Treasury would promise up to $100 billion in taxpayer money to the companies. The catch was that the companies would go under government conservatorship. Those who held preferred stock were wiped out, but all debts of the two companies would be honored.[69]

LEHMAN BROTHERS

In the summer of 2008, the market was unstable. Bear Stearns had already gone down and the street was looking for who would be next. Lehman Brothers posted a $2.8 billion loss for the second quarter.[70] Short sellers circled like vultures. Since no one was buying Lehman stock, there was excess supply. Lehman Brothers, like Bear Stearns, Fannie, and Freddie, found it difficult to borrow once it was perceived as being in trouble. Investors closed accounts, making problems worse.

There were two possible buyers for Lehman Brothers, Bank of America and Barclays. Bank of America, based in Charlotte, North Carolina, was looking to move into the investment arena and compete with Citigroup. Barclays, based in London, was interested in the broker dealer business. As the negotiations with the two parties went on, Bank of America declined to bid, setting its sights instead on Merrill Lynch. Barclays determined late in the game that it would not be able to do the deal.

The Fed did not step in and rescue Lehman Brothers. Perhaps the reason for not stepping in to help Lehman Brothers was the heat that it took for helping Bear Stearns land in the lap of JPMorgan Chase with taxpayer money. Another reason was that the possible buyers went away. Neither buyer really wanted Lehman Brothers. Bank of America wanted Merrill Lynch and Barclays just wanted parts of Lehman Brothers. When the Barclays deal fell apart, then president of Lehman Brothers Bart McDade called CEO Dick Fuld. He told Fuld, "Nobody's saving us." Fuld was speechless.[71]

Lehman Brothers filed for bankruptcy on September 15, 2008, and on the same day Bank of America announced it would acquire Merrill Lynch. It must have stung the executives at Lehman Brothers to see their potential rescuer pulling their rival out of the water instead of them. While the Fed continued to loan money to Lehman Brothers' broker dealer business to keep it open, the bankruptcy announcement caused a huge disruption in the market.

Since Lehman Brothers was allowed to fail, those who lost money have sought justice. As previously stated, then New York Attorney General Andrew Cuomo filed a civil fraud lawsuit against Ernst & Young, the accounting firm for Lehman Brothers, over the practice of Repo 105. There have also been multiple lawsuits against Lehman Brothers by angry investors alleging that the marks had been false and the CFOs had signed off on them.[72]

MERRILL LYNCH

Merrill Lynch had massive losses in 2008 of $27.6 billion.[73] Announced on the same day as the Lehman Brothers bankruptcy, Bank of America chose Merrill Lynch over Lehman Brothers because it had a higher comfort level with Merrill Lynch than with Lehman Brothers, specifically with the value of the marks on the assets.[74] Bank of America agreed to purchase Merrill Lynch for $29 per share, which was a premium on the price at the time of $17 per share.[75] While there was plenty of encouragement from the Fed, there was no taxpayer money to offset toxic assets on Merrill Lynch's books. The deal that JPMorgan Chase got with Bear Stearns' assets, the so-called "Jamie Deal" for JPMorgan Chase CEO Jamie Dimon, was not likely to be repeated, as there was a more pressing issue on the Fed's radar: AIG.

AIG

AIG's credit rating had been downgraded. The credit default swaps AIG had issued were all based on their reputation and good credit rating. It had not put up any collateral. Now that its rating was downgraded, it was now required to put up collateral. AIG was already paying on defaults, now it had to come up with collateral as well. When you have a cash flow problem and your stock is dropping, no one wants to loan you money. Like Bear Stearns, Lehman Brothers, and Merrill Lynch, AIG was in trouble.

On September 16, 2008, one day after the announcement of the Lehman Brothers bankruptcy and the Merrill Lynch acquisition, the government loaned AIG $85 billion in exchange for a 79.9 percent of the company.[76] By March 2009, the Fed and Treasury had put $183 billion into AIG.[77]

TARP

U.S. Treasury Secretary Tim Geithner had already been thinking that trying to save companies one at a time was not the best strategy. Internally, Geithner's people called the plan "break the glass," as in "In Case of Emergency, Break Glass." He had asked Congress for $700 billion to buy troubled assets from Wall Street firms and try to stabilize the market. On September 29, 2008, the House of Representatives voted the bill down, 228 to 205, and the Dow Jones Industrial Average fell 778 points, its largest one-day drop to date.[78] It would lose 1,096 points for the week, and another 1,874 the next week for a two-week drop of 2,970 points.[79]

The house reconsidered a new version of the bill a week later on October 3. Fifty-seven members changed their votes (33 Democrats and 24 Republicans) and the measure passed. What Congress did not know was that everything it had been told about what the funds would be used for had changed in the mind of the Treasury Secretary. He had reconsidered Troubled Asset Relief and was now planning to invest directly in individual banks rather than buy toxic assets.[80] Buying up toxic assets was complicated. As the rapid decline of Bear Stearns, Fannie Mae, Freddie Mac, and Lehman Brothers had shown, "there was too much room for fudging the numbers when it came to valuing them."[81]

On Sunday October 12, 2008, Geithner invited the heads of the nine largest banks to appear at Treasury the next day. He would give them an offer they couldn't refuse. The following day each of the nine banks was told to take a capital injection on generous terms. If they refused the capital, and then asked for capital in the future, the terms would not be as good. The nine banks were offered the following in a take-it-just-take-it deal:

Citigroup – $25 billion
JPMorgan Chase – $25 billion
Wells Fargo – $25 billion

Bank of America – $15 billion

Merrill Lynch – $10 billion

Goldman Sachs – $10 billion

Morgan Stanley – $10 billion

Bank of NY Mellon – $3 billion

State Street – $2 billion[82]

TARP funds as they ultimately got used were meant as a liquidity cushion, so the banks would start lending again. However, they also gave Congress the right to call Wall Street executives to Washington to be grilled about excessive pay, incentives that were out of alignment, and possible regulatory reforms to replace the ones Wall Street had lobbied to remove. Everyone said all the right things.

Soon the TARP recipients were paying back the money to the government. First to repay was Goldman Sachs in the summer of 2009, then JPMorgan Chase, Morgan Stanley, Citigroup. As investigative reporter and author Vicky Ward put it, "... the devil was back in the casino—and was eager to spin the wheel again."[83]

TOO BIG TO FAIL POLICY

Looking back, what was the policy of the federal government regarding financial firms that were too big to fail during the Great Panic? Here is what actually happened:

- Bear Stearns was acquired in a deal subsidized by $30 billion in taxpayer money, preventing bankruptcy.
- Fannie Mae and Freddie Mac were put under government conservatorship.
- Lehman Brothers was allowed to go bankrupt. No subsidy was offered to potential merger partners.
- Merrill Lynch was acquired in a deal with no subsidy.
- AIG was nationalized for $183 billion.
- The top nine banks were given boatloads of money.

What we see is that there was no real policy. Investors and creditors could not be sure what would happen because the government did something different every time. This only increased the instability. The main purpose of Too Big to Fail policy is to prevent instability. Here are the three main reasons given for the government's Too Big to Fail policy:[84]

1. Preventing instability in the banking system from occurring and spilling into the rest of the economy
2. Protecting uninsured depositors and creditors
3. Protecting credit allocation

WAS ANYONE DOING THINGS RIGHT?

The reason that many banks were chasing profits on risky financial instruments was that banking, and the financial industry in general, was in flux. Many investment banks abandoned risk management strategies when regular fee income from handling accounts, which had long been propping up the business model, eroded thanks to discount brokers. Many commercial banks embraced the higher fees of subprime lending. The old customer service models were no longer profitable.

Rather than using gimmick financial instruments, perhaps banks should have been looking for opportunities for innovations in their legacy enterprise applications, with the multiple layers of applications held together with middleware and proprietary code. The financial services industry has some of the oldest technology of any industry.[85] If a bank wanted to differentiate themselves from other players in the industry who were busy risking the farm, there were two good ways:

1. Innovate: Find a better way to manage customer accounts.
2. Reiterate: Don't abandon your risk management principles.

ING Direct and Hudson City Bancorp were two companies that did not drink the Kool-Aid and had success to show for it, the first by innovation, the other by reiterating its commitment to risk management principles. ING Direct had deposits of $651 million at the end of 2000.[86] Those deposits grew to more than $81.8 billion by the first quarter of 2011.[87] This growth rate, which was nearly 10 times the average growth rate of U.S. banks in the same time frame, was due in large part to an innovative business model that looks to the Internet.[88] ING Direct offers high yield rates marketed primarily on their Web site. It also has modern cybercafés in seven U.S. cities. By offering paperless online checking accounts, ING Direct is tapping into the wave of the future. According to an American Banking Association survey, the preferred method of banking for persons under 55 years of age is the Internet.[89] Mobile phone subscribers are doubling every year. Forecasts are that by 2015, 244 million people will conduct financial transactions on their mobile phone.[90]

Hudson City Bancorp stuck to its conservative lending practices and passed on subprime mortgages. Choosing slow, steady growth over short-term risky windfalls, Hudson City Bancorp avoided the fray that claimed many banks, as can be seen by the following increase in bank failures between 2008 and 2010:[91]

2008 – 25
2009 – 140
2010 – 157

Although it initially took criticism for not seeking the higher returns, depositors sought out Hudson City Bancorp in 2008. While others faltered, Hudson City Bancorp's deposits increased, and it reported a year-to-year net profit increase of 64 percent in 2008.[92] Since it went public in July 1999 through year-end 2010, Hudson City Bancorp not only grew earnings at an average rate of 19 percent a year, but growth accelerated during the recession.[93] Ironically, after the smoke cleared from the Great Panic, Hudson City Bancorp was being penalized for its good behavior by the government's forced need to support a fractured mortgage market created by the reckless behavior of other financial institutions.

LOOTING: AKERLOF AND ROMER

At the beginning of this chapter, we asked a question based on the work that George Akerlof and Paul Romer from the University of California performed in 1993. Their paper, "Looting: The Economic Underworld of Bankruptcy for Profit," theorized that given the right conditions, managers would run their firms into bankruptcy for personal profit. The conditions were:

1. Poor accounting
2. Lax regulation
3. Low penalties for abuse
4. Precedent or expectation of government bailout[94]

All of these were present during the period of the Great Panic. This strategy has many colorful descriptions: "heads I win, tails I break even;" "gambling on resurrection;" and "fourth-quarter football" to name just a few. However, the paper written in 1993 by Akerlof and Romer also discussed the spreading of the activity to other firms with contracts that could not be honored. This prophetically describes the practice of shady subprime lenders signing of mortgage contracts with borrowers that could not repay, just to fill the CDO pipeline:

> Looting can spread symbiotically to other markets, bringing to life a whole economic underworld with perverse incentives. The looters in the sector covered by the government guarantees will make trades with unaffiliated firms outside this sector, causing them to produce in a way that helps maximize the looters' current extractions with no regard for future losses. Rather than looking for business partners who will honor their contracts, the looters look for partners who will sign contracts that appear to have high current value if fulfilled but that will not-and could not-be honored.[95]

Akerlof and Romer described this activity by flawed managers as criminal. Whenever these factors come together the tendency toward this behavior will be the same. Akerlof and Romer saw it in the data of thrifts from the 1980s, and it held true for the Great Panic of 2008.

Those who cannot remember the past are condemned to repeat it.
—*George Santayana*, Reason in Common Sense

NOTES

1. Credit for linking the Akerlof and Romer paper, which was based on the savings and loan bailouts of the 1980s, to the Great Panic of 2008 goes to Yves Smith in *Econned*, (New York:

Palgrave MacMillan, 2010), 164–166; George A. Akerlof, Paul M. Romer, Robert E. Hall, and N. Gregory Mankiw, "Looting: The Economic Underworld of Bankruptcy for Profit," *Brookings Papers on Economic Activity*, vol. 1993, no. 2 (1993), 1–73, www.jstor.org/pss/2534564.

2. With apologies to Nicole Gelinas, who begins her book, *After the Fall*, with the story of Samuel Insull, (New York: Encounter Books, 2009).
3. Mark T. Williams, *Uncontrolled Risk* (New York: McGraw Hill, 2010), 40.
4. Kaye Bonnick, *Why Too Big to Fail?* (Bloomington, IN: Author House, 2010), 16.
5. Nicole Gelinas, *After the Fall* (New York: Encounter Books, 2009), 48.
6. Gelinas, *After the Fall*, 49.
7. Gary H. Stern, *Too Big to Fail* (Washington, DC: Brookings Institute, 2004), 42.
8. Barry Ritholtz, *Bailout Nation* (Hoboken, NJ: John Wiley & Sons, 2009), 71.
9. Ibid., 72.
10. Stern, *Too Big to Fail*, 36.
11. Ibid., 142.
12. Robert Scheer, *The Great American Stickup* (New York: Nation Books, 2010), 54–55.
13. Ibid., 7.
14. Ibid., 57.
15. Ritholtz, *Bailout Nation*, 139.
16. Ibid., 132.
17. Gillian Tett, *Fools Gold* (New York: Free Press, 2010), 147.
18. Ritholtz, *Bailout Nation*, 140.
19. Ibid., 139.
20. Bethany McLean and Peter Elkind, *The Smartest Guys in the Room* (New York: Penguin, 2003), 136.
21. Ritholtz, *Bailout Nation*, 102.
22. Richard Bitner, *Confessions of a Subprime Lender* (Hoboken, NJ: John Wiley & Sons, 2008), 13.
23. Michael Lewis, ed., *Panic* (New York: W.W. Norton, 2009), 317.

24. Yves Smith, *Econned* (New York: Palgrave MacMillan, 2010), 6.
25. Lewis, *The Big Short* (New York: W.W. Norton, 2010), 129.
26. Bitner, *Confessions of a Subprime Lender*, 90.
27. Lewis, *The Big Short*, 129.
28. Ritholtz, *Bailout Nation*, 111.
29. Charles Gasparino, *The Sellout* (New York: Harper, 2009), 191–192.
30. Lewis, *Panic*, 320.
31. Lawrence G. McDonald and Patrick Robinson, *A Colossal Failure of Common Sense* (New York: Random House, 2009), 200.
32. Ibid., 200.
33. Bitner, *Confessions of a Subprime Lender*, 105.
34. Ibid., 100–101.
35. From Opening Statement of Chairman Christopher Dodd, U.S. Senate, Committee on Banking, Housing, and Urban Affairs, *Mortgage Market Turmoil: Causes and Consequences* Hearing, March 22, 2007, quoted in Lewis, *Panic*, 310.
36. Lewis, *Panic*, 314.
37. Bitner, *Confessions of a Subprime Lender*, 101.
38. Matt Taibbi, *Griftopia* (New York: Random House, 2010), 83.
39. Williams, *Uncontrolled Risk*, 126.
40. Ibid., 123.
41. Michael W. Hudson, *The Monster* (New York: Times Books, 2010), 156–159.
42. Ibid., 234.
43. Hudson, *The Monster*, 245, 261.
44. Taibbi, *Griftopia*, 100.
45. Ibid., 99.
46. Lewis, *The Big Short*, 71.
47. Tett, *Fools Gold*, 134.
48. Lewis, *The Big Short*, 129.
49. Williams, *Uncontrolled Risk*, 127.
50. McDonald and Robinson, *A Colossal Failure of Common Sense*, 254–255.
51. Greg Farrell, *Crash of the Titans* (New York: Crown, 2010), 415.
52. Sorkin, *Too Big to Fail*, 163.

53. Jake Bernstein and Jesse Eisenger, "The 'Subsidy': How a Handful of Merrill Lynch Bankers Helped Blow Up Their Own Firm," *ProPublica*, December 22, 2010, www.propublica.org/article/the-subsidy-how-merrill-lynch-traders-helped-blow-up-their-own-firm.
54. Sorkin, *Too Big to Fail*, 164.
55. Ibid., 120.
56. Ibid., 124.
57. David E. Y. Sarna, *History of Greed* (Hoboken, NJ: John Wiley & Sons, 2010), 276–277.
58. Ibid., 34.
59. Report of Anton Valukas, *Lehman Brother Holdings Inc v Debtors*, Chapter 11, Southern District of New York, Case # 08–13555, 732–733.
60. Liz Rappaport and Michael Rappaport, "Ernst Accused of Lehman Whitewash," *Wall Street Journal*, December 21, 2010, online.wsj.com/article/SB10001424052748704259704576033540546160536.html.
61. Sorkin, *Too Big to Fail*, 99.
62. Ibid., 98.
63. Vicky Ward, *Devil's Casino* (Hoboken, NJ: John Wiley & Sons, 2010), 158.
64. Sorkin, *Too Big to Fail*, 163.
65. David Wessel, *In Fed We Trust* (New York: Three Rivers Press, 2010), 151.
66. Ibid., 168.
67. Ibid., 172.
68. Ibid., 182.
69. Wessel, *In Fed We Trust*, 185–187.
70. Kaye Bonnick, *Why Too Big to Fail?* (Bloomington, IN: Author House, 2010), 62.
71. Sorkin, *Too Big to Fail*, 351.
72. Ward, *Devil's Casino*, 223.
73. Bonnick, *Why Too Big to Fail?*, 69.
74. Sorkin, *Too Big to Fail*, 367.
75. Ibid., 333.
76. Wessel, *In Fed We Trust*, 195.
77. Ibid., 194.
78. Ibid., 227.

79. Ibid.
80. Sorkin, *Too Big to Fail*, 485.
81. Ward, *Devil's Casino*, 218.
82. Wessel, *In Fed We Trust*, 239.
83. Ward, *Devil's Casino*, 218–219.
84. Stern, *Too Big to Fail*, 53.
85. Louis Hernandez, *Too Small to Fail* (Bloomington, IN: Author House, 2010), 64.
86. Ibid., 59.
87. Philip van Doorn, "GE's ING Bid May Overhaul Profit Engine," *The Street*, June 7, 2011, www.thestreet.com/story/11145032/1/ges-ing-bid-may-overhaul-profit-engine.html.
88. Hernandez, *Too Small To Fail*, 59.
89. Ibid., 60.
90. "Mobile Banking Subscriber Numbers Doubling Every Year," *PYMNTS.com*, February 18, 2010, www.pymnts.com/mobile-banking-subscriber-numbers-doubling-every-year/.
91. "FDIC Failed Banks – Bank Failures 2011, 2010, 2009, 2008 and 2007," www.calculatorplus.com/savings/advice_failed_banks.html.
92. Lindsay Blakley, "Hudson City Bancorp: One Bank That Didn't Drink the Kool-Aid," *BNET.com*, December 1, 2008, www.bnet.com/article/hudson-city-bancorp-one-bank-that-didnt-drink-the-kool-aid/253410.
93. Chuck Carnevale, "Hudson City Bancorp, Short Term Risk Long Term Opportunity?," *SeekingAlpha.com*, January 29, 2011, seekingalpha.com/article/249498-hudson-city-bancorp-short-term-risk-long-term-opportunity?source=yahoo.
94. Akerlof, Romer, Hall, and Mankiw, "Looting: The Economic Underworld," 2.
95. Ibid., 3.

CHAPTER 11

Designing a Robust Fraud Prevention Program

EXECUTIVE SUMMARY

All entities need a robust fraud prevention program staffed with savvy and experienced fraud examiners. The Certified Fraud Examiner (CFE) certification is the gold standard in fraud detection and prevention, and all corporate investigators should be so certified. Forensic accountants and forensic data analysts are also needed in fraud prevention units. A financial integrity concept should be used in protecting the organization from all forms of fraud and abuse while reducing the risk of financial and reputational harm. The program should be aligned with the internal audit function, as there are great synergies to be achieved with such a partnership. Interaction with internal auditors will result in increased discovery of fraud and abuse issues. The fraud prevention program should include the detection, investigation, and prevention of all frauds including financial statement fraud, asset misappropriation, and bribery and corruption schemes. The investigative unit needs a wide variety of fraud detection software and technology solutions as well as excellent cross-group collaboration throughout the company.

Companies face numerous fraud risks. There are the financial risks from fraud losses, shareholder lawsuits, government investigations, prosecutions, convictions, and fines. Along with financial risk goes the reputational risk and damaging media attention from fraud. Vicarious liability, in which a company may be responsible for the actions of an employee even if those actions are unauthorized and contrary to company policy, stands out as another serious risk. Organizations can be held liable for criminal acts committed as a matter of organizational policy. They may also be held liable for the criminal acts of their employees if those acts are done in the course and scope of their employment. Once well-respected companies have been destroyed by fraud. Consider the personal devastation to the thousands of innocent Enron employees who believed in their company but were deceived by their senior executives. They lost their jobs, their savings, and their pensions and face years of emotional and financial issues.

ONLY ROBUST WILL DO

Fraud prevention has come a long way in the last decade. Corporate executives realize that preventing fraud is critical to the long-term existence of a company. The concept of preventing fraud is more than just a good business practice; it is a requirement that is critical to proper company management. Every company that wants to be serious about compliance needs a fraud-detection and investigative response. Building a state-of-the-art fraud prevention program requires effort to ensure integrity, transparency, honest reporting, and a culture of compliance. Only a robust fraud prevention program will do. Robust can be defined as having or exhibiting strength or vigorous health, firm in purpose or outlook, and strong. It is about being proactive rather than just reactive.[1] What makes a program robust are a number of elements. Highly experienced fraud examiners and forensic accountants understand the reasons people commit fraud and know how to detect it. They stay current with local, national, and world events related to fraud in order to integrate best practices into a company's program. It is about always adding new strategies to a fraud prevention tool chest. Most importantly, it is a commitment to excellence and innovation.

A robust fraud prevention program must build a predictable response model to allegations of fraud or financial improprieties, providing thorough and timely results in support of management action, including related business, legal, and human resources decisions. The primary focus should be on stopping misconduct, driving continuous improvement in policies, procedures, internal controls, and compliance, including Sarbanes-Oxley Act certifications and whistleblower provisions. Experience has shown that once a robust fraud prevention program is established, many instances of previously hidden frauds will be disclosed. The existence of a well-communicated reporting mechanism for employees and others to report allegations of fraud and noncompliance with company policy will lead to the identification and resolution of previously unresolved matters. The types of fraud and abuse addressed will run the gamut of traditional financial fraud and abuse, ranging from low-risk areas such as expense reporting fraud and petty cash abuses, to higher risk areas including financial accounting issues, conflicts of interest, hidden business relationships, kickbacks, and bribes.

THE INVESTIGATIVE RESPONSE

A robust fraud prevention program will include awareness of fraud issues, fraud risk assessment, detection, education, prevention, and responsive investigations. Preventative programs, no matter how good, will not stop all fraud. Therefore, an investigative response component through which company investigators can quickly respond to allegations of fraud is needed for all prevention programs. The fraud investigative unit must be responsible for the detection, investigation, and prevention of fraud and must have the strong support of senior management and the Audit Committee.

Any unit created by a company needs to be staffed with experienced fraud investigators. Due to the complexities of fraud schemes and their myriad forms, it takes many years for someone to gain the experience and skills to be an expert in fraud detection and investigation. Consideration should be given to hiring former law enforcement professionals, corporate investigators, forensic accountants, and others with extensive investigative experience as well as those certified in related disciplines. Certified Fraud Examiners (CFE), Certified Compliance and Ethics Professionals (CCEP), Certified Public Accountants, Certified Protection Professionals (CPP), Professional Certified Investigators (PCI), and other highly skilled investigative and forensic experts should be part of every organization's investigative function.

In particular, the Certified Fraud Examiner certification has become the gold standard in fraud detection and prevention. CFEs are known the world over as fraud-fighting experts. To become a CFE, a fraud examiner must meet strict standards of education and experience in investigating fraudulent financial transactions and other fraud investigations and must also have knowledge of legal elements of fraud, accounting, criminology, and ethics. Thus, CFEs have extensive knowledge investigating fraud and antifraud control measures. They should also be part of any robust fraud prevention program. Beyond just their investigative skills, investigators must also be agents of change and the voice of compliance convincing upper management (and then all levels below) of the importance of fraud prevention.

The hiring of these fraud professionals demonstrates the company's commitment to high integrity, and with their assistance, will help the company embrace a robust fraud prevention and investigation program. The investigators' skills should also be supplemented with high-tech tools and resources to further their investigative efforts. Ongoing training of the investigative staff is also required. A sound recommendation is that each investigator should receive a minimum of 40 hours of training each year with emphasis on fraud detection, investigative procedures, employment law, and other legal aspects. The message that needs to be conveyed is that the company is ready, willing, and able to respond quickly and appropriately to the allegations of fraud.

Consideration should also be given to developing an investigative framework for all investigations conducted. This framework would provide a detailed step-by-step process for investigative excellence and oversight. There should be an intake process for how compliance issues are routed for review and an investigative determination. An assignment process must also be included to decide who actually conducts the investigation and under what oversight. Prior to the start of an investigation, a detailed investigative plan should be created that identifies the scope of the investigation and all related elements. Included in the plan should be what documents will be analyzed, what tools will be needed in the investigative process, who will be interviewed, who will lead the investigation, what investigative assistance will be needed from human resources, legal, investigative vendors, and others, the timeline for completion of the investigation, and other key elements of an investigation.

THE FINANCIAL INTEGRITY CONCEPT

Consider calling the fraud prevention unit something other than the "fraud investigation group" or a similar name. The unit could be called the *financial integrity unit* to emphasize the focus on the preservation of financial integrity, process improvements, and prevention rather than just reactive investigations. The term "financial integrity unit" sends a strong message that the overall mission is protecting the financial health and promoting financial stewardship and integrity of the organization. "Financial integrity unit" also conveys a different and better message to employees that there is more than just a response to fraud. Incorporating the words "financial" and "integrity" sends a very positive message that the unit is protecting them as well as the company.

The financial integrity investigation unit should have a charter or mission that provides clear objectives and definitions of the organization-wide fraud prevention program. The charter or mission must be communicated to key stakeholders in the company. See Exhibit 11.1 for a sample financial integrity unit charter.

The financial integrity unit must have written policies and procedures and should work closely with other company departments. A *needs and capabilities analysis* should be conducted that identifies a series of recommendations for key program elements, a proposed organizational structure, and team capabilities for the unit. A good start-up strategy includes the following factors:

- Program and process development, including a company-wide fraud risk profile
- Policy integration and close interaction with other company organizations, including senior executives, legal, office of compliance, human resources, internal audit and finance, procurement, and public relations

- Case management for event and trend tracking and reporting
- Development of technology solutions to identify fraud and abuse
- An investigative protocol for conducting investigations
- A company-wide communication program to disseminate fraud risk and prevention strategies

---

The Financial Integrity Unit (FIU) is established as an integral element of Internal Audit to assist the General Auditor, Chief Financial Officer, General Counsel, Chief Compliance Officer, and other members of management and the Board of Directors in the effective discharge of their responsibilities over financial integrity. To this end, the FIU is authorized to respond to any reports or allegations of financial improprieties or violations of the company's code of conduct and other related code of conduct violations that could negatively impact the company's financial integrity. The FIU has a worldwide charter. The FIU's responsibilities include the following:

- Conducting timely and professional investigations into allegations of financial improprieties or violations of codes of conduct that could negatively impact on the company's financial integrity. Investigations will be conducted under the direction and supervision of the office of general counsel, and investigative reports will be issued to the office of general counsel and other members of management as appropriate for resolution.
- Identifying and making recommendations to correct control weaknesses and process deficiencies that increase the risk of financial improprieties; making recommendations to adopt industry best practices.
- Partnering with the controllers' community and other finance personnel to provide a proactive, comprehensive, and effective program aimed at preventing, detecting, and investigating incidents of fraud, waste, and abuse.
- Collaborating with business groups in their continuing efforts to improve finance-related processes and contribute to cost efficacy.

EXHIBIT 11.1   Sample Financial Integrity Unit Charter

INVESTIGATIONS CODE OF CONDUCT

Another best practice to consider is the creation of a specific *investigations code of conduct*. While almost all companies have employee business conduct codes, very few have specific codes of conduct for their investigative staff. Such a code details how investigation professionals must conduct themselves when engaged in investigation activities.

The role of corporate investigators and the internal investigative process has been the focus of media reporting over the last few years involving Fortune 500 companies. There were a number of issues raised regarding the behavior of their investigators including spying on employees and journalists, surveillance techniques, using pretexting and subterfuge to obtain personal information, and other questionable investigative techniques. The result has been a greater oversight of the investigative role in business organizations. Above all else, investigators must not permit any bias, prejudice, or preconceived opinions to impede an investigation and always report facts accurately and completely.

An investigations code of conduct should require adherence to company policies as well as the highest ethical and legal standards. Thus, the creation of a specific investigations code that embodies professional conduct, best practices, compliance with laws and policies, and prohibits inappropriate and unethical conduct is another process that can further protect an organization from reputational and financial risk. The investigations code of conduct should address the following requirements:

- Investigators will conduct their investigations with honesty and integrity.
- Investigators will use investigative techniques approved by the company and always within the highest professional standards.
- Investigators will gather evidence and report facts accurately and completely.
- Investigators will not permit any bias, prejudice, or preconceived opinions to interfere with the investigation.
- Investigators will not participate in any investigation where they have an actual or perceived conflict of interest.
- Investigators will not use subterfuge or use false statements in their investigations.
- Investigators will respect the privacy rights of witnesses and subjects of investigations.
- Investigators will safeguard all evidence obtained in investigations.
- Investigators will ensure that any investigative vendors or contractors that assist in company investigations will adhere to the same standards as this code of conduct.
- All investigators and authorized vendors and contractors will comply with annual certification requirements.

TECHNOLOGY SOLUTIONS

Today's modern fraud prevention unit must have an extensive array of technology tools and solutions to conduct successful fraud investigations. Forensic data analysis tools must be used to identify anomalies or irregularities in electronic data that are indicative of fraud or abuse. The unit must be familiar with the fraud detection software on the market and must also have the technical expertise to develop in-house applications specific to particular fraud risk issues. It is recommended that each unit have a dedicated forensic data analyst to support complex investigations by identifying, designing, maintaining, and using appropriate technologies to mitigate fraud. Almost every case of fraud today has some connection to computers, e-mail, and the Internet. Thus, digital evidence recovery capabilities must exist for identifying, preserving, recovering, and examining electronic evidence. The unit needs to become competent in this area or, at the minimum, have access to skilled professionals who can examine digital evidence.

EMBEDDING A FRAUD PREVENTION PROGRAM IN INTERNAL AUDIT

Many fraud investigation units are based within the corporate security department. This has been the traditional approach: The fraud response is aligned with physical security, theft investigation, workplace violence, and executive protection functions. Enhanced fraud prevention programs require a continuous interaction with a company's internal audit function as well. In today's world, "internal audit must have a solid understanding of measures intended to prevent and detect fraud and be able to evaluate and test antifraud control effectiveness."[2] More and more fraud prevention programs are now being placed within internal audit. As accounting firm PricewaterhouseCoopers states, "Some larger internal audit functions are creating internal units to address prevention, detection, investigation, and remediation of fraud and issues stemming from forensic investigations."[3] There are great synergies to be achieved with a partnership of fraud prevention and internal audit. The interaction with the internal auditors allows a free exchange of information and a quicker response to potential fraud matters for investigation. Professional fraud investigators can take the "red flags" found by auditors and determine whether there is a basis for them. A well-functioning financial integrity unit should be based within internal audit or at the very least have close interaction with that department.

The internal audit department is an independent appraisal function to examine and evaluate a company's activities as a service to management and the board of directors. To accomplish this, internal audit must be authorized to direct a broad, comprehensive program of internal auditing throughout the company. In carrying out their duties and responsibilities, members of internal audit will have full, free, and unrestricted access to all company activities, records, property, and personnel. This is also the function of a fraud prevention unit, so a close interaction of the two groups is beneficial to all.

Another positive benefit when the financial integrity unit is aligned with internal audit is ready access to the findings of both the internal and independent auditors. A member of the fraud investigative unit of a major technology company confided that his group has little if any interaction with the internal audit department. Furthermore, he wondered if having a closer interaction with internal audit would result in increased referrals regarding potential fraud issues arising from audits conducted. Effective fraud investigation units need to be proactive, and review of audit findings for the red flags of fraud is critical. Wherever the unit is based, it must be staffed with a sufficient number of experienced investigators who have extensive fraud detection experience, forensic accounting skills, and CFE certifications.

WHERE FRAUD WILL BE FOUND

The types of fraud that a company may find are varied but generally can be broken down into three broad categories:

- **Fraudulent Financial Statements,** including fraudulent financial accounting, revenue recognition, improper asset valuations, abuse of accounting systems, and side letters (written or unwritten agreements not included in contracts).

- **Asset Misappropriation,** including fraudulent disbursements, larceny, and skimming. Common embezzlement schemes include contract fraud, false billing, fraudulent expense report submissions, relocation fraud, time and attendance fraud, and false disability claims.
- **Corruption,** including bribery, kickbacks, economic extortion and conflicts of interest, including insider trading, employees with hidden ownership of companies doing business with them, and spouses of employees with undisclosed ownership in vendor companies.

In the authors' experience, many companies will find that fraud involving expense reporting is the biggest fraud problem they have, followed by conflicts of interest and then vendor kickback schemes.

As much as a corporate executive may think a company has no fraud problem, it does. Once a fraud prevention program is up and running, it will uncover issues that have been ongoing for many months or years without discovery. In any population, including those within a company, a certain percentage of employees will have their own illicit agendas and will commit fraud when given the opportunity.

ABUSE CANNOT BE IGNORED

Fraud is not the only problem facing an organization. As big a problem as fraud is, the issue with abuse is bigger. More importantly, whereas fraud is usually addressed, abuse is often ignored. Although fraud and abuse have two different meanings, abuse mitigation must be part of a robust fraud prevention program. Abuse can be defined as "improper use, misuse, to use wrongly, unjust or wrongful practice."[4] Abuse typically involves policy violations, such as the inappropriate use of corporate resources for personal reasons. It might involve taking home a box of company pens for personal use, consistently arriving at work late and going home early, using the photocopier to make personal copies, or using sick leave when one is not ill. Other examples are violating employee authorized purchase limits by splitting invoices to stay within the approved limits, excessive travel and entertainment spending such as $400 bottles of wine at a dinner, and first-class travel when coach is mandated. If abuse is not appropriately addressed, it can lead to fraud by giving the false impression that this behavior is condoned.

EMPLOYEE COOPERATION WITH COMPANY INVESTIGATIONS

When people are confronted about possible fraudulent activities and misconduct, admissions and truthfulness are paramount. It's all or nothing when it comes to being truthful; half-truths are not acceptable. Investigator skill and experience play a key factor in obtaining the truth from employees when one is conducting interviews. Professional interviewing techniques and treating all people with dignity and respect go a long way in getting to the truth.

The cooperation of employees in internal investigations is critical to determination of the facts of the case and a successful outcome. Witnesses will provide great insight and context for allegations. The collection of documentary and supporting evidence along with witness interviews may help to prove or disprove the allegations before having to confront the subject employee. An interview with a subject is made easier with this approach, and when an employee is confronted with substantial evidence of wrongdoing, it is easier to obtain an admission.

Therefore, the company code of conduct should include a statement that employees are required to cooperate fully and truthfully with any authorized company investigation. Employees who are subjects of investigations cannot be forced to speak with investigators, but the failure to meet and discuss the allegations can be used by human resources and management in a determination of final disciplinary action.

INVESTIGATIVE PLAN

Prior to the start of the actual investigation, an investigative plan should be prepared outlining the anticipated steps of the investigation. The plan should cover the scope and objectives of the investigation and should be in writing unless determined not to by legal counsel. Determine if the investigation will be conducted in-house or by outside counsel. Identify key business, legal, human resources, audit, and other contacts for assistance in gathering documents, identifying witnesses, and explaining business operations. Consider contacting the company's public relations department so it is alerted to possible external communication issues. Internal investigations need to be coordinated, not only between the company's inside counsel and outside counsel but also with other corporate functions. This includes corporate security, human resources, internal audit, and the appropriate business groups. Also consider whether there is a need to disclose the investigation to the external auditor at this stage or at the conclusion of the investigation.

Identify key contacts in business, finance, and compliance at company headquarters and, if appropriate, in the country or region. Review and analyze all gathered documents. Identify in-house or external counsel for legal assistance in foreign venues for an understanding of local employment and criminal laws especially around fraud and corruption. Identify all potential interviewees including witnesses, subjects, supervisors of complainants, and others. Establish if any of the interviewees are nonemployees or located outside the United States requiring a further understanding of local laws for interviews. The issue of any employee indemnifications should be considered as well as a review of the directors and officers (D&O) insurance policy for coverage and limitations.

It is always advantageous to prepare a timeline of the issues and events in the case to provide a better understanding of the who, what, when, where, why, and how. Determine if any advance notice will be given to interviewees. Prepare for the possibility of workplace searches if allowed. Consider privacy and privilege issues. Is the company a union shop requiring the presence of a union representative in interviews? The investigation plan should be approved by appropriate legal authority. Remember that the course of an investigation can invariably change resulting in changes to the investigation plan. Therefore, the plan is a living document that should be revised as appropriate through the many steps of the investigation.

At times, there may be parallel government investigations occurring where both federal prosecutors and civil regulatory agencies are conducting inquiries into the same set of facts. These parallel government investigations may be taking place while the company is conducting its own internal investigation. This may be an opportunity to have a dialogue with the government to learn more about their investigation and how the company is viewed. It is also possible that the government may request the company to share results of the internal investigation.

In planning the investigative steps for any internal investigation, it is a best practice to reflect on the lessons learned from prior investigations, both internally and externally. The lessons, both good and bad, from prior investigations can help advance a professional investigation and avoid repeating pitfalls that create greater risk. One problematic area that arose in prior government investigations was the destruction of documents by the subject company and its employees. This can pertain to subpoenaed documents and other documents not yet under subpoena but may very well have an investigation nexus. The two cases that come to mind are *United States v. Arthur Andersen* and *United States v. Quattrone.*

In *United States v. Arthur Andersen*, Andersen was the external auditor for Enron and anticipated being served a government subpoena for Enron-related documents related to the government's corporate fraud investigation. Ahead of that, an in-house counsel for Andersen recommended that a notice be sent out reminding the Andersen engagement team of their document retention policy. This was a thinly veiled attempt at encouraging destruction of documents related to the Enron engagement that was the subject of the government investigation.[5]

David Duncan, the Houston-based partner in charge of the Enron audit engagement, met with Enron executives and other members of the Andersen engagement team and after that organized a wholesale destruction effort to shred documents and delete e-mails. Subsequently, Andersen was indicted for obstruction of justice for shredding documents and deleting computer files in order to protect its client, Enron. Duncan pled guilty and was a cooperating defendant for the government at trial. Although Andersen was convicted after trial, United States Supreme Court overturned the conviction in May 2005 on procedural grounds related to jury instructions.[6]

In *United States v. Quattrone*, Frank Quattrone was an investment banker at Credit Suisse First Boston (CSFB) charged by federal prosecutors in April 2003 with obstruction of justice relating to the destruction of subpoenaed documents. Quattrone forwarded an e-mail to his staff containing a reminder of the company's document retention policy and the possibility of damaging civil litigation based on the government's criminal investigation. The government eventually indicted Quattrone and he was convicted at trial and sentenced to prison. In March 2006, the Court of Appeals for the Second Circuit threw out Quattrone's conviction on grounds of improper jury instructions but the court commented that the evidence was sufficient to sustain a conviction.[7] Quattrone was never retried on the charges.

CONDUCTING INTERVIEWS

In conducting interviews of company employees, it is imperative that employees understand the role of corporate or outside counsel and the company's right to use and disclose anything that is said during the interviews. That includes disclosure to law enforcement authorities of any employee statements and evidence obtained. Employees need to understand that attorneys representing the company are not representing them and they may have adverse interests. These cautionary statements to employees are called *Upjohn warnings* and they need to realize the potential impact of admissions to wrongdoing while employed at a company.

In *Upjohn v. United States*, the Supreme Court decided that, in federal proceedings applying federal law, corporate entities could claim attorney-client privilege and that the scope of the privilege should depend on the subject matter of the communication, not on who was doing the communicating. As long as the communication involves the subject matter of the representation on whatever legal issue counsel is working on for the company, it does not matter if the communication was with management, lower-level employees, or agents. Prior to this, federal courts used a "control group" test to determine privilege and it is still used in some states. The privilege applied only to members of the control group, those senior leaders responsible for the highest level of decision making. The Supreme Court in *Upjohn* extended attorney-client privilege to a wide group of employees beyond the previous control group.[8]

Although the *Upjohn* case was not actually a warnings case, warnings would need to be given in order for companies to retain the discretion to disclose the results of internal investigations to third-parties. "Corporate Miranda" warnings have become almost mandatory in internal investigations. The Upjohn warning provides a clear understanding of what protections are, and are not, afforded to the employee and protects the attorney–client privilege between counsel and the corporation.

If employees who are interviewed request counsel, the company has to decide if it will provide counsel or whether employees retain their own counsel at their own expense. If the company decides to provide representation, it must consider the issue of multiple representation and conflicts of interest. While it might appear simpler and cheaper to have one law firm represent all employees who ask for an attorney, this is a path fraught with peril. The company may have totally different issues than the employee. Employees may have different interests from each other and these interests may change over time creating significant legal issues for the company.

When conducting interviews, it is highly recommended that two investigators participate. This provides increased documentation of the interview as one person can take detailed notes while the other conducts the interview. Having two investigators present provides greater protection from allegations of fabricated investigator misconduct by subjects. While this is an infrequent occurrence, it does happen and it is always better to be protected in advance. Taking copious notes is a must for all interviews. At the completion of the interview, the notes should be carefully reviewed for any necessary clarifications and additional recollections. If allowed by company policy and law, consider tape recording interviews. While there are needed protocols around tape recording, this practice removes many issues around what was actually said and what was not. Whether tape-recording or not, interview notes should be formalized in a memorandum of interview.

Develop a working chronology of the investigation and update frequently as the investigation progresses. At appropriate intervals of the investigation, prepare detailed reports of investigation replete with exhibits. Report writing is a critical skill and takes time and effort to become good at it. Always check with legal counsel to determine if written reports are required as there may be a determination by counsel not to prepare a report. Consider using privilege during the investigation and reporting phases. Companies should provide ongoing training on internal investigations, interviewing, and report writing to its investigators using outside counsel, consultants, and other subject matter experts to ensure a professionally trained investigative group and work product.

ROLE OF HUMAN RESOURCES

Once an investigation has concluded that the subject employee has committed a fraud or other violation of company policy, management, legal counsel, and human resources must take appropriate disciplinary action. Assuming that the violation rises to the level requiring termination, the employee is removed from the company. Zero tolerance for fraud is the standard. Whether one dollar or one million is stolen, fraud in any form cannot be tolerated. A person with no integrity must leave the organization. Although some might assume that the problem has been resolved with a termination, experience has shown that this may not be the case. It is not enough just to remove the fraudster from a company. The person responsible for the fraud should be prevented from returning to the company in another employment capacity.

If human resources does not list the employee as ineligible for rehire, it is quite possible that the terminated employee might apply for employment months or years later. In companies of significant size that have a high turnover in human resources departments, it is impossible to retain the institutional knowledge of who was fired and why without appropriate records being maintained. Employees terminated for fraudulent conduct may return to the company that fired them as contingent staff or vendors. Although it is always possible that the terminated employee has reformed and will not commit a fraud ever again, one must always remember that the best indicator of future performance is past performance. Be on the safe side. If a worker was terminated for wrongdoing, a company would do well to place that employee on an ineligible for rehire list and always refer to it before hiring new employees.

INTERACTION WITH CORPORATE EXECUTIVES AND THE AUDIT COMMITTEE

A critical element for any financial integrity unit is acknowledgment and involvement at the executive level. CEOs and CFOs need not be subject matter experts in fraud detection and prevention, but they need employees who are. The executives also need to know what their fraud detection professionals are doing to protect the company's interests. The fraud prevention unit must have access to the top executives for the program to be successful. The leadership of the fraud prevention unit should meet regularly with the CFO, Director of Compliance, Audit Committee, internal auditors, and other appropriate personnel. There should be a discussion of the fraud and abuse issues investigated at the company as well as recommendations for improvements in process and internal controls.

Regular meetings with the CFO or other appropriate corporate executives are recommended to discuss the work of the financial integrity unit including detection, investigation, prevention, and recovery. Included should be discussions of recent investigations conducted, how the issues were discovered, what internal control failures allowed the fraud to occur, employee terminations and other disciplinary actions, referrals for prosecution, recoveries and cost avoidance, and prevention and fraud awareness training of employees. Ongoing meetings with senior executives will open their eyes to the fraud and corruption risk and the importance of a robust program, as well as demonstrate their support of the program and tone at the top. This visibility within the highest reaches of the company will reinforce for all employees the commitment of the company to a culture of compliance and integrity. In addition to a close interaction with senior executives, the financial integrity unit must have key interactions with corporate security, legal counsel, finance, public relations, human resources, and other corporate groups to ensure cross-group collaboration.

PROSECUTION AS A FRAUD DETERRENT

Companies should consider referring internal and external fraud cases to law enforcement for prosecution. A certain percentage of the criminal element is deterred from committing fraud by knowing they may face a prison term for their actions. Holding a fraudster responsible is important in the pursuit of justice and the protection of the business. It can send a strong message to employees that the company is protecting their interests in a fraud-free environment and is willing to hold accountable those who break the law. A consideration for not referring cases to law enforcement is when the dollar loss is very small and not within prosecution guidelines in various districts. Another consideration is whether disclosure is in the best interest of the company based on the facts of the case. A company's legal counsel should make the final determination for any prosecution referrals.

RECOVERY OF DEFRAUDED ASSETS FROM FRAUDSTERS: MAKING FRAUD LESS PROFITABLE

A well-defined fraud prevention program must encompass recovery of defrauded assets to remove the financial gain from fraud. Fraud losses come out of the bottom line, so any recovery is beneficial. Recovery sends another strong message that not only will fraud not be tolerated, but also every effort will be made to recover the stolen assets. Consider civil actions, support and encourage criminal forfeiture in cases prosecuted, institute consent agreements to recover assets, and eliminate bonuses and other incentive compensation to employees who have defrauded the company.

Cost efficacy is about cost containment and reducing expenses while improving the bottom line. Equally important are measuring fraud losses, recovery, restitution, and cost avoidance. It is important to track losses and recoveries to know the full extent of the problem and the response. It is always hard to quantify fraud losses and the benefits of a fraud prevention program. One way to show the value of the program is through the amount of money recovered. Another way is by demonstrating the cost avoidance by early detection. When a fraud is discovered, consider extrapolating the losses over the next 12 months to show what the fraud amount might have been had it not been detected and stopped. Corporate executives are always concerned about profit, and recoveries and cost avoidance can demonstrate the financial benefit of a strong financial integrity program.

Another consideration in taking the profit out of fraud is the issuance of IRS Form 1099s to employees and others who have committed fraud or theft against the company either internally or externally. It is a given that fraudsters will not be declaring their ill-gotten earnings on their tax returns. We are aware of several companies that use this procedure, but it has not been universally accepted. It is quite possible that companies have never considered this possible course of action. There is no reason why it should not be at least considered and then possibly instituted. Issuing 1099s is an extension of good corporate governance and citizenship by reporting to the government the proceeds received by those who defrauded the company. It sends a strong message to those who commit fraud that the company will take strong measures, including reporting the embezzled funds to the IRS for whatever action the IRS deems appropriate. It is important to let employees and others know that the company has this process of IRS reporting.

It is quite conceivable that a person who has been discovered defrauding an organization will make restitution, knowing that he or she will ultimately have to deal with the IRS through the 1099 reporting procedure. That alone should strike fear into a fraudster and will add to cost efficacy and reimbursement of defrauded proceeds. Once this company policy is widely known, it should have a therapeutic effect and should increase fraud prevention. The resulting deterrence will add to an already effective culture of compliance. A sample company 1099 reporting policy is shown in Exhibit 11.2.

INTERNATIONAL INVESTIGATIONS

Fraud and corruption violations are increasing throughout the world, and there is little chance that this will change. Companies with an international reach need investigative coverage in all countries where they operate. Accounting fraud, embezzlements, and bribes to government officials can and do occur everywhere in the world. If a company's operations are based in the United States, it needs an investigative presence at the headquarters office. If there are significant operations outside the United States, investigative units need to be in those regions too. It is important to remember that the manner in which investigations are conducted in one country may differ widely from how they are done in other countries. This is due not only to different cultures but different labor and employment laws, as well as business practices. Thus, the need for guidance from legal counsel is critical in protecting the interests of the company.

In some countries, the authorities have the ability to detain people for prolonged periods without charging them, while subjecting them

The company has initiated a policy in which income derived from illegal activity including fraud, embezzlement, and theft perpetrated against the company by an employee, former employee, vendor, contractor, partner, or any other person or persons will be reported to the IRS by the company's tax department via IRS Form 1099. The amount that will be reported is based on the actual loss amount suffered by the company as a result of the activity by the employee or others or, if actual numbers are not available, on a reasonable figure as determined by the legal department and the investigative group conducting the investigation. The amount reported to the IRS should be able to be justified in the event the amount is ever challenged by the former employee or other external persons. According to IRS regulations, income obtained from illegal means is taxable to the person who benefited. The company's investigative group will maintain detailed records by case of each potential 1099 reporting. At the end of the calendar year, the head of the investigative group will report to the company's tax department the relevant information needed so a 1099 can be issued to the employee or others by the IRS notification deadline of January 31. Before the information is submitted to the IRS, the loss amounts will be carefully checked to ensure accuracy of reporting. Annual loss reports will be maintained by the investigative group, the legal department, and the tax department. These reports will contain the following:

- Name of employee or other person
- Title and work unit
- Mailing address
- Social Security number
- Amount to be reported to the IRS
- Case number
- Details of the violation of business conduct and how the amount was quantified

The reported amount will appear on a 1099 Miscellaneous Form, Box 3 (Other Income). Restitution of embezzled funds does not affect the reporting requirement. Income is recognized at the time the embezzler takes control of the funds and, is therefore, not affected by subsequent restitution.

EXHIBIT 11.2   Sample Company 1099 Reporting Policy

to constant interrogation and intimidating tactics. At one company's operation in a foreign country, a large number of its local employees found themselves detained without access to counsel or company resources. The company found itself without critical employees needed to operate its business. More importantly, the company was unable to interview these confined employees in order to perform its own internal investigation. In addition, the authorities seized computers and files, which also had an impact on the business and the company's ability to "get its arms around" the government's investigation.

Preparing employees for the possibility of government enforcement activity can be difficult due to the variability in individual and company rights in foreign countries. However, knowing what those rights are, establishing communication protocols, systemic back-up of data, as well as proper document retention policies can prove to be invaluable in such circumstances.

ONGOING DISCUSSIONS WITH COMPANY LEADERS

Fraud prevention and the reporting of fraud are critical to company management. With the enactment of Sarbanes-Oxley, CEOs and CFOs must now certify that their financial statements are truthful and free from misstatements and fraud. No more fuzzy financial accounting is allowed, unless that CEO and CFO want to land in jail. Section 302 of Sarbanes-Oxley requires certification by CEOs and CFOs that SEC Forms 10K (annual reports) and 10Q (quarterly reports) do not contain untrue statements, that financial information is fairly presented, and that disclosure controls and procedures are effective. Sarbanes-Oxley has a specific requirement that the company disclose "any fraud, whether or not material, that involves management or other employees who have a significant role in the company's internal controls."[9] Violation of this certification requirement is a federal felony punishable by up to 20 years in prison.

The fraud prevention unit has a key role in helping executives certify that their books and their companies are in compliance. In addition to ongoing meetings with the CEO, CFO, and other executives, the financial integrity unit needs to meet regularly with other senior executives, General Counsel, the Chief Compliance Officer, the General Auditor, and others as appropriate to discuss the current fraud cases that may or may not need to be reported to the Disclosure Committee, the Audit Committee, the SEC, and/or the Department of Justice. Meetings may be more frequent if serious issues of fraud are disclosed that need to be reported. The financial integrity unit should prepare a report detailing all the various fraud and abuse cases, ranking them by risk level. This report should be presented at the regularly scheduled fraud discussion meeting by the manager of the financial integrity unit, who will provide specific details on each case as well as answer any questions.

QUARTERLY FRAUD DISCUSSIONS WITH THE EXTERNAL AUDITOR

An additional step to reduce the risk of fraud and promote transparency is to hold regular meetings with the company's external auditor. The American Institute of Certified Public Accountants' Statement on Auditing Standards (SAS) 99, Consideration of Fraud in a Financial Statement Audit, established standards and guidance for auditors in detecting fraud in the financial statements of companies. Because of SAS 99, auditors must look for fraud throughout the audit process. The auditors must ask probing questions and determine whether the company is in compliance with the requirements of SAS 99. The external auditor needs to work closely with the financial integrity unit to ensure that a robust fraud prevention program is in place.

It is recommended that the financial integrity unit meet on a quarterly basis with the external auditor to discuss the fraud prevention program in place at the company, including detection, investigation, recovery, and prevention aspects. In addition to the manager of the financial integrity unit, senior executives, General Counsel, the Chief Compliance Officer, the General Auditor, and others as appropriate should attend this meeting. The manager of the financial integrity unit should discuss relevant issues with the external auditor to demonstrate compliance and transparency. External auditors will be interested in the company's response to cases of fraud but will be just as interested in learning about what the company is doing proactively to identify fraud risk and communicate fraud prevention and a culture of compliance with policy, procedures, and laws.

NOTES

1. See *Webster's Third New International Dictionary*, 1986 ed., s.v. "robust."
2. PricewaterhouseCoopers, *The Emerging Role of Internal Audit in Mitigating Fraud and Reputation Risks* (2004), 15.
3. Ibid., 6.
4. See *Webster's Third New International Dictionary*, 1986 ed., s.v. "abuse."

5. *United States v. Arthur Andersen LLP*, 544 U.S. 696 (2005).
6. Ibid.
7. *United States v. Quattrone*, 441 F.3d 153 (2d Cir. 2006).
8. *Upjohn v. United States*, 449 U.S. 383 (1981).
9. *Sarbanes-Oxley Act*, U.S. Code Title 15, Section 7241(a)(4)(B).

CHAPTER 12

Whistleblowers and Hotlines

EXECUTIVE SUMMARY

Whistleblowers and hotlines are important elements in the detection and prevention of fraud and corruption. The Federal Sentencing Guidelines, Sarbanes-Oxley, the Dodd-Frank Act, and other corporate governance enhancements all discuss the importance of whistleblowers and hotlines, as well as the standards to implement them. Tips from employees are the most common means of fraud detection, and a hotline is the reporting mechanism of choice. Creating a state-of-the-art reporting system and properly communicating its existence allows employees and others to report violations of business conduct and other issues. In addition, legitimate whistleblowers, who have evidence of fraud, must be confident that they will be protected from retaliation in reporting allegations. Failure to build this protection into a program will guarantee civil and criminal repercussions. Numerous requirements in setting up a successful hotline must be understood and carried out in protecting a company. One major requirement is the use of a third-party provider for the hotline to ensure independence and confidentiality.

WHAT ARE WHISTLEBLOWERS?

Now may be the best time to be a whistleblower. There are more whistleblower statutes and more protections than ever before. The potential for huge payouts has extended beyond just qui tam cases and the huge monetary rewards are helping overcome the stigma of being an informant. The Dodd-Frank Act's Whistleblower Provisions and the IRS Whistleblower Office are new reporting avenues open to tipsters with knowledge of fraud, corruption, and abuse.

Today's executive needs to have a greater understanding of potential risks than ever before, and few things are more important than knowledge of whistleblowers and hotlines. If those entrusted with protecting their corporation's interests either intentionally hide the existence of fraud or fail to discover it, there are those who will assume that responsibility. They are the whistleblowers, who risk their careers to expose significant allegations of financial fraud or other wrongdoing by public or private organizations.

Experience teaches that fraud is often uncovered and exposed by people with inside knowledge, including employees, vendors, customers, and others. The long-time secretary or bookkeeper who has been with the company for ages may know where all the "bodies are buried" and if given the opportunity will give valuable information to an all-too-willing-to-listen federal agent, prosecutor, or news reporter. In addition to being referred to as whistleblowers, these people are also called *confidential informants* (CIs), *confidential sources*, *informed employees*, or, as the ACFE calls them, *sentinels*. They are citizens willing to come forward—regardless of personal or professional sacrifices or consequences—to expose corporate fraud and corruption at the highest levels.[1]

Some people think that whistleblowers are simply disgruntled employees looking for an easy way to get back at their employers. In some cases this may be true, but clearly not all. This may have been the defense previously used by employers in dismissing a whistleblower's allegations of corporate wrongdoing. Often it is easier to discredit the whistleblower than to investigate thoroughly and determine whether the accusations are true. Being fired is sometimes not the worst consequence for a whistleblower. Business and professional colleagues often turn against whistleblowers rather than be identified with their cause. Whistleblowers have lost friends and families, and some have turned to alcohol to ease their personal pain and depression.[2]

It is safe to say that no one ever aspires to be a whistleblower. In fact, people usually do not use the term when referring to those who "blow the whistle" on fraud and abuse. They are called rats, stool pigeons, snitches, betrayers, and much worse. All too often it is the whistleblower standing alone against a wrongdoer. "The lone wolf whistleblower is often set up against a powerful corporate or government entity with more resources and power," commented James E. Fisher, director of the Emerson Electric Center for Business Ethics at St. Louis University. He goes on to say, "From the get-go, you have the likelihood of retaliation."[3]

Retaliation is the big "R" word facing whistleblowers. This fear has no doubt kept many individuals with personal knowledge of corporate fraud from going public. Organizations that use retaliation as a weapon of silence may have succeeded in the past. There has been a focus on reducing retaliation with the strengthening of the False Claims Act as a means to extract civil and criminal punishment in government fraud cases, the whistleblower protection afforded by Sarbanes-Oxley and the Dodd-Frank Act, and the good press given to the role of whistleblowers over the last decade.

THE GOVERNMENT'S USE OF INFORMANTS AND WHISTLEBLOWERS

It can be argued that the government's success against corporate fraud has been in large part because of the assistance of cooperating informants, cooperating defendants, and whistleblowers. In the Arthur Andersen case, the government had a cooperating defendant, former Arthur Andersen partner David Duncan. He testified for the prosecution and helped convict Arthur Andersen of obstruction of justice for shredding documents and deleting computer files in order to protect its client, Enron. Although the conviction was overturned by the U.S. Supreme Court in May 2005, it was not because of Duncan's cooperation. In the prosecution of WorldCom CEO Bernard Ebbers, the government had cooperating defendant and former CFO Scott Sullivan testify, as well as other cooperating WorldCom defendants who helped convict Ebbers on all counts of corporate fraud. In countless other cases, defendants decided to plead guilty and cooperate with the government in the hopes of receiving a lighter sentence.

A cooperating defendant is just that, a person who has committed a crime, pleads guilty to that crime, and agrees to cooperate with law enforcement authorities to provide evidence against co-conspirators in the hopes of receiving a reduced sentence. A whistleblower "is someone in an organization who witnesses behavior by members that is either contrary to the mission of the organization, or threatening to the public interest, and who decides to speak out publicly about it."[4] Simply put, a whistleblower is an informant who wants to expose and stop wrongdoing in an organization.

It has been said that if one wants information on crimes, it is more likely to come from criminals than from honest citizens. Every defense attorney will attack the credibility of a cooperating defendant, especially one who originally was part of the conspiracy and decided to break from his fellow criminals. The prosecution does not always have the luxury of using witnesses with high moral and ethical standards. Although one would prefer witnesses without "baggage" for the defense to attack, the fact is that prosecutors have to play the cards they are dealt and that includes using criminals to testify against other criminals. No one has better knowledge of fraud than fellow fraudsters.

WHISTLEBLOWERS ARE CORPORATE SENTINELS

A number of well-publicized and lesser known whistleblowers have been involved in the corporate scandals of the last decade. The best known of the group are Enron's Sherron Watkins and WorldCom's Cynthia Cooper, who exposed corporate fraud at their respective companies. Their actions gained new respectability for whistleblowers and the gratitude of the investing public. "Whistleblowers can be a source of valuable firsthand information that may otherwise not come to light," commented then SEC Chairman Mary L. Shapiro. "These high-quality leads can be crucial to protecting investors and recovering ill-gotten gains from wrongdoers."[5]

It is vital for a company to foster a culture in which employees feel empowered to come forward to report allegations of wrongdoing. Watkins thought she was doing just that when, in August 2001, she sent a six-page letter to then Enron CEO Kenneth Lay detailing what she had uncovered about accounting abnormalities and possible fraud at the energy giant. She characterized it as "an elaborate accounting hoax."[6] She must have felt some level of trust and comfort in sending the letter to Lay rather than to an outside source such as law enforcement or the media. Obviously, she thought that Enron would take more action than it did in response to her letter.

The magnitude of Watkins's allegations greatly concerned her and was a harbinger of bad things to come for Enron. Watkins must be credited with having the courage to pen such a detailed letter of corporate wrongdoing and sending it to her CEO, yet, there are some who might question why she sent her whistleblower letter only to Lay and not others outside the company. Why did she not also send the letter to the FBI, the SEC, or the media? The question will probably never be answered, but suffice it to say that whistleblowers probably have their own level of risk tolerance.

Not all whistleblowers gain notoriety. Some just come forward, do their duty, and try to go back to their prior lives. Most also do not write books capitalizing on their blowing the whistle on corporate fraud. Take the case of Maureen Castaneda, the director of foreign exchange and sovereign risk for Enron. When she was laid off by Enron in January 2002, she took home a box of paper shredding to use as packing material for a household move. She had no idea what the shredding contained until by accident she noticed a familiar name on a piece of paper. The shredded paper contained financial records of the fraudulent off-the-books partnerships that would result in indictments of many Enron executives.

Castaneda came to learn that the shredding continued long after the SEC had announced a formal investigation into Enron's finances. Castaneda told her lawyer about her discovery, and he promptly disclosed it to the government. The shredded documents were later used to verify that Enron employees were illegally destroying evidence. Castaneda told CNN's Jack Cafferty in an on-air interview, "There was a lot of arrogance at the company, I mean to the point where—an arrogance at the level where you think you can lie to Wall Street and get away with it. You can't get more arrogant than that."[7]

The ACFE has recognized the importance of the corporate sentinel who, without malice or a hidden agenda, wants to expose impropriety. In response, the ACFE has created an award called the Cliff Robertson Sentinel Award that is bestowed annually on a person who, "Without regard to personal or professional consequences, has publicly disclosed wrongdoing in business or government." The award is named for the late Oscar-winning actor who blew the whistle on fraud in Hollywood in the 1970s and who was the first recipient of the award in 2003. In 1977, Robertson discovered that the head of Columbia Pictures was embezzling funds due him and reported the fraud to authorities. Hollywood power brokers were unhappy with Robertson's whistleblowing and blacklisted him for several years. The ACFE's Sentinel Award carries the inscription, "For Choosing Truth over Self." The award is significant because Robertson was a famous Hollywood actor who dared to come forward at great risk to his professional career to expose corporate corruption at the highest levels in Hollywood.

SARBANES-OXLEY WHISTLEBLOWER REQUIREMENTS AND PROTECTIONS

Sarbanes-Oxley's Title III (Corporate Responsibility), Section 301 (Public Company Audit Committees) requires that each Audit Committee establish procedures for "the receipt, retention, and treatment of complaints received by the issuer regarding accounting, internal accounting controls, or auditing matters; and the confidential, anonymous submission by employees of the issuers of concerns regarding questionable accounting or auditing matters."[8] This translates into the requirement for public companies to have a mechanism and process that provides confidentiality and anonymity for employees and others to report issues of financial impropriety. Clearly, the mechanism alluded to is a hotline.

Title IV (Enhanced Financial Disclosures), Section 404 (Management Assessment of Internal Controls) requires an annual assessment by the issuer and its external auditor "of the effectiveness of the internal control structure and procedures of the issuer for financial reporting."[9] This translates into the requirement of an assessment of the mechanism for receiving complaints and how they are investigated and resolved. Unless a company has set up an effective process from creating a hotline, to properly communicating its existence, to conducting professional and thorough inquiries, to taking appropriate action when necessary, to reporting the results to the Audit Committee, there will be no way that a company will be in compliance with Section 404.

Title VIII (Corporate and Criminal Fraud Accountability), Section 806 (Protection for Employees of Publicly Traded Companies Who Provide Evidence of Fraud) details the civil action that employee whistleblowers can take to protect themselves against retaliation for reporting allegations of fraud at their companies.[10] Title XI (Corporate Fraud Accountability), Section 1107 (Retaliation against Informants) makes it a federal felony to retaliate against a whistleblower who provides assistance to law enforcement. The penalties include up to 10 years in prison for managers and others who are convicted of retaliation.[11] The actual criminal penalties are detailed in the amended section of Title 18, United States Code, Section 1513, which reads, "Whoever knowingly, with the intent to retaliate, takes any action harmful to any person, including interference with the lawful employment or livelihood of any person, for providing to a law enforcement officer any truthful information relating to the commission or possible commission of any Federal offense, shall be fined under this title or imprisoned not more than 10 years or both."[12]

Role of OSHA

The mission of the Occupational Safety and Health Administration (OSHA) of the Department of Labor (DOL) is to ensure the safety and health of American workers by setting and enforcing standards and by working with employees and employers to create better working environments. The DOL (OSHA through inference) have been designated by Sarbanes-Oxley to enforce its whistleblower protections. OSHA provides detailed information on the protection of whistleblowers and reporting of possible retaliation against whistleblowers.[13] OSHA now administers 21 whistleblower protection provisions. There have been a number of new whistleblower protection statutes enacted in the last few years including the Affordable Care Act, FDA Food Safety Modernization Act, and the Dodd-Frank Wall Street Reform and Consumer Protection Act.

Legal Protection When Reporting Corporate Fraud

People who work for a publicly traded company or brokerage firm, or their contractors, subcontractors, or agents, have special whistleblower protection under Section 806 of Sarbanes-Oxley. All companies with a class of securities registered under Section 12 of the Securities Exchange Act or those that are required to file reports under Section 15(d) of the Act, or their contractors, subcontractors, or agents are covered. Although most companies are covered under this provision, it is important to check with the SEC at www.sec.gov and search the EDGAR database for the specific company, contractor, or agent.

Under Sarbanes-Oxley protections, a company may not discharge or discriminate in any manner against a person who has provided information, caused information to be provided, or assisted in an official government investigation including law enforcement, securities regulators, or Congress, or an internal company investigation relating to alleged violations of mail fraud, wire fraud, bank fraud, securities fraud, SEC rules or regulations, or other federal laws relating to fraud against shareholders. This also includes disclosing information to a supervisor or other person at the company. The protected employee must reasonably believe the misconduct is a violation of federal law or SEC rules. In addition, there is a ban on discharging or other discrimination for filing a complaint or otherwise assisting in a proceeding relating to a potential violation. There is a strict ban on any form of retaliation including the following:

- Discharge
- Demotion
- Suspension
- Threats
- Harassment
- Failure to hire or rehire
- Blacklisting
- Other discrimination or disciplinary action

Requirements for Filing Complaints

To be protected under OSHA, a person must file a complaint not later than 180 days after the date of the alleged violation or when the person became aware of the violation. OSHA will review the complaint and determine whether it will conduct an investigation into the allegation. OSHA will then issue findings and an order on the complaint. After OSHA issues its findings and order, either party may request a hearing before an administrative law judge of the DOL. There is an appeal process for any administrative law judge's decision and order. If a final agency order is not issued within 180 days of the date the complaint was first filed, the complainant can bring an action in the appropriate U.S. District Court.

Whistleblower Relief

Whistleblowers who prevail can expect to be made whole with compensatory damages providing:

- Reinstatement with the same seniority status
- Back pay with interest
- Compensation for special damages including litigation costs, reasonable attorney's fees, and expert witness fees

There is always the possibility that a person will falsely allege wrongdoing on the part of company. An employee may have a personal agenda, anger, or resentment against a particular person such as a supervisor for any number of reasons. This may result in a false claim. OSHA recognizes this, and if a complaint is found to be frivolous or brought in bad faith, the false accuser may be held liable by both the government and the victim company.[14]

DODD-FRANK ACT

The Dodd-Frank Wall Street Reform and Consumer Protection Act was signed into law by President Obama on July 21, 2010. Commonly called the Dodd-Frank Act after its primary sponsors, former Senator Chris Dodd and Representative Barney Frank, it was the government's response to the financial crisis to lessen another economic meltdown. The act contains a voluminous list of laws, regulations, and changes in how Wall Street will do business. Within the act is the Section 922 Whistleblower Provisions that provides whistleblowers with huge financial incentives for reporting of securities laws violations and strong protection from retaliation. This strengthening of the SEC's whistleblower program is expected to significantly increase both the number of cases reported and monetary awards.

In order to be eligible for an award, "a whistleblower must voluntarily provide the SEC with original information about a violation of federal securities laws that leads to the successful enforcement by the SEC of a federal court or administrative action in which the SEC obtains monetary sanctions totaling more than $1 million."[15] Whistleblowers can receive between 10 and 30 percent of the amount recovered by the SEC over the first $1 million recovered. Section 922 covers publicly traded companies, private equity funds, and hedge funds. There are limitations as to who can receive whistleblower awards. People who are excluded from the award program include:

- Individuals with a preexisting legal or contractual duty to report wrongdoing
- Attorneys who use information obtained from client engagements to make whistleblower claims for themselves unless otherwise permitted
- Independent public accountants who obtain information through an engagement required under the securities laws
- Foreign government officials
- Individuals who learn about violations through a company's internal compliance program or who are in positions of responsibility for an entity, and the information is reported to them in the expectation that they will take appropriate steps to respond to the violation[16]

The last exclusion "is intended to prevent company personnel from 'front running' legitimate internal investigations" as long as the company self-discloses violations to the SEC in a timely manner.[17] Whether intentional or not, the whistleblower provision has the potential to seriously undermine corporate compliance programs by incentivizing employees to bypass their internal reporting channels to go directly to the government to gain a big payday. In late 2010, more than 260 companies sent a letter to the SEC warning that the whistleblower provisions could turn fraud into a "gold mine" for employees and others. The companies were concerned that Dodd-Frank would substantially weaken compliance programs. The SEC listened and made proposals to soften the impact including:

- Individuals reporting a violation would not be disqualified from an award if they first report a problem internally at their company, as long as they then report the wrongdoing to the SEC within 90 days.
- The SEC would give higher percentage awards to informants for first reporting the wrongdoing through internal company channels and then to the SEC.
- The SEC would bar compliance personnel and those in responsible positions of authority from receiving awards.

Compliance Program Concerns

Time will tell just how significantly corporate compliance programs will be impacted by Dodd-Frank. However, it is fair to say that there will be more whistleblower reporting by individuals as well as more self-reporting by companies. The SEC has reported a surge in fraud tips since the enactment of Dodd-Frank. Once large bounties begin to be paid out, there will be even more reporting. Organizations will need to assess their whistleblower programs and nonretaliation protections. Effective compliance programs are designed so that employees and others will come forward to report misconduct allowing the company to conduct a full and objective investigation. Dodd-Frank may change that with whistleblowers going directly to the government and receiving a financial windfall in the process. Another concern is whether the lure of a large bounty will cause employees to report minor complaints or other issues that have not been fully investigated by the organization.

Especially problematic for companies will be the impact of Dodd-Frank on Foreign Corrupt Practices Act (FCPA) cases. While the majority of enforcement actions result from corporate self-reporting, Dodd-Frank has the potential for employees to jump the gun on reporting. Employees and others with knowledge of corruption violations could report them to the government before a corporation has completed its investigation and made a decision on self-reporting. There have been whistleblowers in FCPA cases before but the financial incentive could significantly increase the number of cases. The SEC has reported that it is getting at least one FCPA tip each day. The result may be that more companies will self-report out of concern that others will beat them in the rush to the government's door.

Ongoing evaluation and modification of compliance programs are hallmarks for effective compliance. With Dodd-Frank even more emphasis is needed in compliance program design, implementation, and modification. This includes thoroughly vetting complaints, conducting internal investigations, fair and balanced disciplinary decisions and remediation, communicating standards of business conduct, whistleblower protection and nonretaliation, and incorporating internal control enhancements.

IRS WHISTLEBLOWER PROGRAM

The 2006 Tax Relief and Health Care Act implemented a significant change to the existing IRS Whistleblower Program for reporting tax fraud violations. The Act greatly increased the maximum payouts, made reward payments mandatory for truthful information, and created an appeals process for fairness when disputes arise over the outcome of a claim. Similar to the False Claims Act, successful whistleblowers can collect between 15 and 30 percent of the proceeds recovered based on certain rules. The IRS Whistleblower Office administers the informant program and payment of awards.

The IRS is looking for "specific and credible information" that "results in the collection of taxes, penalties, interest or other amounts from the noncompliant taxpayer." The IRS wants "solid information, not an educated guess or unsupported speculation" and "a significant Federal tax issue." There are different types of awards depending on if a business entity or an individual is the target and on dollar thresholds.[18] Yet it took several years for the first case to come to fruition with a reward payment.

On April 7, 2011, the IRS paid a record $4.5 million reward to an in-house accountant of an unnamed Fortune 500 financial services firm for blowing the whistle on a $20 million underpayment of tax by the company. The accountant told his employer that the company had not paid the taxes to the government but its management made a conscious decision not to self-report or correct the matter. So, the accountant took matters into his own hands and went to the IRS in 2007 to report the tax fraud. The investigation took several years and the accountant needed to hire an attorney to push the IRS into action but the result was the first such payment by the IRS Whistleblower Office under the 2006 Act. "It ought to encourage a lot of other people to squeal," stated Senator Charles Grassley who pushed for establishment of the Whistleblower Office.[19]

This well-publicized reward payment should drive others with knowledge of tax fraud to report it to the IRS. The law firm that represented the accountant feels the same way and created a Web site with the name www.first-tax-fraud-reward.com. The site documents the case, the firm's successful efforts on behalf of their client, the 2006 Act, the IRS whistleblower program and how private citizens can report wrongdoing related to unpaid taxes, and tax fraud while potentially recovering substantial rewards.

HOTLINES: BUILD IT RIGHT AND THEY WILL CALL

"Build it right and they will call" should be the mantra for today's well-run employee hotlines. On the same day in January 2002, both Enron Vice-President Sherron Watkins and former CEO Jeff Skilling testified before Congress about the Enron implosion. They sat next to each other but gave opposite testimony. Skilling said that as far as he knew, everything was in compliance at Enron. Then Watkins detailed how she tried to "blow the whistle" to then CEO Kenneth Lay, but he would not listen. Watkins detailed to Lay an "elaborate accounting hoax." Instead of being hailed as a hero for reporting the fraud, she felt Enron's wrath. The company confiscated her computer hard drive, moved her from her executive office and even considered firing her.[20]

All companies, public or private, benefit from hotlines. Confidential hotlines and business conduct lines are excellent ways to receive allegations of fraud and other wrongdoing. Hotlines allow employees and others outside the company to communicate compliance concerns to the company for appropriate action. Hotlines reveal hidden issues; company employees know that their financial futures are linked to the successful existence of their companies. If a company does not already have a hotline in place, it is putting itself at risk. Hotlines are here to stay. Whistleblowers and hotlines together provide a potent mix that can protect a company.

Other than the Sarbanes-Oxley requirement for having a hotline, some key statistics also support the benefit. The ACFE's *2010 Report to the Nations on Occupational Fraud and Abuse* found that tips were the most common way that frauds were detected. This occurred with a far greater frequency than through management review, internal audit, or even by accident. Exhibit 12.1 shows the source and percent of tips for the 2010 study. When one looks at the makeup of the tipsters, one sees that the greatest number came from employees, followed by customers, vendors, and then anonymous individuals.[21] Exhibit 12.2 shows the detection of frauds by disclosure method and percent of cases for the 2010 study.

Other findings from the *2010 Report to the Nations* also support the need for hotlines. The presence of hotlines increases the number of

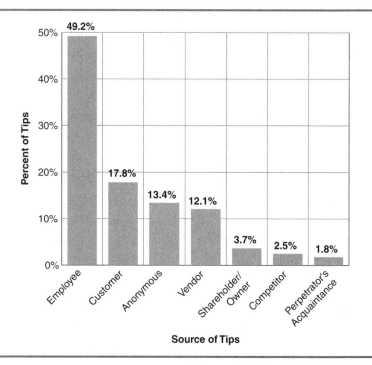

EXHIBIT 12.1   Percent of Tips by Source
Source: Reprinted with permission from the *2010 Report to the Nations on Occupational Fraud and Abuse*, Association of Certified Fraud Examiners, Austin, Texas © 2010.

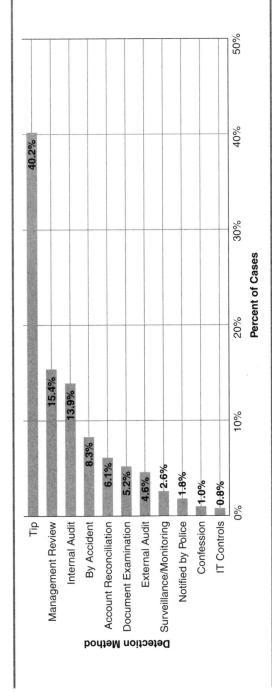

EXHIBIT 12.2 Detection of Fraud by Disclosure Method and Percent of Cases

Source: Reprinted with permission from *the 2010 Report to the Nations on Occupational Fraud and Abuse*, Association of Certified Fraud Examiners, Austin, Texas © 2010.

tips received and therefore, the number of fraud cases discovered. In organizations with hotlines, 47 percent of fraud was detected through tips. In organizations without hotlines, only 34 percent of frauds were detected by tips.[22] In further support of the need for hotlines, the study also found that 67 percent of fraud cases resulted from anonymous tips to a company's hotline.[23]

The Need for Hotlines

Another key statistic from the *2010 Report to the Nations* points to the beneficial aspects of having a hotline. Organizations that implemented hotlines and other confidential reporting mechanisms significantly reduced fraud losses. The median loss for organizations that had hotlines was $100,000. The median loss was more than twice that amount, $245,000, for organizations that did not have such confidential reporting mechanisms.[24] There is no doubt that tips to hotlines greatly increase the detection and reporting of fraud.

An interesting finding from the *2010 Report to the Nations* was that only 15 percent of small businesses had a hotline, while 64 percent of large organizations had one. The lower number of hotlines in place at smaller businesses may seem remarkable; the fact is that many organizations do not realize the full potential of hotlines. Smaller organizations with fewer controls in place are often more susceptible to fraud, especially if they do not use hotlines. Hotlines are nothing new, but they work. There is no reason for any company, no matter how small, not to have some manner of confidential and anonymous reporting such as a hotline.

One of the authors was involved in an investigation that started as a result of a hotline call. The caller stated that if the company had not had a hotline, the allegation would not have been reported. The caller wanted anonymity, and a hotline was the only mechanism that provided that level of comfort and trust. The whistleblower used the hotline call to report a fraud scheme involving an employee and a vendor totaling thousands of dollars.

Choose the Right Name

The term *hotline* is the common default for a confidential and anonymous reporting tool. Texas Instruments' *Accounting and Auditing*

Hotline, Pepsico's *Speak Up Hotline*, and Citigroup's *Ethics Hotline* all use "hotline" in the name. Although a hotline conveys the idea of a quick and direct telephone line for information, it may also give a connotation that any call received may bring bad news. Callers will do more than just report fraud. They may inquire as to appropriate business practices, policy and procedure clarification, or matters totally unrelated to mechanism hotline's purpose. A company may consider using a term other than hotline that better signifies the intent. General Motor's *Awareline*, Merck's *Advice Line*, Altria's *Integrity HelpLine*, and Microsoft's *Business Conduct Line* all are "hotlines," but they use a more inclusive and less threatening title. The appropriate name sends a message to employees and others about the importance of the reporting mechanism.

Some companies' hotlines are not easy to find on the company Web site. If the intent is to provide a means to report violations of business conduct and foster good corporate governance, one can ask why the hotline is not in a prominent location on the home page. Build it right and they will call.

Confidential vs. Anonymous

Most hotlines are confidential and anonymous so as to provide a level of comfort to the caller. Maintaining the confidentiality and anonymity of hotline callers is absolutely critical to the success of the hotline. Violate the trust between the caller and the organization, and there is little chance of ever restoring confidence. If the caller's identity is not kept confidential and anonymous, it is a good bet that few people will call and report violations of business conduct. There is a difference between confidentiality and anonymity, however.

Confidentiality implies that the caller's identity and information will not be communicated broadly and only to those with an absolute need to know. If a person calls a hotline and provides a name along with the allegations, it must be understood that this information will be made known to officials at the company, such as the legal department, the investigative unit, human resources, and other appropriate personnel. Confidentiality should ensure that the communication is only disclosed to the minimum number of authorized people in order to resolve the issue. If a person's name is provided, the organization has a duty to protect the confidentiality of that person. If it cannot do this, the organization may have far bigger problems than whatever the caller is reporting. There is an argument to be made that it might be better for a whistleblower not to provide a name or other identifying information when reporting wrongdoing.

Anonymity provides secrecy and nondisclosure for the caller's identity but not the information provided. True anonymity involves the removal of any reference to a caller's gender or other identifying information, even if a name is not provided. Safeguards must be in place to protect the caller's identity in case certain personnel at the company attempt to determine it for any reason. Anonymity promised must be anonymity kept. It is important to always advise that the confidentiality of anyone reporting a possible violation will be maintained within the limits allowed by law.

Hotline Basics

A number of basic rules apply when it comes to hotlines. The hotline number must be easily accessible. It must be available to callers in every country where the company operates. As globalization of business increases, it makes good sense to be able to receive calls from anywhere in the world. The number must be toll-free from within the United States and other countries where such a number can be dialed. In countries where a toll-free number is not available, there must be an international number that can be called collect. As previously stated, the hotline must be confidential and anonymous. It must be available 24 hours a day, seven days a week, to capture all possible calls. Employees may not want to call from work, where there is the chance they may be discovered, so a call at night from home is more likely. In fact, 40 percent of hotline calls are made outside of normal business hours.[25] In addition, with callers from other countries and time zone differences, round-the-clock availability is a must.

The hotline must be staffed by "live" people. The interaction with a live person cannot be duplicated in any other way. Having a telephone line with an answering machine to take calls after hours is not state-of-the-art compliance in today's world. The hotline must have language capability for all employees in all countries where the organization has operations. This means translators with excellent language skills must be available to speak to any caller. The caller should be advised that the calls are not recorded or traced. For callers who want to remain anonymous, any reports provided should be gender neutral to protect the caller's anonymity. Operators must be thoroughly screened and trained. The questioning of callers must be professional in nature, focusing on the information or allegation provided. Callers should be provided a callback code word or number in case they want to call back and provide more information or ask about the status of any investigation resulting from their information. A good policy should be never to advise the caller of the details of any ongoing investigation. At the conclusion of any investigation, the organization's legal department should decide what information, if any, should be communicated to the caller.

Types of Reporting Mechanisms

Potential reporters of fraud and abuse should have as many available means of communication as possible. This includes reporting by telephone, e-mail, letter, or fax. The more and varied types of reporting that a company has, the greater the chance that important information will be provided. When reporting is done by e-mail over the Internet, the third-party vendor should remove the header and other contact information before forwarding it to the organization. Anonymous e-mail accounts are easy to open for this purpose. When a number of different reporting systems are available, there is the potential for information to be missed or routed to the wrong person. Whoever maintains the hotline for an organization must have appropriate systems and safeguards in place to receive and respond to each type of report.

Kinds of Calls to the Hotline

An organization's hotline should take any and all kinds of calls. When calls are limited only to those related to financial accounting issues, as mandated by Sarbanes-Oxley, the hotline is not being used to the fullest extent possible. A hotline should take calls covering all kinds of wrongdoing, whether it is fraud, corruption, theft, sexual harassment, workplace violence, or other violations of business conduct. Hotlines should also take any other type of call even if it is not related to a wrongdoing. Callers with questions and requests for information about policy, procedures and ongoing deals should be encouraged. It is far better to be able to advise an employee on a potentially problematic issue earlier than later. All reports from calls should be communicated to an appropriate official at the organization for further action.

Questions to Ask of Callers

The operators of the hotline need to ask probing questions but not appear to be conducting an interrogation. Professionalism and experience play an important role in asking key questions and getting the answers without intimidating the caller. The tone and demeanor of the operator, the respect provided to the caller, and how the questions are asked will provide either a positive or negative result. The process to be completed and the information to be documented are as follows:

- Advise that the call is confidential and that nothing is provided to identify the caller unless the caller specifically requests to be identified.
- Record the time and date of the call.
- Record the operator's name, identification number, and location.
- Assign a specific caller identification code or number.
- Is the caller an employee, vendor, contractor, or other?
- What is the business conduct violation or other wrongful act(s)?
- How is the caller aware of this information?
- Who are the people involved? In addition to the names, the operator should ask the caller to provide as much detailed information as possible, such as titles, addresses, and other contact information.
- When did it occur?
- Where did it occur?
- How long has it been going on?
- It is still ongoing?
- How often has it been occurring?
- Does the caller have any documentary evidence related to the allegation?

- Has the caller ever reported this before? If so, provide details.
- Have the caller provide as much information as possible, as there may be only one chance to capture it.

Use Third-Party Hotline Providers

Although some companies may feel it is more cost effective to maintain the reporting system in-house, this is not a best practice and can lead to serious independence issues. To ensure transparency and a culture of compliance, there is nothing better than having an independent third-party vendor take hotline calls. In fact, it is highly recommended that a company's hotline be administered by an external third-party vendor to provide an increased level of trust and confidence and to avoid the "concern that 'anonymous calls' will go to a company person who will recognize the tipster's voice."[26] By outsourcing this function, the company is protected from accusations of covering up evidence of fraud. There is just too much risk if a company's in-house hotline receives an allegation of financial accounting fraud by a CEO or CFO and the company then finds the allegation without merit. There may always be that nagging feeling that a thorough and impartial investigation was not conducted and the matter was swept under the rug. Although this will not be true in most instances, it is not necessary to take the chance.

Third-party vendors of hotlines with many years of experience and many corporate clients are best able to receive and respond to all types of calls. They have trained professionals handling the calls, and they understand the importance of confidentiality and the reputational risk they face if the calls are not handled professionally. Hotlines can be built for the individual needs of each client. Of course, all hotline vendors may not have the same level of experience and skills. Before signing a contract, a careful vetting must be conducted. The vetting requires that the company obtain certain information and ask questions that must be appropriately answered, such as:

- How long has the company been in business?
- Who is (are) the principal owner(s)?
- Is there more than one physical office location?
- How many clients does the company have?

- Has the company received any complaints? If so, what are the details?
- Ask them to provide several references.
- Check the Better Business Bureau for complaints.
- Are there operators available around the clock to take calls?
- What is the experience level of the operators?
- What kind of educational requirements are needed to be an operator? All operators should at least have college degrees. Some vendors require postgraduate degrees in social work, psychology, or a related field.
- Are background checks including criminal checks and credit checks performed on all operators with periodic updates?
- Do all vendor employees (ownership and operators) sign nondisclosure agreements?
- What kind of training program do the operators complete?
- Is the training program general in nature or specific to the client's operation?
- How long are the operators trained before they can take calls?
- Is there an ongoing training program to keep the operators up to date on changes and process improvements?
- What is the operator turnover rate and why?
- How many languages are available and what is the proficiency level for each?

The third-party vendors should report allegations and other issues to several points of contact to ensure transparency and action. Among the people who should receive the information are the Chief Compliance Officer or Director of Compliance, the Ethics Officer, the Chair of the Audit Committee, the head of Internal Audit, and the Director of Corporate Security or Financial Integrity. There are many experienced third-party providers of hotlines and related services. Potential clients of hotline services are encouraged to do their homework and find the most experienced provider that suits their needs.

Communicating the Existence of the Hotline

A reporting system will not be successful unless all employees are aware of it and have a reasonable assurance that the company will act on allegations based on factual belief. A good test is for managers to ask employees about their knowledge of the hotline at one-on-one meetings and group training sessions. It might be surprising to find that a good number of employees are unaware that a reporting mechanism even exists in the organization. However, a company is only half protected unless the hotline is known by people outside the organization. People outside the company are as likely to call as those within if they have knowledge of violations of business conduct. Thus, there is a constant need to communicate the existence of the hotline both inside and outside the company. There are a number of ways to do this, including the following:

- Prominently displaying information about the hotline on the company's Web site.
- Including hotline information in the company code of conduct as well as other codes used such as procurement, vendor, and finance.
- Placing hotline information on the company Intranet, office bulletin boards, in newsletters, on posters, in break rooms, on employee access badge holders, on table-tents in cafeterias, and other places where employees congregate.
- Sending letters to all company employees at their home address announcing the hotline.
- Communicating that the organization has an independent third-party vendor taking the calls.
- Sending letters to all company vendors and partners announcing the hotline.
- Printing the hotline number on all company checks paid to vendors. The benefit is that a supplier may call in and report a violation.[27]
- Being sure to communicate that appropriate action will be taken against those who are found to have reported false allegations.

Corporate Response to Hotline Calls

Responding to hotline calls must be a top priority for an organization. A quick response will build confidence and also remove potential doubts about the company's commitment to ethical behavior and a culture of compliance. The hotline provider should communicate all allegations and other reported information to appropriate officials at the organization. All reports should be immediately logged into a case management system for future reporting to the CEO, CFO, Audit Committee, and, if necessary, external auditors and government regulators.

Vetting the Hotline Calls

Third-party receivers of hotline calls will not normally test the validity of the information received or provide any commentary as to the legitimacy of the information. This is the organization's responsibility. Be aware that some people may use an anonymous reporting mechanism for their own sinister designs. Using live interviewers who can ask probing questions may lessen the possibility that a person will report false information. When the organization receives an allegation of fraud or other business conduct violation through a hotline, it is important to test and corroborate the allegations received. Detailed vetting for independent corroboration of allegations is critical. Financial integrity units are the logical choice to receive and investigate fraud allegations received through the hotline.

The content of calls that are received must undergo a further examination to corroborate the allegations. A number of questions need to be asked and answered, including the following:

- Is the allegation detailed and specific or just general, such as saying there is fraud at the company?
- Is the allegation reasonable or so outlandish that it may have no basis in fact?
- Is someone actually named in the allegation?
- If a person is named by the anonymous caller, is it even possible that the person could have committed the violation?
- Does the person named have the position and opportunity to commit the alleged fraud?
- Is evidence provided to substantiate the allegation or is information provided so as to find the evidence?
- Does it appear that the caller has a hidden agenda?
- Can a preliminary corroboration of the allegations be made?
- Does the caller make additional calls to the hotline providing additional information?

Another element needs to be added to this process. When a call is received and referred to an investigator for follow-up, advise the third-party vendor of the name and contact information for the investigator assigned to the matter. In case the whistleblower calls back, the investigator's name can be provided to the whistleblower, who may decide to contact the investigator directly to provide additional information. There is a great benefit when an experienced investigator has the opportunity to actually interview a hotline caller to learn more about the allegation and whether it has merit. Sometimes the whistleblower then calls the investigator directly and provides even more useful information.

It is also important to test the effectiveness of the hotline when third-party vendors are used. A checks and balances approach will ensure that hotline calls are being routed by the vendor to the appropriate personnel at the company. An organization may consider having designated company personnel call the hotline and anonymously provide a specific but made-up allegation. Test how quickly and correctly the allegation is communicated to the company. In addition, make test calls on Sarbanes-Oxley-related issues and see whether they are referred to the Audit Committee by the hotline as they should be. Make these calls from the United States and various other countries where the company has offices. The calls outside the United States can be made by investigative or legal personnel while they are traveling to foreign countries on business.

THE FALSE CLAIMS ACT

For whistleblowers, possibly the best recourse for exposing fraud in government contracts has been the False Claims Act (FCA). This federal law was enacted to encourage private citizen whistleblowers to file lawsuits in the name of the U.S government charging false claim violations by government contractors, health care providers, and other businesses and persons who receive or use government funds. The greatest impact from FCA whistleblower actions has been in the health care industry. Physicians, hospitals, medical service and equipment providers, and pharmaceutical companies typically receive federal funds. Organizations and individuals who commit fraud involving federal funds face the possibility that employees or others who have knowledge of the fraud may use the FCA not only to expose the criminal wrongdoing of the organization but also to reap huge monetary rewards from reporting it.

The FCA was passed in 1863 after Congress uncovered widespread instances of fraud on the part of military contractors to the Union Army, resulting in defective weapons as well as price gouging during the Civil War. President Lincoln urged its passing to combat rampant fraud and restore needed funding for the war effort. In fact, it is often called the "Lincoln Law" because of President Lincoln's strong support of its enactment. The *qui tam* (short form of the Latin phrase that means "who sues on behalf of the king as well as himself") provision of the FCA encourages private citizens to uncover and disclose fraud and as a result benefit financially. Although the FCA was initially intended to fight military procurement fraud, it applies to all government contractors and federal programs when government funds are involved.

The original federal law of 1863 allowed a relator (plaintiff) to file a lawsuit, but there were a number of obstacles to overcome. The relator had to bear all the costs of the lawsuit, and the government could join the lawsuit at any time and completely take over the case. In later years, the government made it even harder for relators to prevail. The maximum monetary amount that could be awarded to a relator was reduced from 50 percent to 25 percent if the government did not join in the case with the relator. If the government entered the case, the maximum that a relator could receive was 10 percent. These restrictions resulted in little use of the FCA.

That changed in 1986 with the emergence of new government contracting and procurement frauds. This long-forgotten FCA gained new popularity when Congress reinforced it with strengthened amendments. Defendants faced increased damages and penalties. The relator's share of recovered proceeds was now between 15 and 25 percent if the government joined the lawsuit. The maximum payout of 25 percent would be based on the whistleblower's significant contribution to the case. If the government did not join the case, the whistleblower could recover at least 25 percent but not more than 30 percent of what the government recovered. The amount awarded to the relator is based on the amount recovered and not the actual fraud loss. In addition, prior government knowledge of the fraud did not affect the ability of a relator to file a qui tam action and prevail.

EXECUTIVE INSIGHT 12.1: A WHISTLEBLOWER FINDS THE GOLDEN GOOSE

Whistleblowers who utilize the False Claims Act not only find justice but often discover the Golden Goose along the way: The windfall can be huge for plaintiffs who prevail after blowing the whistle on fraud. Jim Alderson is one who hit the jackpot after successfully filing whistleblower claims. In one case, he received $20 million and in another, he split $100 million. In 1990, Alderson was employed as Chief Financial Officer at a hospital in Montana and was fired for refusing to maintain two sets of books. One set of books contained falsified numbers to be used for Medicare reimbursement and another set was only for the hospital's internal use, allegedly containing the true accounting numbers. Even though he was fired, Alderson continued digging and found massive fraud. He filed a wrongful termination lawsuit that eventually became *qui tam* actions against Quorum Health Group, Inc. and Columbia/HCA, two of the largest health care management companies in the United States. The Department of Justice joined Alderson's civil lawsuits in 1998, and the cases were eventually settled in the government's and Alderson's favor. He was richly rewarded for the heartache of 13 years of legal battles. Alderson now lives the good life knowing that he helped expose fraud and in the process took the defrauded proceeds from the offenders.[i] As Senator Charles Grassley (R-Iowa), who helped enhance the act in 1986, said, "Whistleblowers shed light on why something is wrong, and their insights can help hold the bad actors responsible, fix problems and achieve reforms."[ii]

---

[i]Siobhan McDonough, "Whistleblowers Rake in the Dough," *Seattle Times*, November 27, 2004, A28.

[ii]Associated Press, "For Some Whistleblowers, Big Risk Pays Off," New York Times.com, November 28, 2004, A1.

Whistleblowers can file civil actions under seal in district courts that will be reviewed by the local U.S. Attorney's Offices. If the prosecutors feel the cases have merit, the government can bring in federal agents to conduct a related criminal investigation. The addition of these resources would help to bring about a successful prosecution and greatly benefit a relator's civil case and subsequent monetary reward.

Whistleblower protection is also included in the False Claims Act. The FCA prohibits an employer from any form of retaliation against an employee who attempts to report allegations of fraud against the federal government. The retaliation protection covers discharge, demotion, suspension, threats, harassment, or other discrimination as a result of lawful acts by employees or employees on behalf of others in furtherance of a False Claims Act action. The affected party or parties "shall be entitled to all relief necessary to make the employee whole" and "shall include reinstatement with the same seniority status such employee would have had but for the discrimination, two times the amount of back pay, interest on the back pay, and compensation for any special damages sustained as a result of the discrimination, including litigation costs and reasonable attorneys' fees."[28]

As a result of the 1986 enhancements, the False Claims Act has become very popular with whistleblowers by offering them significant financial incentives to expose wrongdoing. There has been a steady increase in the number of lawsuits filed and recoveries of funds. In 1987, 33 cases were filed; in 1995, 274 cases were filed; and in early 2011 the government disclosed that more than 1,300 *qui tam* cases were under investigation. In November 2010, the Department of Justice reported that it had recovered $3 billion in False Claims Act cases in Fiscal Year 2010 and more than $27 billion since 1986.[29] The top 10 FCA settlements and relator rewards are shown in Exhibit 12.3.

In recent years, the scope and reach of the FCA has been expanded through new legislation including the Fraud Enforcement and Recovery Act of 2009, the Affordable Care Act of 2010, and the Dodd-Frank Act. The enhancements include expansion of the definition of what constitutes a false claim, removal of the intent requirement and replacing it with just a materiality requirement, simplification of the conspiracy element for violations, added liability for retention of overpayments, increased protections for relators from the previously

EXHIBIT 12.3 Top 10 False Claims Act Settlements and Relator Rewards

Date	Company	Allegation	Settlement Amount	Relator Reward
September 2009	Pfizer, Inc.	Illegally promoted several drugs not approved by the FDA and kickbacks to physicians and others	$1.0 B	$102 M
June 2006	Tenet Healthcare	Kickbacks, upcoding, bill padding, and other unlawful billing practices	$900 M	$150 M
December 2000	HCA, Inc. (formerly Columbia/HCA	A number of health care fraud violations including kickbacks to physicians, upcoding, billing for lab tests not medically necessary or ordered by physicians	$731 M	$100 M
February 2008	Merck	False Claims Act violations including pricing fraud and kickbacks to health care providers	$650 M	$68 M
June 2003	HCA, Inc. (formerly Columbia/HCA	A number of health care fraud allegations including cost report fraud and kickbacks to physicians	$631 M	$151 M
October 2010	GlaxoSmithKline	Systematic deceit on product contamination and dosage irregularities	$600 M	$96 M
October 2005	Serono	Kickbacks to physicians and pharmacies, illegal off-label marketing of a drug, and other fraud	$567 M	$52 M
October 2001	Taketa-Abbot Pharmaceutical	Fraudulent drug pricing and marketing, kickbacks to physicians	$559 M	$95 M
July 2009	New York State & New York City	Improper and questionable billing for school-based health care services during a seven-year period	$540 M	$10 M
April 2010	AstraZeneca	Illegally marketing an anti-psychotic drug for uses not approved as safe and effective by the FDA	$520 M	$45 M

Source: U.S. Department of Justice press releases on False Claims Act Settlements, www.justice.gov.

covered employees to the now covered contractors and agents, and other amendments that in total will increase civil and criminal cases.

Fraud fighting tools such as the FCA and the *qui tam* provision allow whistleblowers to team up with the federal government in a potent partnership to fight fraud. It is expected that the steady flow of *qui tam* cases will continue as people with knowledge of fraud become aware of the existence of the FCA. Organizations without fraud detection and prevention programs will find that whistleblowers will do their work for them with negative implications.

NOTES

1. Association of Certified Fraud Examiners, "Awards and Special Recognition," www.acfe.com/membership/awards.asp.
2. Fred C. Alford, *Whistleblowers: Broken Lives and Organizational Power* (Ithaca, NY: Cornell University Press, 2001), 19–20.
3. Marci Alboher Nusbaum, "Blowing the Whistle: Not for the Fainthearted," *New York Times*, February 10, 2002, B10.
4. Fr. Floriano C. Roa, *Business Ethics and Social Responsibility* (Manila: Rex Books Store, Inc., 2007), 145.
5. U.S. Securities and Exchange Commission, "SEC Proposes New Whistleblower Program under Dodd-Frank Act," Securities and Exchange Commission Release No. 2010–213, November 3, 2010, www.sec.gov/news/press/2010/2010–213.htm.
6. Charlene Oldham, "Diary of Deception," *Dallas Morning News*, February 3, 2002, 1H.
7. "Ex-Enron Exec: Shredding Went on after Probe Began," *CNN.com*, January 22, 2002, edition.cnn.com/2002/LAW/01/22/castaneda.cnna.cnna/.
8. *Sarbanes-Oxley Act*, U.S. Code Title 15, Section 301.
9. Ibid., Section 404.
10. Ibid., Section 806.
11. Ibid., Section 1107.
12. Ibid., Section 1513.
13. Occupational Safety and Health Administration, United States Department of Labor, "The Whistleblower Program," www.osha.gov/dep/oia/whistleblower/index.html.

14. Ibid.
15. U.S. Securities and Exchange Commission, "SEC Proposes New Whistleblower Program under Dodd-Frank Act."
16. Ibid.
17. Ibid.
18. Internal Revenue Service, "Whistleblower – Informant Award," www.irs.gov/compliance/article/0,,id=180171,00.html.
19. Maryclaire Dale, "IRS Awards $4.5M to Whistleblower," Associated Press, April 8, 2011, www.usatoday.com/money/perfi/taxes/2011–04–08-irs-whistleblower-taxes-reward.htm.
20. "Bitter Row Dominates Enron Hearing," *BBC News*, February 26, 2002, //news.bbc.co.uk/1/hi/business/1841824.stm.
21. Association of Certified Fraud Examiners, *2010 Report to the Nations on Occupational Fraud and Abuse* (Austin, TX, 2010), 17.
22. Ibid., 18.
23. Ibid., 17.
24. Ibid., 43.
25. Timothy L. Mohr and Dave Slovin, "Making Tough Calls Easy," *Security Management*, March 2005, 51.
26. Ibid., 52.
27. Ibid. This recommendation is based on a company that received such a call after it printed its hotline number on its checks.
28. *Civil Actions for False Claims*, U.S. Code 31, § 3730 (h).
29. U.S. Department of Justice, "Department of Justice Recovers Record $3 Billion in False Claims Cases in Fiscal Year 2010," press release (November 22, 2010), www.justice.gov/opa/pr/2010/November/10-civ-1335.html.

Time to Do Background Checks

EXECUTIVE SUMMARY

It has often been said that the best indicator of future performance
is past performance. Vetting all employees through background
investigations is an absolute necessity today. During a difficult
economic climate, fraud in the workplace has increased. The FBI
has stated that employee theft is the fastest growing crime in
the United States.[1] The level of scrutiny in a background check
should be commensurate with the employee's role and responsibilities. Background investigations cost money, but this is money
well spent. Companies have been embarrassed and worse when
the star CEO was found to have skeletons in the closet that easily could have been discovered through a simple public records
search. Well-regarded CEOs also have had their reputations damaged when they joined start-ups without doing appropriate due
diligence. Due diligence and background checks also are important in the world of mergers and acquisitions. Even the best background checks conducted at the time of hire will not help if there
are no periodic updates to develop any subsequent arrests, civil
actions, or adverse media reports regarding employees.

If you have decided to adopt the recommendation of the Committee of Sponsoring Organizations (COSO), as well as other compliance initiatives, to start screening job applicants, you have taken a great first step. Now what? One of the easiest ways to establish a strong moral tone for an organization is to hire the right employees. Hiring the right employees not only reduces fraud but also reduces workplace violence. Some two million American workers are victims of workplace violence each year.[2] Employers face liability for acts of workplace violence under the OSHA "General Duty Clause."[3] Many factors surrounding workplace violence create liability for employers, including negligent hiring and retention.[4] Major corporations such as Wal-Mart, Ford, General Motors, and IBM conduct background checks on all job applicants.

Organizations should conduct thorough background checks on all employees. County-level criminal checks should be used in conjunction with statewide checks and national sex offender searches. For those in financially sensitive positions, credit checks are also recommended. Many studies have shown that those in financial difficulty are much more likely to commit workplace fraud. While many employers have become reluctant to supply employment references for former employees, every attempt should be made to obtain as much information as possible from prior employers. Many employment verifiers have found increasing instances of candidates listing nonexistent prior work experiences.

All employers should be aware of the progress of state and federal data privacy legislation, its notice requirements, and associated regulations. As of the writing of this chapter, most states have enacted security breach notification laws, which apply to companies that retain consumer information electronically, including employers who retain information derived from background checks. In addition, all companies engaging in employment screening must have a thorough familiarity with the Fair Credit Reporting Act and various state and local restrictions on obtaining personal information with respect to employees and candidates. For example, Oregon specifically prohibits an employer from obtaining or using a consumer credit report for purposes of making a hiring decision unless the employer can prove that the credit history is "substantially related" to the performance of the job.[5]

FCRA REQUIREMENTS

The Fair Credit Reporting Act (FCRA) is one of the federal statutes that govern employment screening. For employment purposes, each applicant should sign a consent form before any checks are made into their criminal or credit histories. If derogatory information is found, applicants have the right to receive a copy of this information if they want to inspect or challenge any incorrect information from the original consumer credit company or courthouse that is the official keeper of this information. Companies are encouraged to develop consent forms that authorize the search of criminal, civil, and credit histories of applicants.

WHAT IS A BACKGROUND CHECK?

The Society for Human Resource Management (SHRM) research shows that "the top reasons why organizations conduct credit background checks are to limit theft and embezzlement in the workplace, reduce liability for negligent hiring, assess the overall trustworthiness of the job candidate, and comply with applicable state laws requiring a background check for particular positions."[6]

So, what kinds of information should an employer attempt to develop about a candidate? Typical elements of a background check might include:

- Work history
- Nature and length of work experience
- Related work experience in the same industry
- Education and certifications including professional credentials
- Personal references
- Driver's safety history
- Criminal history
- Credit history

Different emphasis on each element or additional types of background history may be sought depending on the nature of the position to be filled. A position that requires arduous and expensive training in order for the individual to become productive may place a greater value on longevity in a candidate's work history than on extensive education. A project management position, on the other hand, may place more value on an applicant's wide variety of work experiences obtained from multiple employers.

Unfortunately, in today's litigious environment, employers may be reluctant to provide an accurate assessment of a former employee's work history including strengths, weaknesses, and disciplinary actions. They fear that such a candid assessment might expose them to liability for defamation or negligent referral.[7] It is becoming increasingly difficult to obtain any useful information from former employers.

THERE IS NO ONE-STOP SHOPPING FOR CRIMINAL RECORDS

"Wait a minute, isn't there a national criminal history search?" The answer is no, not for employment screening. The FBI's National Crime Information Center (NCIC) is for law enforcement use only. Companies that are conducting background checks for the first time have many decisions to make about how much checking they want to do and how much they want to spend. The fact is that more and more companies are conducting criminal checks on job applicants, with 92 percent of employers conducting checks in 2009 up from 80 percent in 2004.[8] This indicates that background screening is increasing in midsize and smaller companies.

Numerous firms offer background screening services, and they make many claims about what kind of criminal checks can be done. Some companies claim they can do nationwide criminal checks on applicants. The only true database that tracks all criminal records from anywhere in the country is the NCIC. Although this same information is sometimes marketed as "National Wants and Warrants" by some background check vendors, this information is not legally available, and the vendors are breaking the law if they are selling data from NCIC. NCIC is accessible only by law enforcement and cannot be sold to perform background checks. If the background check vendor has compiled data from multiple databases to try to get national coverage, this is legal and available, but it is not a true national search. It is as close as you will get. A national sex offender database exists, which is recommended for screening all applicants.

Many levels of criminal records are available for background check purposes, some automated and some not. Some states have statewide criminal check capabilities and some do not. States such as Delaware have only three counties, whereas others have close to a hundred. The employer should not attempt to inquire about arrests; only convictions are permitted to be used in making employment decisions.

A U.S. District Court federal criminal check will produce any records that the candidate may have been a party to nationwide but only for federal violations. This relates to crimes investigated by the FBI, the Drug Enforcement Administration (DEA), the U.S. Customs, the U.S. Postal Inspection Service, and other federal law enforcement agencies. The results would not show all criminal records in the United States, only those from federal courts. Federal violations are a small minority of all convictions. When one is hiring for entry-level positions, which may be filled by high-school and college-aged applicants, it is unlikely that the FBI or DEA has arrested any of these applicants or that they have federal convictions. Federal criminal record searching is more suited for executive applicants.

State convictions are also a minority of all convictions. These include serious felonies like murder and rape. Many states maintain a database for all those convicted in the state. However, if a conviction occurred on the county level, which is the large majority, the conviction might not have been recorded in the statewide database. So, even if one were to pay for a U.S. federal criminal check and a statewide criminal check from each of the 50 states that had such a database, there would be no guarantee of finding all the convictions a person might have. The only way to ensure that all possible convictions that a subject has in one state are obtained is to check each county in the state one by one. Therefore, to do a real nationwide criminal check on one person would involve checking all counties in all states and would cost thousands of dollars.

To make the process workable, an initial search is run in public records using the Social Security Account Number (SSAN) of the applicant as a filter. Once verified, the SSAN can be linked to all the past addresses of the subject. This identifies which counties in which states to check for possible criminal records. Do not use the address history provided by the subject, as the subject may leave out any jurisdiction in which he may have a criminal conviction. If the subject has lived only in one county in one state for the previous 10 years, only one county's records need to be checked.

Any case in which an applicant is discovered to have more than one SSAN should be investigated. This is often caused by a typographical error or other mistake in the public records; but it could have resulted from a stolen identification or a deliberate attempt to hide a true identity. Advise the applicant of the issue and work together to solve it.

A check of the statewide database is a good idea if the state has one. However, a county check should also be done in the counties where the subject lived during the previous seven years. If the subject has lived in multiple counties, this could be expensive. Some background check firms offer to check all counties in which an applicant has lived in the previous seven years for a set price. What these firms lose monetarily on rare multiple-county checks is made up by the fact that most checks are on applicants who resided in just one county.

The downside to this method is that convictions will not be found for areas in which the subject did not live. However, the majority of convictions are in the county of residence. As an example, suppose an applicant lives in Jefferson City, Missouri (Cole County), but holds season football tickets to the University of Missouri Tigers in Columbia, Missouri (Boone County). For the most part, the applicant is a law-abiding person. However, the applicant has a tendency to overindulge in beer and has been arrested a few times over the years at these football games. A background check that only examines county records where the applicant resides will not uncover this information. Furthermore, Boone County is not obligated to send conviction records to any state conviction repository. Even if Missouri has a state convictions list, the Boone county records might or might not be there.

The cost of county-level criminal checks depends on many factors, such as whether the county seat is easily accessible or requires significant travel by a records searcher; whether the county has digitized its information making it easier to find information relative to the specific candidate under consideration; and whether the county itself charges an "access fee" to obtain the records. For example, as of this writing, New York charges a $65 access fee, and Florida charges a $24 access fee. This varies widely from jurisdiction to jurisdiction. Some states have free statewide criminal record databases on the Internet;

however, let the buyer beware. Every state that makes its data available via the Internet also posts a strong disclaimer about the accuracy of the information. And they mean it. A true background search requires an experienced searcher to go to the courthouse and use his or her skills to find the required records. Each courthouse is different, so you should find a searcher that goes to the specific courthouse frequently and knows the systems the Clerk of Courts has established.

Not all convictions are listed on the statewide databases. Especially suspect are those databases operated by the state Department of Corrections (DOC), rather than the state police. There is a combined 38-state DOC database check that can be run for a minimal fee; although there are free DOC databases also available. This is the closest one can get to a nationwide search. Once again, some background check vendors offer "National Wants and Warrants." Beware! If the data are taken from NCIC it is illegal to purchase this information. However, as of September 2005, a national warrants database is commercially available through Tracers Information Specialist, Inc.

There is a value in requesting criminal checks. But do not be lured into a false sense of security and do not overspend for unnecessary checks. Criminal checks are recommended for all employees. Credit checks are recommended for all employees who will handle money, financial information, credit card numbers, or valuable merchandise. This includes bank tellers, cashiers, security guards, and many others. Any employee who has a problem with bad debt (written off by the creditor or turned over to collection) in the previous three years that cannot be appropriately explained should not be hired for these types of positions. Remember what Donald Cressey said about financial pressure and opportunity. An employee who is in a financial crisis is more likely to steal from an employer when an opportunity presents itself and the employee can rationalize the action.

Credit checks usually vary in cost depending on the bureau providing the information, and you can usually negotiate discounts for volume searching; the price may come down as the number of checks per year requested by the company increases. There are vendors that will include the national sex offenders search for free as a package deal. A statewide search is a good idea if that state has such a database, but do not use the state check to replace the county-level search! Remember that doing one background check at the time of hire is good, but follow-up checks are also important, especially for those employees in financially sensitive positions. Driver safety records for those that drive company vehicles should be conducted on a regular basis. It is recommended that follow-up checks be conducted every five years.

Additional questions may come to mind about drug screens, credit checks, and whether it is enough to do criminal checks alone. As there is no way to cover all the bases, a company must do its best with the budget it has and the associated risk.

EXECUTIVE INSIGHT 13.1: JOHN SCULLEY AND A DEN OF THIEVES

The failure to conduct appropriate due diligence and background checks can result in serious financial and reputational issues whether a business is hiring an employee for an important role or considering a merger and acquisition. It is just as important for an employee to consider due diligence when deciding to join a new venture, as John Sculley unfortunately learned in 1993. Up to that point, Sculley was a renowned corporate executive with experience as the Chairman at Apple Computer and CEO at Pepsi-Cola.

Sculley shocked the technology world when he suddenly announced in October 1993 that he was joining a little-known company with no profits in the then-emerging field of wireless communications. The company was Spectrum Information Technologies, Inc., headquartered in Manhasset, New York. Sculley had recently left Apple and was looking for new challenges. When Spectrum President Peter Caserta demonstrated the company's wireless technology for sending messages over cellular airwaves, Sculley was intrigued.[i] He decided to take Caserta's offer to be the new chairman and CEO of Spectrum. When Spectrum announced on October 18, 1993, that Sculley was joining the company, the stock jumped 46 percent.[ii]

However, all was not as it seemed. What Sculley did not know was that in May 1993, after signing a patent-licensing agreement with AT&T, Caserta had proclaimed that the deal would bring Spectrum "hundreds of millions of dollars" in royalties. Although this statement initially caused Spectrum shares to jump, they quickly fell the next day when AT&T publicly announced that the deal was actually worth only a few million dollars.[iii] This reckless assertion on the part of Caserta should have caused Sculley some concern had he known about it.

Caserta had claimed to be a "key management engineer on the Apollo space program," but he had no college degree and only a two-year certificate from a defunct training school.[iv] A resume claimed he was an electrical engineer.[v] A thorough background check of public information databases would have revealed that Caserta and the consulting companies he controlled had been the subject of litigation over the years from clients who sued "for fees for services that the client companies claim were never rendered."[vi] Additionally, once Sculley joined Spectrum, Caserta and two other company executives exercised their stock options. The three made millions of dollars capitalizing on the soaring stock price that had benefited from Sculley's reputation and good name.[vii]

Within a few months of joining Spectrum, Sculley was starting to feel uneasy about the company's practices. In December 1993, he fired the company's external auditor, Arthur Andersen, and retained another. The new auditor quickly found that Spectrum's accounting practices were "overly aggressive in that it recognized revenue for license fees the company had not yet received."[viii] In addition, the SEC was conducting an investigation of Spectrum emanating from Caserta's comments about the AT&T deal of May 1993. Caserta never told Sculley about the investigation until it became public in January 1994. This was unacceptable to Sculley, who felt that Caserta had lied to him. On February 7, 1994, Sculley resigned from Spectrum and said, "Recent events have made it clear that certain aspects of Spectrum's business are not what they were represented to be when I joined the company."[ix]

Sculley got out not a moment too soon. On March 22, 1994, 50 Postal Inspectors raided the offices of an investment firm that had been owned by Caserta and arrested five employees for mail fraud.[x] In April 1995, Caserta and nine others were indicted for operating an advance fee scheme whereby they allegedly "defrauded hundreds of companies around the country out of $6 million."[xi] Caserta eventually pled guilty to the fraud and in October 1996 was sentenced to 27 months in prison.[xii] Caserta was also charged by the SEC for "artificially boosting" Spectrum's stock price.[xiii]

Looking back, part of the problem was that Sculley trusted the word of Peter Caserta and failed to do his own due diligence. When Sculley was considering joining Spectrum, he asked Caserta whether there were any problems he should be concerned with and Caserta said no.[xiv] What he should have done was trust but verify.

[i] John J. Keller, "Sculley Suddenly Quits New Job and Accuses a Top Officer of a Plot," *Wall Street Journal*, February 8, 1994, A1.
[ii] James Bernstein, "Explosive Exit," *Newsday*, February 8, 1994, 3.
[iii] Keller, "Sculley Suddenly Quits."
[iv] Ibid.
[v] James Bernstein, "Just Who Is Peter Caserta?" *Newsday*, March 7, 1994, 31.
[vi] Keller, "Sculley Suddenly Quits."
[vii] Ibid.
[viii] Bernstein, "Explosive Exit."
[ix] Ibid.
[x] Robert E. Kessler, "Investment Firm Raid," *Newsday*, March 23, 1994, 37.
[xi] Robert E. Kessler, "Caserta, Cronies Indicted: 10 Charged in Alleged Advance-Fee Loan Scam," *Newsday*, April 4, 1995, 35.
[xii] Robert E. Kessler, "Hi-Tech Con Man Sentenced," *Newsday*, October 1, 1996, 31.
[xiii] James Bernstein, "Feds Charge 3 in Spectrum Fraud," *Newsday*, December 5, 1997, A77.
[xiv] Keller, "Sculley Suddenly Quits."

THE BEST INDICATOR OF FUTURE BEHAVIOR IS PAST BEHAVIOR

How a background check program is designed depends on what the goal is for conducting background checks. If the goal is to reduce fraud and workplace violence in general, there are several facts to consider:

- Those who have a record of stealing are likely to steal again.
- Those convicted of theft did it many times before getting caught and convicted.

- Drug abusers are more likely to steal than non-drug abusers.
- Those who have financial difficulties are more likely to steal than those who don't.
- Those who have been violent in the past are more likely than others to be violent again.

Companies would do well to screen for drug use and for criminal convictions involving theft, drugs, or violence and also to check credit histories. County-level criminal checks are adequate for most entry-level positions, as federal convictions represent fewer than 5 percent of all convictions.

The actions described earlier will reduce the risk of fraud, but they will not stop fraud from happening. Some people who steal from their employers never stole before, never used drugs, and always paid their bills on time. Background checks are a tool. A company does not need the best and most expensive tool, but one tool is not enough to do this job.

THE TREND TOWARD RESTRICTING USE OF BACKGROUND SCREENING TO PREDICT JOB PERFORMANCE

Terry Becker was an auto mechanic who was struggling to find work. It all started with medical bills he incurred when his 10-year-old son began having seizures when he was a toddler. In one year alone, Becker ran up $25,000 in medical debt. During four and a half months, Becker was turned down for more than eight positions after allowing the prospective employers to obtain his credit report. Former Wisconsin State Representative Kim Hixson called that "discrimination based on credit history" and drafted a bill to ban that practice.[9]

Employer use of credit history as a screening tool was the subject of testimony before the U.S. Equal Employment Opportunity Commission at its meeting of October 20, 2010.[10] One of the presenters was Christine V. Walters, who has 25 years experience in human resources administration, management, employment law practice, and teaching. She stated, "To be clear, we believe that employment decisions should be made on the basis of an individual's qualifications—such as education, training, professional experience, demonstrated competence—and not on factors that have no bearing on one's ability to perform job-related duties." She continued by stating that SHRM believed, "... there is a compelling interest in enabling our nation's employers ... to assess the skills, abilities, and work habits of potential hires."[11]

Since it is becoming more and more difficult for potential employers to obtain meaningful references from prior employers, they have turned to additional information about the candidate that can be legally obtained from third-party information gathering agencies. While credit histories are rarely used as the sole factor in assessing a candidate's suitability for a specific position, it may sometimes be used as the deciding factor when two candidates appear to be equally suited for a position. Since employers have a fiduciary responsibility to safeguard the company's assets and sensitive information, credit histories have taken on increasing importance in hiring decisions. However, employers should be cautioned that derogatory credit histories do not automatically indicate a propensity for theft or other malfeasance ... particularly during times of economic hardship.

In 2010, SHRM conducted a survey of credit history use in the background checking process. It found that credit checks on all job candidates were the exception, with only 13 percent of organizations conducting credit checks on all candidates. Another 47 percent of employers consider credit history only for candidates for select jobs. Four out of 10 companies do not check credit histories at all.[12] Those companies that do conduct credit checks typically do so only for positions with financial or fiduciary responsibilities, senior executive positions, and ones with access to highly confidential employee information. Finally, the survey found that employers overwhelmingly use credit checks at the end of the hiring process and not to screen out applicants up front. Medical treatment debt normally is not considered during the hiring decision process and employers regularly allow candidates to explain their credit histories.

Nonetheless, starting in 2009, many states began questioning the use of credit reports to evaluate job-seekers' qualification for many positions. In the summer of 2009, a bill was introduced in Congress to prohibit the use of credit reports in evaluating employee candidates.[13] Sixteen states have proposed bills to ban credit checks, stating that derogatory credit reports may trap people in debt and keep them from finding work to ameliorate their credit problems because of past credit history. Hawaii and Washington already ban credit checks for most job applicants. Employers should carefully monitor the status of a number of bills introduced in Congress that would regulate the use of credit histories and other elements of employment background screening.

Mike Aitken, SHRM's director of government affairs, has stated that a blanket ban on the use of credit reports in making hiring decisions could remove a tool that helps employers to make good hiring decisions. In their last several reports on occupational fraud and abuse, the Association of Certified Fraud Examiners found that the two most common red flags for employees who commit workplace fraud are (1) living beyond their means and (2) having difficulty meeting financial obligations. While that is true during times of "normal" unemployment, is it equally true during times of high unemployment? SHRM found that the majority of employers obtain credit reports only after a job has been offered and allow candidates to explain their credit histories before a final hiring decision is made. Even then, only specific credit factors such as pending lawsuits and accounts in debt collection are used to influence the employment determination. Most employers do not consider home foreclosures or medical debt.

The use of credit reports is not the only element of a background check that is being scrutinized. In August 2010, the National Center of Public Policy Research issued a press release stating that the Equal Employment Opportunity Commission (EEOC) was warning employers that "it is illegal to use a prospective employee's past conviction records, even for serious felonies, as an 'absolute measure' as to whether they should be hired because this 'could limit the employment opportunities of some protected groups.'"[14] The EEOC was cautioning employers based on Title VII of the Civil Rights Act of 1964 prohibiting discrimination on the basis of race, color, national origin, and so on, that blacks and Hispanics were overrepresented among felons. However, the National Center of Public Policy Research objects to this interpretation of Title VII by stating that it does not ban discrimination based on character, and states that the EEOC is attempting to "micromanage private hiring decisions beyond the authority given to it by Congress." This debate is likely to continue and employers should keep it in mind when making hiring decisions.

RESUME FRAUD AND AN ADEQUATE BACKGROUND REVIEW

This chapter has focused on the need for criminal records and credit checks in evaluating a prospective employee's propensity to commit fraud or violence in the workplace, and rightly so, since these checks are the most relevant to a candidate's probable future performance. However, every employer needs to evaluate the requirements of each position being filled and then decide the extent of the background check to be made.

Resume fraud is a huge problem. Every job-seeker attempts to show his or her work history in the best possible light, and a certain amount of euphemism or even "puffery" may be expected. That is how janitors came to be "sanitation engineers." But too many job applicants have supplied employers with either gross exaggerations or significant omissions in their resumes, leading to serious hiring errors. Four common discrepancies found in resumes include:

- Falsifying the degree or credential earned
- Inflating salary history or title of previous position
- Concealing criminal records
- Exaggerating dates of past employment[15]

Therefore, if a particular job requires a certain level of education, the background check should include verifying the applicant's degree directly with the educational institution. The employer should not accept a copy of a diploma from the applicant, as these are easily forged. Likewise, all professional licensing should be verified directly with the license issuing agency. Most reputable employment background screeners at least encourage verification, if not comprehensive reference interviews, directly with previous employers. It is also suggested that the screener obtain a telephone number or address with the previous employer and not rely on the telephone number or address provided by the candidate, as applicants have been known to supply the telephone numbers of friends or relatives to give employment references rather than that of the previous employer. There may be other significant aspects of a specific job that dictate exactly which elements of an applicant's background should be verified.

IT IS NOT NECESSARY TO BE FORT KNOX

There are companies that demand verification of military service, verification of high school and all college credits, a federal-level criminal check, a state-level criminal check, Social Security number verification, reference checks with all former employers, and so on. This standard is applied to all positions no matter what level. Reason and logic may need to be applied here. If the position for which the organization is hiring does not require a college degree, and a high school diploma is sufficient, why verify college? If no preference is given for being a veteran, is it necessary to verify military service for this applicant? These companies may not be unreasonable in their background check requirements; they may just be using a little overkill for entry-level employees. Of course, this kind of intense background check is necessary when one is hiring auditors, accountants, investigators, and other financial managers, officers, and directors.

How does this apply to an industry in which a huge turnover in entry-level positions exists? Take large call centers, for example; if an international call center company has 60,000 employees, most of those employees will be in entry-level, call center positions. There is a high turnover in the call center industry. If this company has 40,000 call center agents and the annual turnover is 50 percent, more than 20,000 agents a year are hired. If the background checks are $100 each, the cost would be $2 million a year just on background checks. By doing those checks that give the most protection for the dollar, it is possible to cover most of the bases for a reasonable, cost-effective percentage of the corporate budget. Duplicating Fort Knox is not necessary, only the practice of reasonable due diligence.

ARE BACKGROUND CHECKS WORTH THE COST?

Story 1

A company decided to begin conducting criminal checks on its applicants and to track the results. In the first six months of checking, more than 60 applicants were found to have felony convictions. That was ten felons a month that the background checks kept out of the company. These were applicants who had claimed to have no convictions on their applications.

Story 2

One of the authors investigated bank fraud at one point in his career. He took a confession from a bank employee, and she was allowed to plead guilty to embezzlement, pay restitution, and serve one-year probation. She still had a federal felony conviction on her record, but she didn't go to jail. The author had reason to contact her a few months later to get her to sign some documents regarding the restitution. When he called her home, her mother answered the phone and said that her daughter was at work. The mother provided the phone number. Imagine the author's surprise when the call went to a bank. It had hired a convicted bank embezzler who was still on probation!

Story 3

A well-respected employment screening company was searching for an administrative assistant to manage the services that the company provided to one large international client. Several acceptable candidates were interviewed, but one stood out above the rest because of her charismatic manner, which would be required to handle the often difficult client. The candidate authorized a background check to include a credit history. The credit report indicated some derogatory credit history, but the employer requested an explanation and was told that the candidate's first husband had died five years before, leading to a period of financial distress for her and her three children. The results of the candidate's criminal check were delayed, and the employer (wanting to relieve himself of his duties with the difficult client) hired the charismatic candidate without the benefit of the criminal history.

Two weeks later, the criminal history arrived and indicated a conviction for welfare fraud a year after the loss of the husband. The background screening company might have been able to accept a prior fraud conviction for which the sentence had been served;

however, the candidate had not disclosed it on her application or during the interview. The company subsequently hired one of the less charismatic candidates after all the elements of the background check had been completed.

Story 4

In 2003, Penn State University's faculty searches focused on teaching and research credentials, but did not necessarily include criminal backgrounds. Penn State University hired Paul Krueger as an assistant professor to teach workforce development, and he later became the Director of the Institute for Research in Training and Development. During his tenure with Penn State, he had a spotless teaching record. What the university didn't know was that Krueger was convicted in the mid-1960s for the murder of three fishermen in Corpus Christi, Texas. He was paroled in 1979.

To this day it is unknown whether Krueger volunteered any information about his conviction or whether the search committee ever asked. When a reporter asked whether Krueger was to retain his position at Penn State after the murder conviction finally came to light, Penn State officials said they had been unable to speak with Krueger, though they expected him to return to the main campus to teach in the fall semester. However, the same officials learned later that week that Krueger had signed a contract to become an associate professor of business at National University in La Jolla, California. When asked, a National University spokesman stated that they were not aware of his criminal past. Sheldon Steinbach, then general counsel with the American Council on Education stated, "The background checks for part-time and full-time faculty members are porous.... They're not compatible with good 21st century human resources practices."[16]

Story 5

On November 28, 2010, the *Philadelphia Inquirer* published a story about a man who was sentenced to life in prison 40 years ago for the murder of a 12-year-old girl. His conviction was based on evidence provided by Agnes Mallatratt, a forensic technician who analyzed most of the microscopic analysis of the evidence used at his trial. Ms. Mallatratt was very highly respected in the Philadelphia District Attorneys office, and had been the subject of several city newspaper stories in the early 1960s extolling her accomplishments.

At the trial, she stated she had worked on at least 35 high-profile cases of robbery, rape, or homicide. She had won several awards for her lab work. On the stand she said she had taken courses at Temple University in forensics, biology, botany, zoology and criminal law, and that she had a certificate in medical technology. She said she taught courses in forensics at Temple and that over eight years had worked on 4,000 or 5,000 cases and testified in 50 or 60 cases.

In a subsequent case, several defense lawyers discovered that she had never earned a degree from Temple; indeed, she never even finished junior high school! She had claimed a favorable review from the American Society of Forensic Pathologists, an organization that doesn't even exist. The officials at the American Academy of Forensic Pathologists, which does exist, had no record of her ever being a member. On the basis of her testimony, the subject of the news article was convicted and incarcerated for more than 40 years. Two other men in different cases were sentenced to death.[17]

THE ROLE OF HUMAN RESOURCES IN BACKGROUND CHECKS

While the fraud prevention unit can strongly recommend the use of background checks, locate vendors, and even recommend policy, it is the responsibility of the human resources department to make sure that a background check appropriate to the position is conducted on all applicants. Employment managers should handle the day-to-day implementation of the background check policy and have direct contact with the background check vendor.

NOTES

1. "Industry Fast Facts," 2010, *HireRight*, www.hireright.com/ Background-Check-Fast-Facts.aspx; and Profiles International,

"Leaders Guide to Managing Workplace Fraud, Theft and Violence," Executive Briefing, 2010, 8, img.en25.com/Web/ProfilesInternational/Fraud_Theft_Violence-SocialMedia.pdf?fromWebsitePressReleases=Fraud_Theft_Violence-Overview.

2. U.S. Department of Labor, Occupational Safety and Health Administration, "Workplace Violence," OSHA Fact Sheet, 2002, www.osha.gov/OshDoc/data_General_Facts/factsheet-workplace-violence.pdf.

3. *Occupational Safety and Health Act of 1970*, 29 U.S.C. § 654, 5(a) 1, www.osha.gov/pls/oshaweb/owadisp.show_document?p_id=3359&p_table=OSHACT.

4. Liability based on negligent hiring arises when employers fail to diligently investigate the individuals they hire. The Restatement (Second) of Agency, § 213 (1958) states, "A person conducting an activity through servants ... is subject to liability for harm resulting from his conduct if he is negligent or reckless: ... (b) in the employment of improper persons ... involving the risk of harm to others: ...."

5. Oregon Revised Statute, § 659A.885, Civil action, www.oregonlaws.org/ors/659A.885.

6. Statement of Christine V. Walters, before the U.S. Equal Employment Opportunity Commission, October 20, 2010, www.eeoc.gov/eeoc/meetings/10-20-10/walter.cfm.

7. Linnea B. McCord, "Defamation vs. Negligent Referral," *Graziadio Business Review* 2 (1999), gbr.pepperdine.edu/2010/08/defamation-vs-negligent-referral/.

8. "Employment Screening Benchmarking Report," *HireRight*, 2010, go.hireright.com/forms/201012_blog_12_17_10.

9. Wisconsin Legislature, "Taylor/Hixson Bill Assisting Job Seekers Receives Public Hearing," press release (December 15, 2009), www.wispolitics.com/1006/091215_Hixson_Taylor.pdf.

10. Walters statement before EEOC; See also Statement of Michael Eastman, Executive Director of Labor Law Policy, U.S. Chamber of Commerce, www.eeoc.gov/eeoc/meetings/10-20-10/eastman.cfm.

11. Ibid.

12. Kathy Gurchiek, "Credit Checks Are Legitimate Screening Tool," November 2, 2010, www.shrm.org/about/news/Pages/LegitimateScreeningTool.aspx.

13. HR 3149, the Equal Employment Act for All, was introduced to amend the FCRA by prohibiting employers from using consumer credit checks for both prospective and current employees for the purpose of making employment decisions, except in situations of national security or for an FDIC clearance, with state and local government agencies that otherwise require use of consumer reports, or in a supervisory, managerial, professional, or executive position at a financial institution. The bill did not get out of committee.

14. National Center for Public Policy Research, "EEOC Warns Employers: If You Don't Want to Hire Felons, You Need a Good Reason," August 16, 2010, www.nationalcenter. org/PR_EEOC_Felon_081610.html.

15. "Employment Screening Benchmarking Report."

16. Bill Schackner, "Penn State professor murdered 3 in 1965," *Pittsburgh Post-Gazette,* July 26, 2003, www.post-gazette.com/localnews/20030726krueger0726p1.asp.

17. Faye Flam, "In Philadelphia, a Bid to Give a Lifer, 82, Another Day in Court." *Philadelphia Inquirer,* November 28, 2010, articles.philly.com/2010-11-28/news/24953647_1_crime-lab-worker-bad-science-crime-scene/4.

Training, Training, and More Training

EXECUTIVE SUMMARY

Training at all levels in an organization, from the CEO down the ranks, is an absolute requirement in preventing fraud and creating a culture of compliance. Training reinforces an entity's commitment to ethical conduct and compliance with company policies, as well as government laws and regulations. The training should encompass the code of conduct, the risk of fraud, the employees' role in preventing fraud, and the company's strong commitment to being a good corporate citizen. There are many ways to deliver quality training; all of them must be considered in designing an effective company-wide training program. An organization's fraud investigators should be involved in providing fraud prevention training. They are the ones involved with fraud and fraud prevention on a daily basis and can provide insight and context to the problem. Managers are role models for their direct reports and are the first line of defense in detecting and preventing fraud. Appropriate training of managers can provide great benefits to an organization.

BUILDING FRAUD AWARENESS THROUGH TRAINING

Fraud prevention begins with training. Education and awareness of the fraud risk, the types of fraud an organization may face, the impact on a business, how employees' lives are impacted by wrongful behavior, and what can be done to stop fraud are key elements in any fraud awareness and prevention program. Good companies recognize that fraud awareness and prevention training are essential for reducing the impact of fraud and abuse and for maintaining effective corporate governance. However, even good companies are limited in how much training they can provide, and the training budget is often the first to be cut in a downturn.

Training and reinforcement of policy and procedure should be required for all employees from the executive level on down. The difference is in the type and length of a particular training. Training comes in many different forms; all forms can be effective if they are properly conceived and implemented. In-house training, seminars offered by professional organizations, Web-based interactive training modules, or college courses are all possible avenues of training. The Committee of Sponsoring Organizations (COSO) recommends that "internal auditors and corporate accountants should study the forces and opportunities that contribute to fraudulent financial reporting, the risk factors that may indicate its occurrence, and the relevant ethical and technical standards."[1] Certified Public Accountants (CPAs), Certified Fraud Examiners (CFEs), and others with professional certification are required to complete a specific number of Continuing Professional Education (CPE) hours each year. It is recommended that all professionals in the organization, whether certified or not, receive a minimum of 40 CPEs per year, with at least eight hours related to fraud prevention and an equal amount for ethics and compliance training.

Even a well-designed complaint reporting mechanism can fail without adequate training for employees. Companies must train employees on the reasons for the reporting mechanism, the type of complaints that may be reported, how to use the reporting procedure, and how to maintain confidentiality. Without this type of training, the system crumbles.[2]

Effective fraud awareness training has four main parts:

1. Give a simple definition of fraud: fraud is lying, cheating, and stealing.
2. Discuss how fraud negatively impacts a company's bottom line and reputation.
3. Give examples of various fraud schemes employees might discover, such as an offer for kickbacks or the illegal use of customers' credit card numbers by other employees.
4. Tell employees what they are supposed to do if they suspect fraud.[3]

Obtaining employee buy-in for fraud training and then embracing the concept of fraud prevention is critical to success in training. The benefits of training need to be effectively communicated to all employees no matter where in the world they are located. "Education of employees should be factual rather than accusatory. Point out that fraud—in any form—is eventually very unhealthy for the organization and the people who work there. Fraud and abuse impact raises, jobs, benefits, morale, profits, and one's integrity. The fraud educated workforce is the fraud examiner's best weapon—by far."[4] The support of training for all employees by executive leadership sends a strong message about the tone at the top and throughout the organization.

Neither Sarbanes-Oxley nor the SEC specifically mentions education or training in employee conduct, ethics, and fraud prevention. However, both the New York Stock Exchange (NYSE) and NASDAQ corporate governance guidelines reinforce the need for continuing education and training of directors. The Federal Sentencing Guidelines for Organizations, promulgated by the United States Sentencing Commission, include ongoing training and communication as part of an effective compliance and ethics program. The Federal Acquisition Regulation (FAR), the principal set of rules in the Federal Acquisition Regulation System, now include a requirement for most companies that do business with the federal government to provide ongoing, effective training to their employees.

THE ROLE OF FRAUD INVESTIGATORS IN TRAINING

Any ongoing fraud prevention training should include presentations from the organization's fraud investigators. They have first-hand experience investigating various kinds of fraud and unique insights that are invaluable in educating employees. They can detail the elements of the fraud triangle for specific cases that were investigated; they can explain how frauds were detected through red flags, and they can outline the best practices to prevent them. Because of the nature of the fraud investigators' work, their experiences are of great interest to employees. Fraud investigators should make ongoing presentations to employees at all levels throughout a company. Depending on the size of the organization, the fraud prevention unit may spend a significant amount of their time in educating employees.

Informing employees that there is a professional investigative unit within the company that responds to allegations of fraud sends a strong preventative message. It also sends an important message that improper conduct has consequences and that fraud is not tolerated. As a result of the training conducted by the fraud investigative unit, increased reporting of fraud allegations should be expected. Experience has shown that when employees are educated about the many kinds of fraud impacting a company and the associated red flags, they are much more likely to recognize possible wrongdoings and report them.

TRAINING FOR CHIEF EXECUTIVES AND DIRECTORS

Although every public and private company has a responsibility to educate and train all its employees in ethics, compliance, and fraud prevention, no group is more in need of this training than chief executives and directors of boards. Even though the number of ethically challenged chief executives is small, there is always something new for CEOs and directors to learn because of ever-changing corporate compliance requirements. COSO recommends that "Participants in the financial reporting system must first understand the multidimensional nature of fraudulent financial reporting to be able to address it with appropriate responses."[5] COSO details how a public company needs to educate its directors, management, and employees about fraudulent financial reporting; it is especially important for the Audit

Committee "to be alert to the risk of such fraud and to educate its members and the rest of the board about the forces and the opportunities" that can lead to fraud.[6] Executives and directors also need an understanding of other kinds of internal and external frauds that can attack a company. The Association of Certified Fraud Examiners presents a number of excellent fraud awareness and prevention training sessions. Their training can be customized to fit the needs of any organization. More information about custom antifraud training is included in Executive Insight 14.1.

EXECUTIVE INSIGHT 14.1: CUSTOM ANTIFRAUD TRAINING

Custom-designed antifraud training taught by fraud examination professionals may be the ideal solution for businesses. Such training can be focused on the unique needs of a public or private company to improve fraud detection and prevention. A course on developing effective anti–money-laundering programs may be appropriate for a financial services organization. A course on conducting internal investigations might be perfect for a company starting up a fraud investigation unit. A course on the impact of the Foreign Corrupt Practices Act and detection and prevention strategies is beneficial for a company doing business in high-risk countries where bribery and governmental corruption are common.

Bringing such training in-house has many advantages; it is convenient, comprehensive, motivating, and cost effective. The leader in antifraud training is the Association of Certified Fraud Examiners (ACFE). The ACFE provides custom training to a wide variety of clients including corporations and government agencies. Courses are taught by Certified Fraud Examiners who are experts in fraud detection, investigation, and prevention and who provide practical training in an interactive learning environment.

The ACFE has a number of excellent training courses that are available to organizations worldwide including Principles of

Fraud Examination, Fraud Risk Management, Auditing for Internal Fraud, Professional Interviewing Skills, Conducting Internal Investigations, Financial State Fraud, Contract and Procurement Fraud, Bribery in International Business Transactions, Investigating by Computer, Investigating Conflicts of Interest, and Fraud Prevention. These courses and others offered by the ACFE can be adapted to any size audience and should be considered by any organization looking to improve its understanding of fraud and fraud prevention. More information about the ACFE's antifraud training can be found at www.acfe.com.

NEW EMPLOYEE ORIENTATION

The first day of hire for a new employee is a perfect time to start developing a culture of compliance for that particular person. Typically, a company has some form of introduction to the business for a new hire. Although the subjects covered in a new employee orientation may include general information about the company, employee benefits, policies and procedures, and compliance with the code of conduct, an introduction to the risk of fraud should be considered. A new employee feels inundated with new information, and much of it may not be remembered, but a short and general introduction to the company's strong stand against fraud and abuse at any level is a good starting point. Consideration should be given to providing some key bullet points about how fraud can affect an organization. Some important messages can be highlighted including the types of fraud; key ACFE fraud statistics including how an average organization loses 5 percent of its annual revenue to fraud and abuse; how most frauds are discovered by tips or by accident; and how employees can report allegations of fraud and abuse.

MANAGERS ARE ROLE MODELS

Good managers are role models to their employees. They provide guidance and mentoring. They show employees how to succeed, and they instill honesty and integrity by their actions. Managers who provide great oversight and lead by example can have a major impact in preventing fraud. "Trust but verify" should be every good manager's mantra. When employees see their managers are following policy and procedure and are closely monitoring their group's operation, fraud is harder to commit and get away with. As an example, expense reporting fraud can be greatly reduced by increased manager scrutiny of expense claims and receipts. The credibility of "tone at the top" begins with a first-line manager.

On the other hand, poor managers can contribute to a fraudulent culture through a lack of engagement and leadership. Managers who are not well versed in an organization's policies and procedures or who fail to follow them can send the wrong message to their direct reports. A manager who is not engaged or committed to the company's code of conduct and who does not live it every day can do little to promote compliance by employees. The authors have seen numerous examples over the years of fraud occurring under the very noses of poor managers who never detect it.

Training of managers in fraud detection and prevention provides an opportunity for reinforcing and enhancing the skills of great managers while improving those of poor or uninformed managers. A unique approach to obtain manager buy-in is to appeal to career advancement. Provide examples of how managers had their careers derailed when fraud occurred on their watch and they failed to detect or report it. No one wants to have a career stopped dead in its tracks for failure to protect the organization from fraud. Good managers can stop fraud before it occurs.

NEW MANAGER TRAINING

Many organizations provide training to new managers when they assume their new roles. There is no better way to start off the career of new managers than to educate them about the risk of fraud and their role in addressing that risk. Experience has shown that new managers often report allegations of fraud at a greater rate than existing managers. This is because new managers are learning their new roles, probing, asking questions, and often finding fraud and policy violations not detected by the managers who came before them.

Providing both fraud prevention tools and knowledge to new managers, as well as all managers, aids them in evangelizing compliance to their direct reports. This training yields unexpected benefits in protecting an organization.

FRAUD PREVENTION TRAINING FOR FINANCE EMPLOYEES

It is recommended that all finance employees including internal audit personnel receive fraud prevention training. The recent improvements in corporate governance now require greater involvement and review by the finance function to protect an organization. An excellent introductory training course is Fraud and the CPA created by the ACFE and the American Institute of Certified Public Accountants. This eight-hour computer self-study course provides an introduction to the problem of fraud; the CPA's fraud detection and reporting responsibilities; the basics of financial statement fraud, asset misappropriation, and corruption schemes; the reasons employees commit fraud; and methods for detecting and preventing fraud schemes. The course incorporates video clips of fraudsters detailing how they committed fraud and how they concealed it. Although this course is especially useful for CPAs, it is just as beneficial for any finance, procurement, or other employee within an organization. Because it is computer based, the course can be provided to large numbers of employees at an economical cost.

There are other opportunities for employees to receive fraud prevention knowledge through degree programs such as those offered in colleges and universities. Executive Insight 14.2 provides information about an excellent graduate program in economic crime management at Utica College.

EXECUTIVE INSIGHT 14.2: BECOMING A MASTER IN ECONOMIC CRIME MANAGEMENT

Thanks to technology, experienced professionals can gain fraud prevention skills and knowledge and also earn an academic degree in the comfort of their homes or offices. Utica College, in Utica, New York, is the first college to offer a master's degree in Economic Crime Management (ECM) integrating online learning.[i] Established in 1999, the program is offered in a distance learning format, only requiring students to be on campus for one four-day-long residency for each of the two years. The rest of the courses are presented online with faculty-directed study.

The ECM curriculum focuses on fraud and risk management strategies, current economic crime challenges, and applying innovative technological and analytical solutions to preventing fraud. The program has been designed to meet the growing security demands placed on experienced personnel in law enforcement, private corporations, government, and the military. The curriculum, based on the four themes of management, technology, analytical methods, and economic crime, was developed in collaboration with experts in private industry, government, and law enforcement, and is continually updated to meet societal changes.

The ECM program's distance learning format allows full-time professionals to complete a master's degree without having to relocate and/or take a leave of absence from employment. Two courses start in each of the six terms. The intensive learning experience allows students to complete the courses on the Internet, using sophisticated learning software. The communication and discussion during the 14 weeks following each residency are crucial to the learning process. Students are given access to online library resources, including LexisNexis^{TM}, and applications such as i2 Inc.'s Analyst's Notebook, to provide them with the research tools necessary to advance their studies.

The two-year program is fully integrated, so the two courses that the students take each semester build on the courses they have completed. The 12 integrated courses (36 credit hours) cover organizational theory and management, research methods, economic crime, legal issues, Internet and computer security, and fraud analysis. Students are required to complete a professional project as a capstone to their academic experience. More information about the online Master's in Economic Crime Management can be found at www.ecii.edu.

_____

[i]Coauthor Martin T. Biegelman is Chair of the Economic Crime Institute's Board of Advisors.

TRAIN YOUR ACCOUNTS PAYABLE DEPARTMENT: LOOKING FOR FRAUD ON THE FACE OF THE INVOICE

There are several strategies for searching payables proactively for fraud. An organization can ensure that its auditors are trained to conduct computerized data mining. It can also train accounts payable employees to look for clues to fraud on the invoices themselves. Making the accounts payable (AP) department "fraud aware" can result in increased detection of issues.

Many asset misappropriation schemes involve inserting a fraudulent invoice into the system. The AP clerk, not the auditor, is the person in the best position to catch this fraud. For example, a false invoice from a known vendor has been placed into the AP system using an address that is different from the true address of this known vendor. This type of fraud will be caught if the addresses on vendor payments are always checked against the approved vendor file. A fraudster who inserts such a phony invoice will forget to fold the invoice—as it would have been had it actually arrived in the mail. An AP clerk should know to look for that clue (see Exhibits 14.1 and 14.2 for examples).

A March invoice has arrived from a known vendor with a past due notice for the February invoice. When the AP clerk pulls the February invoice, the clerk notices that the address on the February invoice is different from the "usual" address on the invoice from March. The February invoice that was paid is for much more ($7,580) than is usual from this vendor. The different address from the February invoice is the logical place to begin this fraud investigation. Someone, probably an employee, removed and discarded the real February invoice from International Enterprises and replaced it with one that was created—for much more money—to a different address.

INVOICE

International Enterprises
341 S 4th Street
Anytown, USA

March 25, 2006

Invoice #063511

For services rendered January 19, 2006 - PAST DUE.............$1,032
See invoice #063378
And February 20, 2006..$1,300

Total due on receipt: $2,332

EXHIBIT 14.1   Invoice #1

INVOICE

International Enterprises
2503 West Linden
Anytown, USA

February 5, 2006

Invoice #064832

For services rendered January 19, 2006.............................$7,580

Total due on receipt: $7,580

EXHIBIT 14.2   Invoice #2

The fraudster hoped that AP would recognize the vendor as a valid one but would not notice the different address. Searching the records for payment of a February invoice numbered 063378 to International Enterprises for the amount past due reveals no record that invoice #063378 was paid. Here is the critical moment. If the approving authority for this invoice does not recognize this for what it is, a fraud, there is a chance that the approving authority will assume that there were two invoices for February and that the one listed as past due has not been paid. If proper fraud awareness does not exist, this fraud might escape detection. What should an AP clerk do if the approving authority just authorizes the second payment for February? Should the clerk notify the fraud examiner? This is a prime example of the need to train AP clerks to be alert for anomalies such as unusual addresses for known vendors. There is a possibility that the approving authority is the one who slipped this fake invoice into the system. Is the address on the February invoice for $7,580 the address of the person approving the invoice?

Here are other red flags that are best looked for on the face of the invoice by AP employees rather than auditors using data mining:

- Invoices with no telephone number
- Invoices with handwritten notes from the approver explaining unusual circumstances
- Any invoice that calls for rebates, retrofits, or refunds
- Invoices that mention delivery of goods to a site other than the company
- Invoices with large amounts just under the maximum approval authority of the approver
- Invoices with unusual lack of detail
- Invoices that have not been folded, since they were probably not mailed
- Invoices from a vendor that are a month apart but the invoice numbers are consecutive or close

An invoice should display the name, address, and telephone number of each vendor. Vendors with a PO Box or a mail drop for an address may require additional scrutiny. The telephone number should be called to verify the address. It is also a good idea to check Web sites for all vendors. Only after proper due diligence has been done should the vendor be added to an approved vendor list. Until a vendor is placed on this list, no payments should be sent. Each invoice should be compared with the vendor as listed on the approved vendor list.

TRAIN THE AUDIT STAFF TO DATA MINE

Computerized data mining strategies can be used to look for disbursement amounts that do not fit the expected pattern. Benford's Law states that naturally occurring sets of data have more small items than big items. Any deviation from this pattern raises a red flag.

Frank Benford was a physicist at GE Research Laboratories when he noticed that he used logarithms for numbers that began with low digits more often than he used logarithms for numbers that began with high digits. His log table book was much more worn in the beginning than it was at the back. Like any good physicist, he set out to find the law that made this so. He was able to find the specific formula that identifies these skewed frequencies of first-digit values.[7]

In any group of normal numbers (not assigned or having built-in maximum or minimum values), there is a greater probability that the first digits will be ones, and then twos and threes, all the way up to nines. The higher the number, the less probable it is that it will be the first digit in an amount. These skewed frequencies became known as Benford's Law.

If any group of amounts results in a positive spike of more than 5 percent out of this pattern, the figures should be reviewed in detail. There are systems and programs that are commercially available to run checks using Benford's Law (see Exhibit 14.3). One such product is the audit software available from ACL™ (www.acl.com).

Employees committing fraud inside an organization typically want to use figures that begin with nines. It is more efficient to steal $900 than $100 nine times. A common example is when an organization requires receipts for expenses over $75 and a fraud-minded employee submits phony expense claims for $74.99, just under the receipt threshold. Therefore, testing financial records using Benford's Law exposes fraudulent amounts. This type of data mining using Benford's Law can also be done by looking at the frequency of the first two digits.

EXHIBIT 14.3   Benford's Law[a]

First Digit	Probability
1	.30103
2	.176091
3	.124939
4	.09691
5	.0791812
6	.0669468
7	.0579919
8	.0511525
9	.0457575

[a] http://mathworld.wolfram.com/BenfordsLaw.html.

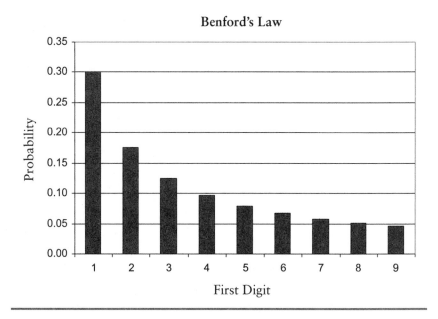

Benford's Law

The use of Benford's Law in an AP audit at one particular company showed an inordinate number of payments of $50. This caused an investigation into the $50 charges, most of which were for car batteries. However, the company had paid for twice as many car batteries in one year than they had cars. Someone was selling the car batteries.[8]

In addition to using ACL™ to apply Benford's Law, auditors can also look for red flags in payables using tools such as Business Objects™, Crystal Reports™, Microsoft Access™, ActiveData for Microsoft Excel™, and IDEA™. Fraud detection software is essential for any fraud prevention program. There are several obvious areas to keep in mind when looking for possible fraud inside an organization. The first places to look are in employee and vendor records. Employee records give the home addresses of employees. It is obviously a red flag if any of the vendors have the same address as an employee. A business can data mine using Microsoft Access to compare a table of employee addresses against a table of vendor addresses. This is called a "relational table query."

Relational Table Query

Such comparison checks between vendor and employee addresses are not easy without Access, which has the ability to search not only for exact matches but also close matches. This is important, as vendor records are seldom in the same address format as employee records. Address information such as 200 1st Street might be in the address line in the employee records, but the address line in vendor records could show 200 1st STR. This will not be caught by an exact match check but would be caught by the close match relational table query in Access. Care must also be taken to cross-compare address lines one and two, as well as the telephone numbers (see Exhibit 14.4).

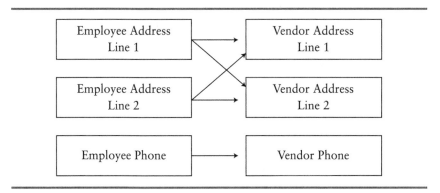

EXHIBIT 14.4 The Two-Line Address Problem

It is quite possible that a vendor and an employee could have the same address of 400 High Street, but one table could have that value in address line 1, whereas the other had that value in address line 2. Also causing problems are abbreviations for Street, which could be entered as St., ST, or Str. or written out as Street. These differences can foil a literal computer match. Fraudsters are known to misspell the name of their street intentionally for the sole purpose of defeating such exact searches and data comparisons.

Find Duplicates Query

When an Access table titled "paid invoices" is created (Microsoft Excel spreadsheets can be imported into Access format), duplicate payments can be found by running a "find duplicates query." Access has a query wizard that creates the query easily. Pick the table and the fields in that table to be searched for duplicates, and the results appear. Duplicate payments might be a mistake, but they could also be a red flag for kickbacks or other types of fraud such as interception of the duplicate payments by an insider, who then converts them for personal use.

In most payment systems, invoices associated with approved purchase orders are paid with little question. Access can review all invoices paid on purchase orders to ensure that the approver of the invoice was an authorized approver. Therefore, a master list of persons with authority to approve purchase orders should be maintained. This file can become an Access table called "PO Approvers" that is then compared with a "Purchase Order" table that has a field for "approver." This is an "unmatched query"—looking for any approver in the Purchase Order Table that does not appear on the PO Approver table. The "unmatched query" can also determine whether any vendors have been paid who are not on the approved vendor list.

Between Ranges Query

To find invoices that are just under the dollar limit of the approver, query using the "between" expression. If the approval authority is $10,000, query for all invoices approved when the amount is between

$9,000 and $10,000. If fraud exists, it is very likely that there are an inordinate number of invoices within this range. This red flag can also be uncovered using Benford's Law, as the frequency of invoices that begin with a 9 are above the expected norm.

Simple Data Mining

Data mining, also called *data profiling* or *digital analysis*, is evaluating key number fields using filtering. The goal is to find anomalies or outliers. Some common strategies include finding the highest or lowest values in various fields. Other good tactics include looking for transactions just below various limits or examining the transactions of customers with the most of anything: purchases, refunds, referrals, and the like. Microsoft Excel is a perfect tool for sorting. The sort can rearrange the entire spreadsheet into ascending or descending order for whatever column the investigator or auditor chooses to sort. Excel files used over time can be formatted using "conditional formatting" to have the cells change color when the amounts go over or below certain set thresholds. (If using Excel 2007 and later versions, click Home tab, Conditional Formatting, and then Color Scales.)

Data mining is searching for patterns in large amounts of data using mathematical processes. When dealing with simple computer programs, it is best to remember they must be told exactly what you want them to do every step of the way. This is why there is such a problem with false positives in fraud data mining. The program can only apply the rules you provide and can only learn from what you give it.

Writing every rule for a robot to cut your grass would be a complicated process. You would have to tell it the coordinates of the grass you want cut, and what you don't want cut (flower beds or the neighbor's grass). A fraud data mining model is similar in that you want to eliminate the false positives and only find the fraudulent entities or transactions you want. It can be very hard to exclude what you don't want when the fraud is complicated and unknown.

Peer Grouping

Peer grouping is placing similar entities together so that they are only compared with each other rather than the entire universe of data.

For example, if you were looking for possible fraud in the claims of doctors, you would probably not want to group a family practice doctor from rural Alabama with a surgeon from a major metropolitan medical center. The billing patterns of these two physicians are unlikely to be similar. Comparing all rural family practice physicians together reduces false positives and brings the outliers to the top.

Predictive Modeling for Fraud

In order to create a good predictive model, you need examples of past frauds to feed into the model. Good results often require a lot of analysis and reworking the models a few times. Predictive modeling or artificial intelligence is a set of techniques that uses past events and behaviors to predict similar future events and behaviors. This is called *supervised learning*. The predictive modeling methods that use supervised learning include: (1) decision trees, (2) logistic regression, and (3) neural networks.

Decision Trees

While most people who use predictive modeling techniques have teams of statisticians who write SQL code and have very expensive software, simple decision trees are relatively easy to understand and can be created without the help of expensive software. The steps are:

1. Define the scope and type of fraud you want to predict. For example, predict which credit card transactions are likely to be fraudulent.
2. Prepare the data. Make sure you get the data right, because the prediction is only as good as the data.
3. Identify indicators usually present in fraudulent credit card transactions. Predictive modeling software like SAS business analytics software actually helps you pick the observations that it thinks are best. However, this can be done with the right amount of sorting and analysis just using a program like Excel.
4. Build a decision tree. (Exhibit 14.5 shows a modeling example that uses fictional data.)

EXHIBIT 14.5   Decision Tree with Fraudulent Transaction Indicators
Present

Transactions	Fraudulent Transactions	Fraud Percent
Total transactions: 9620	Fraudulent transactions: 96	Fraud Percent: 1%
Electronics transactions: 630	Fraudulent transactions: 31	Fraud Percent: 5%
Price >$250 transactions: 310	Fraudulent transactions: 22	Fraud Percent: 7%
# transactions/day >2: 120	Fraudulent transactions: 12	Fraud Percent: 10%
Transactions with all 3 Rules: 14	Fraudulent transactions: 12	Fraud Percent: 85.7%

The claims with all three rules have a fraud probability of 85.7 percent. While there were only 12 transactions that fell into this category out of the 9,620 transactions, when you can find rules that show over 85 percent of one type of claim to be fraudulent, it is wise to block it and do manual reviews. Another interesting point is that the total transactions in these three categories are 11 percent of all the transactions (1,060 out of 9,620) but account for over 67 percent of the fraud transactions (65 out of 96). Decision trees can become very complex predictive models. When that occurs, programs such as SAS are used to make sure that the right choices have been made for the optimal detection and prevention of fraud. The complexity of the tools required is often determined by the complexity of the data.

Logistic Regression

This is a statistical type of predictive model that works best for predicting events where there is some dependent variable or variables. Linear variables are in constant proportion, while nonlinear variables do not remain in constant proportion. A good example of logistic regression is thefts of inventory or cash committed over a long period of time. Logistic regression could determine who worked on the days of every theft, if there were certain days or hours that were common to all thefts, and so on. This can help narrow the list of suspects and identify who committed the thefts.

Neural Networks

Neural networks involve specialized software and are very complicated. While the network is supposed to recognize patterns of past frauds and find similar, but not identical patterns in the rest of the data, it requires a large number of examples before it can learn the pattern. Therefore, a neural network is best suited for the prediction of fraud at the transaction level. Since a neural network can have hundreds of decision nodes, it can be almost impossible to explain the reasoning process behind the selection of the items to be investigated. This "black box" may not be acceptable for some situations where the reasons for selecting certain outliers are required to be identified, such as cases being referred to prosecution.

Other Resources

There are various resources available to help with data mining, books that include sample queries, ACL and IDEA mining ideas, and predictive fraud models for various types of possible fraud scenarios. A search on any of the major book sellers' Web sites will reveal several from which to choose. The use of data mining in fraud prevention and identification is no longer a "nice to have." It is an essential part of the fraud fighter's arsenal to protect today's companies.

NOTES

1. The Committee of Sponsoring Organizations of the Treadway Commission, James C. Treadway Jr., Chairman, *Report of the National Commission on Fraudulent Financial Reporting*, October 1987, Chapter 5, Section V, www.coso.org/publications/NCFFR_Part_5.htm.
2. Marian Exall and Jack Capers Jr., "Establishing the New Complaint Procedures," *Fraud Magazine*, November–December 2004, 24.
3. Kenneth Dieffenbach, "Recruiting an Anti-Fraud Foot-Soldier Army," *The White Paper*, March–April 2004, 34.

4. Joseph T. Wells, *Corporate Fraud Handbook: Prevention and Detection* (Hoboken, NJ: John Wiley & Sons, Inc., 2004), 406.
5. *Report of the National Commission on Fraudulent Financial Reporting*, Chapter 5, Section I.
6. Ibid., Chapter 5, Section VI.
7. Mark Nigrini, "Digital Analysis: A Computer-Assisted Data Analysis Technology for Internal Auditors," *IT Audit*, December 15, 1998, www.theiia.org/itaudit/ index.
8. Ibid.

Global Fraud and Corruption Risk*

EXECUTIVE SUMMARY

An organization's fraud and corruption risk does not end at the border of the United States. In many ways, it is even greater outside the country. This is especially true when a company has operations and employees based in foreign countries. The Foreign Corrupt Practices Act (FCPA), UK Bribery Act, and other laws that outlaw bribery of foreign government officials have significant penalties, both for individuals and companies. Knowing those risks and being able to appropriately respond to them are critical for successful and compliant business operations. An entity's compliance and ethics program must take into consideration the risk of fraud and corruption and institute internal controls, policy, training, and other critical program aspects.

GLOBAL CRACKDOWN

Like no time before, there is a growing global crackdown on bribery and corruption. The United States has been joined by other countries in this fight. There have been more investigations and prosecutions of both businesses and their employees in recent years than at any time in the past 30 years. "Crimes of official corruption threaten the integrity of the global marketplace and undermine the rule of law in the host countries," said Lori Weinstein, the Justice Department prosecutor who oversaw the Siemens bribery case.[1]

Corruption and bribery are the insidious elements of the dark side of business. Illegal payments by public and private corporations to foreign government officials to induce business dealings have long been an unscrupulous practice. These bribes, in the form of cash and a host of other means including gifts and gratuities, trips and entertainment, charitable contributions, forgiveness of debt, and more, are illegal and have been outlawed by the United States for many years. A rash of business corruption cases in the 1970s and a Congressional focus resulted in the enactment of the FCPA in 1977 that prohibits bribes to foreign government officials. Since the enactment of the FCPA, Nigeria has had the most prosecutions by country. Nigeria is followed by Iraq, China, Indonesia, India, Azerbaijan, Canada, Costa Rica, Rwanda, Egypt, Kazakhstan, and South Korea in number of cases. Countries in every region of the world have seen FCPA enforcement. By far, Asia has seen more cases than any other region, with Africa a distant second.

DEVASTATING COST OF CORRUPTION

The sad fact is that corruption is pervasive and entrenched on a global scale. A culture of corruption is still embraced as a way of doing business in many parts of the world. "Each year one trillion U.S. dollars is lost in bribes and other forms of corruption around the world," said Alan Boeckmann, Chairman of the Board of Fluor

---

*Material in this chapter is adapted from *Foreign Corrupt Practices Act Compliance Guidebook: Protecting Your Organization from Bribery and Corruption*, by Martin T. Biegelman and Daniel R. Biegelman, ©2010, John Wiley & Sons, Inc., reprinted with permission.

Corporation. "Consider this: the trillion dollars lost each year to bribes could feed up to 400 million starving people for the next 27 years."[2] These impactful words reinforce the devastating cost of corruption and bribery on a global scale.

Corruption often occurs in the worst possible locales. They include developing and emerging countries and regions that suffer the most from corruption's evil consequences. Corruption fuels poverty, hunger, disease, illiteracy, contempt, and disillusion. Corruption drains the funds necessary for the very programs that people in developing countries most need. Corrupt government officials in countries with rich natural resources such as oil, timber, and minerals "accumulate enormous personal wealth, taking millions in bribes from corporations looking to secure lucrative contracts" while the very poor live in abject poverty.[3] The resulting bribes and graft destroy honest government and business. The corruption turns the populace to distrust, ambivalence, acceptance, and ultimately, participation.

FCPA PROVISIONS

The FCPA has two main parts: the antibribery provision and the accounting provision. The FCPA mandated that corporate records contain accurate statements concerning the true purpose of all payments made by the company. The law makes it a crime for American companies, domestic concerns, or foreign nationals doing business in the United States, as well as individuals and organizations acting on their behalf, to bribe any foreign government official in return for assistance in:

- Obtaining or retaining business, or directing business to any particular person
- Influencing a foreign government official to do or to omit an act in violation of his duty
- Influencing a foreign government official to affect an act or decision by a foreign government[4]

The FCPA not only makes it a crime to pay bribes to foreign officials, it also makes it a crime for publicly traded United States companies to make payments of any kind that are not recorded on the books. Bribes are almost always disguised on the books as another business expense rather than the true nature of the payments.

This reduces the government's evidentiary burden because the very evidence the government will need in prosecutions can be found in the internal books and records. Government prosecutors do not have to prove a bribe, only that a payment was made and not recorded properly on the company's books.

While the Department of Justice (DOJ) is responsible for bribery violations of the FCPA, the Securities and Exchange Commission (SEC) handles accounting violations of the FCPA. It is interesting to note that it is not a crime under the FCPA for an American company to pay bribes in a country where bribes are legal. There are also specific exceptions granted in a 1988 amendment to the FCPA. American companies can make facilitating payments. Facilitating payments includes fees to expedite permits, licenses, papers, visas, mail, and phone service, and to expedite the movement of perishable cargo. Further, it is not considered a bribe to reasonably reimburse public officials for expenses such as meals, travel, and lodging while the company is promoting or demonstrating a product, or executing a contract. These expenses must not be excessive and must reflect bona fide charges. However, it must be kept in mind that these actions still may be illegal in the country where they occur.

The FCPA prohibits individuals and companies from "corruptly making use of the mails or any means or instrumentality of interstate commerce in furtherance of an offer, promise, authorization, or payment of money or anything of value to a foreign official for the purpose of obtaining or retaining business for, or directing business to, any person or securing any improper advantage."[5] Furthermore, the FCPA also requires "issuers not only to refrain from making corrupt payments to foreign government officials, but also to implement policies and practices that reduce the risk that employees and agents will engage in bribery."[6] The books and records provision of the FCPA requires certain corporations to create and maintain books, records, and accounts that fairly and accurately reflect company transactions. The knowing falsification of company records is also prohibited.[7] Penalties include both civil and criminal sanctions against the company and culpable employees.

The penalties for violating the FCPA can be severe. Enterprises can be fined $2 million for each violation, and individuals face five years in prison and a $250,000 fine. In addition, the company can be forced to abandon the business won by bribery through business debarments, face disgorgement of the profits obtained through bribery, be denied export licenses, or be disqualified from any U.S. government contracts.

GLOBAL ANTI-CORRUPTION EFFORTS

Olusegun Obasanjo, the former President of Nigeria, who fought bribery and corruption during his years in leadership, called corruption "the greatest single bane of our society today." He should know because Nigeria faced the effects of entrenched corruption since its formation as a country and rule by a succession of corrupt dictators. Corruption is a way of life in Nigeria as it is in many parts of the world. While it's much too early to say that society has turned the corner on this massive problem, anti-corruption activities and initiatives have taken hold and are making a difference. A multitude of countries and organizations such as the United Nations, the World Bank, Transparency International, and many others are united in the fight against corruption. This focused effort has brought needed changes in laws and how business operates throughout the world.

The globalization the world has witnessed has extended beyond business and into the world of law enforcement. Anti-corruption activity is being given the worldwide attention it so desperately needs. Police and prosecutors are working together to prosecute corruption like never before. While once police authorities did not fully share intelligence or cooperate in investigations, there has been a sea change in fighting corruption and bribery. This transformation has resulted in a significant improvement of cross-border cooperation and investigative successes.

There are several reasons for this change. Governments are recognizing that corruption is a destabilizing force that impacts their standing in the world community. Developing countries want to create a level playing field for business competition, no matter where they do business.[8] The United States' increasing enforcement of the FCPA has sent a strong message to other countries. They are slowly adopting FCPA-like statutes and enforcement. "International harmonization of antifraud and anticorruption regulation will lead to more parallel investigations, with the likely consequence of increased penalties."[9]

The DOJ and SEC have become more focused on FCPA enforcement than at any time since the act's enactment. Self-disclosure of FCPA violations has been extraordinary and has caught the attention of foreign regulators and prosecutors. More and more countries are embracing the anti-bribery tenets of the Organisation for Economic Co-operation and Development (OECD) Anti-Bribery Convention. The OECD is increasing pressure on convention signatories to heighten visibility around anti-corruption enforcement. The increasing interactions and cooperation among international enforcement agencies has helped U.S. prosecutors bring record numbers of cases and settlements. Cross-border and collaborative investigations in other countries have grown and will continue to do so. Germany, Brazil, France, Nigeria, Korea, and other countries are increasingly focused on anti-corruption efforts.

Another contributing factor is that over the last two decades, there has been a significant increase in both the adoption of international anti-bribery agreements and the creation of anti-corruption organizations. The many agreements, organizations, and efforts are focused on reducing bribery and corruption through increased legislation, interactions and cooperation, and awareness and prevention.

OECD CONVENTION ON COMBATING BRIBERY

Established in 1961, the Organisation for Economic Co-operation and Development brings together the governments of member countries in an effort to improve democracy and the world economy. The OECD commitments encompass economic development and growth, increasing employment and living standards, maintaining financial stability, and world trade. There are 34 member countries including Australia, Japan, Korea, Germany, France, Turkey, United Kingdom, Mexico, Canada, and the United States.[10]

Although the United States enacted the FCPA in 1977 to attack bribery and corruption, the rest of the world did not act with the same level of urgency. Through many years of efforts by the United States and other interested countries, the OECD decided to act. In November 1997, the 29 member countries unanimously agreed on principles to combat bribery of foreign government officials in international business dealings. On December 17, 1997, the OECD members and non-member nations signed the OECD Convention on Combating Bribery of Foreign Public Officials in International Business Transactions. The signatory nations agreed to enact legislation similar to the FCPA outlawing bribery of public officials, and to create a legal basis for extradition and international cooperation.

The OECD Convention has been signed by 38 countries and its influence is growing. There is no doubt that the OECD Convention has had an impact on anti-corruption activities and legislation. Signatories have a requirement to pass legislation that makes bribery and corruption a criminal offense. This includes individuals or corporate entities that "intentionally offer, promise, or give any undue pecuniary or other advantage, whether directly or through intermediaries, to a foreign public official, for that official or for a third party, in order that the official act or refrain from acting in relation to the performance of official duties, in order to obtain or retain business, or other improper advantage in the conduct of international business."[11] A foreign public official is defined as "any person holding a legislative, administrative, or judicial office of a foreign country, whether appointed or elected; any person exercising a public function for a foreign country, including for a public agency or public enterprise; and any official or agent of a public international organization."[12]

Prior to the signing of the convention, 11 OECD members, including Germany, France, and the UK, allowed tax deductions for bribery of foreign officials as a legitimate business expense. Pressure from other OCED members has helped to enhance both enforcement and anti-bribery legislation. Still, much work needs to be done. According to a 2011 Transparency International report on enforcement of the OECD Convention, only 16 member countries, including Korea, Germany, the UK, and the United States, were either actively or moderately enforcing the principles of the OECD Convention. The report found that the other signatory countries including Brazil, Canada, and Mexico have little or no enforcement.

UK BRIBERY ACT

The UK's criminal law for bribery dates back to the turn of the 20th century and needed updating to meet the requirements of the modern age. Not only was a strong statute necessary to hold those involved in giving and accepting bribes accountable but also to ensure that the long arm of the law can reach those who commit bribery in both the public and private sectors, in the UK or abroad, and ensure a culture of compliance. As a result, the UK enacted a strong anti-corruption statute that has been called the "FCPA on steroids." The Bribery Act was passed by Parliament in April 2010 and is intended to reform existing criminal law "to provide a new, modern, and comprehensive scheme of bribery offences that will enable courts and prosecutors to respond more effectively to bribery at home or abroad."[13]

The Bribery Act covers both active and passive forms of bribery. Active bribery is the giving of bribes and passive bribery is the receipt of bribes. It is the first anti-corruption statute in the UK to include penalties for governmental corruption and commercial bribery. Facilitation payments are a criminal offense. Third-party risk is also addressed by including language on the corrupt offer, promise, or gift made to a foreign public official through "associated persons" including agents and contractors. Unlike the FCPA, the Bribery Act does not contain a books and records provision.

A corporate offense of failure of a commercial organization to detect and prevent bribery is also included in the Bribery Act. This corporate offense applies to both UK companies and those others that have business operations in the UK. There is a defense available if the organization can demonstrate that "adequate procedures" were previously in place and the corrupt activity was not carried out by senior officers or agents acting on their behalf.

On March 30, 2011, the UK Ministry of Justice issued guidance on the adequate procedures requirement of the Bribery Act. The guidance is intended to assist organizations in preventing bribery and limiting corporate liability for noncompliance. Although originally scheduled for implementation in April 2010, the Bribery Act was delayed so the Ministry of Justice could solicit comments and recommendations from those organizations impacted by this legislation. The Bribery Act took effect on July 1, 2011. The guidance reinforces to entities the need to implement a risk-based approach in preventing bribery and developing an effective anti-bribery and corruption compliance program.

Within the guidance are Six Principles that constitute adequate procedures. If successfully put into place, these principles can defend against a charge of failing to prevent bribery. Similar to the Federal Sentencing Guidelines' seven steps to effective compliance, the Six Principles as defined in the new guidance are:

Principle 1—Proportionality

Principle 2—Top Level Commitment

Principle 3—Risk Assessment

Principle 4—Due Diligence

Principle 5—Communication

Principle 6—Monitoring and Review

The issued guidance is formulated around these principles. As stated in the document, the guidance "is not prescriptive and is not a one-size-fits-all" approach.[14] In designing an anti-bribery and corruption compliance program, each organization must assess numerous risk factors and other distinctive elements particular to the entity. While there is much in the guidance for an organization to consider, the following sections discuss key areas of importance.

Assessing Risk and Due Diligence

The guidance supports the premise that operating in the global marketplace implies increased corruption risk that must be addressed through an appropriate risk assessment process. The guidance reinforces the need for organizations to assess their risk of bribery based on a number of factors. These risk factors include country, customer, business sector, transaction, business opportunity, business partnership and third parties, and other risk factors. The guidance advises that risk assessment procedures should be "proportionate to the organization's size and structure and to the nature, scale and location of its activities."[15]

Due diligence is a required part of risk mitigation especially for vendors, contractors, third parties and other associated persons who perform services on behalf of the organization. The guidance reinforces the importance of a thorough vetting when establishing business relationships, especially when working through local country agents. The guidance encourages entities to establish due diligence procedures that prevent associated persons from committing bribery on the organization's behalf. Due diligence processes and procedures need to be proportionate to the risks identified and conducted with a risk-based approach.

Corporate Hospitality

There was a concern that providing corporate hospitality such as meals, travel, and entertainment would constitute a violation of the Bribery Act. The guidance makes it clear that "genuine" hospitality or related business expenses are not prohibited. The guidance recognizes the need for legitimate business expenses to promote corporate interests and differentiates when the intention is to corruptly influence a foreign government official. To be in compliance, hospitality and promotional expenses must be reasonable and proportionate and intended to improve the organization's image, demonstrate products and services, and enhance business relations between the company and customer. Tickets to sporting events, client dinners, travel expenses gifts to clients, and other legitimate forms of hospitality are still appropriate and allowed with the reasonable test always applied. The guidance does call out bribery disguised as hospitality and the need for the entity to be aware of this in designing and implementing adequate procedures.

Facilitation Payments

The guidance reinforced that facilitation payments—small payments to government official to perform routine government services such as obtaining permits, starting utility services and scheduling inspections, are bribes under the Bribery Act as well as in previous law. This is contrary to the Foreign Corrupt Practices Act that allows facilitation payments. Although still a bribe, the UK government recognizes the challenges that organizations face when doing businesses in certain countries and regions. The guidance notes that it will take mutual cooperation between many interested parties and many years to eradicate facilitation payments. Furthermore, the guidance implies that prosecutorial discretion will determine potential prosecution for facilitation payments. Large or repeated payments as a long-standing business practice, and payments in violation of existing compliance policies, will determine whether the organization is prosecuted.

Prosecution Guidance

In addition to the guidance released by the Ministry of Justice, the two major prosecuting offices in the UK issued joint prosecution guidance on March 30, 2011.[16] The Director of the Serious Fraud Office and the Director of Public Prosecutions detailed their general approach to bribery prosecutions with a two stage test: (1) whether there is sufficient evidence of bribery to obtain a conviction; and (2) whether a prosecution is in the public interest. Factors influencing a prosecution include whether a conviction would result in a significant prison sentence; if the offense was premeditated; if other serious criminal offenses were also involved; and if those involved in the bribery are in positions of trust or authority. One important factor weighing against prosecution is if the organization had "a genuinely proactive approach involving self-reporting and remedial action."[17] The adequacy of the anti-bribery and corruption compliance program will be a further determining factor in any prosecution.

TRANSPARENCY INTERNATIONAL

Transparency International (TI) is a leading international nongovernmental organization fighting corruption through awareness and practical solutions. Its members include thought leaders from government, civil society, business, and the media to promote transparency in business, procurement, public administration, and elections. TI was founded in 1993 to be politically nonpartisan and to bring together like-minded people with one common mission: a world without corruption. TI has grown into a global network of more than 90 chapters around the world. TI has been instrumental in widely communicating the damaging impact of corruption, defined as the misuse of entrusted power for private gain, through a variety of references, materials, and tools.

Corruption Perceptions Index

TI may be best known for its annual Corruption Perceptions Index (CPI), published since 1995. The CPI ranks 180 countries by the perceived levels of corruption believed to exist among public officials and politicians. The scoring is determined through expert assessments and opinion surveys. For the index, TI defines corruption as the abuse of public office for private gain. CPI scores range from 10 (least corrupt) to 1 (most corrupt). Several factors are present in those nations that have high CPI scores: accountability, political stability, effective government regulations, and rule of law. The fewer of these factors present, the lower, and worse, the CPI score will be. Exhibit 15.1 lists the top 20 countries with the least amount of perceived corruption for 2010. Exhibit 15.2 lists the bottom 20 countries with the greatest amount of perceived corruption for 2010.

This universally used tool has grown in popularity each year as an indicator of the level of corruption in countries of the world. More

EXHIBIT 15.1   2010 Corruption Perceptions Index: Top 20 Countries

Denmark
New Zealand
Singapore
Finland
Sweden
Canada
Netherlands
Australia
Norway
Iceland
Luxembourg
Hong Kong
Ireland
Germany
Austria
Barbados
Japan
Qatar
United Kingdom
Chile

Source: Transparency International, 2010 Corruption Perceptions Index.

EXHIBIT 15.2   2010 Corruption Perceptions Index: Bottom 20
Countries

Papua New Guinea
Cambodia
Russia
Tajikistan
Guinea-Bissau
Guinea
Venezuela
Kyrgyzstan
Congo, Democratic Republic
Angola
Equatorial Guinea
Burundi
Chad
Sudan
Uzbekistan
Turkmenistan
Iraq
Afghanistan
Myanmar
Somalia

Source: Transparency International, 2010 Corruption Perceptions Index.

and more organizations use the CPI in enterprise risk management for
their operations in the countries surveyed. The countries perceived as
the most corrupt have earned that designation for good reason, and
companies that do business there need to be especially vigilant.

COMPLIANCE PROGRAM DESIGN

In designing an anti-corruption compliance program for an organization, compliance program individuality is a key consideration. Ideally
a compliance program should be both industry-specific and unique to
the organization; it should be tailored to fit the requirements of the individual organization, particular geographic operating locations, related risks, and the overall compliance requirements of its particular
industry, but should also reflect the compliance requirements imposed
on all corporations and the laws that they must follow. The anti-
corruption program must be integrated into the overall compliance

program. Each organization must ensure that their compliance programs are receiving ongoing and individualized evaluation and modification.

Anti-corruption compliance programs must address the inherent risks when doing business in foreign countries. These risks result from the various aspects and forces that come into play in the global business environment. These risks are particularly problematic to the FCPA and anti-corruption laws in various countries. Many companies prosecuted for FCPA violations over the years either outright ignored or were willfully blind to these risks. Their compliance programs were inadequately designed to recognize and mitigate risk. The following are key business issues germane to corruption risk:

- Business contracts, deals, sales, and marketing
- Business partners and third parties
- Dealing with government officials
- State-owned enterprises
- Sales consultants
- Joint ventures
- Mergers and acquisitions
- Conflicts of interest
- Facilitating payments
- Travel and entertainment of foreign government officials
- Gifts to foreign government officials
- Promotional expenses
- Lobbyists
- Charitable donations
- Country risk as defined by Corruption Perceptions Index and other informational sources

An effective anti-corruption compliance program needs to incorporate the following program elements into the overall compliance program:

- Tone at the top
- Anti-corruption standards and procedures
- Reasonable efforts to exclude prohibited persons
- Training and communication

- Mechanisms for reporting violations and seeking guidance
- Third-party due diligence
- Anti-corruption contractual clauses
- Internal accounting controls
- Monitoring, auditing, and evaluating program effectiveness
- Performance incentives and disciplinary actions
- Response to criminal conduct and remedial action

These program elements are not anti-corruption program specific and are interconnected to functions and practices across an organization.

Companies can protect themselves with a compliance program that ensures all employees are specifically aware of which actions are prohibited by the FCPA. Companies can also protect themselves by including special clauses in their contracts whereby local agents and partners confirm that they will not violate the FCPA, as well as other anti-corruption laws. Many companies have tried to circumvent the FCPA by having local joint venture partners commit bribery while the United States companies are willfully blind. This use of third parties will not prevent a FCPA prosecution.

Department of Justice's FCPA Red Flags

A few years ago, the United States Department of Justice published a list of potential red flag indicators of FCPA violations. While this list was in no way comprehensive, it provided some of the many predictors of misconduct and noncompliance. Of note, the DOJ has since removed this red flag list from their Web site. Speculation is that the DOJ did not want to issue what some might think is a comprehensive list and thus deemphasize other possible red flags. Red flags come in all shapes and sizes and must be acted upon once discovered. Each organization needs to determine the particular universe of red flags they may face. The now deleted DOJ list included:

- Unusual payment patterns or financial arrangements
- A history of corruption in the country

- Refusal by the foreign joint venture partner or representative to provide a certification that it will not take any action in furtherance of an unlawful offer, promise, or payment to a foreign public official in violation of the FCPA
- Unusually high commissions
- Lack of transparency in expenses and accounting records
- Apparent lack of qualifications or resources on the part of the joint venture partner or representative to perform the services offered

CONTROL COMPONENTS, INC.

If there is a recent case that exemplifies the strong stance that government authorities are taking in pursuing FCPA violations, the prosecution of Control Components, Inc. (CCI) is that one. CCI is a California corporation that designs and manufactures control valves for the nuclear, oil and gas, and power generation industries throughout the world. Between 1998 and 2007, CCI, through its officers, employees, and agents, made more than 200 corrupt payments to employees of state-owned enterprises and private companies in 36 countries. These countries included China, Korea, Malaysia, and the United Arab Emirates. The bribes totaled $6.85 million and earned CCI $46.5 million in net profits.

CCI's business strategy employed corruption and bribery to drive revenue and senior management was involved in this decade-long conspiracy along with employees and agents. The CEO and others devised a sales model euphemistically called the *friend-in-camp* (FIC) *program*. The FIC program cultivated relationships with employees of both state-owned enterprises and private companies that included the payment of bribes to obtain and retain business. FICs were primarily people who had the authority to award contracts or at least steer a contract to CCI. Code words such as "flowers" were used to refer to bribes. Consultants were retained whose sole purpose was to funnel bribe payments to recipients. In addition to corrupt payments, the company provided bribes in the form of lavish trips to Disneyland, Las Vegas, and Hawaii. College tuition was paid for the children of executives at state-owned enterprises.[18]

In 2004, when CCI's parent company conducted an internal audit of suspect commission payments, CCI executives tried to obstruct the audit. Information was purposely withheld from auditors. False information in the form of phony invoices to conceal bribes was provided to the auditors. When outside counsel was hired to conduct an internal investigation, CCI personnel made false statements to obstruct the inquiry. Incriminating documents were destroyed.[19]

Prosecutors used a variety of tactics to unravel the pervasive conspiracy, a move that is indicative of the new approach to fighting FCPA violations. Both the corporation and individuals were prosecuted. In fact, the eight CCI defendants is the single largest number of individual defendants in a FCPA case. There was cross-border law enforcement cooperation resulting in the prosecution of a UK official implicated in the bribery probe. Both government corruption and private company bribery were charged in this case. The Travel Act was used to charge commercial bribery. The Travel Act prohibits using interstate or foreign commerce to promote unlawful activity including bribery and corruption in violation of state law.

In April 2009, six former CCI executives including the CEO, director of sales for China and Taiwan, director of worldwide sales, vice president of worldwide customer service, head of sales for Europe, Africa, and the Middle East, and president of the CCI Korea office were indicted. Two other executives, including the former CFO, have pled guilty. In July 2009, CCI pled guilty to violations of the FCPA and the Travel Act and was sentenced to three years of probation and a criminal fine of $18.2 million. The company will have to retain an independent monitor for three years and implement an effective compliance program.

The lesson that CCI and other organizations learned from the government in this case is clear and simple: FCPA compliance is not an option and violations will be vigorously prosecuted. "The number of individual prosecutions has risen—and that's not an accident," said former DOJ official Mark Mendelsohn. "That is quite intentional on the part of the Department. It is our view that to have a credible deterrent effect, people have to go to jail. People have to be prosecuted where appropriate. This is a federal crime. This is not fun and games."[20] Self-reporting of FCPA violations is the expected norm according to the DOJ.

NOTES

1. Siri Schubert and T. Christian Miller, "At Siemens, Bribery Was Just a Line Item," *FRONTLINE*, February 13, 2009, www.pbs.org/frontlineworld/ stories/bribe/2009/02/at-siemens-bribery-was-just-a-line-item.html.
2. Alan Boeckmann, CEO, Fluor Corporation, "Help Us Fight Against Corruption!" (statement for Partnering Against Corruption Initiative, World Economic Forum), YouTube video, December 8, 2008, www.weforum.org/issues/ partnering-against-corruption-initiative/index.html.
3. "Spotlight: The Victims of Corruption: The Human Cost of Bribery in the Developing World," *FRONTLINE*, February 24, 2009, www.pbs.org/frontlineworld/stories/bribe/2009/02/spotlight-the-victims-of-corruption.html.
4. *Foreign Corrupt Practices Act*, U.S. Code Title 15, Section 78dd-2(a).
5. Ibid., Section 78dd-3.
6. *U.S. v. SSI International Far East, Ltd.*, criminal information unsealed on October 16, 2006, United States District Court, District of Oregon, 24.
7. Ibid.
8. PricewaterhouseCoopers, *Corruption Crackdown: How the FCPA Is Changing the Way the World Does Business*, July 27, 2009, 3.
9. Ibid.
10. The complete list of OECD member countries includes: Australia, Austria, Belgium, Canada, Chile, Czech Republic, Denmark, Estonia, Finland, France, Germany, Greece, Hungary, Iceland, Ireland, Israel, Italy, Japan, Korea, Luxembourg, Mexico, Netherlands, New Zealand, Norway, Poland, Portugal, Slovak Republic, Slovenia, Spain, Sweden, Switzerland, Turkey, United Kingdom, and United States.
11. Organisation for Economic Co-operation and Development, *OECD Convention on Combating Bribery of Foreign Public Officials in International Business Transactions*, Article 1, Section 1, www.oecd.org/dataoecd/4/18/38028044.pdf.
12. Ibid.

13. Draft Bribery Bill, United Kingdom Ministry of Justice, www.justice.gov.uk/ publications/draft-bribery-bill.htm.
14. UK Bribery Act of 2010, 6.
15. Ibid., 25.
16. Serious Fraud Office, "UK Bribery Act of 2010: Joint Prosecution Guidance of the Director of the Serious Fraud Office and the Director of Public Prosecutions," March 30, 2011, www.sfo. gov.uk/media/167348/briberyactjointprosecutionguidance.pdf.
17. Ibid., 7.
18. *U.S. v. Control Components, Inc.*, Criminal Information, CR No. 09-00162, United States District Court, Central District of California, July 22, 2009.
19. Ibid.
20. "Mendelsohn Says Criminal Bribery Prosecutions Doubled in 2007." *Corporate Crime Reporter*, September 16, 2008, www.corporatecrimereporter.com/ mendelsohn091608.htm.

The Feds Are Watching

What to Know and Do Now

EXECUTIVE SUMMARY

The federal government has had a strong response to the many corporate frauds over the last decade. Using the full range of law enforcement actions and new laws, federal agents and prosecutors have used a "shock and awe" strategy against corporate fraudsters. "Flipping" lower-level employees to testify against higher-ups, cooperation agreements, grand jury subpoenas, and search warrants are but a sampling of the weapons in the government's arsenal. Hopefully all businesses will embrace a culture of compliance; if not, the feds will be watching and will be ready to pounce. Organizations must also be prepared in the event the government makes them the focus of a fraud investigation. The right or wrong response at the beginning of the investigation may set the tone that follows. Entities that acknowledge wrongdoing early and "give up" their corrupt executives will do far better in surviving and emerging from a major fraud investigation. Companies must also have a policy as to legal recourse when it is discovered they have been the victims of fraud.

There is a new war on crime in America today, and it is being waged by the government to stop corporate fraud and corruption. In the past decade, titans of industry have succumbed to fraud and in their wake were left the many victims. This war is not being fought solely by the government. Businesses must now take appropriate action to detect and prevent fraud of all kinds. Sarbanes-Oxley was enacted because some corporate executives failed to ensure ethical operations and the protection of shareholders and employees. Fraud prevention and enhanced internal controls help, but organizations must also know the strategies of law enforcement and be prepared to take action when allegations of fraud are discovered.

THE GOVERNMENT'S "SHOCK AND AWE" STRATEGY

In years past, it often took a lengthy period to investigate white-collar crime cases thoroughly. Considering the complexity of sophisticated corporate fraud, the vast numbers of documents to be obtained and analyzed, the numerous interviews to be conducted, the resource constraints, the court proceedings, and the legal maneuvering, it was not uncommon for investigations to continue for years. That changed as a result of the corporate scandals. The government and the public have little sympathy or patience for corporate fraudsters, and justice demands quick resolution to allegations.

As a result, federal law enforcement has also changed its modus operandi for investigating white-collar criminals. In the past, the FBI and other federal investigative agencies often spent years developing every possible criminal violation against a subject or subjects of an investigation. The purpose was to make an airtight case, but valuable resources were often not available for similar investigations. The approach was "deterrence" rather than the development of every possible criminal charge. In the investigation of HealthSouth Corporation for a massive accounting fraud, the government adopted a "shock and awe" strategy against corporate fraud. Federal prosecutors and the FBI in Birmingham, Alabama, used new levels of cooperation among various federal agencies, search warrants, the new laws from Sarbanes-Oxley, a push for plea bargains, and cooperation from codefendants. In a matter of weeks after first announcing the investigation against HealthSouth in March 2003, the government had obtained 12 guilty pleas from company officials, and this was just the beginning.[1]

The cooperating defendants provided evidence against other corporate officials, who also pled guilty and agreed to work with the government. They provided even more significant evidence of the fraud, which allowed the case to progress rapidly and, most importantly, pointed directly to CEO Richard Scrushy. Alice H. Martin, the U.S. Attorney in Birmingham, whose office prosecuted HealthSouth said, "Your case doesn't have to be perfect. You don't have to prove every crime. If you've got enough evidence to back up a few good charges, don't work for another year nailing down every shred of evidence for every possible charge that might be there."[2] She added that the Department of Justice sent out a strong message to prosecutors and federal agents that it "wanted real-time prosecution of corporate crime."[3]

Unfortunately, this approach did not work in the government's trial of Scrushy. In fact, Ms. Martin's words about not needing a perfect case came back to haunt the prosecutors. Scrushy became the first chief executive charged and acquitted under Sarbanes-Oxley. The Scrushy jury bought the "Mr. Magoo Defense" of the CEO who has no idea that a massive fraud is occurring inside the company. Clearly, the government was at a disadvantage. The trial was held on Scrushy's home turf of Birmingham, where he had strong support from religious groups and others in the community.

The defense team did an amazing job of portraying the defendant as the only innocent person in a den of thieves and created reasonable doubt. The fact that Scrushy did not take the stand and face cross-examination also helped in his acquittal. Even though the CEO was not convicted, there is no denying the depth and breadth of the accounting fraud at HealthSouth. Exhibit 16.1 provides a list of the many HealthSouth employees who were charged by the government for this fraud and the prosecution results. Executive Insight 16.1 provides insight into the mindset of former CFO Aaron Beam in both the fraud he committed with others and his cooperation with the government against Scrushy.

Part of the government's strong approach in fighting corporate fraud has been to treat corporate fraudsters no differently with the

EXHIBIT 16.1 HealthSouth Prosecution Results

Date Charged	Defendant	Title	Status
March 19, 2003	Weston Smith	CFO	Convicted
March 26, 2003	William T. Owens	CFO	Convicted
March 31, 2003	Emery Harris	VP, Finance and Assistant Controller	Convicted
April 3, 2003	Rebecca Kay Morgan	Assistant Controller	Convicted
April 3, 2003	Cathy C. Edwards	VP	Convicted
April 3, 2003	Ken Livesay	Chief Information Officer and Assistant Controller	Convicted
April 23, 2003	Michael Martin	CFO	Convicted
April 23, 2003	Virginia B. Valentine	Assistant VP	Convicted
April 23, 2003	Angela C. Ayers	VP	Convicted
April 23, 2003	Malcolm McVay	CFO	Convicted
April 24, 2003	Aaron Beam	CFO	Convicted
July 9, 2003	Jason Brown	VP, Finance	Convicted
July 31, 2003	Richard Botts	Senior VP, Tax	Convicted
July 31, 2003	Will Hicks	VP, Investments	Convicted
September 26, 2003	Catherine Fowler	VP, Treasury and Cash Manager	Convicted
November 4, 2003	Richard Scrushy	CEO	Acquitted

Source: U.S. Attorney, Northern, District of Alabama, HealthSouth criminal investigation prosecutions.

media than organized crime figures. Perp walks are routinely used to showcase white-collar defendants. Federal agents are going to fraudsters' homes and arresting them, rather than allowing them to surrender. Handcuffing is not optional. Defendants are being charged with more than just typical fraud and securities violations. Although some prosecutors are using the "quick hit" approach, others are using all the weapons in their arsenal when necessary. Money laundering, conspiracy, and racketeering, as well as the criminal charges resulting from Sarbanes-Oxley are also being used. Federal prosecutors are using asset forfeiture statutes to take back the ill-gotten gains of corporate criminals. A defense attorney who has represented both organized crime figures and corporate executives explains that the government's strong approach is a result of "the public demanding that white-collar criminals be sent to prison, and prosecutors are playing tough.... There's no more white-glove treatment."[4]

EXECUTIVE INSIGHT 16.1: AARON BEAM: REFLECTIONS ON A LOST OPPORTUNITY TO STOP FRAUD

"After losing possessions, serving prison time, and fully coming to terms with what happened, I understand that I have committed a terrible, white-collar crime that hurt many people. Because of a lack of conviction, I will always be remembered as the guy that committed the fraud instead of the co-founder of one of America's most successful health care companies."[i] With those painful words, former HealthSouth CFO Aaron Beam recalls how he went from corporate visionary to corporate fraudster. Beam was the company's first CFO and together with former Chairman and CEO Richard Scrushy grew HealthSouth into an extremely successful company and a darling of Wall Street.

The most tragic thing about HealthSouth was that unlike Enron and other failed companies, the business model was sound. However, the seed for fraud was present from day one. Beam's moral compass went haywire the first time he met Scrushy, which was during a job interview in the years before they started HealthSouth. "Something about him told me that the things he promised were just too good to be true," lamented Beam. Yet, Beam took the job. During his first day at work, Scrushy shocked him by lying to another executive about a relatively small issue. Both Beam and Scrushy knew it was a lie. "I always wondered if he tested me that first morning on the job—to see if I would go along with him," commented Beam.[ii] Beam went along and said nothing. "As brilliant as Richard was in his business dealings, he was equally diabolical, callous and cruel in his justification for attaining success."[iii] Yet Beam was seduced by the money, which gave him multiple homes, cars, and the lifestyle of the nouveau rich.

Many years later the warning signs Beam feared, that Scrushy would resort to fraud, proved to be right. It was June 30, 1996. For the first time in the company's history, HealthSouth would not meet Wall Street's expectations and report a bad quarter. Beam and the company controller dreaded having to tell Scrushy the bad news. Scrushy responded as expected and told them there was no way they could disappoint the Street. "Fix the numbers," he ordered them and they were unable to say no.[iv] Once they started cooking the books, they couldn't stop. Each subsequent quarter failed to meet expectations and each quarter they falsified the financial statements. The fear of discovery and prison ate at Beam and by the next year, he knew he had to do something.

He quickly discounted becoming a whistleblower, seeking legal advice or trying to convince Scrushy to change his ways. Instead, Beam decided to retire. Even in retirement, he kept looking over his shoulder for the day when he would be held accountable. That day came in 2003, just months after the enactment of Sarbanes-Oxley and greater scrutiny of public companies. The government investigation of HealthSouth began in earnest and the huge accounting fraud came to light. To his credit, Beam reached out to federal authorities, agreed to cooperate, and pled guilty. It is never easy admitting one's wrongdoing especially if it involves billions of dollars in fraud. Yet Beam accepted responsibility and told what he and others did. He testified at Scrushy's trial and was shocked and angered by the acquittal. "It was unfair. In my eyes, and in the eyes of many, justice simply was not served," Beam later said.[v] He served his prison term and today operates a lawn care business and speaks on business ethics and preventing corporate fraud. Beam is forever haunted by one question: What would have happened if he stood up to Scrushy and refused to cook the books?

---

[i] Aaron Beam with Chris Warner, *HealthSouth: The Wagon To Disaster* (Fairhope, AL: Wagon Publishing, 2009), 7.
[ii] Ibid., 19
[iii] Ibid., 12.
[iv] Ibid., 78.
[v] Ibid., 159.

Just a few short months after Scrushy's acquittal, he was indicted in October 2005 on new charges of bribery, money laundering, extortion, obstruction of justice, and racketeering stemming from a federal corruption probe in Alabama. This time, he was convicted after jury trial and in June 2007 was sentenced to six years and 10 months in prison. In January 2011, Scrushy lost his appeal of a $2.88 billion civil case judgment for his role in the accounting fraud at HealthSouth.

Prosecutors have asked for bail in the millions of dollars to ensure that defendants appear for court proceedings. In the case of former Tyco CEO Dennis Kozlowski, the New York County District Attorney's Office obtained a $10 million bail on the indicted executive, causing his defense attorney to utter incredulously, "This is not a narcotics case."[5] Prosecutors are using every possible advantage to get defendants to plead guilty and cooperate against other defendants, even using a loved one as leverage. The Enron Task Force charged former Enron CFO Andrew Fastow with fraud, money laundering, and conspiracy. This was not enough to get him to cooperate. Fastow was then indicted on new charges, but this time his wife, Lea Fastow, was also charged. Lea Fastow had been a former assistant treasurer at Enron and was charged with helping her husband and other executives perpetrate the massive fraud at Enron. She was arrested, handcuffed, and given her perp walk. Clearly, the intention was to put pressure on the husband to cooperate now that his wife and the mother of his children was facing many years in jail if convicted. After lengthy negotiations, both Andrew and Lea Fastow agreed to plead guilty. Andrew agreed to a 10-year prison term, forfeiture of $24 million in cash and property, and cooperation with the government in the continuing case. Lea received a misdemeanor charge of filing a false tax return and was sentenced to one year in prison.

There was a time when a corporate plea was more acceptable than having a corporate executive take a fall for fraud. In the late 1980s, one of the authors investigated a security guard services company in a scheme to defraud commercial airlines operating out of John F. Kennedy Airport in New York by overbilling for guard services and other crimes. More than 20 lower-level employees were convicted. When the investigation began to focus on higher-level executives, the company wanted to take a corporate plea rather than have any of their top executives prosecuted. The government went along with this approach. The company pled guilty to wire fraud and paid a $1 million fine. This may not happen today; corporate executives are now being held more accountable and businesses understand the impact of a criminal conviction.

EXECUTIVE INSIGHT 16.2: COMPUTER ASSOCIATES AND THE "35-DAY MONTH"

In today's world, protecting the viability of a business is paramount. Computer Associates—now called CA Technologies[vi]—is an example of a company that has learned from the past and taken strong steps to promote good corporate governance while protecting its investors and employees. Computer Associates is one of the world's largest management software companies. It was founded in 1976 and is a global business leader with operations in more than 100 countries. It is listed on the New York Stock Exchange with a market capitalization of $13.14 billion.

What is remarkable about what Computer Associates did lies not in the fraud committed by senior executives, although securities fraud and obstruction of justice charges are not to be taken lightly, but in the fact that the company's board took charge and put the interests of shareholders over those of corporate executives.

In 2002, the SEC and the U.S. Attorney for the Eastern District of New York started a probe into accounting practices at Computer Associates. The government felt that the company was not being totally cooperative in producing documentary evidence and asked the Board of Directors to start its own investigation, which it did. Computer Associates' Audit Committee Chair drove the internal investigation.

In October 2003, the company announced that it "found improper booking of sales."[vii] Investigators working for the Board turned over evidence including e-mails, documents, and results of internal interviews in which executives had lied. The Board fired or forced out numerous employees including top finance people and the General Counsel. Computer Associates knew that the level of cooperation, the replacement of "responsible management," and the "pervasiveness of the criminal conduct" were all factors that the government used in determining whether to charge the company criminally.[viii]

The SEC investigation found that employees conducted a fraudulent accounting practice known internally as the "35-day month" because company accountants would extend the booking of revenues in the final month of a fiscal quarter several days beyond the actual end of the month.[ix] In Fiscal Year 2000 alone, Computer Associates prematurely recognized more than $1.4 billion in revenue.[x] The internal investigation conducted by Computer Associates discovered that corporate executives "snipped date-stamps off faxed documents and added fake dates to contracts" to hide the fraud from outside auditors.[xi]

In January and April 2004, four former senior executives, including the CFO, pled guilty to securities fraud and obstruction of justice charges. The securities fraud charges involved "a long-running, company-wide scheme to backdate and forge licensing agreements in order to allow the company to meet or exceed its quarterly earnings projections during multiple fiscal quarters."[xii] The obstruction of justice charges related to "the defendants' lying to the government investigators and concealing evidence of the securities fraud."[xiii] The U.S. Attorney for the Eastern District of New York prosecuting the case stated that the guilty pleas of executives and their allocutions to their crimes "demonstrate the corrupt culture in Computer Associates' management."[xiv]

On September 22, 2004, former CEO Sanjay Kumar was indicted for his "alleged participation in a long-running, company-wide accounting fraud scheme and subsequent efforts to obstruct the government's investigation."[xv] On the same day, Computer Associates agreed to pay the government $225 million to settle the SEC lawsuit and avoid criminal prosecution. The company's agreement with the government included accepting responsibility for its criminal conduct and continued cooperation with the government. Computer Associates also agreed to the appointment of new management, the addition of independent members to the Board of Directors, and the appointment of an independent examiner to review compliance with the terms and conditions of the agreement with the government. In short, it would continue implementing remedial steps throughout the organization to ensure that fraud would not re-cur. In return, Computer Associates received a deferred pros-ecution for the criminal conduct of its former officers, exec-utives, and employees. It would face possible prosecution if it violates the terms of the agreement or commits any other crimes.[xvi]

Computer Associates posted details of the deferred prosecu-tion agreement and related information at the Investor Relations section of its Web site. The posting states that the resolution of the government investigation "marked the end of a troubling period" for the company and that it "has agreed to implement controls and governance measures to ensure that such past prac-tices are never repeated."[xvii]

[vi]In 2005, Computer Associates changed its corporate name to CA, Inc. In 2010, it again changed its name to its current CA Technologies. The original name, Computer Associates, is in keeping with the events and documentation discussed here.

[vii]Steve Hamm, "A Probe—and a Bitter Feud," *Business Week*, April 12, 2004, 78.

[viii]Charles Forelle and Joann S. Lublin, "Kumar Gives up Leadership Posts under Pressure," *Wall Street Journal*, April 22, 2004, A1.

[ix]Charles Forelle, "Ex-CFO at Computer Associates to Enter Plea in Accounting Probe," *Wall Street Journal*, April 8, 2004, A1.

[x]Charles Forelle, "CA Ex-Executives Plead Guilty, Call Fraud Pervasive," *Wall Street Journal*, April 9, 2004, A3.

[xi]Ibid.

[xii]Corporate Fraud Task Force, "Second Year Report to the President," July 20, 2004, www.usdoj.gov/dag/cftf/2nd_yr_fraud_report.pdf.

[xiii]Ibid.

[xiv]Charles Forelle, "CA Ex-Executives Plead Guilty, Call Fraud Pervasive," *Wall Street Journal*, April 9, 2004, A3.

[xv]Press Release issued by the United States Attorney's Office, Eastern District of New York, September 22, 2004.

[xvi]Ibid.

[xvii]*United States of America v. Computer Associates Int'l, Inc.*, Cr. No. 04–837 (ILG), Deferred Prosecution Agreement, September 22, 2004, http://news.findlaw.com/wp/docs/ca/usca904defpagr.pdf. Deferred Prosecu-tion Agreement between the Government and Computer Associates posted on the Computer Associates Investor Relations Web site, September 22, 2004, http://investor.ca.com/phoenix.zhtml?c=83100&p=irol-govdeferred. (No longer available; copy of agreement on file with authors.)

SNAPPING THE BONDS OF LOYALTY: JOINING TEAM AMERICA

An attorney with a white-collar defense practice in New York was fond of giving federal prosecutors and agents baseball hats with the words "Team America 5K1.1" emblazoned on the cap. "5K1.1" refers to the Federal Sentencing Guidelines Section 5K1.1 that pertains to a possible reduction in the criminal sentence for a defendant who has provided substantial assistance in the investigation or prosecution of another person who has committed an offense. This usually means becoming a federal informant and witness. This attorney represented many fraudsters who, because of the enormity of the evidence against them, decided to cooperate with the government in the hope of receiving a reduced sentence. The defense attorney would joke that since he and his client had joined the "team" and were now working on behalf of the "red, white and blue," it was only proper that everyone have some kind of uniform accoutrement. Although many thought this was humorous, in reality the practice of defendants "joining Team America" to help prosecute other fraudsters is quite common and is a very useful weapon in the government's war on corporate fraud and corruption.

The government uses the power of prosecution and long prison terms as a strong inducement to plead guilty and cooperate against other defendants. As the United States Court of Appeals for the Second Circuit stated so well in the case of *U.S. v. Rosner* in 1973, "in human experience, the pressure of imminent incarceration tends to snap the bonds of loyalty."[6] The possibility of long periods of incarceration has been known to convince even the most hardened individual to cooperate with the government in the hope of a reduced sentence. White-collar criminals are usually not in the same league as organized crime figures, who subscribe to the code of "omerta" or the vow of silence. For fraudsters, prison is something to be feared. Fraudsters are not used to prison life and all the harshness and violence associated with it. Factor in the increased penalties that translate to much longer jail time, and one can see how cooperation with the government begins to look appealing.

A former federal prosecutor, who is now in a white-collar defense practice and represents a number of the corporations under investigation, had some interesting things to say about the new compliance environment. A number of his clients are well-known public companies, and their corporate executives are under investigation for fraud involving revenue recognition and other issues. His view is that executives are now facing what amounts to life sentences if convicted for corporate fraud, and they are fearful. As a result of the new landscape, executives need to understand that willful blindness plus conscious avoidance equals knowledge under the law. Prosecutors are using this threat to obtain cooperation. Now it is how quickly one can get to the prosecutor's office to cooperate and tell all. "Take five," as this defense attorney calls invoking the Fifth Amendment right against self-incrimination, is no longer an option. Corporate boards are no longer protecting the chief executives and are the ones now turning them in to the government when wrongdoing is discovered. The attorney's advice to clients is to question every deal and every accounting procedure in which they are involved, to ensure that everything is above board, and to blow the whistle early and often when fraud is found.

THE CHALLENGES OF RUNNING A BUSINESS WHILE ATTEMPTING TO PROSECUTE A COMPLICATED CIVIL FRAUD CASE

For a business, there may be no more disruptive and challenging event than prosecuting a civil fraud claim against former officers and directors who have defrauded the company. The challenges are numerous and substantial. First, the company must conduct an internal investigation to determine what occurred and decide what, if any, communication must be made to governmental agencies, including law enforcement agencies, about the relevant events. Then the company leadership must decide what steps are to be taken to pursue compensation from those former insiders who committed fraud. Although the principal decision-maker will almost certainly want to pursue recovery of any funds that the wrongdoer may have stolen, executing that decision can be difficult and disruptive to ongoing business.

This section offers some practical guidance into what a lawyer retained to pursue civil insider fraud for a business will consider in prosecuting the case successfully. It also provides some insight into how long it will take to pursue a successful action as a plaintiff. The section's main themes can be summed up in four words: capture, cooperation, cost, and patience.

Capture

It is axiomatic that prosecution of any case requires evidence. White-collar cases may require the production of thousands of documents. Document control is both expensive and time consuming. Moreover, all this production must occur while management simultaneously rebuilds its reputation and remains profitable.

"Capture" refers to preserving the record that will prove the fraudulent actions by the former employee. The less complete the documentary trail, the more difficult prosecution becomes. If documentation is lost or destroyed, then the case against the wrongdoer is jeopardized through the legal doctrine of "spoliation." "Elements of a spoliation claim are (1) the existence of a potential civil action; (2) a legal or contractual duty to preserve evidence which is relevant to the potential civil action; (3) destruction of that evidence; (4) significant impairment in the ability to prove the lawsuit; (5) a causal relationship between the evidence destruction and the inability to prove the lawsuit; and (6) damages."[7] Moreover, the negligent destruction of relevant evidence can be sufficient to give rise to the spoliation inference, allowing a jury to conclude that the destroyed evidence would have been unfavorable to the offending party.[8]

Consequently, a business must capture the record as quickly and as thoroughly as possible. This process is complicated by the fact that critical databases change literally every second of every day at virtually every businesses. Therefore, it is important for a business to have in place a procedure for capturing data as soon as it discovers a fraudulent act. Taking that data "snapshot" will immensely assist the prosecution of litigation, and failing to take this "snapshot" jeopardizes the case.

Document capture is a highly involved process. It should involve employees from a company's technology, accounting, and legal departments. The process will need to be closely managed and may require that specific personnel be dedicated solely to this task. It also may require the retention of outside consultants and attorneys. For example, a forensic accountant can assist with the reconstruction of illicit insider transactions, whereas an investigator can interview employee witnesses who may have knowledge about events.

No matter how prevalent or outlandish the fraud, nothing can be proved without capturing the record. Capture is critical.

Cooperation

Personnel of a business that has become the victim of internal fraud may be uncomfortable and reluctant to cooperate with any external entity, including outside counsel or investigators retained to assist with an internal investigation. Therefore, cooperation with these entities must be a priority of top management, and top management must emphasize this to all employees. Cooperation should extend to governmental agencies, including law enforcement. The business will be far better served by quickly disclosing to law enforcement any fraudulent acts that may qualify as crimes. The top management of public corporations faces additional disclosure obligations as set forth by Sarbanes-Oxley.

Informing the company's general counsel about the problems that confront it will probably be the most effective strategy for successful prosecution against any wrongdoer. First, adept counsel will be able to focus on the most salient issues. Counsel also will be able to temper the impractical emotions of righteous indignation that executives may feel toward those suspected of defrauding the company. Finally, fully informed counsel should be able to be the leader of the team charged with performing any internal investigation, shaping that investigation toward the goal of prosecuting those who have breached their fiduciary duties.

Failure to make substantive disclosures both inside and outside the company jeopardizes any civil action that management may pursue against former employees, officers, and directors who have defrauded the company. Moreover, a failure to cooperate in an attempt to protect the company's "dirty laundry" is unlikely to be successful. In most cases, there are simply too many individuals who have knowledge of what has occurred for the salient facts to remain secret. Any party attempting to maintain the secret is probably spending entirely too much time on the ultimately fruitless task of protecting that secret.

Cost

Pursuing a fraud case is expensive. Understanding the economic factors associated with the prosecution of a civil fraud claim is critical to successful resolution of that claim. Unfortunately, a company's motivation in pursuing a wrongdoer for fraudulent acts often exceeds its litigation budget. Sometimes the company has lost so much money to the wrongdoer that scarce resources must be devoted to getting the business back on track rather than spending big to pursue a Pyrrhic victory. Spending $1 million to recoup $100,000 is not fiscally prudent. Additionally, the target of the investigation may have become "judgment proof," meaning that any monetary judgment against the wrongdoer may not be collectable if the wrongdoer has few assets.

The biggest expense for a company pursuing an action against a wrongdoer is the retention of experts needed to assist with investigation and prosecution efforts. From the start, the company will probably need to retain forensic accounting experts to reconstruct suspicious transactions. The company also will need to hire attorneys with experience in white-collar crime issues to prosecute any action and to interact with governmental authorities, including law enforcement personnel. Investigators may be needed to interview witnesses and to conduct background checks on suspects. Additionally, the company may need to retain technology consultants to comb through data housed on its computer networks. The lawyers will insist on placing any and all documentation that the company has captured in its "snapshot" on an independent database under their control for purposes of doing their own review and assisting with the production of documents when discovery in any litigation commences.

One constant is that costs to prosecute the case will exceed all initial expectations. It is incumbent on the executive charged with litigation management to understand the rationale for all services that its experts believe necessary to do their respective jobs. This does not mean that the professionals retained are attempting to exploit the company's predicament. It rather means that virtually every professional services firm can name a product, piece of software, or employee that can assist with the prosecution of the case; however, simply because the item may assist marginally with the task at hand does not mean that it is in the economic interest of the company to possess that tool.

One way to control costs is to appoint a company manager who does not have a vested interest in the outcome of the litigation. In other words, the individual who feels most "wronged" by the fraudulent acts should not also be the point person for litigation management. The likelihood of conflicts of interest for that individual are simply too great. The "wronged" party may be too willing to spend freely on the prosecution, feeling a need to recoup the company's losses. Such individuals may also be unwilling to divulge all they know to those they have retained, in an attempt to protect their reputations. The task of litigation management is thus best left to an independent manager who had little, if anything, to do with the original problem.

Patience

In addition to being expensive, the pursuit of a fraud case is time consuming. Reconstructing the transactions that resulted in the fraudulent acts is time consuming. Witness interviews are time consuming. Moreover, managers and employees will be compelled to spend time on nonproductive activities, such as document review. This consumption of time represents a significant opportunity cost to the company.

In addition, the entire judicial system is designed to be time consuming. In the federal courts, it is not uncommon for civil cases to continue for three to five years from the filing of the first complaint. Therefore, the time from initial discovery of the fraudulent acts to the successful conclusion of a trial can represent a multiyear project for a company, with the company lacking control over much of that timeline. Collection of any judgment will take additional time. Appeals are also a possibility. Any company contemplating the prosecution of a fraud claim must therefore guard against "claim exhaustion." It is difficult to have the same feelings of righteous indignation after two years of investigation and civil discovery that one had when initially discovering the fraudulent act. Personnel often leave the company, and memories lapse. Consequently, as with the cost factor, it is valuable to have someone in place who can objectively balance the benefits of pursuing claims against the time that will be needed to prosecute the case successfully.

Staying the Civil Proceeding

It is quite possible that in today's compliance-driven climate, a business will self-report significant fraud to the government as soon as it was reasonably certain of the crime. At this point, the government might ask the entity to stop any further investigation while the government put its own investigation into gear. It is also possible that the courts might intervene during a civil prosecution if a conflict with the government's criminal proceedings appeared to be a possibility.

There is a legal test regarding whether a court will stay a civil proceeding when there is a criminal proceeding. "The court has the inherent power to stay civil proceedings, postpone civil discovery, or impose protective orders when the interests of justice so dictate. In determining whether a stay should be granted in a civil trial based on the existence or potential existence of a criminal proceeding, the court considers six factors: (1) whether the two actions involved the same subject matter, (2) whether the two actions are brought by the government, (3) the posture of the criminal proceeding, (4) the public interests at stake, (5) the plaintiff's interests and possible prejudice to the plaintiff, and (6) the burden that any particular aspect of the proceedings may impose on the defendants."[9]

"The decision to grant or deny a stay is within the court's broad range of discretionary powers."[10] "The similarity of the issues underlying the civil and criminal actions is considered the most important threshold issue in determining whether or not to grant a stay. The strongest case for deferring civil proceedings until after completion of criminal proceedings is where a party under indictment for a serious offense is required to defend a civil action involving the same matter."[11]

Making a Business Decision

Although corporate fraud is often perceived as a victimless crime, it most emphatically is not. The corporation itself loses greatly. It loses fiscally. It may experience productivity losses and may have its public reputation besmirched. Ultimately, investors and shareholders lose. Once the fraud is discovered, management's immediate reaction may be to launch a lawsuit to get the "bad guys." Often this is the proper, although not always effective, approach, but sometimes it is not. If the fraud is significant, the government may launch its own criminal prosecution. In fact, the government may request the company to hold off on any civil prosecution until completion of the criminal case. Like every business decision, only after a rational analysis of the "capture, cooperation, cost, and patience" factors should the decision be made as to whether to pursue justice through the initiation of a civil suit.

MAKING THE BEST OF A BAD SITUATION: WHAT TO DO IF THE FEDS SHOW UP AT YOUR DOOR

Hopefully this day will never come, but a company must be prepared for the eventuality of federal agents showing up asking questions, with subpoenas, or, worse yet, with search and arrest warrants. In years past, businesses generally reacted with anything but full cooperation with the government. At the first sign of a federal agent attempting to interview a company employee, the company would hire the best attorney money could buy to represent that employee before any questioning. The rest of the company would typically "lawyer-up" and either refuse to answer questions or at least make it as hard as possible to obtain information. In the past, it was rare for a company to provide the government with the results of an internal investigation, disclose wrongdoing on the part of employees, or waive attorney-client privilege.

Federal agents and prosecutors have a powerful set of tools when they are conducting fraud investigations. They use grand juries, subpoenas, confidential informants, and undercover operations. They also use proffer agreements, euphemistically referred to as "Queen for a Day Letters," to learn what a cooperating defendant can offer in a criminal investigation, "flip" defendants into cooperators, and have them "wear a wire" to get evidence that moves up the corporate ladder. Federal authorities use a little fish to get the bigger fish, and even use a big fish such as former WorldCom CFO Scott Sullivan to flip, plead guilty, and testify against an even bigger fish, former WorldCom CEO Bernard Ebbers. The government knows how to use the domino effect in investigating and prosecuting corporate crime.

As federal agents, the authors have investigated fraudulent employee conduct and tried to obtain assistance from companies in corroborating the fraud. Employees under investigation would refuse to be interviewed, and the companies did nothing to make them comply. One attorney hired by the company would typically represent all other potential witnesses. That attorney would be present during all interviews and would report back to the company what transpired in every meeting. There was no doubt that the government would be getting little help from the company, and there was no incentive or requirement to do anything different.

In the post-Sarbanes-Oxley and enhanced Federal Sentencing Guidelines world, everything has changed. Cooperation with government investigations is now a requirement. CEOs, CFOs, and board members face civil and criminal risk for not being compliant and truthful. It is therefore necessary to have a plan in place whenever federal, state, or local authorities approach an organization and ask for information. Businesses have contingency plans for business interruption, natural disasters, strikes, and other possible risks. A contingency plan and response to a government investigation is just as appropriate.

In developing a response plan, an organization's legal department should take the lead role. Assistance from experienced outside counsel should be considered in designing the plan. Former federal prosecutors and agents with extensive experience conducting corporate investigations can work with a company to design and then implement a robust response. They can also brief appropriate company personnel from their experience on what to expect during a government investigation. The following factors should be considered in particular:

- A written company policy requiring cooperation with any government investigation and possible ramifications for not cooperating fully with the government
- Awareness of this policy by corporate executives, the board of directors, and all employees
- Assignment of specific legal department personnel to have ownership of the program and be an initial point of contact for law enforcement conducting an investigation related to the company
- The role of corporate security during any law enforcement action

- The response when government investigators ask to interview a specific employee or employees, including determination of whether outside counsel will be retained to represent them
- The response when government agents serve subpoenas on the company and referral to appropriate legal counsel
- The response when government agents conduct search warrants, including a policy of noninterference with the search
- A decision about whether designated company personnel should monitor any search being conducted, including videotaping the actual search by law enforcement
- The response when agents take privileged material and proprietary information
- Follow-up with the government to obtain copies of important documents taken as a result of a search warrant
- The response when agents announce they have an arrest warrant for an employee, including whether the employee should be arrested at this work location or should be asked to report to a private area and then be arrested

What a company does at the beginning of a government inquiry can set the tone for all further interactions and outcomes. Cooperation is key throughout the process. There must be an appropriate response and compliance with subpoenas, search warrants, and requests for employee interviews. At the first knowledge of an allegation of fraud or wrongdoing, an organization should conduct an unbiased and impartial internal investigation to determine the facts. The results of such an investigation may very well be provided to the government at some point. In fact, releasing the internal investigation reports, findings, and evidence goes a long way in demonstrating cooperation with a government investigation. Attorney–client privilege must be considered before this is done, and guidance from legal counsel is required.

NOTES

1. Ann Carrns, Carrick Mollenkamp, Deborah Solomon, and John R. Wilke, "HealthSouth Case Unveils a Shock Strategy," *Wall Street Journal*, April 4, 2003, C1.

2. Ibid.
3. Ibid.
4. Edward Iwata, "Prosecutors Give CEOs the Mobster Treatment," *USA Today*, October 4, 2002, 1B.
5. Ibid.
6. *U.S. v. Rosner*, 485 F.2d. 1213 (2d Cir. 1973).
7. *Florida Evergreen Foliage v. E.I. DuPont De Nemours and Co.*, 336 F. Supp.2d 1239 (S.D. Fla. 2004).
8. *Mosaid Tech. Inc. v. Samsung Electronics Co., Ltd.*, 348 F. Supp.2d 332 (D. N.J. 2004).
9. *Doe v. City of Chicago*, 360 F.Supp.2d 880 (N.D. Ill. 2005).
10. *Maloney v. Gordon*, 328 F.Supp.2d 508 (D. Del. 2004).
11. Ibid.

A Fraud Prevention Culture
That Works

EXECUTIVE SUMMARY

Building a fraud prevention culture that works is no longer an option in today's business world. It is a requirement for survival. The Sarbanes-Oxley Act, Federal Sentencing Guidelines for Organizations, Dodd-Frank Whistleblower Provisions, and other corporate governance enhancements require accountability and oversight. Fraud prevention was a requirement before Sarbanes-Oxley, and embedding that concept within the framework of an organization makes even better business sense now. This means that every organization, public or private, must have a zero tolerance for fraud of any kind. Fraud risk management based on a "checklist" mentality is not conducive to success in fighting fraud. Outstanding companies view compliance enhancements as opportunities to create a stronger fraud prevention program and an internal control system that ultimately give them a competitive advantage.

CRITICAL ROLE OF COMPLIANCE

At the height of the financial crisis, the SEC was so concerned that organizations would consider cutbacks in compliance spending and staff that it took a very unusual step to reinforce the critical importance of compliance programs. It sent a letter to all CEOs of SEC-registered firms warning that the last thing companies should do in response to the Great Recession was reducing its commitment to compliance. The letter discussed how "compliance is a vital control function that helps to protect the firm from conduct that would negatively impact the firm's business and its reputation."[1] The SEC added that "providing adequate resources to compliance programs and ensuring CCOs and compliance personnel are integrated into the activities of the firm are essential to that process."[2]

It should come as no surprise to business executives or managers that a heightened awareness of fraud and fraud prevention is critical to an organization's success. Implementing enhanced corporate governance requirements is just the beginning of a culture of compliance. A true commitment, beginning with the appropriate and ongoing tone at the top that incorporates all the elements of effective compliance and ethics programs can greatly lessen and even prevent fraud.

FRAUD NEVER TAKES A HOLIDAY

If there is one thing we know, fraud is constant. The economic and reputational toll on organizations and individuals is no different today than in the past. Fraud and corruption continues to occur. It would be naïve to think that we can totally prevent the corporate scandals of the recent past or the many recent instances of economic crime. Case after case demonstrates that fraud and other misconduct are ever-present and companies need to be vigilant in detection and prevention. The following cases studies highlight the continuing risk and that wrongdoers can be found both in the corporate suites and throughout the ranks.

Kickback Scheme: Not a Small Fry

In late 2008, a top executive at Fry's Electronics was charged in a $65 million embezzlement and kickback scheme. The scheme started in 2005 and was discovered in 2008. Asuf Umar Siddiqui, a vice-president of merchandising and operations at the privately held electronics retailer, convinced the company to allow him to work directly with suppliers supposedly as a cost-savings approach. This cut out the normally used independent sales representatives and allowed Siddiqui to negotiate directly with vendors. Siddiqui "allegedly charged vendors commissions of as much as 31 percent in exchange for agreeing to buy merchandise at inflated prices."[3] The exorbitant commissions came back to him in the form of kickbacks.

Siddiqui used the embezzled funds to enjoy a lavish lifestyle. He bought expensive cars and clothes. He was a frequent visitor to Las Vegas casinos where he was a high roller. He gambled and lost millions, even once losing $8 million over the course of several hours.[4] The discovery of this large fraud came as a result of a tip from a Fry's employee. The employee went into the executive's office and "found spreadsheets detailing millions of dollars in secret payments that Siddiqui allegedly received from companies that sold products to Fry's."[5] Of interest, the employee reported the fraud to the IRS and not the company.

Fry's Electronics fired Siddiqui when it learned of the kickback scheme. In 2009, he was indicted by federal authorities in California on multiple counts of wire fraud and money laundering. The indictment only charged $5.7 million of embezzled funds involving only two of the involved vendors. The vendors that participated in the kickback scheme were primarily based in the Asia–Pacific region. They have not been prosecuted. In 2011, Siddiqui pled guilty.

Insider Trading: It's What You Know

On April 19, 2007, Joseph Nacchio, the former CEO of Qwest Communications International, Inc., was found guilty on 19 counts of insider trading on charges stemming from his sale of more than $100 million in Qwest stock while in possession of material, nonpublic information regarding the company's financial health. Nacchio was sentenced to six years in prison and received the maximum $19 million fine on July 29, 2007. An appeal of the sentence resulted in a two-month reduction and a reduction of the $52 million forfeiture to $44.6 million. A former CFO pled guilty to insider trading.[6]

Foreign Corrupt Practices Act: The Government Calling

In an SEC filing, Avon Products, Inc. disclosed an internal investigation of possible bribery of foreign government officials that began in 2008. The investigation first focused on suspected corrupt payments in China but subsequently included similar payments to officials in Brazil, Mexico, Argentina, India, and Japan.[7] The company inquiry resulted from an employee letter to Avon's CEO "alleging improper spending related to travel with Chinese government officials."[8] As a result of the internal investigation, Avon fired its former head of global internal audit and security and three top China executives and more terminations are a possibility. The company reported that it spent $35 million in 2009 on the investigation and $96 million in 2010. The DOJ and SEC subsequently began their own investigation and the company is cooperating as the inquiry expands.

Making a Federal Case Even Worse

In September 2005, the SEC filed civil fraud charges against a Massachusetts biotechnology company, Biopure, and three of its executives in a case that was compounded by further wrongdoing. The SEC alleged that the company made "misleading public statements about the company's efforts to obtain FDA approval for its primary product, a synthetic blood product, while at the same time Biopure was raising millions of dollars from investors."[9] Subsequently, the company, along with the CEO and General Counsel, settled the fraud charges with the government. Howard Richman, Biopure's Senior Vice President of Regulatory Affairs and Operations, decided to contest the SEC charges.

Richman obstructed the SEC case and justice by falsely claiming he had terminal colon cancer and was unable to participate in the legal proceedings. He impersonated a doctor, submitted a phony doctor's note, and said he was undergoing chemotherapy. As a result, the hearing judge dismissed the case. Subsequently, Richman's lawyers informed the SEC and the judge of their client's misconduct. Richman was then charged with obstruction of justice. He pled guilty in March 2009 and in November 2009 was sentenced to three years in prison. Richman also reached a settlement with the SEC in the original civil fraud case, paid a $150,000 fine, and was barred from serving as an officer or director of a public company.[10]

HAVE A ZERO TOLERANCE FOR FRAUD AND MEAN IT

When Jack Welch, the legendary former CEO of General Electric, appeared on *The Tonight Show* on April 25, 2005, host Jay Leno asked him why the general public had such a poor opinion of CEOs. In his inimitable fashion, Welch said, "Because so many of them were skunks." Indeed, a number of corporate executive "skunks" succumbed to greed and fraud and put their personal interests above those of investors and employees. The many perp walks and convictions show that executives are now being held accountable. All corporations and employees must be responsible to both the spirit and the letter of the law as well as policies and procedures, at all levels of the organization. No executive today will ever say that fraud is a good thing. However, if there are different standards of disciplinary action for executives and employees, the message is that fraud is condoned for some and not for others.

Corporate codes of conduct should address the problem of fraud by clearly stating that there is a zero tolerance for fraud of any kind. Whether it is a $50 inflated expense report or a $50 million revenue recognition issue, an organization must take appropriate action against all fraud. A good rule to follow is that the amount of the fraud is immaterial and any fraudulent activity that is disclosed and proved through professional investigation should result in termination of the employee. In addition, organizations should consider referring fraud by employees, vendors, and others to the appropriate law enforcement agency for criminal prosecution. The general counsel should be the focal point for the final decision as to criminal referrals. Companies should also consider publicizing prosecutions of employee fraudsters to reinforce a culture of compliance and a zero tolerance for fraud.

John McDermott is a subject matter expert in the investigation of corporate fraud. He was a United States Postal Inspector for more than 23 years and managed a fraud investigations team in New York. He is currently a corporate compliance investigator at CA Technologies. Over the years, he has conducted and supervised high-profile fraud cases including Symbol Technologies, Spectrum

Technologies, and Hanover Sterling, a huge stock fraud case that resulted in more than 60 convictions of brokers, stock promoters, and company executives. McDermott is a strong believer in criminal prosecution and punishment as a driving force for fraud prevention and compliance. He has said, "If the threat of doing twenty years or life in jail doesn't scare anybody straight, I don't know what would. I certainly wouldn't take any risk by signing 10Ks or 10Qs that were fraudulent, when I knew the risk was going to jail."[11]

McDermott also hopes "that the corporate executives reading this book would have learned these lessons from those who were foolish enough to commit crimes" and do a "better job of self-policing."[12] His experience in investigating corporate fraud has led him to believe that corporations must improve "teaching ethics and morals to their corporate executives" and do "a better job of listening to their internal and external auditors" when compliance issues are raised.[13]

Organizations can also send a great signal to employees, shareholders, and the government that they take fraud detection and prevention very seriously by hiring former federal agents and prosecutors with experience investigating and prosecuting fraud and white-collar crime for their internal investigation and legal departments. Smart companies know that by bringing in fraud detection talent, they are improving their compliance programs and lessening their fraud risk.

Probably the biggest sea change for corporations has been how they deal with the government in cases of fraud and corruption. Gone are the days of "us versus them" when businesses would hire the best defense attorneys money could buy and fight the government at every turn. Today, fighting the government can mean more than just losing the case if the allegations of fraud are true. Business organizations with FCPA violations can face debarment if convicted. The great majority of FCPA cases result from corporate self-disclosures to the DOJ and SEC. Self-disclosure and cooperation with government investigations must be a considered strategy.

GATEKEEPER ROLE OF THE AUDIT COMMITTEE

Under certain circumstances, members of an organization's audit committee may be liable for failing in their oversight duties as gatekeepers of corporate governance. In February 2011, the SEC filed civil charges against three outside directors of DHB Industries who served on its audit committee. The charges stemmed from a major scandal at DHB, a military contractor that sold body armor to the government, where the CEO David Brooks and other senior officers perpetrated a $185 million accounting fraud and looting of company assets for lavish personal expenses, including Ferraris and dozens of purebred horses.[14]

The SEC complaint against the directors alleges that they "wholly failed to carry out their responsibilities as 'independent' directors and Audit and Compensations Committee members" and willfully ignored the many red flags of accounting fraud and the myriad other violations occurring under their watch.[15] These three directors were longtime friends of Brooks and maintained various business relationships with him as well. In fact, their lack of independence and their loyalty to Brooks were why they were selected in the first place. There was no reason to believe that they could not have known about irregularities and payments for which there was no legitimate purpose, such as for prostitutes. These payments were discussed at board meetings but were omitted from the official minutes.[16] Furthermore, the directors allegedly made no effort to even understand their roles or their importance. They overlooked manipulated financial reports as well as woefully inadequate internal controls in the face of repeated red flags. They also neglected concerns raised by the company's controller and the combined resignations of and material weakness letters issued by successive auditors.[17]

Does this mean that the SEC will more aggressively pursue audit committees, which in some cases have been criticized as just "check-the-box groups who mechanically follow procedures aimed at assuring compliance with the law" but do nothing to institute true compliance measures?[18] Of course, one case does not a trend make, and none of the directors have at the time of this writing admitted any wrongdoing. The accusations here go beyond mere negligence; therefore, directors should have no fear of prosecution for an inadvertent oversight or a reasonable business decision. Nevertheless, the DHB case should encourage audit committees to take a closer look at their companies. As corporate gatekeepers, they can and must play an important role in asking the tough questions and enhancing compliance.

THE *WALL STREET JOURNAL* RULE

What should keep an executive up at night? One big worry is the possibility of fraud occurring at the company, whether potentially fatal fraudulent financial accounting or even asset misappropriation. Once detected, how a fraud occurrence is communicated to investors, employees, government authorities, and the press can make a big difference in the final resolution. Today, it is harder than ever to contain the existence of a fraud quietly. With the abundance of whistleblowers and self-reporting requirements for companies and corporate executives, it is extremely difficult to hide fraud. It is also foolhardy even to consider any form of concealment. Bad news always seems to be made public. How would one react if an act by a company were published on page one of the *Wall Street Journal*? A good rule to follow is to always think of this worst-case scenario and do everything possible to prevent it from happening.

A FRAUD PREVENTION VISIONARY: INTERVIEW WITH DR. JOSEPH T. WELLS ON THE FUTURE OF FRAUD AND FRAUD PREVENTION

Dr. Joseph T. Wells is the founder and Chairman of the Board of the Association of Certified Fraud Examiners (ACFE), the world's largest antifraud organization, with nearly 60,000 members in more than 140 nations. A CPA, Certified Fraud Examiner, and former FBI agent, Dr. Wells founded the ACFE in 1988. In addition to his administrative duties as Chairman, Dr. Wells researches, writes, and lectures to business and professional groups on white-collar crime issues. He is also an Adjunct Professor of Fraud Examination at the University of Texas in Austin. Dr. Wells has received numerous honors for his teaching and writing. In 2002, the American Accounting Association named him the Accounting Education Innovator of the Year. On several occasions, he has received the top writing awards from both the *Journal of Accountancy* and *Internal Auditor Magazine*, and for nine years, Dr. Wells was named to *Accounting Today* magazine's annual list of America's "Top 100 Most Influential People" in accounting.

Dr. Wells is truly a fraud prevention visionary. He was promoting the professionalism of fraud examination and education as fraud deterrence long before it was fashionable. In the following wide-ranging interview, Dr. Wells provides insightful comments on the future of corporate crime, fraud prevention, and compliance.

Q: **Do you think Congress will blink and reverse some of the regulations resulting from Sarbanes-Oxley?**

A: As we know, the Sarbanes-Oxley Act was passed in a flurry of activity resulting from some of the large accounting frauds. The pressure for Congress to act at that time was tremendous. Generally, these "hurry-up" laws are seriously flawed and overreaching. As just one example, the penalties for mail fraud have been quadrupled from 5 to 20 years. I term this "feel-good legislation." Although the penalties have been quadrupled, the resources devoted to the criminal justice system that would implement these laws have not. As a result, fewer people—not more—will likely find themselves in our crowded prisons. Besides, volumes of research by criminologists have failed to document a connection between lengthy prison terms and deterrence.

Some aspects of Sarbanes-Oxley are good and overdue. The accounting profession—of which I have been a member for nearly four decades—has historically shown that it is unable or unwilling to regulate itself. Switching the regulatory authority to the Public Company Accounting Oversight Board (PCAOB) will probably turn out to be a good thing. Additional protection for whistleblowers may prove useful. Financial statement certifications by executives won't deter those who are hell-bent on cooking the books, but overall, this procedure can't really hurt, either. Board members of public companies who are completely independent are a step in the right direction, too.

It seems that passing a law in the first place is much easier than getting bad legislation repealed. So I am not expecting Congress to blink any time soon. But my guess is that whether or not Sarbanes-Oxley is a good law won't be known for many years. It will take that long to see if it really reduces the incidence of financial statement frauds.

Q: In the 1980s, we had the savings and loan frauds, in the early 1990s, we had insider trading, and in the last decade [2000–2010] we had the massive financial statement frauds. What's next?

A: First, we have not seen the end of massive financial statement frauds, regardless of Sarbanes-Oxley. The law does nothing to remove the root cause of the problem, which is caused by companies under great pressure to perform in the short term. Fifty years ago, investors bought stock to see it grow over the long haul. That simply isn't the case anymore. Now, in part because of the speed of the Internet, investors and day traders will turn stock over in a matter of hours. They aren't concerned about what a company makes or its long-term innovation; it's more like playing corporate poker using company management as the chips. Unless and until we can change the investing mentality, we will continue to see executives pressured to cross the line.

Second, because of the aging baby boomers (like me) I am seriously concerned with our pension funds. We've already seen cracks in the dike; many companies are filing bankruptcy in order to avoid their pension fund obligations. Other companies have simply spent the money reserved for their retirees on other things. So, I am concerned that the net effect of stock market manipulations and pension plan frauds could have a devastating economic impact.

Third, because of the increased globalization of business, I think that transnational investment swindles are likely to increase. This is exacerbated by the fact that there are no uniform accounting standards worldwide. China, for example, is likely to be a major economic force in the 21st century. But currently its economy, because of pyramiding growth, has a "wild west" aura. As financial opportunities there (and in other emerging economies) increase, can investors trust the numbers? Ponzi schemes still abound. Although Madoff in the U.S. was the poster child for lax government oversight that permitted him to illegally operate for so long, many nations have almost nonexistent governmental enforcement.

Q: What do you think is the best way to convince corporate executives to allocate more resources to fighting fraud?

A: I think the best way is to appeal to their sense of profit. Currently, the approach is to teach ethics, as if ethics really needs to be taught. Don't misunderstand; we all need to be reminded of what ethical conduct is all about. But, normally socialized individuals know right from wrong. And if they don't, all of the ethical training in the world is not going to fix that. What seems to get lost in the shuffle is that fraud prevention is one of the best investments that a business can make. I've seen studies that suggest the return on fraud prevention programs can be 50:1. So, I think that executives should be told, "Fraud prevention doesn't cost much money at all, and it pays huge dividends." I think that they should also be reminded that so-called "immaterial" frauds could have very material consequences. One example is the former investment firm of E.F. Hutton, which imploded in the 1980s. You may recall that the corporate "money management" strategy was actually to kite checks. Now, the kiting itself was immaterial to the financial statements as a whole. But the reputational damage drove E.F. Hutton out of business. There are many more examples like that. So the simple message to management is that tolerating fraud, in any form and at any level, is bad business; nothing good can come from it.

Q: **What more must corporate executives do that they are not doing now to prevent fraud and abuse?**

A: Once you get down from the executive level, two things become critically important. The first is the well-used phrase, "tone at the top." Should executives not walk the talk, then the people below them won't. If mid-level managers are dishonest, so too will be the employees. It is necessary, indeed vital, to lead by example. Second, there is a perception that occupational fraud can be prevented with adequate internal control. Controls are a necessary part of any fraud prevention effort, but control is not the root cause of fraud; it is dissatisfaction with the company or with workplace conditions. A number of landmark research projects, including one by Hollinger and Clark, clearly document that workers who are well treated, respected, and adequately compensated are much less likely to take out their hostility on the company. Executives need to understand that.

Q: How do we move compliance from an initiative to a cultural mind-set?

A: Regrettably, our society seems to have adopted a "get rich quick" mentality. In part, we can thank the mass media for that. By featuring the lifestyles of the rich and famous, people—quite naturally—are convinced that they deserve the same things and they become dissatisfied with what they already have. Sociologist Robert Merton developed an anomie theory to explain the disconnect between what we have and what we want. And in his view, this dissatisfaction is at the root of much crime.

   Many compliance laws are enacted to protect us from ourselves. But that is not really a fix; it is the equivalent of trying to put out the forest fire with a garden hose. What is needed is a realignment of society's priorities, where honesty and integrity are more important than fame and fortune. However, that becomes extremely difficult when we see our leaders and role models lie, cheat, and steal. Psychologists tell us that our values are formed very early in life. And if they are not instilled in us by our parents at an early age, we'll never adopt them. So, the only true—and permanent—solution is to teach the right things to our children and they to theirs.

Q: How is fraud prevention being instituted outside the United States?

A: According to the saying, "When America sneezes, the world catches cold." Our European and Canadian neighbors often look to us for guidance and have similar programs to prevent fraud. We're now seeing movement on other continents, too. Although there are no concrete studies, my suspicion is that Europe specifically has less fraud overall because the gap between the "haves" and "have nots" is generally smaller. European society tends to take better care of its underprivileged than we do in the United States. In Eastern Europe, where they are still recovering from the Soviet era, fraud and corruption are rampant. I suspect it will take them at least another decade or two to get where we are. In Japan and much of Asia (excluding China), cultural prohibitions against dishonesty probably equate to less fraud than in America. In Latin America, especially in Mexico and Colombia, the dependence on the drug trade to help fuel the economic system has created a huge underground economy. The efforts of the United States to control illicit narcotics through interdiction, as well-meaning as it might be, has actually worsened the drug problem by driving up prices.

Worldwide, I don't see fraud coming down until around the mid-21st century. Fraud is the crime of the older and better educated perpetrator. Street crimes are for the young and dumb. Society is aging, and it's more educated; that is one of the reasons we see less violent crime today than at any time in the last 30 years. Technology may offer some solutions, but it is not a panacea. Without being an alarmist, I think fraud is going to get worse before we see it get better.

Q: **What is your vision of the future for the fraud prevention field?**

A: The study of fraud prevention is in its infancy. For example, we can take two companies or individuals with indistinguishable characteristics. One will experience fraud while the other will not. We really don't know why. The only hope is that additional research may provide some of the answers. But, we do know what doesn't work: punishment after the fact. As we say here in Texas, that is like closing the barn door after the horses are gone. That's not to imply that people who commit crimes shouldn't be punished; it's something that must be done in a civilized society. However, we didn't experience a rise in fraud overnight, and this seemingly intractable problem won't be solved quickly.

FROM A COMPLIANCE INITIATIVE TO A CULTURAL MIND-SET

As stated by the SEC regarding internal controls, "A one-size-fits all, bottom-up, check-the-box approach that treats all internal controls equally is less likely to improve internal controls and financial reporting than reasoned, good-faith exercise of professional judgment focused on reasonable, as opposed to absolute, assurance."[19] Fraud risk management based on a "checklist" approach is not conducive to success in fraud prevention because fraudsters are very adaptive and imaginative in their schemes. What is better is a principles-based system because "it is impossible to develop comprehensive rules for every situation."[20] World-class companies understand that fraud prevention and enhanced internal controls is not just a project or a one-time idea and requires embedding sound principles of fraud prevention into the "cultural mind-set" of all employees.

In announcing its intent to amend existing organizational sentencing guidelines on April 13, 2004, the United State Sentencing Commission strongly stated the importance of effective compliance and ethics programs for an organization. The Commission's "focus on ethical corporate behavior is a unique development in the [then] 13-year history of the organizational sentencing guidelines," but it is altogether not surprising given the magnitude of recent corporate crime.[21] The message it sent to all corporate executives is as follows:

> *A fundamental component of the organizational sentencing guidelines, promulgated by the Commission in 1991, is the effective compliance and ethics program. The Commission made the standards for the compliance and ethics program more rigorous and put greater responsibility on boards of directors and executives for the oversight and management of compliance programs. In particular, directors and executives now must take an active leadership role for the content and operation of compliance and ethics programs. Companies that seek reduced criminal fines now must demonstrate that they have identified areas of risk where criminal violations may occur, trained high-level officials as well as employees in relevant legal standards and obligations, and given their compliance officers sufficient authority and resources to carry out their responsibilities. Under the revised guidelines, if companies hope to mitigate criminal fines and penalties, they must also promote an organizational culture that encourages a commitment to compliance with the law and ethical conduct by exercising due diligence in meeting the criteria.[22]*

To ensure a cultural mind-set of fraud prevention, the following key elements must be in place in an organization and must stay in place.

Tone at the Top

Chief executives, officers, and directors set an important tone with every word and action they take. They must lead by example. Their accountability, integrity, responsibility, and how they push the message down to the lowest level employee may be the most important aspect of building a fraud prevention culture that actually works. No employee can be expected to follow company policy or obey laws if their leaders are not doing the same.

The "Policing" Role of the Board of Directors and the Audit Committee

Along with the entire Board of Directors, Audit Committee members are truly the "police officers" of an organization; they ensure compliance with company rules and policy, as well as laws and regulations. Sarbanes-Oxley requires that boards take an active role in corporate governance, acting as "checks and balances" to executive leadership. Yet that does not always occur. Strong and independent Audit Committees ensure compliance, whereas weak and ineffectual ones foster the criminal behavior seen at disgraced companies. Directors who abdicate their important roles face the prospect of being held accountable, both civilly and criminally.

The Challenge to Internal Audit

Internal audit departments must accept the challenge to take a leadership role in fraud prevention. The importance of internal audit departments has been reinforced with the enactment of Sarbanes-Oxley and the overall climate of enhanced fraud prevention and detection. In a perfect world, internal audit should uncover issues before they become headlines in the *Wall Street Journal*. The fraud detection, investigation, and prevention component should be a part of internal audit to ensure linkage and continuous interaction with the auditing function. Adding needed professionals to the internal audit team, training and empowering them, giving them reporting to executive leadership and the audit committee, and providing high visibility in the company are steps that should be considered.

The Important Role of Managers in Fraud Prevention

Managers must provide oversight to their employees and be held accountable for preventing and reporting fraud. Managers are role models in developing their direct reports and ensuring compliance with both company policies and governmental regulations and laws. Managers must know how fraud can infect an organization and how to detect the warning signs. Understanding how to report potential violations of standards of business conduct is paramount for any manager. Strong and committed managers are an important element in an effective compliance program.

Integrity and Honesty for All

Integrity and honesty are core values for all employees, and there can be no exceptions. A successful fraud prevention program must constantly reinforce these values among all employees at all levels wherever the organization operates. Disciplinary actions must be applied equally throughout and no matter the employee level. Having a zero tolerance for fraud goes hand in hand with integrity and honesty at an organization.

Training and Communication

Training and communication are key elements in reducing fraud and reinforcing compliance. Organizations must provide ongoing, company-wide training in fraud prevention as well as overall compliance and ethics. Evangelize the code of conduct, policies, procedures, and a culture of compliance. Use interactive, scenario-based training covering asset misappropriation, corruption, financial accounting issues as well as procurement, expense reporting and other fraud risks. Provide training at all levels of the organization including new and existing employees, executives, managers, board members, and vendors and other third parties.

A Well-Communicated and Responsive Reporting System

Every organization, public or private, large or small, must have an effective reporting mechanism such as a hotline to allow employees and others outside the company to report financial fraud or other violations of standards of business conduct. People must feel empowered and safe so they can anonymously and confidentially report issues and know whistleblowers will be protected from retaliation. Whatever the form of the reporting mechanism, it must be well-communicated and easily accessible to ensure full reporting of all issues.

Cross-Group Collaboration

Consistency, strong interaction, and linkage of all components within an organization are essential and translate to effective cross-group collaboration among chief executives, officers, directors, and the various legal, compliance, internal audit, finance, human resources, investigative, and corporate security functions.

Embracing a Culture of Compliance

Truly outstanding companies view Sarbanes-Oxley and other compliance enhancements as an opportunity for improved corporate governance. They understand and embrace the importance of creating a stronger fraud prevention program and internal control system that ultimately provides a competitive advantage. The Appendix to this book contains a checklist from the Association of Certified Fraud Examiners to help organizations test the effectiveness of their fraud prevention measures.

THE ROAD AHEAD

The purpose of our book is to provide a roadmap for reaching the highest levels of compliance in fraud prevention and internal control. The trip is not always easy and there can be many roadblocks and detours—but stay the course. The route can be successfully navigated with the many tools, programs, and insights provided by the authors. Building a fraud prevention culture that works is no longer an option in today's business world. It is a requirement for survival. Sarbanes-Oxley, the Federal Sentencing Guidelines for Organizations, Dodd-Frank Whistleblower Provisions, and other corporate governance enhancements require accountability and oversight on an ongoing basis. However, there is another simple and straightforward reason for compliance and that is because it is the right thing to do.

An executive director of the Corporate Executive Board has said that "Virtually every organization today has one (or several) pockets where a scandal is festering—the leadership team just doesn't know it," No truer words were ever spoken. It is just a matter of time before the ticking time bomb of fraud goes off in an organization. Fraud can happen anywhere, and its damaging effects go far beyond the financial loss. The impact to reputation can be long lasting and often fatal. Understanding fraud is really quite simple. It is lying, cheating, and stealing. It is motive, opportunity, and rationalization. What is far more important than the definition is how to prevent it. "The potential of being caught most often persuades likely perpetrators not to commit the fraud. Because of this principle, the existence of a thorough control system is essential to fraud prevention."[23] Fraud prevention is about being proactive rather than just reactive. Accountability and integrity along with strong compliance and ethics programs stop fraud.

NOTES

1. Lori A. Richards, "Open Letter to CEOs of SEC-Registered Firms," Securities and Exchange Commission, December 2, 2008, www.sec.gov/about/offices/ ocie/ceoletter.htm.
2. Ibid.
3. Miguel Bustillo, "Fry's Official Faces Fraud Charges," *Wall Street Journal*, December 24, 2008, B3.
4. Richard C. Paddock, "High rollers' paradise lost to debt, fraud case," *Seattle Times*, February 15, 2009, A1.
5. Ibid.
6. Corporate Fraud Task Force, "2008 Report to the President," April 2, 2008, www.justice.gov/archive/dag/cftf/corporate-fraud2008.pdf.

7. Ellen Brown, "Avon Bribe Investigation Widens," *Wall Street Journal*, May 5, 2011, B1.

8. Ibid.

9. *Securities and Exchange Commission v. Biopure Corporation, Thomas Moore, Howard Richman and Jane Kober*, Litigation Release No 19376, September 14, 2005, United States Securities and Exchange Commission, www.sec.gov/litigation/litreleases/lr19376.htm.

10. Trista Morrison, "BioPure Exec Sentenced to Three Years for Faking Cancer to Avoid SEC Probe," *CBS Interactive Business Network*, November 16, 2009, www.bnet.com/blog/pharma/biopure-exec-sentenced-to-three-years-for-faking-cancer-to-avoid-sec-probe/5338.

11. Statement to the authors on April 22, 2005.

12. Ibid.

13. Ibid.

14. Securities and Exchange Commission, "SEC Charges Military Body Armor Supplier and Former Outside Directors with Accounting Fraud," press release, February 28, 2011, www.sec.gov/news/press/2011/2011-52.htm; and Thom Weidlich, "DHB Ex-Chief Guilty of Fraud at Military Contractor," *Bloomberg News*, September 14, 2010, www.bloomberg.com/news/2010-09-14/dhb-industries-ex-chief-brooks-guilty-of-fraud-at-u-s-military-contractor.html.

15. *SEC v. Jerome Krantz, Cary Chasin, and Gary Nadelman*, Complaint for Injunctive and Other Relief, CV-60432, February 28, 2011, (S.D.Fla. 2011), 1–2.

16. Ibid., 9.

17. Ibid., 11–13. In the later material weakness letter, the replacement auditor concluded that the Audit Committee itself was a material weakness. Ibid., 17. The law firm also resigned after conducting an investigation, and the consultants were fired for uncovering other misdeeds. Ibid., 24; 30.

18. Floyd Norris, "For Boards, S.E.C. Keeps the Bar Low," *New York Times*, March 4, 2011, B1.

19. Securities and Exchange Commission, "Commission Statement on Implementation of Internal Control Reporting Requirements," May 16, 2005, 2005-74, www.sec.gov/news/press/2005-74.htm.

20. Peter Morton, "Risky Business," *CAMagazine.com*, May 2005, www.camaga zine.com/index.cfm/ci_id/26177/la_id/1.htm.

21. United States Sentencing Commission, "Sentencing Commission Toughens Requirements for Corporate Compliance Programs," press release, April 13, 2004, www.ussc.gov/PRESS/rel0404.htm.

22. Ibid.

23. Association of Certified Fraud Examiners, Fraud Examiners Manual (Austin, TX: ACFE, 2006), 4.601.

ACFE Fraud Prevention Checklist*

The most cost-effective way to limit fraud losses is to prevent fraud from occurring. This checklist is designed to help organizations test the effectiveness of their fraud prevention measures.

1. Is ongoing anti-fraud training provided to all employees of the organization?
   * Do employees understand what constitutes fraud?
   * Have the costs of fraud to the company and everyone in it—including lost profits, adverse publicity, job loss and decreased morale and productivity—been made clear to employees?
   * Do employees know where to seek advice when faced with uncertain ethical decisions, and do they believe they can speak freely?
   * Has a policy of zero tolerance for fraud been communicated to employees through words and actions?
2. Is an effective fraud reporting mechanism in place?
   * Have employees been taught how to communicate concerns about known or potential wrongdoing?
   * Is there an anonymous reporting channel available to employees, such as a third-party hotline?

*Source: 2010 Report to the Nations on Occupational Fraud and Abuse. Reprinted with permission from the Association of Certified Fraud Examiners, Austin, Texas © 2010.

- Do employees trust that they can report suspicious activity anonymously and/or confidentially and without fear of reprisal?
- Has it been made clear to employees that reports of suspicious activity will be promptly and thoroughly evaluated?

3. To increase employees' perception of detection, are the following proactive measures taken and publicized to employees?
   - Is possible fraudulent conduct aggressively sought out, rather than dealt with passively?
   - Does the organization send the message that it actively seeks out fraudulent conduct through fraud assessment questioning by auditors?
   - Are surprise fraud audits performed in addition to regularly scheduled fraud audits?
   - Is continuous auditing software used to detect fraud and, if so, has the use of such software been made known throughout the organization?

4. Is the management climate/tone at the top one of honesty and integrity?
   - Are employees surveyed to determine the extent to which they believe management acts with honesty and integrity?
   - Are performance goals realistic?
   - Have fraud prevention goals been incorporated into the performance measures against which managers are evaluated and which are used to determine performance-related compensation?
   - Has the organization established, implemented and tested a process for oversight of fraud risks by the board of directors or others charged with governance (e.g., the audit committee)?

5. Are fraud risk assessments performed to proactively identify and mitigate the company's vulnerabilities to internal and external fraud?

6. Are strong anti-fraud controls in place and operating effectively, including the following?
   - Proper separation of duties
   - Use of authorizations
   - Physical safeguards
   - Job rotations
   - Mandatory vacations

7. Does the internal audit department, if one exists, have adequate resources and authority to operate effectively and without undue influence from senior management?
8. Does the hiring policy include the following?
   - Past employment verification
   - Criminal and civil background checks
   - Credit checks
   - Drug screening
   - Education verification
   - Reference checks
9. Are employee support programs in place to assist employees struggling with addiction, mental/emotional health, family or financial problems?
10. Is an open-door policy in place that allows employees to speak freely about pressures, providing management the opportunity to alleviate such pressures before they become acute?
11. Are anonymous surveys conducted to assess employee morale?

About the Authors

Martin T. Biegelman, CFE, CCEP, has been fighting fraud and corruption for more than 35 years in various roles in law enforcement, consulting, and the corporate sector. He is currently a Director in Navigant Consulting's Global Investigations and Compliance Practice where he focuses on FCPA and anti-bribery compliance, financial investigations, litigation consulting, due diligence, and corporate compliance design and implementation. He has conducted and managed hundreds of complex and high-risk internal investigations in more than 70 countries. Prior to joining Navigant, Martin founded and led Microsoft Corporation's Financial Integrity Unit, a highly acclaimed global fraud prevention and anti-corruption program. During his more than eight years of leadership as Director of Financial Integrity, he created a reactive and proactive coverage model with offices and staff in Redmond, Singapore, Beijing, Delhi, Moscow, Paris, Prague, Dublin, and Ft. Lauderdale while protecting Microsoft from financial and reputational risk.

Prior to joining Microsoft, Martin was a Director of Litigation and Investigative Services in the Fraud Investigation Practice at BDO Seidman, LLP. He is a former law enforcement professional having served as a United States Postal Inspector in a variety of investigative and management assignments. As a federal agent, he was a subject matter expert in fraud detection and prevention. He retired as the Inspector in Charge of the Phoenix, Arizona, Field Office of the Postal Inspection Service. Earlier in his career, he was a criminal investigator with the San Francisco District Attorney's Office, where he investigated economic crime and official corruption.

Martin is widely recognized as a thought leader in fraud and corruption prevention and is both a Certified Fraud Examiner (CFE) and Certified Compliance and Ethics Professional (CCEP). He is the Chair of the Board of Advisors for the Economic Crime Institute at

Utica College and also serves on the Accounting Advisory Board for the School of Business at the University at Albany, State University of New York. In 2008, he was appointed by Washington State Governor Christine Gregoire to serve on the Washington State Executive Ethics Board with his appointment ending in 2011. In 2009, he took a leave of absence from Microsoft to accept an appointment as Assistant Director and Deputy Chief Investigator with the Financial Crimes Inquiry Commission to investigate the root causes of the financial crisis.

He is a sought-after speaker and instructor on white-collar crime, corruption, the FCPA, identity theft, fraud prevention, and corporate compliance and has written several authoritative books on these topics. He is the 2008 recipient of the Cressey Award bestowed annually by the Association of Certified Fraud Examiners for lifetime achievements in the detection and deterrence of fraud. In 2010, Martin received an honorary doctorate of laws from Utica College for his leadership role on behalf of students and faculty of the college as well as lifetime contributions to fraud prevention and anti-corruption compliance.

Martin holds a Master's degree in public administration from Golden Gate University and a Bachelor of Science degree from Cornell University.

Joel T. Bartow, CFE, CPP, is an Operations Director for Integri-Guard, LLC managing medical review of Medicare Part A and B claims. He has more than 25 years of experience in fraud prevention, fraud investigation, and security management in countries all over the world, including Russia, Estonia, Ukraine, Antigua, Switzerland, Greece, Israel, Kenya, Nigeria, and the Philippines, as well as across the United States from Sacramento, California, to San Juan, Puerto Rico.

Joel served as a Special Agent for the FBI for 10 years from 1987 to 1997. During that time, he worked on bank fraud and public corruption cases in Alabama and was a member of the original Russian organized crime squad in New York City, conducting complex money laundering investigations and working directly with the Russian Ministry of Internal Affairs.

After leaving the FBI, Joel lived and worked in the Former Soviet Union as a police liaison and loss recovery specialist for an American company in Kiev and Moscow. Upon returning to the United States, he became a partner at The Worldwide Investigative Network, LLC, a fraud consulting and investigations firm near Philadelphia. Joel initiated the fraud prevention program at ClientLogic, an international outsourcing company that had 20,000 employees at more than 40 locations in North America, Europe, the Philippines, and India, where he served as the Director of Fraud Prevention and Investigation for five years. He has also served as Director of Program Integrity for the Department of Defense TRICARE pharmacy benefit program at Express Scripts in St Louis, Missouri.

Joel holds a Master of Arts degree in social science and a Bachelor of Arts degree from Lincoln University in Missouri. He is a Certified Fraud Examiner (CFE), a Certified Protection Professional (CPP), and a Certified Business Manager (CBM). He has written several articles for *Fraud Magazine,* a publication of the Association of Certified Fraud Examiners.